ENCYCLOPAEDIA OF DALITS IN INDIA

Human Rights: Problems and Perspectives

ENCYCLOPAEDIA OF DALITS IN INDIA
(Series)

Volumes Published

1. GENERAL STUDY
2. STRUGGLE FOR SELF LIBERATION
3. MOVEMENTS
4. LEADERS
5. RESERVATION
6. CONSTITUTION
7. SOCIAL JUSTICE
8. EMANCIPATION AND EMPOWERMENT
9. WOMEN
10. EDUCATION
11. LITERATURE
12. HUMAN RIGHTS: PROBLEMS AND PERSPECTIVE
13. HUMAN RIGHTS: ROLE OF POLICE AND JUDICIARY
14. HUMAN RIGHTS: NEW DIMENSIONS IN DALIT PROBLEMS

ENCYCLOPAEDIA OF DALITS IN INDIA

(In 14 Volumes)

HUMAN RIGHTS: PROBLEMS AND PERSPECTIVES

(Volume 12)

Editors
Dr. Sanjay Paswan
Dr. Pramanshi Jaideva

PUBLICATIONS

KALPAZ PUBLICATIONS
DELHI - 110052

ENCYCLOPAEDIA OF DALITS IN INDIA

HUMAN RIGHTS: PROBLEMS AND PERSPECTIVES

(Education, Literature, Political Science, Sociology, Women Studies)

(14 Volume Set)

ISBN: 978-81-7835-066-0 (Set)
ISBN: 978-81-7835-127-8 (Vol. 12)

Published in 2003 in India by
Kalpaz Publications
C-30, Satyawati Nagar
Ashok Vihar-III, Delhi-110052
e-mail: kalpaz@hotmail.com

Laser Typeset at: Alphabet, Delhi
Printed at: Mehra Offset Press, New Delhi.

Contents

Preface

The present title *Encyclopaedia of Dalits in India: Human Rights* is studied in comprehensive volumes: *Problems and Perspectives; Role of Police and Judiciary; New Dimensions in Dalit Problems.*

The concept of human rights should intervene to remove the basic hurdles in the process of human development of downtrodden people. In a rudimentary form Christianity and Islam introduced the notion of all-pervasive human rights into their societies way back in history. But the Brahmanical religion, on the contrary, did not allow the very notion of human rights to come into its orbit.

It believed that except its own self no other social sections should have any rights, whatsoever. As a result of such a notion of Brahmanism the state institutions basically remained of *danda* wielders and the civil society produced gods who resolved human conflict only through violence.

Even today, the popular images of many Hindu gods appear in aggressive modes and not in benign human form. The notions of some beings *Devatas* (deities) and others being *Rakshasas* as (demons) present a picture of dehumanisation and degradation of all producing castes of India. In fact, the Brahmanical language constantly reproduces the consciousness of violation of human rights of the Dalits Bahujans.

The first major effort of the human rights movement should be abolition of untouchability in this country, while carrying on a general campaign against the caste system itself. As long as untouchability exists, no civilised country can claim that human rights are safeguarded in that country. So far, the NHRC has been focusing only on the violation of human rights by the state agencies as against individuals. The widespread civil-societal violation of human rights centering on the caste system has yet to be addressed.

It is now time for the NHRC to launch a massive campaign against untouchability. The government has been carrying on a massive campaign against polio to reach the message to the entire child population of the country. A similar campaign against untouchability is necessary, and it does not involve much money. Such a campaign in every nook and cranny of the country—urban and rural – will force the Indian society to re-examine the notion of the caste system and more particularly untouchability.

The second campaign should be on abolition of the practice of not sharing food with the SCs both in rural and urban areas. This pernicious practice is particularly widespread in rural India. Even today, there are restaurants with separate tumblers and cups for Scheduled Caste users. In community functions in the village the SCs are not allowed to dine with the rest of the villagers. The so-called upper castes are debarred from the social and the familial functions organised by the SCs, now would they invite the SCs for their social gatherings.

Educated Scheduled Caste persons in the villages are naturally put off by such a social environment. When they strive for a better human environment the upper castes react violently resulting, in many cases, in violence against the protestors. Human rights organisations respond only at that stage and talk about violation of human rights of the Dalits. The NHRC should concentrate, at least from now on the cause rather than on the effect.

The third issue which is causing tension on the human rights front between the practitioners of the Brahmanical religion and the Dalit Bahujans intercaste marriage. Irrespective of rural and urban differentiation, Dalit Bahujans marrying upper caste boys and girls leads to attacks on the Dalits Bahujans only. There are cases of 'public hanging of Dalit boys or girls and their parents' responsible for such marriages. There have also been cases of "public burning to death" of such brides and grooms. One does not come across such brutal killings for marrying persons from particular sections of the community in the human rights history of western countries.

In completing these volumes, I have taken support from various sources, like books, journals, and other secondary sources. I am thankful to all those eminent writers and scholars whose works have been utilised in these volumes.

This is a twelfth volume of the series entitled *Encyclopaedia of Dalits in India: Human Rights*. We are trying our best to cover all the aspects on the issue in our forthcoming volumes.

Editors

Introduction

The idea of rights of a human being arise out of the moral conviction of the west that every human being is sacred. The claim that every human being is sacred is often violated. For some categories of certain people like women, tribes, Dalits, Negroes etc. are not the categories that would rank equal to others where the issue of human rights is concerned. The idea that some human beings are sacred and others are not suggest that there are pseudo-humans or sub-humans. This notion is deep rooted in the Indian, more so, the Hindu ether. The basic structure of Indian society is based on the graded inequality. In this regard, the rights of Dalits assume great significance.

In India, even the minimum needs of human beings are often denied to human beings. Recognising this, our Constitution has made certain provisions to restore some basic rights to Dalits. On getting independence from the British, opportunity came our way to include such provisions while drafting the new Constitution. Major step in this direction has been taken like Protection of Civil Rights Act (PCRA).

Our Constituent Assembly tried to make our Constitution the best in the world. It incorporated all the good points found in the Constitutions of other progressive countries and adapted them in such a way as to suit the needs and the culture of our people. Amongst other things, the Constitution guaranteed 'equality of status' and 'dignity of the individual'.

Under the Constitution the untouchability was abolished and its observance was made a cognizable offence. In all the States, legislation was passed to abolish social disabilities of the so-called untouchables. The states vied with each other in appointing separate welfare boards for the scheduled castes and included in an untouchable as minister in the cabinet. Same thing was also practised at the centre. Special facilities, more funds and greater goodwill for re-integration of the untouchables seen flowing from both official and non-official questions. It looked as though the untouchables had turned the corner and soon would merge into the mainstream of the Hindu society. But it was a short-lived dream. Gandhiji, the apostle of non-violence, fell prey to the gun shots of a Hindu fanatic.

This removed a great benefactor of the untouchables from the scene. Soon after the sunshine disappeared and dark clouds of despondency spread across the sky. Universal sympathy dried up mysteriously. The Hindu mind quickly withdrew itself in the shell of caste rigidity and Hindu society conveniently forgot the pledges given to the untouchables. Even state governments changed their stance. Most of them abolished specially created Harijan departments and untouchables were removed from the ministry. Grants for welfare programmes and projects for advancement of Dalits were pruned. The long awaited Independence failed to bring about any tangible change in the living condition of Dalits. One is made to wonder whether the position of untouchables is any better today than in the past.

Poverty for generations has been a permanent feature of Indian life. At many poverty ridden places, one meal a day is common practice. Eating carrion is also common. It is irksome to note that while millions go without a morsel of food, a few enjoy great riches. This stark contrast has always existed and continues to exist in the Indian society. Most of Dalits have been at the lower end of the social ladder, living in abject poverty.

The talk of welfare of Dalits which reverberated soon after the Independence, has been heard once again loudly towards the end of 20th century. In the beginning of this century it continues to make noises and the society is definitely taking note of this. Rights of Dalits are being demanded and law has been on their side. It is hoped that things will change for better and Dalit speak will make its influence and ultimately they will be brought on a par with the rest of the society. Time factor is also crucial. The way things are moving it may take another few centuries for things to get better. Fast action is the need of the hour so that Dalit rights are restored to them at the earliest.

Dr Ambedkar was the leader who led the fight for the rights of Dalits. But after him, no leader of his stature appeared on scene and this led to large scale violence and atrocities being committed on Dalits in post-independent India.

Violence and atrocities along with the economic exploitation as well as sexual abuse has been the basic of Dalits. The economic policies persued by successive governments since independence have not resulted in any major advancement of Dalit community. Human right bodies, conventions and protocols find limited application in India as India has not even signed some of the International Human Right Treaties. Some rights like right to land, education, basic health services, drinking water, shelter, right to work are very basic and essential to human existence. But these are not often available to Dalits.

In the chapter on fundamental rights, the Indian Constitution guarantees human rights to every citizen. It gives adequate powers to both the centre and the state governments to effectively deal with human rights violations. Dalits being socially at the lowest rung and also economically very weak, are a vulnerable lot and have been the victim of human rights violation. Despite laws being in place, very little has been done to stop such violation and for this the centre and the state, the law enforcing machinery have to take the blame.

And this is where NGOs come into the picture. NGOs have a greater duty to perform where the government fails. They have the skill and the experience to deal effectively and in a human itarian manner with the situation. The only problem they might face is of funding these operations. Government, on its part, should make funds available to the performing NGOs industrial houses with a bent towards social causes can also contribute their bit.

India is a pluralistic society. More than one billion people here speak more than 20 major languages, as also a number of dialects. There are followers, in India, of almost all the existent religions in the world. The existing inequalities in the social order here stand in the way of healthy respect to the human rights. The disparity and inequalities are slowly moving out but the level of movement is exceptionally slow.

There are many factors that are behind human rights violation and commitment of atrocities on Dalits. The forms and magnitudes of violations in case of scheduled castes who have successfully improved upon their socio-economic position. But it is more crude in those cases where backwards having some amount of awareness try to improve their lot.

In order to control such a situation, the provisions of Constitution sometimes appear inadequate. Socio-economic justice that needs to be granted to the depressed and oppressed lot is simply not available. Some cases of atrocities, follow up action taken and end result gained have been mentioned in this book which throw a light on the glariy failure of the legal measures.

Spreading of awareness is the need of the hour which can only be done with the spread of education. But even those who have acquired some awareness and are trying to assert their rights are not being taken very kindly by some. When they assert their rights and demanded their fundamental rights, vested interest try to terrorise them and force them to remain dumb and meek.

There are numerous laws to deal with commission of atrocities on Dalits. The Scheduled Castes and the Scheduled Tribes (Prevention of Atrocities) Act was passed in 1989 by the Indian Parliament. The Act provides for setting-up of special courts for the trial of offences under it and also for the relief and rehabilitation schemes of the victims of such offences. A detailed discussion on this law has been incorporated in the book.

The book in fact deals with the major legislative arrangements provided the Constitution to ensure the availability of human rights to Dalits. It also highlights the causes of failure to protect the human rights of Dalits.

1

Human Rights and Dalits

The western moral conviction that every human being is sacred basically gave rise to the idea of rights of human beings. The secular version of human rights arise out of the experiences of the humanity with the brutality of religious practices and as a dialectic of protestantism and science. The claim that every human being is sacred is violated by a number of people. Only some persons are considered to be really human beings and others such as women, tribes, Dalits or Bosnian Muslims, etc. are not truly human. Michael J. Perrys in his recent book *The Idea of Human Rights,* says that, "this is because, the first part of the idea of human rights—the claim that every human being is sacred—is the claim that every member of the species *Homo sapiens* is sacred (or at least every born member); it is claimed that the sacredness of a human being (*Homo sapiens)* does not depend on his or her "race, colour, sex, language , religion, political or other opinion national or social origin, property, birth or other status". The language of the Universal Declaration of Human Rights in Article 2 appears to have been influencing the ideology of human rights in many countries. The idea that some human beings are sacred and others are not, indicate that there are pseudo-humans or sub-humans. This ideology suits the Indians, particularly the Hindu ethos. In India the status of an individual is religiously determined by birth of the person in a caste.

Therefore, the ritual status of the individuals is determined by the religious leaders. The moral code, the basis on which human relations are maintained in India seems to be unequal. They are unequal as the ideas of inequality, fraternity, and democracy have different meanings in the Indian context. The basic structure of the society is based on graded inequality, first sanctioned by the religious scriptures and internalised by individuals by practice. It is in this context, the rights of the Dalits play a very important role in universalising the human rights. The mere declaration of Human Rights and the Bill of Rights comprising of :

(1) Universal Declaration of Human Rights, 1948,
(2) The International Covenant on Economic, Social and Cultural Rights, 1966, and
(3) The International Covenant on Civil and Political Rights, 1966, may not ensure the rights to Dalits in India.

The Dalits have been treated as sub-humans and even as non-humans by the mainstream society for a long period of time in human history. The slaves in the United States and other European societies were better placed regarding certain minimum access to civilised life such as education and training. But, in India even those minimum needs of human beings were denied to Dalits. It is in recognition of this discrimination that the Constitution of India restored some of the basic rights and through constitutional provisions such as Article 17 (abolition of untouchability) in recognition of this discrimination.

Harrassed Community

Some studies indicate that majority of the Scheduled Castes and Scheduled Tribes belong to the indigenous groups, though the mainstream upper caste and western educated anthropologists do not agree with the fact that Dalits are the original inhabitants of India. It was the Aryan invaders who threatened them and destroyed the harmony with nature with which they were living as an eco-community. The Dalits have developed their own systems of justice based on liberty, equality and community living. However, this was destroyed by the rise of a Hindu nation-state and made them foreigners in their own homeland. Therefore, the inalienable rights of the Dalits are taken away by the dominant classes. Dalits have lived in this country without a right to life, security and minimum needs for centuries together.

Social reformers like Mahatma Phooley in the west, Periyar in the south, and Ambedkar at the all-India level, came on to the scene and championed the cause of the Dalits. Though the British appeared to have done some sympathetic charity by way of enacting laws in preventing untouchability and caste discrimination, they have done precious little for the amelioration of the conditions of the Dalits. They were always interested in keeping the balance of power in the country on the advice of the *Babus* who belong to upper castes, mostly the Brahmins. Therefore, it was left to the independent leadership that came up during the first part of 20th century among the Dalits, more particularly after Ambedkar and Rao Bahadur Srinivasan and others who represented the Dalits in the Round Table Conference..It was after independence, that an opportunity was given to Ambedkar to incorporate some Articles in the Constitution to abolish untouchability and bring social equality in the Indian society through the Draft Constitution.

Various measures, legislatures or otherwise, were resorted to implement the constitutional obligations. The restoration of the rights of the Dalits has been made possible through the protection of Civil Rights Act. Unlike that of the civil rights movements in United States of America under the leadership of Martin Luther King, no leader of that stature has emerged in India after Ambedkar to lead the civil rights movements. Many atrocities on the Dalits have been committed in the country during the post-independent India, as its consequence.

Atrocities Against Dalits

Dalits have been subjected to atrocities throughout the country along with economic oppression, sexual abuse and acts of inhuman treatment. The civil society had been hostile to the enjoyment of rights given to the Dalits in the Constitution. A campaign has been launched by the elite against the Dalits that reservation of jobs and equality of opportunities are created for them without taking into account the question of efficiency. This prompted many an unscrupulous elements particularly the communal elements, to treat the Dalits as a hostile group and that has resulted in the increase in the atrocities of Dalits. The economic policy pursued by the successive governments during the post-independent period did not result in the amelioration of the conditions in the same proportion as the rise in investments made on them. The difference between the Dalits and upper castes in terms of economic opportunities have increased. This has led to increase in the atrocities on them. The data in the Table 1.1 show the atrocities on this class they have increased 37-fold during the period 1970-1995. The intensity of the atrocities can also be noticed in terms of the kind of atrocities committed. They are of the nature of murder, rape, arson, etc.

Quantum of Atrocities

To reveal the brutality and alienation of Dalits from the

mainstream society, some evidence can be produced from government sources. The annual reports of the Commissioner of SCs and STs published annually, show the quantum of atrocities committed against Dalits. In her recent report to the Parliament, Maneka Gandhi, Minister for Social Welfare, mentioned that untouchability is prevalent in twelve states even today. As on 1997, there are 8,500 cases of reported crimes against SCs of which 261 are murders and 302 are rapes. Reports reveal that 92,000 Dalits were deprived of their allotted land in 1997 in Uttar Pradesh alone in 1997.

TABLE 1.1
Atrocities and Harassment of SCs and STs during the Fifty Years of Independence

Year	*Scheduled Castes*					*Scheduled Tribes*				
	Murder	*Injury, Violence*	*Rape*	*Other IPC Offences*	*Total*	*Murder*	*Injury, Violence*	*Rape*	*Other IPC Offences*	*Total*
1970-71	370*	—	—	474*	847	—	—	—	—	—
1980-81	383	1,398	425	11,678	13,884	34	95	64	1,971	2,164
1994-95	552	4,365	847	25,623	31,387	66	652	350	3,955	5,023

* Average of 1967, 1968, 1969.

Owing to major projects undertaken by the government during the post-independence period the number of disabled persons amount to two crores. Most of them are Dalits and *adivasis*. It is said that every hour two Dalits are assaulted, everyday three Dalit women are raped, and two Dalits are murdered every day. This is reported here only to illustrate that these people in India are treated as aliens in their homeland. The Constitution of India has created certain safeguards and various Acts have been enacted to protect the Dalits. But they are being exploited everyday. This is happening even with the support of the caste state. The Indian State is slowly being moulded into a caste state where the oligarchy of a few dominant castes control the state power and resources. In this context, the state is collaborating with upper caste forces against the interests of Dalits. The institution and structures such as judiciary, police, etc., of the caste state have also become part of the caste oppression. Therefore, Dalits do not have a resource to the gifts of universal declaration of human rights. The instruments of UN human rights, such as human rights bodies, conventions and protocols have limited application in India as India did not sign some of the treaties. This calls for an international campaign for the declaration of the rights of Dalits as human rights. This is essential to regard the rights of the Dalits to enforce within the framework of the Constitution through human rights organisations such as National Human Rights Commission, State Human Rights Commission, etc. A special campaign to recognise Dalit rights as human rights is necessitated because of the fact that the international community and the UN system of human rights treaties do not recognise problems like untouchability which is a unique feature of the Indian society.

Rights like the right to land, education, basic health services, drinking water, shelter, right to work, etc., are basic for life sustenance. But, these basic rights are denied to the Dalits in India due to their alienation from the mainstream. It is in this context, that a charter of Dalit rights have been drafted as human rights by a group of Dalit intellectuals including K.S. Chalam. They include the following:

1. They claim that Dalit rights are human rights.
2. They affirm that the denial of basic requirement of the Dalits is a gross violation of Dalit human rights.
3. They want the inclusion of caste discrimination and untouchability in the international convention on racial discrimination.
4. They claim that the perpetrators of untouchability should be severely punished according to the provisions of SC/ST Atrocities Act and Rules.
5. They claim full protection of Dalits in the *Panchayat Raj* institutions and other democratic institutions of the country.
6. They also want that the land usurped by the state and private bodies, be restored to the Dalits.
7. They need reservations to Dalits in all private bodies and organisations.
8. They demand that special steps be taken for the protection of the rights of Dalit women.

9. They demand that Dalits, irrespective of their religious faith, be regarded as SCs.
10. They demand right to freedom of thought and expression.
11. They demand a white paper to be placed in the Parliament on atrocities committed on Dalits and reservation facilities actually granted to Dalits from 1947.
12. They demand that Dalit human rights be explicitly and constitutionally guaranteed in the Asian countries where Dalits are domiciled.

Human Rights Violations and the Remedial Measures

The Preamble to the Universal Declaration of Human Rights (UDHR) serves as the foundation and philosophy of human rights. It states, "If man is not to be compelled to have recourse, as a last resort, to rebellion against tyranny and oppression, then human rights should be protected by the rule of law". The Preamble clearly indicates that man as the last resort rebels against oppression in the absence of the rule of law. Rebellions are always cause social chaos. Therefore, maintaining social harmony and peace, which are prerequisites for a nation's progress and prosperity, are proclaimed by the U.N. General Assembly in the UDHR as a general standard of a achievement for all the people and all nations. There are now a host of international conventions including those for prevention and punishment of genocide and elimination of all forms of racial and gender-based discriminations besides torture. Today what a government does to its own people is not only its own concern but is also the concern of the UNO, the UNHRC and other international bodies. The work of our NHRC which was set up in 1993 by the Government of India, will be under the observation of different UN bodies.

The United Nations Convention Against Torture and Other Cruel, Inhuman or Degrading Treatment or Punishment, Article 4 enjoins on every signatory nation to "ensure that all acts of torture are offences under its criminal law" and to make those offences punishable by appropriate penalties. Article 8 make acts of torture extraditable offences.

Indian Constitution and Dalit Rights

The Preamble to the Constitution of India defines the aim of the Constitution as: to secure justice, liberty, equality and fraternity to all the Indian citizens. In the chapter on Fundamental Rights, the Indian Constitution guarantees human rights to every citizen. It also sufficiently empowers the Central and State Governments to eliminate human rights violations in the country. The Indian Constitution provides for socio-economic, educational, cultural, political and service safeguards for the SC/STs (Dalits). Unfortunately, these constitutional safeguards have not improved the socio-economic condition of the SCs/STs nor have they reduced the incidence of atrocities committed on the SCs/STs. Article 17 of the Constitution has abolished "untouchability" and its practice in any form. It was followed by the Protection of Civil Rights Act, 1955. Since atrocities did not end, the Scheduled Castes and Scheduled Tribes (Prevention of Atrocities) Act, 1989 was enacted. The special officer mentioned in Article 338 (1) was designated as early as 1950 by the first President of India, Dr. Rajendra Prasad. The duty of the special officer as specified in Article 338 (2) is to investigate all matters relating to the safeguards provided for the SCs and STs under the Constitution and advise the President on the working of such measures.

Under pressure from the demand by SCs/STs members of Parliament the Special Officer under Article 338 was replaced by a multi-member Commission with more functions and powers and the National Commission for the SCs/STs became a statutory body in June 1990. The Commission does not have powers to impart verdicts or issue directions. It can only give its findings and recommendations. Despite all the constitutional safeguards and the machinery provided for their enforcement, the number of cases of atrocities against the SCs/STs has been rising every year. Does it mean that the constitutional rights have become a mere paper declaration? No, on the contrary, it is a great step forward from the previous law of the land based on inequality as defined in the *Manusmriti*. In spite of the historical distortions of the Hindu society that have divided people, the Indian Constitution has made available the tools in the hands of the people to assert themselves against the onslaught of the organised few. People can go to courts for redressal of their grievances—including violations of human rights. If the atrocities are committed on the Dalits despite the constitutional safeguards, the only logical conclusion that one can draw is, the government has failed to implement the provisions of the law. The failure of constitutional safeguards to deter the tortures—mostly the high caste Hindus—raises the pertinent question: how best can the NHRC reduce the incidence of atrocities against the Dalits, if not but not end them altogether? The agenda which was circulated to chief ministers of the states on the eve of the conference on human rights held on September 13, 1992 in New Delhi brought out the fact that government is well aware of the violation of human rights in the country.

Apart from dealing with the necessity of setting up an NHRC, the agenda included such items as custodial crimes, atrocities against vulnerable sections of society, prison reforms, training in human rights issues, etc. Doubts about the motives of the Central Government in proposing a Human Rights Commission arose chiefly from two considerations. In the first place, it is widely believed, for good reasons, that the proposal emanated from foreign funding agencies and donor countries. A large number of donor countries are particular that financial aid should be given only to those countries which have shown regard for human rights and democratic principles. However, the value of NHRC is not undermined even if the Commission is the result of the pressure, direct or indirect, of international democratic opinion, direct or indirect.

Innovations on technological front has turned the world into a global village. Communication takes place at hyper speed. Human rights abuses are spread to all parts of the world within no time, and international bodies get involved. For example, at the Bangkok Asia-Pacific Precom conference in February 1993, (prior to the Vienna Conference in June 1993), the following resolution was passed: "Take appropriate steps to eradicate the practice of untouchability which is a crime against humanity by the year 2000, failing which sanctions will be imposed". Following this Dr. Manfred Nowak's report was adopted and published at the end of the plenary session of the Vienna NGO-Forum which reads thus: "the working group urges the United Nations to take appropriate steps to eradicate the practice of untouchability, which it regards a crime against humanity and discrimination on the basis of caste, religion and other factors by the year 2000. To this end, the Working Group recommended the appointment of a Special Rapporteur to carry out a study of the situation of untouchables in South Asia, in particular of bonded labour, child servitude and child prostitution. Additionally, a special committee is called for in order to initiate the process of declaring the untouchables as an indigenous people of South Asia to whom all the UN resolutions on indigenous people should be applicable".

The Vulnerable Lot

In cases of human rights violations against the Dalits, the focus on the victims is for the only objective of publicity in the media. The torturers are forgotten. The victims are economically and socially very vulnerable. Human rights activists, NGOs and the associations of Dalit employees must prepare them mentally, socially and politically to resist the torturers by democratic means. The Scheduled Castes and Scheduled Tribes (Prevention of Atrocities) Act, 1989 must be made use of against the torturers. The token economic assistance given to victims is inadequate. Instead of dismissing the torturer as a sadist, or a maniac, he must be promptly punished.

Crimes committed against individuals can be tackled in this way. But what about hundreds of armed high caste Hindus attacking Dalits? This is a national issue and the state must setup effectively. Time and again successive governments have failed to handle large scale atrocities against the Dalits. The guilty are seldom punished. The cases against them drag in the courts for years and people forget about them. Hence the need for separate courts, as justice delayed is justice denied. The high percentage of illiteracy leaves the Dalits to open oppression. The legacy of *Manusmriti* is still continuing. Successive governments have failed to enforce Article 45 of the Constitution because there is no political will. It is only because they want Manu's code and not the Indian Constitution. The present Government will do well to include this Article in the Chapter on Fundamental Rights.

Equitable development of all regions in the country should also be helpful. Then only distress migration to cities which results in slums can be ended. The high rate of growth of population puts undue pressure on the process of development. Family planning programmes should be given top priority and zero population growth in ten years should be the target. Similarly, basic needs of the people, like drinking water should be provided for all. For example, the majority of Dalit women have to spend many hours a day to fetch water for family needs. The UNO adopted a village in Myanmar for the purpose of water supply. All the households were supplied tap water for 24 hours. It was observed that the income of every family went up. To supply tap water to all the household in ten years should be the target for the government. Empowering not only the Dalits but the NHRC and Courts also needs to be undertaken.

Education should be given in schools and colleges on the subject of human rights. A separate, independent ministry, headed by a cabinet rank minister for overseeing atrocities committed on the Dalit should be created. For speedy disposal of such cases, separate courts must be set up in each district to deal with such offences. For conducting cases in these courts, special public prosecutors are required at the district level court and an Advocate General at the High Court. The UNO should also set up an International Court for conducting cases of human rights violations. The judges of this International Court should attend the special courts set up in India. The NHRC should have more power under the present Act, and should enjoy the status of a statutory body. Controlling posts, like those of principal of college/school, managing director of a company, etc., must be brought under the policy of reservation by passing a special bill in the Lok Sabha and including it in the IXth Schedule of Constitution. Intercaste and inter-state marriages need to be given encouragement by the Central Government and by all State Governments.

In eliminating human rights violations NGOs can play a significant role. They should monitor and report human rights violations and pursue them in different forums. The NHRC and the National Commission for the SCs/STs should be susceptible to complaints from NGO's and promptly act on them. But for this to be effective, the Indian NGOs themselves must discourage the caste system and then take up the issue of human rights violation against the SCs/STs. Even if all the measures mentioned above succeed, unless the mind-set of the upper caste people changes, atrocities will not be stopped. There is need for integration of society in changing the mindset of general public.

In order to achieve this objective every State institution (economic, scientific, educational, civil, etc.) must become multicaste. It can be achieved by enforcing reservation on a caste basis. Only ten per cent of all available jobs come under State institutions. The remaining ninety per cent jobs, which are in the private sector are out of the purview of reservation. Hence the SCs/

STs, have no access to them. Merit is never a criterion for selecting a person for a job in India. Only high caste persons, therefore, are selected for jobs in the private sector, due to their economic/social status. As the jobs in the private sector are the preserve of high caste Hindus, strong opposition from this section is expected to reservation of jobs for the SCs/STs in the private sector. This was clear earlier in the opposition to the implementation of the *Mandal Commission report.* However, in spite of opposition from high caste Hindus, all private sector jobs must be subjected to reservation.

In short, atrocities against the Dalits are perpetrated by high caste Hindus. How to tame and humanise the belligerent section of high caste Hindus society and make it civilised and humane is the challenge before the NGOs, the NHRC, and the serious people of our society. Finally, let us be prepared that if the Dalits are deprived of the right to be human, our country may face chaos, and may even be plunged in a civil war.

Human Rights and Developmental Issues

Indian society is a plural and complex society. It has been the home of almost every major religion in the world; its nearly one billion people speak eighteen major languages, apart from many times that number of dialects. Our cultural diversity has produced a colourful mosaic of which we are legitimately proud. However, there is an equally conspicuous diversity of a different dimension; reflecting a social order characterised by inequalities and lack of opportunities, a social order that has stood in the way of a healthy universal respect for human rights and which has been a drag on our programmes of socio-economic development. Even after fifty-years of independence, these disparities and inequalities continue; awareness about them has been slow in growing; equally slow has been the sensitisation of functionaries involved in eliminating them. It is a truism to say that social disparities based on a rigid caste structure have stood in the way of a free play of economic forces, rise of an entrepreneurial class cutting across social divisions, mobility of labour and a more equal sharing of economic gains.

Referring to the caste system, Jawaharlal Nehru wrote in his book entitled *Discovery of India:* "There can be no equality of status and opportunity within its framework, nor can there be political democracy, much less economic democracy." Dr. Ambedkar was of the firm opinion that "annihilation of caste" was the only solution to India's disunity and poverty. He stated: "The caste-system is not merely a division of labour. It is a division of labourers." Awareness of the situation led the government immediately after Independence to resort to a strategy of planned economic development. Such a development was supposed would help break down the rigidities of the caste system.

Social services sector continues to lag behind, accentuating socio-economic disparities. As a result, even after 45 years of planning, the government is striving to provide basic minimum services to the poor and the socially disadvantaged in order to equip them to reap the fruits of freedom, social justice and economic development. The increasing awareness that socio-economic development must be based on justice, equality of opportunity and respect for the dignity and worth of the human person also contributed to a heighten level of expectation and aspirations. During a recent seminar conducted jointly by the Canadian Human Rights Commission and the National Human Rights Commission of India. A presentation of perception of the complaints of human rights was much violations which the NHRC has been receiving from the length and breadth of the country. I had submitted on that occasion that the complaints reflected, apart from individual grievances and concerns, upheavals in a society making attempts to move towards modernism.

Developmental planning in India is a matter much discussed. However, regarding Article 46 of the Constitution, I would like to highlight some of the aspects of an uneven socio-economic development to the disadvantage of the depressed classes and the attention they deserve in fostering a human rights culture. A pre-requisite for socio-economic development is awareness; awareness of the present, and a vision of the future based on that awareness. The most important factor contributing to this awareness is literacy; the ability to read, write and perceive; to comprehend developments beyond the community or the immediate neighbourhood; to judge for oneself what is good and what is not. As Paulo Frieire, the Brazilian proponent of social activism stated; Literacy *per se*, and even adult education at a fairly advanced stage, may not lead to a radical or qualitative change in the lives of individual learners. It may not lead to an end of the status of landlessness, assetlessness and bondage; but it can certainly be a tool of "critical consciousness" and in that sense can be a significant tool to induce or stimulate change.

Problem of Illiteracy

Even after more than half a century of Independence, the illiterate population of India has far exceeded the total population of the country at the time of Independence. This has been the consequence of undue stress on higher education and the meagre resources allocated to the education sector being consumed largely by universalities and technical institutions. It is a cruel irony that while India ranks among the top nations in technical manpower, it is also carries the burden of the largest number of illiterates. And the worst sufferers in this regard have been the disadvantaged communities. Myron Weiner observed: "Indian education has been largely an instrument for differentiation by separating children according to social class. For this reason, those who control the education system are remarkably indifferent to the low enrolment and high dropout among the lowest social classes. The result is one of the highest rates of child labour in the world, ... and a literacy rate that has fallen behind most of the third world."

The 1991 Census, showing that while the literacy rate was 52.2 per cent for the whole population, it was only 37.21 per cent among the Scheduled Castes. (Some of the State figures for literary among the Scheduled Castes are: 26.85 per cent in Uttar Pradesh; 26.2 per cent in Rajasthan and 19.49 per cent in Bihar; the female literacy rates among the Scheduled Castes in these States are 10.69 per cent, 8.39 per cent and 7.07 per cent respectively.) The literacy level among the Scheduled Tribes was pegged at 29.6 per cent for the country as a whole. In Madhya Pradesh which accounts for nearly twenty-three per cent of the country's total Scheduled Tribe population, the literacy level among them was 21.54 per cent and in Andhra Pradesh 17.16 per cent. In the case of females, the literacy rates for the Scheduled Tribes population was 4.4 per cent in Rajasthan, 8.7 per cent in Andhra Pradesh, 10.2 per cent in Orissa and 10.7 per cent in Madhya Pradesh.

The issue of primary education up to the age of fourteen to be of such critical significance that it has taken a number of initiatives by way of addressing various agencies of the government, according to NHRC. Further, the Chairperson of NHRC felt it necessary to write to the president of all political parties in January 1996 on our commitment to fulfil the promise of Article 45 of the Constitution. In his letter he noted that the grim reality of rising number of illiterates enfeebled the country in every way, whether civil and political or economic, social and cultural. He added that this reality affected the dignity and self-esteem of countless Indians and exposed them to constant violations of their human rights. The Chairperson urged that definite steps be taken in Parliament to provide comprehensive legislative backing to the provisions of Article 45. It was further urged that such legislation be matched with necessary resources required for the purpose. It is a matter of gratification that the Common Minimum Programme of the present government (United Front Government in 1996) recognises this position and purposes to make the right to free and compulsory elementary education (as per Art 45 up to the age of fourteen) a Fundamental Right, as also to substantially raise the outlay for education with special attention to the requirements of truly universalising elementary education. It must also be recognised that only an increased flow of funds into the education sector would not provide a total solution to this issue. What is equally significant is the accessibility of children, particularly of the disadvantaged communities, to schools; the availability of physical infrastructure and manpower and material resources for the effective functioning of the schools. Also, the level of commitment and motivation of parents, teachers as well as that of the children is also significant level.

NGOs and local communities have a major role in this regard. We need a national level effort to galvanise the disadvantaged communities and groups to reap the benefit of a more determined effort that is being mounted now. Providing land to the tiller was a promise made during the Independence movement and this promise is yet to become a reality in several parts of the country. In rural areas, the land owned by the top one per cent is estimated to be equal to the land owned by the bottom fifty-five per cent of the land owning families. The data of land distribution, consequent on the application of land ceiling laws, are often questioned. It is alleged that holdings have been divided and sub-divided among family members of different generations.

Being unable to read and write, among tenants and share-croppers, land is often disguised as owner cultivated. A study conducted in 1989 estimated that a third of all cultivated land is held under concealed and informal tenancy. A report brought out by the Department of Rural Development in 1988 stated: "The rural rich maintain their position through use of muscle power and manipulation of administrative and judicial processes." According to the 1991 Census, ninety-three per cent of the Scheduled Tribe population and eighty-one per cent of the Scheduled Caste population live in rural areas and more than ninety per cent of the working population among Scheduled Tribes and seventy-seven per cent of the working population among the Scheduled Castes were engaged in the primary sector. Prevalence of poverty among the disadvantaged in the rural areas due to landless and low wages is too well known.

The Ministry of Welfare in its annual report for the year 1994–95 tells us along the extent of poverty among the Scheduled Castes and the Scheduled Tribes. In 1983–84, 40.40 per cent of the total population of our country was below the poverty line. The percentage for the Scheduled Tribes during the year was 58.40 while for the Scheduled Castes it was fifty-three. The 1987–88 survey estimates put the percentages as 33.40 for the total population, 52.60 for the Scheduled Tribes and 44.7 for the Scheduled Castes. It may be observed that during the four-year period, a higher percentage of the total population came above the poverty line, than in the case of the Scheduled Tribes though marginally better in the case of Scheduled Castes. In any case the incidence of poverty among SCs and STs continues to be much higher.

The Tribal Sub-Plans and the Special Component Plan were introduced as additional support to the socio-economic development plans for these two groups. The government has itself admitted that despite sincere attempts, "There has not been very significant development in the education, entrepreneurial and others fields among the Scheduled Castes." A report of the Ministry of Welfare further states: "In various States, the exercise for the formulation of SCP (Special Component Plan) is of perfunctory nature." The question that comes up in one's mind is whether apart from earmarking funds, there is an actual appreciation of the developmental needs of these disadvantaged communities. One is not off the mark in saying that in families with low income levels, the immediate victims are women and children. We need to ask the question whether in spite of special programmes, these more vulnerable segments among the socially disadvantaged are receiving the required level of attention.

It may be recalled, in this regard, that on a complaint from a human rights activist, the NHRC enquired into the death of 125 tribal children in a district in Orissa as a result of malnutrition and lack of medical care, and ordered the payment of compensation to the affected families (Reported in the Commission's Second Annual Report). While we are exporting foodgrains, sections of the population continue to suffer from under nourishment. Among the various aspects of the situation is a proper lack of understanding that the coarse grains form the staple diet of some of the tribal communities. While there has been considerable stress on the development of improved varieties of rice and wheat, not much attention seems to have been paid to research on improving the production of coarse grains which form their staple diet. The story of the most comprehensive poverty alleviation programme—the IRDP—has been more or less the same. It has suffered a great deal from want of attention to details of the milieu in which the poorest of the poor as well as the socially disadvantaged live, as also for want of essential forward and backward linkages. Milch animals being given to Scheduled Castes families under this programme is a case in point. Those who were assisted under this programme were not habituated to stall-feeding of animals, which, on being let out in the open, stray into farm lands of the upper castes leading to tension between the upper and lower castes.

The Minimum Wages Act has not been with powerful landlords paying abnormally low daily wages. Even the government fixed rates under many of the income-support programmes for the rural poor are said to be well below the statutorily fixed minimum wages. The growing disparity in the income levels in the rural areas and the rising aspirations of the landless and the poor have found violent expressions in States notably in Bihar and Andhra Pradesh. During its visits to these two States, the NHRC received representations highlighting the immediate need for effective land reforms as also a critical assessment of the developmental requirements of the depressed communities so that the widening gap between the rural rich and the poor do not cause an aggravation of social tension and abuse of human rights. Under Article 17 of our Constitution, "Untouchability' stood abolished, and its practice became forbidden. The Untouchability (Offences) Act, 1955 was passed by Parliament to make provisions for punishment for offences that amounted to observance of 'Untouchability' in any form, in order to enforce the Constitutional Provision.

In order to make the law stringent, the Act was amended and renamed as the Protection of Civil Rights Act, 1955 under which the practice of 'Untouchability' has been made an offence both cognizable and non-compoundable. However, number of convictions under this Act have been very low. Even where the cases ended in conviction, the punishment has been too formal. The following is a critical comment on the extent of punishment meted out in cases under this Act: "...In a rare instance where an offender was brought to Court, the Magistrate fined him for only two rupees. On appeal, the High Court raised the fine to a still inconsequential amount of "fifty rupees."

It is also incumbent upon the Central Government, under the Act, to present a report to the Parliament every year on the measures taken by it and the State Governments. The lack of efficacy of the law is evident in a report presented to the Parliament by the Welfare Ministry: "In view of the increasing trend of atrocities on the Scheduled Castes and the Scheduled Tribes, the existing provisions under the Protection of Civil Rights Act had been found inadequate and an additional legislation called the Scheduled Castes and the Scheduled Tribes (Prevention of Atrocities) Act, 1989, to check and eliminate crimes against them by non-Scheduled Castes and non-Scheduled Tribes was passed and brought into force w.e.f. 30.1.1990." The new Act enjoins upon the government to take various steps including the setting up of Special Courts, provision of legal aid and even the economic and social rehabilitation of victims of atrocities. Data available indicate that the conviction rate under these Acts has been very low (around one per cent). There are a number of socio-economic factors which contribute to the continued ineffective enforcement of the provisions of these statutes and a low rate of conviction. There is need to closely and critically monitor these factors and the instrumentalities involved to deal with the situation.

Efforts of the Government

In March 1992, a scheme was launched by the Government of India to put an end to the inhuman and degrading practice of manual handling of night soil. The scheme operates at two levels: one by the Ministry of Urban Affairs and Employments for the conversion of dry latrines into water-borne flush latrines in homesteads and provision of sewage facilities at the town/city level. The other scheme operated by the Ministry of Welfare provides for the rehabilitation of scavengers in alternative dignified occupations. Considerable amount of funds have been spent under this scheme, but very little appears to have been achieved on the ground. The government itself admits that the progress achieved "is extremely dismal barring a few States." (Annual Report of the Ministry of Welfare, 1994-95). Some of the States have not even completed the survey of scavengers. The district collectors are responsible for the overall implementation of the scheme. The level of awareness and commitment among them to implement the scheme faithfully or for that matter the level of social consciousness and societal support for this scheme for eradicating one of the most demeaning occupations is open to debate. Can we not have NGOs and other activists influencing State Governments and the district administrations in the conducting surveys and drawing up meaningful rehabilitation programmes, and helping out beneficiaries to rehabilitate themselves in better jobs.

A great amount of hydel and mineral wealth of our country lies in the tribal areas. The exploitation of this wealth through the damming or rivers and mining of the land has caused to a large scale displacement of the tribal population and also degradation of the environment. This process has been on the increase in recent years. A report of the Central Water Commission indicated that less than one-fourth of 32 dams of over fifty metres height constructed between 1951 and 1970 were in the tribal areas. However, between 1971 and 1990, out of the 85 additional dams of similar size completed or under construction, around sixty per cent were in tribal areas. Mining not only displaces the local population but also causes severe environmental damages such as pollution of surface water sources, damage to agricultural land through dumping of overburden, destruction of forest cover and air pollution. Displacement from original habitats many times lead to a breakdown of a land based community organisation.

Such instances lead to families getting marginalised and morbidity level going up. Cultural and religious practices which are aspects of the social dimensions of displacement are seriously affected. The land-for-land approach adopted for rehabilitation, often does not reflect a holistic perspective. In a letter to Baba Amte in August, 1984, Mrs. Indira Gandhi said, "I am most unhappy that development projects displace tribal people from their habitat especially as project authorities do not always take care to properly rehabilitate affected population." Displacement of tribal population from their habitat form only one part of the story. There has been large scale movement of nontribals into development project areas, as work contractors, shopkeepers, transporters, labourers, etc. A number of them over a period of time have got permanently settled at the project sites—and at times in places beyond—which are in the midst of vast tracts of tribal habitation. Reports of socio-economic exploitation of tribals by these settlers are legion. The complaints the NHRC has been receiving in this regard, whether they be in relation to Sardar Sarovar Project or the Tehri Dam, are a clear pointer to the continued lack of care in comprehensive planning for megaprojects and rehabilitation of affected tribal people.

The Government of India has drafted a National Policy for Rehabilitation of persons displaced as a result of acquisition of land, addressing primarily the needs of the disadvantaged communities. Though the Draft was prepared in consultation with NGOs and some prominent activists, forums such as this are required to deliberate on the character and content of the draft policy and examine how it respects the right to a life with dignity for the tribal people. Basic to all the developmental efforts for the uplift of the SCs/STs is a respect for their human rights; respect for their right to equality and equal opportunity; a right to life with dignity; a right to enjoy the rights guaranteed by our Constitution. Statutes and schemes are of course important, but they are rendered meaningless in the absence of a commitment to enforce or implement them. Projects and programmes for the uplift of the SCs and STs would remain on paper, or they would get derailed unless the agencies charged with the responsibility of implementing them are not only sensitized but also made effective.

The role of human rights organisation and activists in the sensitisation of government functionaries is of great significance in this regard. This would also call for according to these functionaries a greater degree of importance and standing in the administrative hierarchy than they enjoy at present. Let the message spread that the ablest and the best are picked up for this very important task of social uplift and economic development of the poorest of the poor and the weakest of the weak.

Equally, there is a greater degree of accountability, a greater degree of public scrutiny of the acts of functionaries at the cutting-edge level, punishing the guilty and rewarding those who perform. It is ultimately they who have to make sure that there are no roads and wells dividing communities in a village; there are no classrooms and playgrounds keeping the children apart; there are no complaints of discrimination or harassment in police stations or primary health centres; there are no complaints of essential commodities disappearing from the ration shops meant for the weaker sections; or that there is a correct appreciation on the success and failures of policies and programmes for the uplift of the poor and the depressed. Do the Dalits in India avail themselves of their rights concerning life, liberty, equality and dignity of the individual as guaranteed by the Indian Constitution? As the following account would reveal despite completion of fifty years of independence the violation of human rights of Dalits continues unabatedly.

Violation of Civic Rights

The Protection of Civil Rights, 1976 (earlier called Untouchability (Offences Act of 1955) provides penalties for preventing a person, on the ground of untouchability, from entering a place of public worship and offering prayers or taking water from a sacred tank, well or spring. Enforcing any kind of social disability like denying access to any shop, restaurant, hotel, public entertainment, or denying the use of any road, river, well, tank, water tap, bathing ghat, cremation ground, etc., attracts the provision of this Act. Apart from the Civil Rights Act, the Parliament also enacted the Scheduled Castes and Scheduled Tribes (Prevention of Atrocities) Act, 1989 in order to prevent the commission of offence of atrocities against the members of SC/ST to provide Special Courts for trial of such offences. The need for this Act was felt as "under the circumstances, the existing laws like the protection of Civil Rights Act, 1955, and normal provisions of Indian Penal Code have been found to be inadequate to provide safeguard against the crisis against SC/ST (P.K. Gupta 1991)". The term "atrocity" has not been defined in any law. However, it encompasse all IPC offences in which SC/ST persons are made to suffer victims.

Table 1.2 shows that despite the presence of CR Act during the years 1981 to 1985 the total number of cases registered was 19,378. The number of registered cases against the Scheduled

Castes were 2531 in 1993, 1731 in 1994, and 1773 in 1995. The incidence of CR Cases was relatively higher in UP, Tamil Nadu, Rajasthan, MP, Maharashtra, Karnataka and Gujarat. Many agreed that these numbers are "the tip of the iceberg". There are thousands and thousands of incidences which remain unreported.

TABLE 1.2
Areas of Practice of Untouchability

Area	*Untouchability Practice per cent of respondent*
Hotels	80.5
Temples	77.2
Religious Procession	77.2
Tank Water	68.4
Tap Water	77.2
Social Mixing	70.2
Economic Activities	56.0
Political Activities	29.8

Table 1.3 reveals that, between the five years period from 1981 to 1986 about 91097 cases of atrocities were registered by the Scheduled Castes, and another 23, 958 against the Scheduled Tribes. The number of atrocity cases registered by the Scheduled Castes was 14,938 in 1994 and 12,313 in 1995. Thus, on an annual basis an average of 13,000 to 14,000 cases were registered every year. The break-up of the atrocities for the latest year 1995 shows that this includes 513 murder, 4,000 grievous hurt, 439 arson and 787 cases of rapes. The data June 1981 onward reveals that annually about 500 Scheduled Caste persons were murdered, 4,000 are hurt, 400 to 900 are subject to arson and 10,000 faced other offences giving an average of 15,000 cases of atrocities annually.

Every year 513 murders, on an average take place and can we say that the Scheduled Castes enjoy the right to life? With 4,000 cases of arson annually, can we say that the 'Scheduled Castes' right to safe and secure life is guaranteed? With 700 to 800 cases of rape annually can we say that Dalit women have a safe, secure and dignified life? And finally with 3,000 cases of Civil Rights Violation annually can we say that the Scheduled Castes enjoy the same amount of liberty and equality in social relation as the high caste people do? The macro level or overall picture at times hides more than it reveals about the actual human rights violation of

Dalits. The two evidences given below show the picture more clearly.

A Case Study (in Karnataka)

This study is based on survey carried out 52 villages drawn from 52 taluks with 941 samples. For Karnataka, Dr. Mumtaz Khan (1995) concludes that: "Contrary to the expectations... the practices of untouchability in many areas of human social interactions are very much alive in the rural areas". The author further noted that: as high as eighty per cent respondents say that hotels are still barred for them; and if allowed they have to sit in last rows and use separate cups and saucers.

As many as seventy per cent say temples are barred for them, and an equal per cent say they are not allowed to take part in religious processions. Both the sources of water, i.e., tank and tap are prohibited for majority of them. Seventy per cent say that social mixing is not allowed.

Another Study (in Andhra Pradesh)

Dr. Venkateswarlu (1970) in a study of six villages during 1977 of 396 respondents came with the evidence that:

1. Most of the Dalits feel that temples are still bar to them.
2. Most of them feel that they are not to enter the house of the caste Hindu.
3. Marriage procession by Dalits are objected to on one pretext to another, by a large number of upper caste people.
4. Similarly, if a Dalit wants to draw water from a well or a tap in the caste Hindu locality the latter would object to it and sometimes physically obstruct.
5. Physical violence has been perpetrated against the Dalits. A majority of Dalits respondents reported that they were beaten, ranging from, very frequently, to, rarely, there were also cases of raids on Dalits houses. Sometimes raids were followed by looting, kidnapping, insults, rapes, physical torture, threats and attempts to murder. (pp. 109-113).

Violation of Political Rights

The SC/ST Commission's report does not mention the cases of violation of political rights. However, some micro level studies provided some information on this issue. A study on Karnataka observed that: "Tensions in the political spheres of village life occur quite often because of high caste preventing the Dalits from taking part in political activities, for not voting for a particular candidate. Dr. Venkateswarlu has given enough statistical support in favour of violation of political rights."

Lower Wages to Dalits

In the economic field of village life tension takes place when the labourers demand higher wages, intend to change their traditional occupation to more income earning occupation or when they try to occupy the land allotted by the government. Evidence is given where Dalit labourers are beaten for demanding higher wages. Similarly when the Dalits wanted to change their traditional occupation to some other field which meant partly breaking the traditional occupation, they were harassed by being abused or beaten. So there was restriction on the freedom of occupation.

A number of studies point out the discrimination of Dalits in land, and employment market. Minaksi Das observed discrimination in wage earning also. The Dalit labourer often gets lower wages than the non-Dalit worker.

Discrimination in Schools/Colleges

Various studies observed discrimination of the Scheduled Caste in the school and college. Dr. Geeta Nambissan observed that within the schools it appears that Dalit students continue to experience social discrimination and thus can be noticed both in official curriculum, i.e., in the approved content of education and hidden curriculum of schooling. Scheduled Caste communities and the experience of untouchability rarely form part of school education. Though untouchability and maintenance of social distance from certain communities still continues in most parts of India, such practices are rarely mentioned in school books or discussed in the classroom" (*PUCL Bulletin,* April 1995 edited by Dr. R.M. Pal and published by People's Union for Civil Liberties).

Thus, children belonging to communities that belong to lowest caste social hierarchy continue to be discriminated against within the school and classrooms. The personal experiences of Dalits educated in post-independent period mentioned examples of Dalit children being asked to sit away from their classmates, of being refused drinking water and served in broken tea cups, made to sit separately.

Authorities and Civil Rights Violation

The role of various authorities as analysed by Mumtaz Khan, such as the police and the judiciary. The prosecutors and Civil Rights Directorate as much depend on the goodwill, commitment and efficiency of these Civil Rights Act enforcement authorities. About the role of the police he observed that:

1. The vast majority of Dalits are not happy with the treatment meted out of them by the police. About sixty-one per cent say that treatment was relatively bad.
2. Victims faced multiple problems at the time of registration which include non-availability, refusal to register, efforts to compromise, threats and rude behaviour.
3. The reasons for delay were hatred, fear of caste Hindus and higher officers, and indifference.
4. The attitude of Muslim and Christian officers are different from that of Hindu officers.
5. The Scheduled Castes seem to have no faith in the structure and functions of the judiciary. The main cause which prompts the Scheduled Castes to lose faith in the judiciary is the fact that cases ending in convictions do not even amount to one per cent.

The Caste Ideology and Economic Degradation

In 1947, Dr. Ambedkar argued that there is a link between individual liberty and the shape and form of economic structure and the link between the two is real: "Ask those who are unemployed whether what are called Fundamental Rights of any importance to them. If a person who is unemployed is offered a choice between a job of some sort of wage with an interdict on joining a union and the exercise of his rights to freedom of speech, association, religion, etc., can there be any doubt as to what his choice will be? How can it be otherwise? The fear of starvation, the fear of losing a house, the fear of losing saving, if any, the fear of being compelled to take away children from the school, the fear of having to be a burden on public charity are strong factors which stop a man to stand out for his fundamental rights. The unemployed

TABLE 1.3
Incidence of Rural Labour Household

Social group	*% Rural labour HH*			*% Rural labour HH with land*			*% Rural labour HH without land*		
	1974-75	*1983*	*1987*	*1974-75*	*1983*	*1987*	*1974–75*	*1983*	*1987*
Scheduled Castes	NA	57.41	62.55	44.38	37.76	75.67	55.82	62.24	24.33
Scheduled Tribes	31.03	44.04	49.61	51.29	50.04	83.3	48.71	49.96	16.7
Non-SCs/STs	22.01	29.14	31.15	55.97	45.07	79.56	44.02	54.92	20.43

Source: Rural Labour Enquiry Report 1974, 1983, 1987.

TABLE 1.4

Distribution of Households and Area Owened: 1981-82 (All India)

Size/Categories	*SC*		*Non SC/ST*	
	Household	*Area owned*	*Household*	*Area owned*
1. Landless	12.61	–	10.18	–
2. Marginal farmers	72.40	28.32	52.20	7.60
3. Small farmers	8.40	22.82	18.00	10.00
4. Semi-medium farmers	4.52	24.19	12.05	15.77
5. Medium farmers	1.80	19.19	7.00	51.73
6. Large farmers	0.28 (100)	7.69 (100)	1.32 (100)	13.98 (100)
7. Average size	0.62	1.93	2.12	–
8. Gini ratio	0.81	–	0.78	–

NSS Round 37, 1982.
Table on land holdings

TABLE 1.5
Number of Children (5–14 years) Currently Attending Educational Institution per 1000 Children (all India) – 1987-88

Social group	*Rural Female*	*Urban Female*
Scheduled Tribe	204	527
Scheduled Caste	255	523
Others	392	691

TABLE 1.6
Female Literacy Rates

Social group	*Literacy rate*		*Total*	*Rural*	*Urban*
	1971	*1981*	*1991*	*1991*	*1991*
Scheduled Castes	8.44	10.93	27.76	19.46	42.29
Scheduled Tribes	4.85	8.04	18.79	16.22	45.66
All communities excluding SCs and STs	22.25	29.0	39.29	30.62	64.05

TABLE 1.7
Percentage of 'Unemployed' According to Usual Status Currently Weekly Status and Currently Daily Status
Percentage of Person Unemployed

Schedule group	*Rural female*				*Urban female*			
	US–PS	*US excluding SS workers*	*cws*	*cds*	*US–PS*	*LS excluding*	*cws*	*cds*
Scheduled Tribes	0.18 1.22	0.08 —	1.21 1.23	2.57(1972–78) 2.37 (1983–84)	0.46 2.00	0.46 —	0.83 1.67	1.94 2.75
Scheduled Castes	0.50 2.58	0.23 —	2.16 1.90	4.23 4.09 (1983–84)	0.97 3.95	0.71 —	1.15 2.07	2.10 3.27
Others	0.43 1.53	0.29 —	0.91 1.97	1.72(1977–78) 0.97 (1983–84)	1.05 2.95	0.92 —	1.09 1.71	1.42 1.98

US–PS : Usual Status
cws : Currently weekly status
cds : Currently daily status

TABLE 1.8
Number of Poor among Scheduled Castes, Scheduled Tribes vs. All Population (Millions)

Social group	*Rural*		*Percentage Change*	*Urban*		*Percentage Change*
	1977–78	*1983–84*		*1977–78*	*1983–84*	
Scheduled Castes	53.7	19.6	(–) 7.6	7.7	7.8	( ) 1.3
Scheduled Tribes	33.7	31.3	(–) 7.1	1.3	1.5	( ) 15.4
Rest of the Population	165.7	140.6	(–) 15.1	44.7	40.2	(–) 10.1
All India	253.1	221.5	(–) 12.5	53.7	49.5	(–) 7.8

Source: "Changes in Rural Poverty in India", C.H. Hanumantha Rao, *Mainstream*, January 11, 1986.

TABLE 1.9
Number of Persons Below Poverty Line Scheduled Castes, Scheduled Tribes Vs. All Population (Millions)

Category	*Areas*	*1977–78*	*1983–84*	*Percentage Change*
Scheduled Castes	Rural	64.6	53.1	– 17.8
	Urban	54.3	40.4	– 25.6
	Combined	63.2	50.9	– 19.5
Scheduled Tribes	Rural	72.4	58.4	– 19.3
	Urban	52.6	39.9	– 24.1
	Combined	71.4	57.1	– 20.0
All Population	Rural	51.2	40.4	– 21.1
	Urban	38.2	28.1	– 26.4
	Combined	48.3	37.4	– 22.6

Source : "Changes in Rural Poverty in India", C.H. Hanumantha Rao, *Mainstream*, January 11, 1986.

are thus compelled to relinquish their Fundamental Rights for the sake of securing the privilege to work and subsist" (*State and Minorities*, 1947). The dependence of Dalits for economic survival on the high castes causes men and women to forgo the fundamental rights.

In the late 1980s sixty-three per cent of Scheduled Caste household were wage labour households, but only thirty-one per cent of non-Dalits belonged to this category. Only a small percentage of them own land and seventy-three per cent of those who did were marginal farmers with too little land to live on. The result has been a high incidence of poverty among the Scheduled Castes—fifty per cent as compared to only thirty-seven per cent among the general population in the late 1980s. A number of studies suggest that civil rights violations and atrocities are committed over land dispute and wages. The important reason is thus the economic deprivation of the Scheduled Castes. But the economic reason does not tell the whole truth.

A number of studies identify resentment against manifestation of awareness amongst the Scheduled Castes about their rights and privileges as enshrined in the Constitution and many legislations and executive measures. The empirical studies on Andhra Pradesh, Tamil Nadu, Maharashtra, Karnataka and Orissa, etc., clearly indicate that wherever Dalits have asserted their civil, political and economic rights, they have been subject to violence and atrocities as these acts contradict the interest of the dominant caste.

Dalits and Human Rights

The issue of human rights is of profound historical value in the human endeavour of reconstructing society on egalitarian principles. However, among scholars and intellectual human rights activists, there does not appear to be any agreement on the definition and the scope of human rights. First, the disagreement on the definition and scope of human right is broadly located into the dichotomy between the universal and the specific. Second, it is also located in the difference between societal violence and civilizational violence. And finally, an effort is being made by scholars to a creative interpretation which seeks to define in terms of "right to be human" rather than human rights; and a majority of the scholars seek to define human rights basically regarding their violation by society on the one hand and the state on the other

This varied perception of human rights provides the context in which one can bring up four questions with special reference to the human rights of Dalits.

First, in the dichotomy between the universal and the specific where can one situate the issue of Dalit human rights; second, does the Dalit discourse; if any, remain fettered within their specificity or does it come out of this specificity to be seen in terms of its universal applicability; third, how does the Dalit discourse on human rights regard the framework of civilizational violence as more fundamental than social violence? And finally, is the state centered, legally-oriented framework of human rights enough to understand the question of the violation of Dalit human rights? These are some of the issues that require serious follow-up. In recent years efforts have been made to define human rights without reducing them either to an abstract universality or to the romanticisation of specificity.

Nandita Haksar defines human rights as the expression of cultural politics based on the multiplicity of life. Haksar, therefore, seeks to expand the scope of human rights, to include in human rights, right against illicit dumping of toxic and dangerous substances, right against external debt, the right to cultural values, the right of indigenous people to lead their own way of life and the right of disabled people. However, Haksar rightly sounds a note of caution against politics which fall into the trap of romanticising the marginals; on the contrary, as he further says, one should deepen cultural politics that should be connected with a wider vision. D.R. Nagraj is one of the leading intellectuals making major theoretical intervention on *Bahujan* issues.

Well-known creative writer, academic and human rights intellectual-activist, Dr. D.R. Nagraj died on 12 August 1998 at a very young age. He had attended the Madras workshop. However, he laments that Dalit discourse is causing a sort of cultural vacuum. What he means by this vacuum is that Dalit discourse, while focusing on human rights, does not address itself to the question of civilizational violence through which communities are being wiped out by the process of modernisation. Therefore, he concludes, it is not enough to focus just on societal violence but should keep civilizational violence in view. However, Nagraj's communitarian approach seems to be problematic when it is understood in terms of human rights because, how can one restore the community based occupation which by its very nature involves the violation of human rights, as they result in uprooting the human dignity of a community, for example, scavenging. Secondly, the communitarian approach presupposes that the communities exist side by side harmoniously without any tension. This is not a tenable proposition, because the communities are historicity constituted through the constant struggle for and against domination. And it is this historicity that has always condemned the Dalits to seek the protection for human rights. Thus, the protection of community rights from the onslaught of modernity would not automatically ensure human rights to the Dalits. Considering the limitation of this communication approach one will have to take assistance either from Nandita Haksar or from Upendra Baxi who defines human rights in terms of right to be human. Both these scholars have discussed the human rights of the Dalits in India, though not in great detail. Here an attempt is made to understand the human rights particularly of the Dalits in the light of the framework modelled by these scholars.

It is not a mechanical confirmation of the themes developed by Haksar and Baxi; on the contrary it will be a critical reflection on the writings of the eminent scholars. Nandita Haksar's framework is attractive in that it offers a critique of the state which violates human rights and also offers a certain kind of visibility of the human rights of the Dalits which otherwise face the danger of being ignored or subsumed under the grand framework of either extreme culturalism and universalism, or economic reductionalism. In terms of empirical, theoretical and ontological concerns, there is a need to understand the question of Dalit human rights.

First, let us take up the empirical dimension of human rights, particularly of the Dalits, as it is vital to understand the intensity and the magnitude of their violation. It has been rightly argued by Haksar and many others that it is the state and the upper castes who are responsible for the violation through unleashing violence on the Dalits. Thus, the right to the limb is continuously violated by the State and the upper castes. The violence by the upper castes becomes much more brutal particularly against the Dalits. This is clear from the killings of the Kotwal family in Latur district of the Marathwada region of Maharashtra. In this incident an upper caste mob spurred on by enraged caste feelings, broke open the door of a Dalit household and attacked two young sons and their father with deadly weapons killing all the three, then they dragged the bodies of the victims as decomposed bodies of dogs or cats are dragged out of the village. The repeated mass killings of Dalits by the Ranbir Sena of landlords in Bihar, the gorging out of the eyes of Gawai brother in Akola district in Maharashtra and the violence on a Dahanam Dalit school girl in Tamil Nadu, are also examples of brutal violation of the Dalit right to life and limb. The violation of Dalit human rights has another heinous dimension in the shape of sexual exploitation. Such violence ranges from putting a live lizard in the saris of the Dalit women in Osmanabad district in Maharashtra to the gang rape of Bhanwari Devi in Rajasthan. Even a cursory look at the SC/ST Commissioner's report or the Proceedings of People's courts, organised by certain action groups in Delhi and Bangalore or the investigative reports published in the *PUCL Bulletin* edited by Dr. R.M. Pal, one will come across innumerable cases of sexual violence committed by high caste Hindus and the police. However, it looks as though it is the male sexual urge and brutality which are behind such incidents involving the violation of the social honour of Dalit women, thus making the only dimension of the violation of the rights of Dalit women.

What is lacking in such academic discourses or even in the perception of human right activists, is that the sexual violence against Dalit women and also women from the minority community, have more than just a gender bias. Because along with men high caste women also are found, in certain cases, behind destroying the social honour of Dalit women. This was evident when high-caste women in order to exonerate their men folk took to maligning the image of the victims by charging them with loose morals.

Instances such as the killing of the Kotwals in Marathwada and the stripping and beating of Dalit women in some villages in Mul and Brahmpuri talukas of Chandrapur district in Maharashtra and vicarious voyeurism by the high caste women of sexual violence by their manfolk on Dalit and other women highlight this fact. One can look at this absence of feminine conscience as a reflection of the internalisation of patriarchal violence among upper caste women. This brings up a serious question to feminist discourse and the feminist movement in the country. Such violence should not defined merely in terms of its physical or sexual aspects but has to be understood in terms of its implications for intimidation of Dalits.

Dalit people feel fear in speaking out in the presence of the high caste people who exercise control over public institutions and public assemblies. It is also true that the Dalit women feel as intimidated in the presence of men of their own communities as in the company of educated high caste women. Thus, freedom of expression which is at the core of human rights is often denied to the Dalits both by the state and the non-Dalit reactionary Hindus. This violation signifies the individualistic dimension of human rights. But what is required is to include in the definition of human rights, not only the individual right to expression but the Dalit right to speak for even the non-Dalits.

Today, there is a need to broaden the definition through the inclusion of the Dalit right to acquire space in public discourse, specially after the Bhanwari Devi incident in Rajasthan. This case not only involves the violation of the right to life but also the right to human dignity. In addition her gang rape also reflects the violation of the Dalit right to move away from the immediate to the abstract and acquire the public space. In the feudal social order, the obstructionist Hindu Laws have arbitrarily determined the social location of people in a kind of tight caste hierarchy. In Marathi, for instance, it came to be described as *apilya payrine waga* (meaning your boundaries are religiously fixed and you must respect the boundaries). This confinement of the social location of the oppressed has led to the complete marginalisation of the Dalits.

The right to speak for all sections of society presupposes the supremacy of the high castes leading to Brahmanical ego fed on the strict maintenance of the social boundaries by the Dalits. Bhanwari Devi displayed extraordinary courage in challenging the arbitrary boundaries by intervening into the high caste dominated discourse on patriarchy. She opposed child marriages among the high caste families. It hurt the ego of the high caste people and she had to pay the price for crossing the caste boundaries. The Bhanwari Devi case suggests the violation of human rights of the Dalits is caused by denial to them space in public discourse. Thus, Dalits rights need to be understood not in individualist but collectivist terms. The collectivist idea can be substantiated when one tries to follow the collective implication of the individual act of violation of human rights.

Human rights are denied to Dalits due to their group character; Dalits receive discriminatory treatment due to the group character. To put it more bluntly, resistance of violation by a single Dalit person endangers the life and limb of the whole community. It is for this reason only that Dr. Ambedkar did not embark on any individual adventure and had to withdraw apropos of the Poona Pact involving Gandhiji, for otherwise, the entire Dalit community would have been engaged in the upper caste outrage of the 1930s. This "package deal violence" sparked by an individual act of crossing the traditional boundaries had caused mass violence against the Dalits of a village in Tumkar district of Karnataka in June, 1996. Similarly the Dalits of a village in Ambejogai taluka of Bhir district of Marathwada were terrorised and made to vacate the village by non-Dalits. Thus, the violation of rights acquires group character in as much as violence against individual gets compounded affecting the entire Dalit community. Thus, the magnitude of the violation of rights particularly in caste ridden or ethnically divided societies begins with the violence unleashed against individuals but invariably causes violence against the community. The violation of Dalit human rights through violence against the Dalit community emanates from the fascist ideology of the Hindutva forces.

This ideology is also connected with the ideology and practice of untouchability which is technically the violation of the human dignity of the Dalits and was abolished by the Constitution fifty years ago. The fascist ideology of untouchability is based on a specious concept of "purity pollution line" and practises discrimination against the Dalit. Even at the risk of inviting the wrath of environmentalists, one must cite illustrations relating to 'man animal' comparison to indicate how the human dignity of the Dalits is violated by the *Hindutva* elements, and the State. Some animals are regarded by this section to be sacred while the "untouchables" are identified as sources of pollution. Dr. Ambedkar had said that the Black people or Afro-Americans in the U.S. are slightly better than the Indian Untouchables because the White people of America do not regard them as sources of pollution by touch. Even in the days before the abolition of slavery they were not kept beyond reach. On the contrary, when the Dalits of a village in the Chikkodi taluka of Belgaum district of Karnataka were forced by high caste Hindus to eat human excreta in 1992 they were regarded as sub-human. In Maharashtra the government led by the Shiv Sena and BJP practises discrimination by presenting school uniforms of different kinds for Dalits and the others. *Khaki* shorts and shirts constitute the uniform for non-Dalit pupils in the Zila Parishad schools in the State while Dalit pupils have to wear blue shirts and shorts. The identification by the colour of the dress of Dalits is on account of historical association of blue with the Dalits. In the process the government is protecting the high-caste Hindus who commit atrocities on the Dalits. The government has also withdrawn police cases against high caste Hindu under the 1989 Dalit Act (Prevention of Atrocities Against SCs Act). The reports of the Commissioner for SCs/STs have listed several instances of treating the Dalits as pollutants by the high caste Hindus in different states of the country. The SC/ST Commissioner's report in this respect finds support from Harsh Mander's report.

Role of State Unsatisfactory

The role of the state in protecting human dignity of the Dalits seems to be very unsatisfactory in the sense that it has not been able to stop the practice of scavengers carrying night soil on their heads. Though these Dalits are enumerated as *mehtar* instead of *Bhangi* in the government records, they are treated by the Hindu society as filthy, polluting creatures. The stand of some of the so called voluntary organisations of environmentalist activists in opposing the government's efforts to mechanise the sanitary services is conducive to the continuance of the barbaric practice. It is quite possible that the government may have some vested interest in eliminating the practice by the use of wood pulp but the activists should not turn blind eye to the human rights aspect by seeking the perpetuation of physical carrying of night soil by the scavengers. If they have an objection to the government's proposal they should suggest alternatives to it. Similarly, rag picking is regarded environment friendly. It is done mostly by Dalit women who according to these activists do not regard rag picking as below human dignity. Rag picking brings the human being into identification with dogs and pigs which feed on the garbage.

Simultaneously, the police and many householders regard the rag pickers as potential petty thieves so that there are instances of abuse and physical attacks on rag-picking Dalit women. Finally, the endorsement of rag picking by the upper caste perception is based on exteriority. The elitist and superficial perception of rag picking divides feminist consciousness. It becomes superficial, at times, a reactionary agenda for the simple reason that instead of criticising the economic system which rorces a large section of society to make a living on garbage, it tends to protect the economic system by treating garbage or rag picking as environment friendly. Thus, this kind of partial and sometimes negative opinion of human rights which treats rag picking as an attribute of the welfare liberal state makes us take a radical view of human rights, the post-modernist-statist view which is partial makes it imperative for scholars and human rights activists to develop a radical and integrated view concerning the rights of Dalits.

Along with the fulfillment of the non-material needs of the Dalits, like protecting the human dignity and promoting social fraternity the satisfaction of material needs also becomes a precondition for restoring the right to be human. For instance, certain trades like tanning and sanitation carry the stigma of pollution to the practitioners, mostly Dalits. Or to put it slightly differently, as Harsh Manlar has noted, the dividing line between pollution and poverty is water thin, meaning those who are socially polluting are also necessarily steeped in poverty. Thus, the Dalit perspective would seek societal resources for concretising the right to be human. The right to be human should also enable the person to satisfy his or her most basic wants like food, shelter and clothing. The Dalit perspective on the right to be humans does not take a voluntaristic opinion that human rights are bestowed for all people to enjoy. On the other hand, it assumes that the right to be human, is not state constituted but is historically constituted through the constant struggle for "Manuski" (human treatment) led by Phule, Periyar, Ambedkar and several others. The right to be human therefore, is not the result of charity of the mahatmas or the high caste *pandits* or an ad hoc approach to human rights of the liberal state, but is the outcome of Dalit struggle for parity.

The parity principle within the Dalit perspective has to be organised around dignified conditions of human existence. In this context, the Dalit perspective on human rights is different. Haksar's framework of human rights looks to be attractive because it offers a critique of the state which violates Dalit rights and also offer visibility to human rights, which, otherwise are quite generally either ignored or are subsumed in the framework of an abstract universalism, extreme culturalism or economic reductionism. The Dalit perspective is distinct due to its group character as against the legalistic, individualistic approach of the state towards the human rights of Dalits.

Protection of a single individual does not make the entire Dalit community automatically secure. On the contrary as it happened in case of the 1989 Act recourse to the law by affected Dalit individuals against the higher castes in Marathwada region engulfed the entire Dalit community of the region in a widespread caste outrage after the decision to rename Marathwada University after Ambedkar in 1993. Similarly, the case of Bhanwari Devi in Rajasthan reveals the limitations of the individualistic approach as it does not capture the deep structures of violation of human rights of the Dalits. The case of Bhanwari Devi at the surface level no doubt represent the violation of the right to expression of an individual. But what it does not really capture is that Bhanwari Devi's exercise of right to speak against child marriage causes terrorisation of the entire community which would not dare to speak for others and would not dare to acquire the public space. Thus, the case of Bhanwari Devi indicates that the definition of human rights in the Indian context need to be expanded to include in its gamut not only individual rights but the right of the community to move from the immediate to the abstract.

2

Reservation of Seats for Scheduled Castes and Scheduled Tribes in the House of the People

1. Seats shall be reserved in the House of People for—

(a) the Scheduled Castes;
(b) the Scheduled Tribes except the Scheduled Tribes in the autonomous districts of Assam; and
(c) the Scheduled Tribes in the autonomous districts of Assam.

2. The number of seats reserved in any State or Union Territory for the Scheduled Castes or the Scheduled Tribes under clause (1) shall bear, as nearly as may be, the same proportion to the total number of seats allotted to that State or Union Territory in the House of the People as the population of the Scheduled Castes in the State or Union Territory or of the Scheduled Tribes in the State or Union Territory or part of the State or Union Territory, as the case may be, in respect of which seats are so reserved bears to the total population of the State or Union Territory.

3. Notwithstanding anything contained in clause (2), the number of seats reserved in the House of the People for the Scheduled Tribes in the autonomous districts of Assam shall bear to the total number of seats allotted to that State a proportion not less than the population of the Scheduled Tribes in the autonomous districts bears to the total population of the State.

Explanation. In this Article and in Article 332, the expression "population" means the population as ascertained at the last preceding census of which the relevant figures have been published.

Provided that the reference in the *Explanation* to the last preceding census of which the relevant figures have been published shall, until the relevant figures for the first census taken after the year 2000 have been published, be construed, as a reference to the 1971 Census.

331. Representation of the Anglo-Indian community in the House of the People. Notwithstanding anything in Article 81, the President may, if he is of opinion that the Anglo-Indian community is not adequately represented in the House of the People, nominate not more than two members of that community to the House of the People.

332. Reservation of Seats for Scheduled Castes and Scheduled Tribes in the Legislative Assemblies to the States. 1. Seats shall be reserved for the Scheduled Castes and Scheduled Tribes except the Scheduled Tribes in the autonomous districts of Assam, in the Legislative Assembly of every State.

2. Seats shall be reserved also for the autonomous districts in the Legislative Assembly of the State of Assam.

3. The number of seats reserved for the Scheduled Castes or the Scheduled Tribes in the Legislative Assembly of any State under clause (1) shall bear, as nearly as may be, the same proportion to the total number of seats in the Assembly as the population of the Scheduled Castes in the State or of the Scheduled Tribes in the State or part of the State, as the case may be, in respect of which seats are so reserved, bears to the total population of the State.

3-A. Notwithstanding anything contained in clause (3), until the taking effect, under Article 170, of the re-adjustment, on the basis of the first census after the year 2000, of the number of seats in the Legislative Assemblies of the States of Arunachal Pradesh, Meghalaya, Mizoram and Nagaland, the seats which shall be reserved for the Scheduled Tribes in the Legislative Assembly of any such State shall be,—

(a) if all the seats in the Legislative Assembly of such State in existence on the date of coming into force of the Constitution (Fifty-seventh Amendment) Act, 1987 (hereafter in this clause referred to as the existing Assembly) are held by members of the Scheduled Tribes, all the seats except one;

(b) in any other case, such number of seats as bears to the total number of seats, a proportion not less than the number (as on the said date) of members belonging to the Scheduled Tribes in the existing Assembly bears to the total number of seats in the existing Assembly.

3-B. Notwithstanding anything contained in clause (3), until the readjustment, under Article 170, takes effect on the basis of the first census after the year 2000, of the number of seats in the Legislative Assembly of the State of Tripura, the seats which shall be reserved for the Scheduled Tribes in the Legislative Assembly shall be, such number of seats as bears to the total number of seats, a proportion not less than the number, as on the date of coming into force of the Constitution (Seventy-second Amendment) Act, 1992, of members belonging to the Scheduled Tribes in the Legislative Assembly in existence on the said date bears to the total number of seats in that Assembly.

4. The number of seats reserved for the autonomous district in the Legislative Assembly of the State of Assam shall bear to the total number of seats in that Assembly a proportion not less than the population of the district bears to the total population of the State.

5. The constituencies for the seats reserved for any autonomous district of Assam shall not comprise any area outside that district.

6. No person who is not a member of a Scheduled Tribe of any autonomous district of the State of Assam shall be eligible for election to the Legislative Assembly of the State from any constituency of that district.

333. Representation of the Anglo-Indian community in the Legislative Assemblies of the States. Notwithstanding anything in Article 170, the Governor of a State may if he is of opinion that the Anglo-Indian community needs representation in the Legislative Assembly of the State and is not adequately represented therein, nominate one member of that community to the Assembly.

334. Reservation of seats and special representation to cease after fifty years. Notwithstanding anything in the foregoing provisions of this Part, the provisions of this Constitution relating to—

(a) the reservation of seats for the Scheduled Castes and the Scheduled Tribes in the House of the People and in the Legislative Assemblies of the States; and
(b) the representation of the Anglo-Indian community in the House of the People and in the Legislative Assemblies of the States by nomination,

shall cease to have effect on the expiration of a period of fifty years from the commencement of this Constitution:

Provided that, nothing in this Article shall effect any representation in the House of the people or in the Legislative Assembly of a State until the dissolution of the then existing House of Assembly, as the case may be.

335. Claims of Scheduled Castes and Scheduled Tribes to services and posts. The claims of the members of the Scheduled Castes and the Scheduled Tribes shall be taken into consideration, consistently with the maintenance of efficiency of administration, in the making of appointments to services and posts in connection with the affairs of the Union or of a State.

336. Special provision for Anglo-Indian Community in Certain Services. 1. During the first two years after the commencement of this Constitution, appointments of members of the Anglo-Indian community to posts in the Railway, Customs, Postal and Telegraph Services of the Union shall be made on the same basis as immediately before the fifteenth day of August, 1947.

During every succeeding period of two years, the number of posts reserved for the members of the said community in the said services shall, as nearly as possible, be less by ten per cent than the numbers so reserved during the immediately preceding period of two years:

Provided that at the end of ten years from the commencement of this Constitution all such reservations shall cease.

2. Nothing in clause (1) shall bar the appointment of members of the Anglo-Indian community to posts other than, or in addition to, those reserved for the community under that clause if such members are found qualified for appointment on merit as compared with the members of other communities.

337. Special Provision with respect to an Educational Grants for the Benefit of Anglo-Indian Community. During the first three financial years after the commencement of this Constitution, the same grants, if any, shall be made by the Union and by each State for the benefit of the Anglo-Indian community in respect of education as were made in the financial year ending on the thirty first day of March, 1948.

During the every succeeding period of three years the grants may be less by ten per cent than those for the immediately preceding period of three years:

Provided that at the end of ten years from the commencement of this Constitution such grants, to the extent to which they are a special concession to the Anglo-Indian community, shall cease:

Provided further that no educational institution shall be entitled to receive any grant under this Article unless at least forty per cent of the annual admissions therein are made available to members of communities other than the Anglo-Indian community.

338. National Commission for Scheduled Castes and Scheduled Tribes. 1. There shall be a Commission for the Scheduled Castes and Scheduled Tribes to be known as the National Commission for the Scheduled Castes and Scheduled Tribes.

2. Subject to the provisions of any law made in this behalf by Parliament, the Commission shall consist of a Chairperson, Vice-Chairperson and five other Members and the conditions of the service and tenure of office of the Chairperson, Vice-Chairperson and other Members so appointed shall be such as the President may by rule determine.

3. The Chairperson, Vice-Chairperson and other Members of the Commission shall be appointed by the President by warrant under his hand and seal.

4. The Commission shall have the power to regulate its own procedure.

5. It shall be the duty of Commission—

(a) to investigate and monitor all matters relating to the safeguards provided for the Scheduled Castes and Scheduled Tribes under this Commission or under any other law for the time being in force or under any order of the Government and to evaluate the working of such safeguards;

(b) to inquire into specific complaints with respect to the deprivation of rights and safeguards of the Scheduled Castes and Scheduled Tribes;

(c) to participate and advise on the planning process of socio-economic development of the Scheduled Castes and Scheduled Tribes and to evaluate the progress of their development under the Union and any States;

(d) to present to the President, annually and at such other times as the Commission may deem fit, reports upon the working of those safeguard;

(e) to make in such reports recommendations as to the measures that should be taken by the Union or any State for the effective implementation of those safeguards and other measures for the protection, welfare and socio-economic development of the Scheduled Castes and Scheduled Tribes; and

(f) to discharge such other functions in relation to the protection, welfare and development and advancement of the Scheduled Castes and Scheduled Tribes as the President may, subject to the provisions of any law made by Parliament by rule specify.

6. The President shall cause all such reports to be laid down before such House of Parliament along with a memorandum explaining the action taken or proposed to be taken on the recommendation relating to the Union and the reasons for the non-acceptance, if any, or any such recommendations.

7. Where any such report, or any part thereof, relates to any matter with which any State Government is concerned, a copy of such report shall be forwarded to the Governor of the State who shall cause it to be laid for before the Legislature of the State along with a memorandum explaining the action taken or proposed to be taken on the recommendations relating to the States and the reasons for the non-acceptance, if any, or any of such recommendations.

8. The Commission shall, while investigating any matter referred to in sub-clause (a) or inquiring into any complaint referred to in sub-clause (b) of clause (5), have all the powers of a civil Court trying a suit and in particular in respect of the following matters, namely—

(a) summoning and enforcing the attendance of any person from any part of India and examining him on oath;
(b) requiring the discovery and production of any document;
(c) receiving evidence of affidavits;
(d) requisitioning any public record or copy thereof from any Court or office;
(e) issuing commissions for the examination of witnesses and documents;
(f) any other matter which the President may, by rule determine.

9. The Union and every State Government shall consult the Commission on all major policy matters affecting Scheduled Castes and Scheduled Tribes.

10. In this Article, references to the Scheduled Castes and Scheduled Tribes shall be construed as including references to such other backward classes as the President may, on receipt of the report of a Commission appointed under clause (1) of Article 340, by order specify and also to the Anglo-Indian community.

339. Control of the Union over the administration of Scheduled Areas and the welfare of Scheduled Tribes. 1. The President may at any time and shall, at the expiration of ten years from the commencement of this Constitution by order appoint a Commission to report on the administration of the Scheduled Areas and the welfare of the Scheduled Tribes in the States.

The order may define the composition, powers and procedure of the Commission and may contain such incidental or ancillary provisions as the President may consider necessary or desirable.

2. The executive power of the Union shall extend to the giving of directions to a State as to the drawing up and execution of schemes specified in the direction to be essential for the welfare of the Scheduled Tribes in the State.

340. Appointment of a Commission to investigate the conditions of backward classes. 1. The President may by order appoint a Commission consisting of such persons as he thinks fir to investigate the conditions of socially and educationally backward classes within the territory of India and the difficulties under which they labour and to make recommendations as to the steps that should be taken by the Union or any State to remove such difficulties and to improve their condition and as to the grants that should be made for the purpose by the Union or any State and the conditions subject to which such grants should be made, and the order appointing such Commission shall define the procedure to be followed by the Commission.

2. A Commission so appointed shall investigate the matters referred to them and present to the President a report setting out the facts as found by them and making such recommendations as they think proper.

3. The President shall cause a copy of the report so presented together with a memorandum explaining the action taken thereon to be laid before each House of Parliament.

341. Scheduled Castes. 1. The President may with respect to any State or Union Territory, and where it is a State, after consultation with the Governor thereof by public notification, specify the castes, races or tribes or parts of or groups within castes, races or tribes which shall for the purposes of this Constitution be deemed to be Scheduled Castes in relation to that State or Union Territory, as the case may be.

2. Parliament may by law include in the, or exclude from the,

list of Scheduled Castes specified in a notification issued under clause (1) and caste, race or tribe, or part of group within any castes, race or tribe, but save as aforesaid a notification issued under the said clause shall not be varied by any subsequent notification.

342. Scheduled Tribes. 1. The President (may with respect to any State, or Union Territory), and where it is a State, after consultation with the Governor (thereof by public notification, specify the tribes or tribal communities or parts of or groups within tribes or tribal communities which shall for the purposes of this Constitution be deemed to be Scheduled Tribes in relation to that State (or Union Territory, as the case may be).

2. Parliament may by law include in or exclude from the list of Scheduled Tribes specified in a notification issued under clause (1) any tribe of tribal community or part of a group within any tribe or tribal community, but, save as aforesaid a notification issued under the said clause shall not be varied by any subsequent notification.

THE PROTECTION OF HUMAN RIGHTS ACT, 1993

No. 10 of 1994

(8th January, 1994)

An act to provide for the constitution of a National Human Rights Commission, State Human Rights Commission in States and Human Rights courts for better protection of human rights and for matters connected therewith or incidental thereto.

Be it enacted by Parliament in the Forty-fourth Year of the Republic of India as follows:

CHAPTER I

PRELIMINARY

1. Short title, extent and commencement. 1. This Act may be called the Protection of Human Rights Act, 1993.

2. It extends to the whole of India:

Provided that it shall apply to the State of Jammu and Kashmir only in so far as it pertains to the matters relatable to any of the entries enumerated in List I or List III in the Seventh Schedule to the Constitution as applicable to that State.

3. It shall be deemed to have come into force on the 28th day of September, 1993.

2. *Definitions.* 1. In this Act, unless the context otherwise requires:

(a) "armed forces" means the naval, military and air forces and includes any other armed forces of the Union;

(b) "Chairperson" means the Chairperson of the Commission or of the State Commission, as the case may be;

(c) "Commission" means the National Human Rights Commission constituted under section 3;

(d) "Human rights" means the rights relating to life, liberty, equality and dignity of the individual guaranteed by the Constitution or embodied in the International Covenants and enforceable by courts in India;

(e) "Human Rights Court" means the Human Rights Court Specified under section 30;

(f) "International Covenants" means the International Covenant on Civil and Political Rights and The International Covenant on Economic; Social and Cultural Rights adopted by the General Assembly of the United Nations on the 16th December 1966;

(g) "Member" means a Member of the Commission or of the State Commission, as the case may be and includes the Chairperson.

(h) "National Commission for Minorities" means the National Commission for Minorities constituted under Section 3 of the National Commission for Minorities Act, 1992 (9 of 1992);

(i) "National Commission for the Scheduled Castes and Scheduled Tribes" means the National Commission for the Scheduled Castes and Scheduled Tribes referred to in Article 338 of the Constitution.

(j) "National Commission for Women" means the National Commission for Women constituted under Section 3 of the National Commission for Women Act, 1990 (20 of 1990);

(k) "Notification" means a notification published in the official Gazette;

(l) "Prescribed" means prescribed by rules made under this Act;

(m) "Public servant" shall have the meaning assigned to it in section 21 of the Indian Penal Code (45 of 1860); and

(n) "State Commissions" means a State Human Rights Commission constituted under section 21.

2. Any reference in this Act to a law which is not in force in the State of Jammu and Kashmir, shall in relation to that State, be construed as a reference to a corresponding law, if any, in force in that State.

CHAPTER II

THE NATIONAL HUMAN RIGHTS COMMISSION

3. *Constitution of a National Human Rights Commission.* 1. The Central Government shall constitute a body to be known as the National Human Rights Commission to exercise the powers conferred upon and to perform the functions assigned to it, under this Act,

2. The Commission shall consist of:

(a) a Chairperson who has been a Chief Justice of the Supreme Court;

(b) one member who is or has been a judge of the Supreme Court;

(c) one Member who is, or has been, the Chief Justice of a High Court; and

(d) two Members to be appointed from amongst persons having knowledge of, or practical experience in, matters relating to human rights.

3. The Chairpersons of the National Commission for Minorities, the National Commission for the Scheduled Castes and Scheduled Tribes and the National Commission for Women shall be deemed to be Member of the Commission for the discharge of functions specified in clauses (b) to (j) of section 12.

4. There shall be a Secretary-General who shall be the Chief Executive Officer of the Commission and shall exercise such powers and discharge such functions of the Commission as it may delegate to him.

5. The headquarter of the Commission shall be at Delhi and the Commission may, with the previous approval of the Central Government establish offices at other places in India.

4. *Appointment of Chairperson and other Members.* 1. The Chairperson and other Members shall be appointed by the President by warrant under his hand and seal:

Provided that every appointment under this sub-section shall be made after obtaining the recommendation of a Committee consisting of:

(a)	the Prime Minister	Chairperson
(b)	Speaker of the House of the People	Member
(c)	Minister-in-charge of the Ministry of Home Affairs in the Government of India	Member
(d)	Leader of the Opposition of the House of the People	Member
(e)	Leader of the Opposition in the Council of States	Member
(f)	Deputy Chairman of the Council of States	Member

Provided further that no sitting judge of the Supreme Court or sitting Chief Justice of a High Court shall be appointed except after consultation with the Chief Justice of India.

2. No appointment of a Chairperson or a Member shall be invalid merely by reason of any vacancy in the Committee.

5. ***Removal of a Member of the Commission.*** 1. Subject to the provisions of sub-section (2) the Chairperson or any other Member of the Commission shall only be removed from his office by order of the President on the ground of proved misbehaviour or incapacity after the Supreme Court, on reference being made to it by the President has, on inquiry held in accordance with the procedure prescribed in that behalf by the Supreme Court, reported that the Chairperson or such other Member as the case may be, ought on any such ground to be removed.

2. Notwithstanding anything in sub-section (1), the President may by order remove from office the Chairperson or any other Member if the Chairperson or such other Member, as the case may be—

(a) is adjudged an insolvent; or

(b) engages during his term of office in any paid employment outside the duties of his office; or

(c) is unfit to continue in office by reason of infirmity of mind or body; or

(d) is of unsound mind and stands so declared by a competent court; or

(e) is convicted and sentenced to imprisonment for an offence which in the opinion of the President involves moral turpitude.

6. Term of office of Members. 1. A person appointed as Chairperson shall hold office for a term of five years from the date on which he enters upon his office or until he attains the age of seventy years, whichever is earlier.

2. A person appointed as a Member shall hold office for a term of five years from the date on which he enters upon his office and shall be eligible for re-appointment for another term of five years:

Provided that no Members shall hold office after he has attained the age of seventy years.

3. On ceasing to hold office, a Chairperson or a Member shall be ineligible for further employment under the Government of India or under the Government of any State.

7. Member to act as Chairperson or to discharge his functions in certain circumstances. 1. In the event of the occurrence of any vacancy in the office of the Chairperson by reason of his death, resignation or otherwise, the president may by notification, authorize one of the Members to act as the Chairperson until the appointment of a new Chairperson to fill such vacancy.

2. When the Chairperson is unable to discharge his functions owning to absence on leave or otherwise, such one of the Members as the President may, by notification, authorize in this behalf, shall discharge the function of the Chairperson until the date on which the Chairperson resumes his duties.

8. Terms and Conditions of service of Members. The salaries and allowances payable to, and other terms and conditions of service of, the Members shall be such as may be prescribed:

Provided that neither the salary and allowances nor the other terms and conditions of service of a Member shall be varied to his disadvantage after his appointment.

9. Vacancies, etc. not to invalidate the proceedings of the Commission. No act to proceedings of the Commission shall be questioned or shall be invalidated merely on the ground of existence of any vacancy or defect in the constitution of the Commission.

10. Procedure to be regulated by the Commission. 1. The Commission shall meet at such time and place as the Chairperson may think fit.

2. The Commission shall regulate its own procedure.

3. All orders and decisions of the Commission shall be

authenticated by the Secretary-General or any other of the Commission duly authorized by the Chairperson in this behalf.

11. Officers and other staff of the Commission. 1. The Central Government shall make available to the commission:

(a) an officer of the rank of the Secretary to the Government of India who shall be the Secretary-General of the Commission; and

(b) such police and investigative staff under an officer not below the rank of a Director-General of Police and such other officers and staff as may necessary for the efficient performance of the functions of the Commission.

2. Subject to such rules as may be made by the Central Government in this behalf, the Commission may appoint such other administrative, technical and scientific staff as it may consider necessary.

3. The salaries, allowances and conditions of service of the officers and other staff appointed under sub-section (2) shall be such as may be prescribed.

Functions and Powers of the Commission

12. Functions of the Commission. The Commission shall perform all or any of the following functions, namely;

(a) inquire, *suo motu* or on a petition presented to it by a victim or any person on his behalf, into complaint of—

   (i) violation of human rights or abatement thereof, or
   (ii) negligence in the prevention of such violation;
   by a public servant;

(b) intervenes in any proceedings involving any allegation of violation of human rights pending before a court with the approval of such court;

(c) visit, under intimation to the State Government, any jail or any other institution under control of the State Government, where persons are detained or lodged for purposes of treatment, reformation or protection to study the living condition of the inmates and make recommendations thereon;

(d) review the safeguards provided by or under the Constitution or any law for the time being in force for the protection of human rights and recommend measures for their effective implementation;

(e) review the factors including acts of terrorism that inhibit the enjoyment of human rights and recommend appropriate remedial measures;

(f) study treaties and other international instruments on human rights and make recommendations for their effective implementation;

(g) undertake and promote research in the field of human rights;

(h) spread human rights literacy among various sections of society and promote awareness of the safeguards available for the protection of these rights through publication, the media, seminars and other available means;

(i) encourage the efforts of non-governmental organizations and institutions working in the field of human rights; and

(j) such other functions as it may consider necessary for the promotion of human rights.

13. Powers relating to inquiries. 1. The Commission shall, while inquiring into complaints under this Act, have all the powers of a civil court trying a suit under the Code of Civil Procedure, 1908 (5 of 1908) and in particular in respect of the following matters, namely –

(a) summoning and enforcing the attendance of witnesses and examining them on oath;

(b) discovery and production of any document;

(c) receiving evidence on affidavits;

(d) requisitioning any public record or copy thereof from any court of office;

(e) issuing commissions for the examination of witnesses or documents; and

(f) any other matter which may be prescribed.

2. The Commission shall have power to require any person, subject to any privilege which may be claimed by that person under any law for the time being in force, to furnish information on such points or matters as, in the opinion of the commission, may be useful for, or relevant to, the subject matter of the inquiry and any person so required shall be deemed to be legally bound to furnish such information within the meaning of Section 176 and Section 177 of the Indian Panel Code (45 of 1860).

3. The Commission or any other officer, not below the rank of a Gazetted Officer, specially authorized in this behalf by the Commission may enter any building or place where the Commission has reason to believe that any document relating to the subject matter of the inquiry may be found and may seize any such document or take extracts or copies therefrom subject to the provisions of section 100 of the Code of Criminal Procedure, 1973, in so far as it may be applicable.

4. The Commission shall be deemed to be a civil court and when any offence as is described in Section 175, Section 178, Section 179, Section 180 or Section 228 of the Indian Penal Code is committed in the view or presence (45 of 1980) of the Commission, the Commission may, after recording the facts constituting the offence and the statement of the accused as provided for in the Code of Criminal Procedure, 1973, forward the case to a Magistrate having jurisdiction to try the same and the Magistrate to whom any such case is forwarded shall proceed to hear the complaint against the accused as if the case has been forwarded to him under section 346 of the Code of Criminal Procedure, 1973 (2 of 1974).

5. Every proceeding before the commission shall be deemed to be a judicial proceeding within the meaning of sections 193 and 228 and for the purposes of section 196, of the Indian Penal Code (45 oí 1960) and the Commission shall be deemed to be a civil court for all the purposes of section 195 and Chapter XXVI of the Code of Criminal Procedure, 1973 (2 of 1974)

14. Investigation. 1. The Commission may, for the purpose of conducting any investigation pertaining to the inquiry, utilize the services of any officer or investigation agency of the Central Government or any State Government with the concurrence of the Central Government or the State Government, as the case may be.

2. For the purpose of investigating into any matter pertaining to the inquiry, any officer or agency whose services are utilized under sub-section (1) may, subject to the direction and control of the Commission:

(a) summon and enforce the attendance of any person and examine him;
(b) require the discovery and production of any document; and
(c) requisition any public record or copy thereof from any office.

3. The provisions of section 15 apply in relation to any

statement made by a person before any officer or agency whose services are utilized under sub-section (1) as they apply in relation to any statement made by person in the course of giving evidence before the Commission.

4. The officer or agency whose services are utilized under sub-section (1) shall investigate into any matter pertaining to the inquiry and submit a report thereon to the Commission within such period as may be specified by the Commission in this behalf.

5. The Commission shall satisfy itself about the correctness of the facts stated and the conclusion, if any, arrived at in the report submitted to it under sub-section (4) and for this purpose the Commission may make such inquiry (including the examination of the person or persons who conducted or assisted in the investigation) as it thinks fit.

15. *Statement made by persons to the commission.* No Statement made by a person in the course of giving evidence before the Commission shall subject him, to or be used against him in, any civil or criminal proceedings except a prosecution for giving false evidence by such statement.

Provided that the statement:

(a) is made in reply to the question which he is required by the Commission to answer; or

(b) is relevant to the subject matter of the inquiry.

16. Persons likely to be prejudicially affected to be heard. If at any stage of the inquiry, the Commission:

(a) considers it necessary to inquire into the conduct of any person; or

(b) is of the opinion that the reputation of any person is likely to be prejudicially affected by the inquiry;

It shall give to that person a reasonable opportunity of being heard in the inquiry and to produce evidence in his defence:

Provided that nothing in this section shall apply where the credit of a witness is being impeached.

CHAPTER IV

PROCEDURE

17. Inquiry into complaints. The Commission while inquiring into the complaints of violations of human rights may:

(i) call for information or report from the Central Government or any State Government or any other authority or organisation subordinate thereto within such time as may be specified by it:
provide that

(a) if the information or report is not received withIn the time stipulated by the Commission, it may proceed to inquire into the complaint on its own.

(b) if, on receipt of information or report, the Commission is satisfied either that no further inquiry is required or that the required action has been initiated or taken by the concerned Government or authority, it may not proceed with the complaint and inform the complainant accordingly;

(ii) without prejudice to any thing contained in clause (i), if it considers necessary, having regard to the nature of the complaint, initiate an inquiry.

18. Steps after inquiry. The Commission may take any of the following steps upon the completion of an inquiry held under this Act. namely:

1. Where the inquiry discloses the Commission of violation of human rights or negligence in the prevention of violation of human rights by a public servant, it may recommend to the concerned Government or authority the initiation of proceedings for prosecution or such other action as the Commission may deem fit against the concerned person or persons.

2. Approach the Supreme Court or the High Court concerned for such directions, orders or writs as that Court may deem necessary.

3. Recommend to the concerned Government or authority for the grant of such immediate interim relief to the victim or the members of his family as the Commission may consider necessary.

4. Subject to the provision of clause (5) provide a copy of the inquiry report to the petitioner or his representative.

5. The Commission shall send a copy of its inquiry report together with its recommendations to the concerned Government or authority and the concerned Government or authority shall, within a period of one month, or such further time as the Commission may allow, forward its comments on the report,

including the action taken or proposed to be taken thereon, to the Commission.

6. The Commission shall publish its inquiry report together with the comments of the concerned Government or authority, if any, and the action taken or proposed to be taken by the concerned Government or authority on the recommendations of the Commission.

19. Procedure with respect to Armed Forces. 1. Notwithstanding anything contained in this Act, while dealing with complaints of violation of human rights by members of the armed forces, the Commission shall adopt the following, namely:

(a) it may, either on its own motion or on receipt of a petition, seek a report from the Central Government; and

(b) after the receipt of the report, it may, either not proceed with the complaint or, as the case may be, make its recommendations to that Government.

2. The Central Government shall inform the Commission of the action taken on the recommendations within three months or such further time as the Commission may allow.

3. The Commission shall publish its report together with its recommendations made to the Central Government and the action taken by that Government on such recommendations.

4. The Commission shall provide a copy of the report published under sub-section (3) to the petitioner or his representative.

20. Annual and special report of the Commission. 1. The Commission shall submit an annual report to the Central government and to the State Government concerned and may at any time submit special reports on any matter which, in its opinion, is of such urgency or importance that it should not be deferred till submission of the annual report.

2. The Central Government and the State Government, as the case may be shall be annual and special reports of the Commission to be laid before each house of Parliament or the State Legislature respectively as the case may be, along with a memorandum of action taken or proposed to be taken on the recommendations of the Commission and the reasons for non-acceptance of the recommendations, if any.

CHAPTER V

STATE HUMAN RIGHTS COMMISSION

21. *Constitution of State Human Rights Commissions.* 1. A State Government may constitute a body to be known as the . . . (name of the State) Human Rights Commission to exercise the powers conferred upon, and to perform the functions assigned to, a State Commission under this chapter.

2. The State Commission shall consist of—

(a) a chairperson who has been a Chief Justice of a High Court;
(b) one Member who is, or has been a Judge of a High Court;
(c) one Member who is, or has been, a District Judge in that State; and
(d) two Members to be appointed from amongst persons having knowledge of, or practical experience in, matters relating to human rights.

3. There shall be a Secretary who shall be the Chief Executive Officer of the State Commission and shall exercise such powers and discharge such functions of the State Commission as it may delegate to him.

4. The headquarters of the State Commission shall be at such place as the State Government may, by notification, specify.

5. A State Commission may inquire into violation of human rights only in respect of matters relatable to any of the entries enumerated in List II and List III in the Seventh Schedule to the Constitution:

Provided that if any such matter is already being inquired into by the Commission or any other Commission duly constituted under any law for the time being in force, the State Commission shall not inquire into the said matter.

Provided further that in relation to the Jammu and Kashmir Human Rights Commission, this sub-section shall have effect as if for the words and figures "List II and List III in the Seventh Schedule to the Constitution" the words and figures "List III in the Seventh Schedule to the Constitution as applicable to the State of Jammu and Kashmir and in respect of matters in relation to which the Legislature of that State has power to make laws" had been substituted.

22. *Appointment of Chairperson and other Members of State*

Commission. 1. The Chairperson and other Member shall be appointed by the Governor by warrant under this hand and seal.

Provided that every appointment under this sub-section shall be made after obtaining the recommendation of a Committee consisting of:

(a) the Chief Minister — Chairperson
(b) Speaker of the Legislative Assembly — Member
(c) Minister-in-charge of the Department of Home in that State — Member
(d) Leader of the Opposition in the Legislative Assembly — Member

Provided further that where there is a Legislative Council in a State, the Chairman of that Council and the Leader of the Opposition in that Council shall also be members of the Committee:

Provided also that no sitting judge of a High Court or a sitting District Judge shall be appointed except after consultation with the Chief Justice of the High Court of the concerned State.

2. No appointment of a Chairperson or a Member of the State Commission shall be invalid merely by reason of any vacancy in the Committee.

23. Removal of a Member of the State Commission. 1. Subject to the provisions of sub-section (2), the Chairperson or any other member of the State Commission shall only be removed from his office by order of the President on the ground of proved misbehaviour or incapacity after the Supreme Court, on a reference being made to it by the President, has, on inquiry held in accordance with the procedure prescribed in that behalf by the Supreme Court, reported that the Chairperson or such other Member, as the case may be, sought on any such ground to be removed.

2. Notwithstanding anything in sub-section (1), the President may by order remove from office the Chairperson or any other Member if the Chairperson or such other Member, as the case may be—

(a) is adjudged an insolvent; or
(b) engages during his term of office in any paid employment outside the duties of his office; or
(c) is unfit to continue in office by reason of infirmity of mind or body; or

(d) is of unsound mind and stands so declared by a competent court; or

(e) is convicted and sentenced to imprisonment for an offence which in the opinion of the President involves moral turpitude.

24. Term of office of Member of the State Commission. 1. A person appointed as Chairperson shall hold office for a term of five years from the date on which he enters upon his office or until he attains the age of seventy years, whichever is earlier.

2. A person appointed as a Member shall hold office for a term of five years from the date on which he enters upon his office and shall be eligible for re-appointment for another term of five years:

Provided that no Member shall hold office after he has attained the age of seventy years.

3. On ceasing to hold office, a Chairperson or a Member shall be ineligible for further employment under the Government of a State or under the Government of India.

25. Member to act as Chairperson or to Discharge his Functions in Certain Circumstances. 1. In the event of the occurrence of any vacancy in the office of the Chairperson by reason of his death, resignation or otherwise, the Governor may by notification, authorize one of the Members to act as the Chairperson until the appointment of a new Chairperson to fill such vacancy.

2. When the Chairperson is unable to discharge his functions owning to absence on leave or otherwise, such one of the Members as the Governor may, by notification, authorize in this behalf, shall discharge the functions of the Chairperson until the date on which the Chairperson resumes his duties.

26. Terms and Conditions of Service of Members of the State Commission. The salaries and allowances payable to, and other terms and conditions of service of, the Members shall be such as may be prescribed by the State Government:

Provided that neither the salary and allowances nor the other terms and conditions of service of a Member shall be varied to his disadvantage after his appointment.

27. Officers and Other Staff of the State Commission. 1. The State Government shall make available to the Commission—

(a) an officer not below the rank of a Secretary to the State Government who shall be the Secretary of the State Commission; and

(b) such police and investigative staff under an officer not below the rank of an Inspector-General of Police and such other officers and staff as may be necessary for the efficient performance of the functions of the State Commission.

2. Subject to such rules as may be made by the State Government in this behalf, the State Commission may appoint such other administrative technical and scientific staff as it may consider necessary.

3. The salaries, allowances and conditions of service of the officers and other staff appointed under sub-section (2) shall be such as may be prescribed by the State Government.

28. Annual and special reports of State Commission. 1. The State Commission shall submit an annual report to the State Government and may at any time submit special reports on any matter which, in its opinion, is of such urgency or importance that it should not be referred till submission of the annual report.

2. The State Government shall cause the annual and special reports of the State Commission to be laid before each House of State Legislature where to consists of two houses, or where such Legislature consists of one House, before that House along with a memorandum of action taken or proposed to be taken on the recommendations of the State Commission and the reasons for non-acceptance of the recommendations, if any.

29. Application of certain provisions relating to National Human Rights Commission to State Commissions. The provisions of sections 9, 10, 12, 13, 14, 15, 16, 17 and 18 shall apply to a State Commission and shall have effect, subject to the following modifications, namely:

(a) references to "Commission" shall be construed as references to "State Commission";

(b) in section 10, in sub-section (3), for the word "Secretary General", the word "Secretary" shall be substituted;

(c) in section 12, clause (f) shall be omitted; and

(d) in section 17, in clause (i), the words "Central Government or any" shall be omitted.

CHAPTER VI

HUMAN RIGHTS COURTS

30. For the purpose of providing speedy trial of offences arising out of violation of human rights, the State Government may, with the concurrence of the Chief Justice of the High Court, by notification, specify for each district a Court of Session to be a Human Rights court to try the said offences.

Provided that nothing in this section shall apply it:

(a) a Court of Session is already specified as a special court, or

(b) a special court is already constituted, for such offences under any other law for the time being in force.

31. Special Public Prosecutor. For every Human Rights Court, the State Government shall, by notification, specify a Public Prosecutor or appoint an advocate who has been in practice as an advocate forgot less than seven years, as a Special Public Prosecutor for the purpose of conducting cases in that Court.

REFERENCES AND NOTES

1. As amended in 1965.
2. Formerly eleven.
3. As amended in 1965.
4. Formerly seven.
5. As amended in 1973.
6. Originally eighteen
7. Originally six.
8. As amended in 1968.
9. Formerly seven.
10. Subs. by the Constitution (Forty-second Amendment) Act, 1976, s. 2, for "Sovereign Democratic Republic" (w.e.f. 3-1-1977).
11. Subs. by s. 2, *ibid.*, for "Unity of the Nation" (w.e.f. 3-1-1977).
12. Ins. by the Constitution (Twenty-fourth Amendment) Act, 1971, s. 2.
13. Added by the Constitution (First Amendment) Act, 1951, s. 2.
14. Subs. by the Constitution (Seventh Amendment) Act, 1956, s. 29 and Sch. for "under any State specified in the First Schedule or any local or other authority within its territory, any requirement as to residence within that State".
15. Ins. by the Constitution (Forty-fourth Amendment) Act, 1978, s. 2 (w.e.f. 20-6-1979).
16. Sub-clause (f) omitted by s. 2. *ibid.*, (w.e.f. 20-6-1979).

17. Subs. by the Constitution (First Amendment) Act, 1951, s. 2, for cl. (2) (with retrospective effect).
18. Ins. by the Constitution (Sixteenth Amendment) Act, 1963, s. 2.
19. Subs. by the Constitution (Forty-fourth Amendment) Act, 1978, s. 2, for "Sub-clauses (d), (e) and (f)" (w.e.f. 20-6-1979).
20. Subs. by the Constitution (First Amendment) Act, 1951, s. 3, for certain words.
21. On the enforcement of s. 3. of the Constitution (Forty-fourth Amendment) Act, 1978, Art. 22 shall stand amended as directed in s. 3 of that Act. For the text of s. 3 of that Act, see Appendix III.
22. Ins. by the Constitution (Forty-fourth Amendment) Act, 1978, s. 4 (w.e.f. 20-6-1979).
23. The sub-heading "*Right to Property*" omitted by s. 5, *ibid*. (w.e.f. 20-6-1979).
24. Ins. by the Constitution (Forty-second Amendment) Act, 1976, s. 3 (w.e.f. 3-1-1977).
25. Ins. by the Constitution (First Amendment) Act, 1951, s. 4 (with retrospective effect.)
26. Subs. by the Constitution (Fourth Amendment) Act, 1955, s. 3, for cl. (1) with retrospective effect.
27. Subs. by the Constitution (Forty-fourth Amendment) Act, 1978, s. 7, for "Article 14, Article 19 or Article 31" (w.e.f. 20-6-1979).
28. Ins. by the Constitution (Seventeenth Amendment) Act, 1964, s. 2.
29. Ins. by the Constitution (Seventeenth Amendment) Act, 1964, s. 2, for sub-clause (a) (with retrospective effect).
30. Subs. by the Madras State (Alteration of Name) Act, 1968 (57 of 1968), s. 4. for "Madras" (w.e.f. 14-1-1969).
31. Ins. by the Constitution (Fourth Amendment) Act, 1955, s. 3 (with retrospective effect).
32. Ins. by Constitution (First Amendment) Act, 1951, s. 5.
33. Ins. by the Constitution (Twenty-fifth Amendment) Act, 1971, s. 3 (w.e.f. 20-4-1972).
34. Subs. by the Constitution (Forty-second Amendment) Act, 1976, s. 4. for "the principles specified in clause (b) or clause (c) of article 39" (w.e.f. 3-1-1977).
35. Subs. by the Constitution (Forty-fourth Amendment) Act, 1978, s. 8. for "Article 14, Article 19 or Article 31" (w.e.f. 20-6-1979).
36. In *Kesavananda Bharti* v. *The State of Kerala*, (1973) Supp. S.C.R. 1, the Supreme Court held the provision in italics to be invalid.
37. Ins. by the Constitution (Forty-second Amendment) Act, 1976, s. 5 (w.e.f. 3-1-1977).
38. Ins. by the Constitution (Forty-second Amendment) Act, 1976, s. 6. (w.e.f. 1-2-1977).
39. Subs. by the Constitution (Fiftieth Amendment) Act, 1984, s. 2 for Art. 33.

40. Art. 38 renumbered as cl. (1) thereof by the Constitution (Forty-fourth Amendment) Act, 1978, s. 9 (w.e.f. 20-6-1979).

41. Ins. by 9 *ibid* (w.e.f. 20-6-1979).

42. Subs. by the Constitution (Forty-second Amendment) Act, sec. 7, for cl. (f) (w.e.f. 3-1-1977).

43. Ins. by s. 8 *ibid.* (w.e.f. 3-1-1977).

44. Ins. by the Constitution (Forty-second Amendment) Act, 1976. s. 9 (w.e.f. 3-1-1977).

45. Ins. by s. 10, *ibid,* (w.e.f. 3-1-1977).

46. Subs. by the Constitution (Seventh Amendment) Act, 1956. s. 27, for "declared by Parliament by Law."

47. Subs. by the Constitution (Forty-second Amendment) Act, 1976, s. 11 (w.e.f. 3-1-1977).

3

Constitutional Provisions

Renaissance and social reforms began in India in 19th century with the rise of several social movements. The credit of which goes to the English education, industrialisation, conversions and development of representative institutions. However, the problem of untouchability came to prominence in 1909. This year witnessed the commencement of the Government of India Act, 1909. It was but the inkling of the future which was to start with representative institutions. However, this perturbed the Muslim minority who felt that they would be "outvoted" by the Hindu majority. Hence they requested to the Government in 1909 not to enumerate untouchables as Hindus. The census authorities deliberately or otherwise did not describe the untouchables as Hindus, but as "untouchables", the Hindus who were already disturbed on the conversions of untouchables got one more shock. They met in a conference held in Haridwar in 1915 under the presidentship of Munindra Chandra Nandi where they formed an organization of the Hindus called *Sarvadeshik Sabha,* with the objective of eradication of untouchability.

The grand old man of India, Dadabhai Nauroji, moved a resolution in the Imperial Legislative Council in 1916 for the upliftment of untouchables unsuccessfully. The Indian National Congress in its 1917 session held at Calcutta under the presidentship of Mrs. Annie Beasant passed a resolution urging the people of India to remove all the disabilities based on untouchability. Dr. B.R. Ambedkar, who thought the problem of untouchables was not only humanitation and social, but it was also political, demanded separate electorate with reserved seats while giving his evidence before the Southborough Committee on franchise in 1919, but in vain. Again the same demand was reiterated in the Round Table Conferences held during 1930–32. Ultimately, the British Government accepted the demand of separate electorate, but it did not find favour with Mahatma

Gandhi, the leader of the Indian National Congress, who thought that it may lead to divide the Hindu society into caste Hindus and the untouchables. He started fast unto death in protest of separate electorate to untouchables. Eventually Dr. B.R. Ambedkar constrained to give up the demand of separate electorate, and accepted reserved seats in exchange of the assurance from them to uplift the untouchables. Both the parties concluded an agreement to that effect, which is known as "Poona Pact." Accordingly many Provincial Governments and States passed the anti-untouchability Acts, during 1934 to 1946. Those Provinces and States were, the C.P. and Berar, Madras, Bombay, Malbar, Baroda, Mysore and Orissa. When the Constituent Assembly was formed to frame a new constitution for India before it which was going to become independent sovereign democratic republic, the remaining States including Bihar, East Punjab, United Provinces, West Bengal, Hyderabad, Madhya Bharat, Saurashtra, Travancore-Cochin and Coorg who passed anti-untouchability Acts in their respective States during 1948 to 1949. All those laws were in force till the Protection of Civil Rights Act, 1955 came into being.

Constitution of India

India got independence on 15th August, 1947. The Constituent Assembly which came into existence on December 9, 1946 under the presidentship of Dr. Rajendra Prasad formed a Drafting Committee on August 29, 1947, under the Chairmanship of Dr. B.R. Ambedkar, who was already included in the Cabinet of Pandit Jawaharlal Nehru on August 3, 1947, as a Law Minister. The Draft of the Constitution became ready by 14th November 1949 and the Constituent Assembly finally approved it on 26th November 1949. It came into force on 26th January, 1950. The Constitution of India is the basic and supreme law of our country. It provides, *inter alia,* for the abolition of untouchability and declares the forbidden practice of untouchability as an offence. It provides the philosophy of liberty, equality and fraternity which the conducive for the egalitarian and humanitarian form of society. Therefore, it may be said that the Constitution is the first and foremost law which, *inter alia,* provides for abolition of untouchability.

Provisions with Regard to "Untouchability"

I. There is a Preamble to the Constitution of India, which reveals the philosophy of the Constitution. It is given below:

> "We, the People of India, having solemnly resolved to constitute India into a sovereign socialist secular democratic Republic and to secure to all its citizens— Justice: Social, Economic and Political, Liberty of thought, expression, belief, faith and worship. Equality of status and of opportunity, and to promote among them all fraternity, assuring the dignity of the individual and the unity and integrity of the nation. In our Constituent Assembly this twenty-sixth day of November, 1945, to hereby adopt, enact and give to ourselves this Constitution."

This is a "firm resolve," "a pledge," "an undertaking" or a commitment of the Constituent Assembly in favour of the people of India including the so called untouchables who are legally termed as Scheduled Castes. No doubt it is a Charter of Justice, liberty, equality and fraternity granted to one and all, but it is especially important from the point of view of the so called untouchables. It is a unique occasion in their life to witness such a charter. Therefore, it is more important and assumes more relevance in their respect.

It is the philosophical foundation on which the whole edifice of the Constitution is based. It is deeply rooted in the historic Objectives Resolution passed by the Constituent Assembly on January 22, 1947 at the initiative of Pandit Jawaharlal Nehru, which guarantees to all the people of India, justice, social, economic and political; equality of status of opportunity, and before the law; freedom of thought, expression, belief, faith, worship, vocation, association and action subject to law and public morality and promises to provide reasonable safeguards "for minorities, backward and tribal areas and depressed and other backward classes." The "ideal" embodied in the Objectives Resolution is "faithfully reflected in the Preamble to the Constitution, which summarises the aims of and objects of the Constitution." In the words of Nani Palkhiwala, "The Preamble is a part of the Constitution-Statute but it is not a part of the Constitution." It contains the ideal philosophy of the Constitution, but it is not the Constitutional law as such. For this reason, it is not enforceable in the court of law.

Though, the Preamble of the Constitution does not form a part of the constitutional law, it serves as a key to interpret the

Constitution as and when it is required. It is expected to give such an interpretation to the constitutional provisions which would conform with the ideal embodied in the Preamble. Of course, "where the language of the enacting sections is clear and unambiguous, the terms of the Preamble cannot qualify or cut down that enactment."

(II) Article 5 of the Constitution of India states that "At the commencement of the Constitution, every person who has his domicile in the territory of India and :

(a) who has born in the territory of India, or
(b) either of whose parents was born in the territory of India, or
(c) who has been ordinarily resident in the territory of India for not less than five years immediately preceding such commencement."

As per the Citizenship Act, 1955 passed by the Parliament by virtue of Article 11, any person can be a citizen of India in one of the five provisions. They are:

1. Citizenship by birth,
2. Citizenship by descent,
3. Citizenship by registration,
4. Citizenship by naturalization, and
5. Citizenship by incorporation of territory.

Therefore, all the individuals in respect of their caste, creed, sex or religion, ordinarily domiciled in India at the time of commencement of the Constitution, and born thereafter became citizens. Naturally all the ex-untouchables known as Scheduled Castes are citizens of this country as they are not only domiciled in India at the commencement of the Constitution of India, but from the commencement of India itself. However, they were denied their rights and privileges as citizen of this country since the period unrecorded by historians. Although they came to be treated equally just before the commencement of the Constitution in some parts of India, they were not considered so throughout the country. It is the Constitution of India which confers on all of them the status of citizenship, first of all.

Untouchability and citizenship form an anti-thesis of untouchability. A citizen is a member of the state equally enjoying civil as well as political rights and owing some duty towards the state. The declaration of the Constitution under Article 5 reveals that they are on par with others, they are "citizens" and not "untouchables". Thus, most of the rights incidental or linked to the status of citizenship are now available to them in their beneficial operations as they are to the others.

(III) Under Part III "Fundamental Rights" Article 13 holds importance. It reads :

1. 13(1) All Laws in force in the territory of India immediately before the commencement of this Constitution insofar as they are inconsistent with the provisions of this part, shall, to the extent of such inconsistency be void.
2. The state shall not make any law which takes away or abridges the rights conferred by this part and any law made in contravention of this clause shall, to the extent of the contravention, be void.
3. In this Article, "unless the context otherwise requires:
   (a) 'Law' includes any ordinance, order, bye-law, rule, regulation, notification, custom or usage having in the territory of India the force of law;
   (b) 'Laws' in force includes laws passed or made by a Legislature or other competent authority in the territory of India before the commencement of this Constitution and not previously repealed, notwithstanding that any such law or any part thereof may not be then in operation either at all or in particular areas."
4. Nothing in this Article shall apply to any amendment of the Constitution under Article 368.

Untouchability was considered a "Social Custom" all over India till the commencement of the Constitution. A social custom is "group pattern of habitual activity usually transmitted from one generation to another." It was a vehicle of untouchability which has carried it since the latter's inception. In the pre-Constitution era the Courts were not unanimous in upholding the custom of untouchability. In *Shankarlinga Nandan v. Raja Rajeswari Dorai* (1908). The Privy Council upheld the exclusion of Shannars from a temple and granted damages for its purification. In *Atmaram v. King Emperor* (1924) the Court held that, "when custom that has held for several centuries, ordains that an untouchable, whose very touch is in the opinion of devout Hindus pollution, should not enter the enclosure surrounding the shrine of any Hindu god and when an untouchables with that knowledge deliberately enters and defiles it he has, in my view committed an offence within the purview of Section 295, IPC". In *Chatunni v. Appakuttan* (1945) that Nairs were granted damages for pollution and undertaking the purificatory ceremonies necessitated by Ezhavas bathing in a tank as they had "no such right by reason of the usages of the institution having the force of law."

However, there are some exceptions as well. In *Govinda s/o Mukunda Mahar* (1902) the Bombay High Court reversed the conviction of a Mahar who had drawn water from a well. In *Khajjan Chand v. Emperor* (1926) the Lahore High Court upheld the claim of two Chamars to fetch from a Public well and reversed the order of the District Magistrate demanding security in anticipation of breach of peace if they attempted to draw water from that well. In *Narhari Damodar Vaidya v. Dr. B.R. Ambedkar* (1937) the Bombay High Court held that, "the appellants have not established the immemorial custom which the yallege. Had they succeeded on this point it might have been necessary to view whether the custom was unreasonable or contrary to Public Policy." According to C.K. Allen the test of a good custom is :

(A) it must be based on reason,
(B) it should not be against the public policy, and
(C) it should not be against the fundamental principle of law or statute.

It is submitted that the custom of untouchability cannot fulfil the said tests or conditions, as such it is irrelevant and void.

It will be interesting to observe what the judiciary and commentators have to say in this respect. In *Dashratha Rama Rao v. State of A.P.* (1961) it was held that, "even if there was a custom which has been recognized by law that custom must yield to a Fundamental Right." The custom which imposes unreasonable restriction on the Fundamental Right is inoperative. According to Prof. V.N. Shukla, "It is not the Act of the legislature or subordinate legislation alone, but customs and usages having the force of law are also invalidated. Even binding customs, if they are in derogation of the Fundamental Rights, shall become inoperative after commencement of the Constitution."

In the eye of law, the custom of untouchability has been explicitly abolished under Article 17 of the Constitution. Still, it appears that even otherwise also it would have been inoperative under Article 13 itself, being contrary to the Fundamental Rights. What Article 17 does more is, it makes the said custom is not only inoperative but an offence punishable by law. It leaves no room for any interpretation and it alarms to the society that untouchability is an offence. Thus Article 13 at the very beginning of the Fundamental Rights cuts down the customary source of untouchability.

(2) Article 15(1) states that,

"the state shall not discriminate against any citizen on grounds only of religion, race, caste, place of birth or any of them."

The State, as per Article 12, includes "the Government and Parliament of India and the Government and the legislature of each of the states and all local or other authorities within the territory of India or under the control of the Government of India".

The term "discriminate against" means "to make an adverse distinction with regard to, or distinguish unfavourably from others."

(a) Thus Article 15(1) prohibits "the state" from discriminating against my citizen on grounds only of religion, race, caste, sex, place of birth or any of them and the remedy is available only to citizens, if "the state" discriminate so.

Discrimination would carry no meaning if it is based just on caste consideration and not on economic or social backwardness. The policy of reservation in favour of a caste, under Article 15(4), will not be unconstitutional, if the members of a caste are socially and educationally backward. (b) Article 15(2) states, "No citizen shall on grounds only of religion, race, caste, sex, place of birth or any of them be subjected to any disability, liability, restriction or condition with regard to (a) access to shops, public restaurants, hotels and places of public entertainment or (b) the use of wells, tanks, bathing ghats, roads and places of public resort maintained wholly or partly out of state funds or dedicated to the use of the general public."

The right provided by clause (1) is available to the citizens against the state only while the right under clause (2) is available to the citizens against any person. The present clause stops any person from subjecting any citizen to any disability, liability, restriction or condition regarding access to shops etc., on grounds only of religion, race, caste, sex or place of birth or any of them. However, "a private well or tank does not come within the meaning of this clause: A burial ground shall be of a place of public resort if it is maintained wholly or partly by the state and shall be open to all. Where a place of public resort is not maintained by the state, it must be dedicated by the owner to the use of the general public." The discrimination on the ground only of religion, race, caste, sex, place of birth or any of them is barred. Grounds such as profession, language, health, morality and indecency do not find any mention.

Probably there may be discrimination on these grounds unless such discrimination is barred under some other provisions. Although it is a general clause, it is specifically applicable to the untouchables who were subjected to discrimination only on the ground of their "caste" which was supposed to be lower than all the caste Hindus. Thus it prohibits any discrimination against such untouchable castes with regard to (a) access to shops, public restaurants, hotels and places of public entertainment or (b) the use of walls, tanks, bathing ghats, roads and places of public resort maintained by wholly or partly out of state funds or dedicated to the use of the general public. This article bridges one of the areas of segregation between the untouchables and the upper castes.

(3) Article 16(1) states, "there shall be equality of opportunity for all citizens in matters relating to employment or appointment to any office under the state". However, the State is empowered under clause (4) of Article 16 to make any provisions for the reservation of appointments or posts in favour of any backward classes which in the opinion of the State is not adequately represented in the services under the State. The Constitution maintains *status quo* so far as "the operation of any law which provides that the incumbent of an office regarding the affairs or any religious or denominational institution or any member of the governing body thereof shall be a person professing a particular religion or belonging to a particular denomination."

(4) Article 17 of the Constitution states, " 'untouchability' is abolished and its practice in any form is forbidden. The enforcement of any disability arising out of 'untouchability' shall be an offence punishable in accordance with law."

The long-fought struggle for the abolition of untouchability ultimately brought some results. Constitutionally the evil is abolished. A major section of society which was subjected to inhuman treatments has been freed by the supreme law of the land once for all. It is a landmark in the socio-religious and politico-legal history of India.

(A) "Untouchability" is abolished under the Constitution; but the term has nowhere been defined. While discussing on the provision of the said Article some of the members of the Constituent Assembly expressed their opinion that the term "untouchability" requires clarification. Mr. K.M. Munshi in his effort to clarify the term in question said that "The word 'untouchability' is put purposely within inverted commas in order to indicate that the union legislature when it defines 'untouchability' will be able to deal with it in the sense in which it is normally understood." The Hon'ble Sardar Vallabhbhai Patel while enlightening by his opinion said, "the removal of untouchability is the main idea and if untouchability is made illegal or an offence, it is quite enough".

Once the untouchability in the Fundamental Rights as an offence, all is included adjustment will be made in the law that may be passed by the legislature. Thus the Constituent Assembly left the matter on the Central Legislature to define it. But the Central Legislature also did not give its definition in the "Protection of Civil Rights Act, 1955". In his efforts to define untouchability, Mr. Justice Sreenivasa Rau noted that "the subject matter of Article 17 is not untouchability in its literal or grammatical sense but the practice as it had developed historically in this country". Thus, "untouchability" denotes the disgraceful Hindu Social custom observed in respect of the so-called untouchables as a matter of misconceived notions by the so called upper caste Hindus.

As the custom of untouchability has been overruled by the law of the Constitution explicitly, it has now ceased to be a custom. As such no defendant, would raise a plea of custom in a case against him under the PCRA or under any law. From the positive point of view, with the end of the custom of untouchability a new era was expected to dawn, the era of liberty, equality and fraternity in the society as a whole. The end of untouchability could pave the way for the realization of the philosophy of the Constitution as enshrined in the Preamble.

(B) Further, the said Article states that, "its practice in any form is forbidden". "Practice" means performance. Here practice means the performance or commission of the forbidden act of untouchability; "forbidden" means and suggests a command to refrain from doing some action. "Any form" includes any form and "every form". Thus the Constitution commands to refrain from doing or performing the prohibited act of "untouchability" in any form, whatsoever it may be. "Any form" is a inclusive word, which comprises all the forms and patterns of untouchability. "It would appear to include any invidious treatment associated with the victims membership or origin in an untouchable group, even if the treatment did not involve avoidance of pollution—for example, restrictions on the dress or ceremonials of untouchables.

It seems to extend to private social conducts like avoidance of commensuality and observance of purification after contact." Therefore, in its broader scope each and every form of "untouchability" is a forbidden act. The Protection of Civil Rights Act provides punishment for certain Acts, but it does not mean that all "those acts contemplated in the PCRA" are the only one within untouchability.

(C) Article 17 further states that "the enforcement of any disability arising out of 'untouchability' shall be an offence." "Enforcement" means the act of enforcing or compelling the obedience to get something done. "The enforcement of disabilities involves more than actual physical prevention of the use of facilities or compulsion of customary deference. The untouchability (offences) Act makes it an offence to molest, injure, annoy, obstruct or try to obstruct the exercise of any right accruing to a person by reason of Article 17". Even loud words by worshipper frightening an untouchable boy to go out of a temple have been held to constitute an offence under an Act. According to Prof. Marc Galanter, it is not clear whether it would be "enforcement of a disability to persuade an untouchable voluntarily to abide by an invidious usage." It is difficult to comprehend as to why he is "not clear" whether persuasion amounts to enforcement or not. It is the "practice" of untouchability which is an offence; the "practice" is material; whether it is done by "enforcement" or "compulsion" or "performance" or "persuasion" is immaterial. Here emphasis should be given on "practice" and the "intention" behind the act. Another fact is the practice of untouchability is criminal offence.

Therefore, any criminal offence done even with persuasion will be an offence. One cannot persuade a widow to perform the custom of *Sati*.

There is no way to persuade a woman to profess prostitution or one can not persuade to accept dowry or to be a bonded labour. No human being intends to be victim of any system or custom or act adverse to his benefits. Nobody has any right to persuade others to be victim of some forbidden act. Nobody has any right to exploit one's ignorance or minority. Persuasion may not be coercion, but certainly it amounts to undue influence and fraud if it is done with wrongful intent. Therefore, it is given that so far as Article 17 is concerned "persuasion" means "enforcement".

"Disability" includes any incapacity, disqualification, restriction, prevention, liability, obstruction, molestation, insult, injury or boycott. The enforcement of "any" disability "arising out of" untouchability shall be an offence. It is given that the "enforcement of any disability" is not much different from the "practice in any form".

(D) "Offence" means "any act or omission made punishable by any law for the time being in force". Thus any practice, including the enforcement of any disability arising out of "untouchability" "shall be" an offence punishable in accordance with law. Article 17 not only forbids "untouchability" but it declares 'untouchability' as a whole an offence punishable by law. However, the responsibility of making the law providing punishment for the offences of untouchability was given to the Parliament by Article 35 of the Constitution. But, the Parliament did not pass the "uniform" law till 1955.

Hence, the "Laws in force" were to govern the offence of untouchability. "Laws in force" included laws passed or made by a Legislature or other competent authority in the territory of India before the commencement of the Constitution. Thus all the laws passed by different state legislatures in the pre-Constitution era were in force till 1955.

(E) The enforcement of any disability "arising out of" untouchability is an offence. For constituting an offence under Article 17 of the Constitution the disabilities that are enforced must originate out of "untouchability". Thus there is "root and fruit" relationship between untouchability and the disabilities. It is, however, not needed to prove the 'Intent' or *mens rea* in such cases. What one has to do is simply to establish the relationship between 'untouchability and disabilities' that is all.

(F) While examining the provisions of this Article, Prof. Marc

Galanter observes that, "the Article refers to two overlapping classes of conduct: acts constituting the "practice of untouchability in any form" and acts which are the "enforcement of any disability arising out of "untouchability". The first appears broader than, but not fully inclusive of the latter, while all the former are "forbidden", only the latter are declared an "offence punishable in accordance with law."

The explanation provided by Marc Galander to Article 17 as "practice" part and "enforcement" part to one and the same Article seems to be a little too technical and undesirable. Firstly, Article 17 has a historical background. Almost all the reformers and their movements strived for the removal of untouchability from the Hindu social system, so as to secure social justice to all the people of India. If the Article is divided merely on technical ground between its "practice" part which is just forbidden and its "enforcement" part which is punishable it would negate the very purpose of the provision itself.

Secondly, if the practice part, being unpunishable remained in practice, it would be addition to ambiguity and loopholes; and ultimately of no use. The framers of the Constitution must have never thought to allow such a construction which provides a leophodes it.

Thirdly, the word "practice in any form" is inclusive of "enforcement of any disability" arising out of untouchability. Untouchability, at least in its overt form, exists in some "form", "practice" and "enforcement of certain disabilities". When it is said that "untouchability" is abolished it can be stated that it has been abolished with all its forms, practices and patterns of enforcement of disabilities.

Fourthly, "untouchability" as a whole is a "forbidden" act. Therefore, any act contemplating, conveying or constituting untouchability constitutes an "Offence" punishable by law. Any overt or covert act manifesting hatred, contempt and humiliation of untouchables arising out of "untouchability" is an "offence" punishable in the eyes of the law.

Lastly, the construction given by Prof. Marc Galanter to this Article appears to be against the rule of construction itself. Article 17 is entirely one Article without any clause, sub-clause, or proviso therein and it deals only with one subject, i.e., untouchability. Therefore, it should be construed as a whole. Moreover, it is a rule of interpretation that one has to make such interpretation which shall suppress the mischief and bring forth the remedy.

(G) Now, it would be desirable to seen in brief the difference between the provisions under Article 17 and Article 15(2).

1. Article 17 contains a provision in respect of untouchables whereas Articles 15(2) contains the provisions in general, applicable to touchables and untouchables alike.
2. Article 17 deals with "untouchability" enforced on the untouchables, whereas Article 15(2) deals with "discrimination" in respect of any person.
3. Article 17 states enforcement of disabilities 'arising out of untouchability, is an offence, while Article 15(2) states the grounds of religion, race, caste, sex, place of birth or any of them.
4. Article 17 forbids all forms and practices of untouchability in any field. Its scope is wider than Article 15(2) which prohibits any act with regard to access to shops, public restaurants, hotels and places of public entertainment or the wells, tanks, bathing ghats, roads and places of public resort.
5. Under Article 17 remedy is available against any person or institution or the state but under Article 15(2) the remedy is available only against the state and not against the private individuals.
6. By virtue of Article 35(2) the Parliament alone, not the state legislatures, is empowered to pass the law providing punishment for the offences contemplated under Article 17. In respect of 15(2) the Parliament as well as the state legislatures can pass the law for providing punishment for the discriminatory acts contemplated under it.
7. The nature of Article 17 is prohibitive and punitive whereas the nature of Article 15(2) is merely prohibitive. Article 15(2) does not state that the forbidden acts under it constitute offence as such.

(5) Article 23(1) enumerates that,

"Traffic in human beings and beggar and other similar forms of forced labour are prohibited and any contravention of this provision shall be an offence punishable in accordance with law."

Objective of this is "recognition and restoration of the dignity of man." Traffic in human beings means to deal in men and women like goods, such as to sell or let or otherwise dispose of. It would includes traffic in women for immoral reasons. This evil is comes under the purview of the Suppression of Immoral Traffic in Women and Girls Act, 1956.

"Beggar means involuntary work without payment." It is a Fundamental Right of each and every person not to be compelled to work without due payment. Other forms of forced labour are also violative of Fundamental Right under 23(1). The Parliament by virtue of Article 35 passed "the Bonded Labour System (Abolition) Act, 1976", to deal with beggar and other similar forms of forced labour including Bonded Labour. Of course "(2) Nothing in this Article shall stop the state from imposing compulsory service for public purposes, and in imposing such service the state shall not make any discrimination on grounds only of religion, race, caste or class or any of them."

(6) Article 25 states that

"(1) Subject to public order, morality and health and to the other provisions of this part, all persons are equally entitled to freedom of conscience and right freely to profess, practice and propagate religion".

This Article guarantees the right to religion to all persons, which includes the right "to freedom of conscience and the right freely to profess, practice and propagate religion." Religion includes not only ethical code, but "rituals and observances, ceremonies and modes of worship which are considered as integral parts of religion; and these forms and observances might extend even to such matters of food and dress."

However, the right to religion is not absolute one. The Article itself states that "subject to public order, morality and health and to the other provisions of this part", all persons enjoy equal freedom of religion.

Furthermore, the right to religion is subject to "other provisions" of Part III of Fundamental Rights. Article 17 of the Constitution (Part III) has explicitly abolished the custom of untouchability pertaining to the Hindu Society or Hindu 'religion'. Therefore, no Hindu can lawfully defend "untouchability" on the basis of religious freedom. Now, untouchability finds no ground either in "religion" or in "custom" or in the religious freedom.

Clause (2) of Article 25 states that, "Nothing in this Article shall affect the operation of any existing law or stop the state from making any law.

(b) Providing for social welfare and reform or the throwing open of Hindu religious institutions of a public character to all classes and sections of Hindus."

Explanation II: In sub-clause (b) of clause (2) the reference to "Hindus shall be construed as including a reference to persons professing the *Sikh, Jaina or Buddhist* religion, and the reference to Hindu religious institutions shall be construed accordingly."

Article 25(2) removes the general hinderance which otherwise would have been so in providing for "social welfare" and "reform" or "the throwing open of Hindu religious institutions of a public character to all classes and sections of Hindus."

The Constitution contemplates to throw open all the Hindu religious institutions to all the Hindus as mentioned in the Explanation II.

(i) The right protected by Article 25(2)(b) is a right to enter into a temple for the purpose of worship. But it does not mean that is absolute and unqualified. No member of the Hindu public could claim by virtue of the Article that he should personally perform those services which the *Poojari* alone could perform. The so-called untouchable can enjoy the right to worship in any temple "in the like manner and to the like extent as any other Hindu."

(ii) Article 26(b) itself limits what is said under Article (25)(b). Article 26 states that subject to public order, morality and health every religious denomination or any section thereof shall have the right (b) "to manage its own affairs in matters of religion". It is noted by the Supreme Court in *Venkatraman v. State of Madras* (1958) that during certain ceremonies and on social occasions it is only members of a certain community that have the right to participate therein and that on those occasion all other persons would be excluded, would be a denomination right and protected by Article 26(b).

(iii) The provisions under 25(2) are limited to the Hindu religious institutions which are public or dedicated to the public, and the beneficiaries are only Hindus, as elaborated in Explanation II.

(iv) The right protected by Article 25(2)(b) does not provide any right or claim on the part of the Scheduled Castes. It is an enabling provision to the state to throw open the temples of Hindu religion for all Hindus. This article, however, neither imposes any duty on the state, nor it gives corresponding right or any legitimate claim on behalf of the Scheduled Castes.

(v) Moreover, the term "the state" is ambiguous. It includes, "the Government and Parliament of India", "the Government and the legislature of each of the states" and all local or other authorities within the territory of India. If "the State" means all the authorities under the Union Governments, State Governments and the Local Governments, then it is problematic to locate the responsibility assigned to "the State".

(vi) According to M.C.J. Kagzis the guarantee of religious freedom does not take away the authority of the state to legislate for maintenance of public order, public health and public morality. He states different heads on which the state can make legislation. They are (1) Public order, (2) morality and health, (3) social welfare and reforms, (4) economic, financial and political interests, and (5) respect for the Fundamental Right in general.

(vii) It is submitted that while ascertaining the scope of the denominational right reference should be made to 'equality' stated in the Preamble as well as in Article 25(1). Undoubtedly the religious denomination or any section thereof will have the right to "manage" the matters of religion. However, management does not include "discrimination" or observance of untouchability or any "irreligious" custom which is opposed to the public order, morality and health of the people. Article 26(b) cannot conflict with any other provisions in the Fundamental Rights; and even if it conflicts harmonious construction demands that construction should be such which may avoid it. Religious denomination is a religious sect with a distinctive name and a common faith, e.g. *Advaitaism, Shavism, Vaishnavism* etc. If there is the meaning and scope of "denomination" then it appears "denominations and sections thereof" may exhaust "Hindu" religion itself. After all what constitutes "Hinduism"?

In a way Hinduism is a compendium of certain sects and sub-sects, denominations and sub-denominations. All of them profess "Hinduism" in its different forms and practices. Denomination or any section thereof is their "inner" existence and "Hinduism" is their "outer" existence. Hence recognising their absolute right would render Article 25 redundant.

Article 25(2) tells us in unqualified terms that "Nothing" in this article shall affect the operation of any existing law or stop the state from making any law; providing for social welfare and reform or the throwing open of Hindu religious institutions of a public character to all classes and sections of Hindus. If it is studied minutely, the words such as "Hindu religion" "institutions", "all classes" and "sections of Hindus" it can be said that denominational right may not conflict with the absolute power of the state, under 25(2)(b). When "religious beliefs and practices conflict with matters of social reform or welfare on which the state wants to legislate, such religious beliefs and practices must yield to the higher needs of social welfare and reform."

There is some difference between the provision under Article 17 and provisions under Article 25(2)(b). It may be summarised as under:

(1) Article 25(2) stated a general provision which "extends to all classes of Hindus, not merely to "untouchables" whereas Article 17 confers a particular right on untouchables not to be subjected to 'untouchability'.

(2) Article 25(2) contains 'enabling' provision, empowering the state to make laws in respect of temple entries. Article 17 'forbids' the practices of 'untouchability' as such it is prohibitive and punitive.

(3) Article 25(2) is applicable to the religious institutions, including temples. The state has been empowered to throw open all the Hindu religious institutions for all the sections. Article 17 deals with "untouchability" which includes enforcement of disabilities with regard to entry in the temples and other places. "It would be anomalous to interpret 'untouchability' as excluding temple entry. For one of the immediate effects of forbidding its practice in any form was to nullify the pre-existing enforceable right to exclude untouchables from temples."

(4) It is "the state" which has been enabled to make law in respect of temple entry under Article 25(2), whereas under Article 17 and by virtue of Article 35 it is the Parliament alone which could pass the law.

(5) Article 25(2) is a 'positive' provision enabling the state to make law in respect of temple entry and to secure social welfare and reformation of the Hindu society. Article 17 contains a 'negative' provision abolishing untouchability.

(6) Article 25(2) confers no right or claim as such on the part of the Scheduled Castes; whereas Article 17 confers a right against all the persons and institutions not to be subjected to untouchability.

(7) Article 17 explicitly declares "untouchability" as an offence

being a forbidden act; whereas Article 25(2) does not declare so directly. As it states, "Nothing in this article "shall affect the operation of any existing law" it can be said that owing to the punitive nature of the pre-Constitution law in this respect, it indirectly declares that contrary to the provision of it, would constitute an offence.

(7) Article 29(2) states that

"No citizen shall be refused admission into any educational institution maintained by the State or receiving aid out of the state funds on grounds only of religion, race, caste, language or any of them."

No (citizen) or person having Indian nationality, other things being equal, would be denied admission into any educational institution run by the state or receiving aid out of state funds on grounds only of religion, race, caste, language or any of them.

It is one of the most important Article in the Constitution which is concerned with the ex-untouchables, who were once upon a time deprived of this right. This clause guarantees the right of admission into any educational institution for all the Indian nationals. Now they are equally entitled to not only to admission, but to opt for any courses or subjects including Sanskrit, provided they fulfil the minimum condition mentioned for the same.

Under Article 15(4) the State is given the powers to reserve a minimum number of seat for members of the backward classes including the Scheduled Castes, if they are, in the view of the state socially and educationally backward, notwithstanding anything contained under Article 29(2). However, this Article does not take away the right of an institution to refuse admission or to expel a student on the basis of misconduct or the like (previous training, physical fitness, vaccination, dissociation from injurious association, age, etc.) provided the discretion is not misused.

(8) Article 32 states that, "(1) The right to move the Supreme Court by appropriate proceedings for the enforcement of the rights conferred by this part is guaranteed.

(2) The Supreme Court shall have power to issue directions or orders of writs, including writs in the nature of *habeous corpus, mundamus,* prohibition, quowarrants and *certiorari,* whichever may be appropriate, for the enforcement of any of the rights conferred by this part."

Supreme Court, is the guardian of the Fundamental Rights and it guaranteed under Part III, including right under Article 17 and other relevant Articles, any citizen or person whose rights are infringed may move to the Supreme Court directly through appropriate proceedings for the enforcement of the rights conferred by the said part. Even his right to move to the Supreme Court for enforcement of his rights itself is a Fundamental Right guaranteed under Article 32. "Appropriate proceedings" means such proceedings "which invoke, by original petition the jurisdiction of the Supreme Court to issue according to the nature of the case, writs or orders of the types mentioned in clause (2)".

The significant doubt here that whether an ex-untouchable can approach the Supreme Court for the enforcement of his allegedly infringed Fundamental Rights that are accrued to him to abolition of untouchability under Article 17 ?

Of course, the Parliament has already okayed the Protection of Civil Rights Act, 1955 for enforcement of such rights. Whether or not in view of alternative legal remedy, an ex-untouchable has right to move the Supreme Court under Article 32 ? Whether the statutory right under PCRA may be an alternative for the Fundamental Right under Article 32 ? In this respect what the Supreme Court has to speak is significant. It has stated that "the mere existence of an adequate alternative legal remedy cannot *per se* be a good and adequate ground for throwing out a petition under Article 32, if the existence of a Fundamental Right and a breach, actual or threatened, of such right is alleged and is *prima facie* established on the petition." Thus an ex-untouchable whose rights under Article 17 are infringed may approach the Supreme Court.

(9) Article 35 provides "Notwithstanding any thing in this Constitution (a) Parliament shall have and the legislature of a state shall not have, power to make laws."

(a) For prescribing punishment for those acts, which are declared to be offences under this part; and Parliament shall, as soon as may be after the commencement of this Constitution, make laws for prescribing punishment for the acts referred to in sub-clause (ii).

(b) Any law in force immediately before the commencement of this Constitution in the territory of India with respect to any of the matters referred to in sub-clause (i) of clause (a) or providing for punishment for any act referred to in sub-clause (ii) of that clause shall, subject to the terms thereof and to any adaptations and modifications that may be made therein under Article 372, continue in force until altered of repealed or amended by Parliament."

According to Article 17 "untouchability" is an offence; hence the Parliament along is empowered to pass law for prescribing punishment for the offences under the said article. Article 32(a) explicitly takes out the jurisdiction of the legislatures of the states so far as the power of making laws to govern the offence of "untouchability" is concerned. However, from the commencement of the Constitution right up to the implementation of the Protecting of Civil Rights Act; 1955, i.e., 26th January 1950 to 30th May 1955, the laws passed by different states and provinces during the pre-Constitution period continued to be in force *vide* Article 35(b) and Article 372 of the Constitution.

Concerning the rights under 25(2)(b) (Entry into religious institution including temples) are concerned, the Parliament as well as the legislatures of the states are given the power to pass the laws in that respect; as the subject "charitable and religious endowments and institutions" appears in the concurrent list. "This is confirmed" says Marc Galanter, by the conferring of the power on the "state" which is used in the broad sense of central, state and local governments. Of course, the Parliament, empowered under Article 35 (a) (ii) read with Article 17, has passed "the Untouchability (Offence) Act, 1955", amended as "the Protection of Civil Rights Act, 1955 in 1976".

(10) Article 38 under Directive Principles of state policy, provides that, "the state shall strive to promote the welfare of the people by securing and protecting as effectively as it may a social order in which justice, social, economic and political, shall inform all the institutions of the national life."

Although "shall" is written after "the state" it is qualified by "as effectively as it may written after protecting". Thus the words "welfare" of the "people", "social-order", "justice, social, economic and political" and "national life" which appears to be ambiguous. Also, the courts have no jurisdiction to enforce directive principles.

(11) Article 39-A states, "The state shall secure that the operation of the legal system promotes justice, on the basis of equal opportunity, and shall, in particular, provide free legal aid, by suitable legislation or schemes or in any other way to ensure that opportunities for securing justice are not denied to any citizen by reason of economic or other disabilities."

This principle of directive policy has been included in the Constitution through 42nd Amendment Act, 1976, in order to ensure equal justice to all the citizens. Poverty deprives equal opportunity, equal status and social justice. It leads to disabilities and indignities. The pity is it is a distinct feature of untouchable community as a whole; as it is incidental to or connected with "untouchability". Undoubtedly, the provision may be helpful to all the backward communities generally, but is certainly helpful to Dalits.

(12) Article 46 states, "The state shall promote with special care the educational and economic interests of the weaker sections of the people, and in particular, of the Scheduled Castes and the Scheduled Tribes, and shall protect them from social injustice and all forms of exploitation."

This Article has provisions similar to there under Article 15(4). Article 46 is a directive whereas Article 15(4) is an enabling provision to the state to make any special provision for the advancement of socially and educationally backward classes including the Scheduled Castes. Further the present Article has similarity to Article 16(4) also, which is an enabling provision on the part of the state to make provision for the reservation in favour of any backward classes including Scheduled Castes, if they are not reasonably represented in the services of the state.

(13) Under the chapter of Fundamental duties it is stated under Article 51-A that, "it shall be the duty of every citizen of India (a) to abide by the Constitution and respect its ideals and institutions, the National Flag and the National Anthem."

"(e) to promote harmony and the spirit of common brotherhood amongst all the people of India transcending religious, linguistic and regional or sectional diversities, to renounce practices derogatory to the dignity of women. (h) to develop the scientific temper, humanism and the spirit of inquiry and reform."

It is duty of every citizen "to abide" by the Constitution, which means the whole Constitution including the Fundamental Rights, directive principles, fundamental duties and other provisions and above all the philosophy of the Constitution. It is a fundamental duty of every citizen to promote "harmony" and the "spirit" of brotherhood regardless of such diversities as religious, linguistic, regional or sectional.

It is said futher that every citizen shall develop the "scientific temper", humanism and spirit of inquiry and "reform". This clause appears to be an anti-thesis of neglect, superstitions, barbarism, blind faith and obscurantism.

"Fundamental Rights are" as T.K. Tope observes "specifically made enforceable, the directives shall not be enforceable by any court and as regarding the fundamental duties nothing is said. Hence, it is submitted as there is no specific prohibition for their enforceability, the fundamental duties can be enforced by the judiciary". This means that the Constitution puts an obligation on the part of the citizens not to believe in superstitions and wrong notions including "untouchability". They must develop the spirit of 'humanism' and respect social reforms on the basis of scientific as well as humanistic ground.

(14) Article 164 states that "...in the State of Bihar, Madhya Pradesh and Orissa, there shall be a Minister-in-charge of Welfare of the Scheduled Castes..."

(15) Article 325 states "There shall be one general electoral roll for every territorial constituency for election to either House of Parliament or to the House or either House of the Legislature of a state and no person shall be ineligible for inclusion in any such roll or claim to be included in any special electoral roll for any such constituency of grounds only of religion, race, caste, sex or any of them."

This Article ensures political justice to the ex-untouchables who were consciously deprived of this right in earlier time. Article 330(1)(a) provides reservation of seats in the House of people and Article 332(1) provides reservation for the Scheduled Castes in the Legislative Assembly of every state. Of course the quota of seats for the Scheduled Castes would be decided in accordance with principle as stated under Article 330(2) in respect of the House of People and according to Article 332(3) in respect of State Legislative Assemblies. Accordingly the seats are reserved based on Concentration of the Scheduled Caste population in the particular state.

(16) Article 338 (1) states, "There shall be a special officer for the Scheduled Castes and Scheduled Tribes to be appointed by the President."

338(2) "It shall be the duty of the Special Officer to investigate all matters relating to the safeguards provided for the Scheduled Castes and Scheduled Tribes under this Constitution and report to the President upon the working of those safeguards at such intervals as the President may direct, and the President shall cause all such reports to be laid before each House of Parliament."

The Commissioner for the SC and ST is to "(1) investigate all matters relating to the safeguards provided for the Scheduled Castes and Scheduled Tribes under the Constitution, and (2) to report to the President upon the working of those safeguards". The President shall cause all such reports to be laid before each House of Parliament.

(17) Article 341 states "(1) The President may with respect to any State or Union Territory and where it is a State after consultation with the Governor thereof by public notification, specify the castes, races of tribes or parts of or groups within castes, races or tribes which shall for the purpose of this Constitution be deemed to be Scheduled Castes in relation to that State or Union Territory.

(2) Parliament may by law include in or exclude from the list of Scheduled Castes specified in a notification issued under Clause (1) any caste, race or tribe or part of or group within any caste, race or tribe, but save as aforesaid a notification issued under the said clause shall not be varied by any subsequent notification."

As per Article 366(24) "Scheduled Castes" means such castes, races or tribes or parts of or groups within such castes, races or tribes as are deemed under Article 341 to be Scheduled Castes for the purposes of this Constitution. Although no criteria is laid down specifically under 341 for declaring a particular community as Scheduled Castes, the Constitution (S.C.) Order 1950, Clause 3 lays down the condition that any member staking claim to be Scheduled Caste must belong to either Sikhism or Hindu religion.

Out of all the Articles discussed above, Articles 17 is pivotal one, as it abolishes all the disabilities incident to or linked to untouchability. All those Articles, other than Article 17, touch some aspect of untouchability and remove a part of it, but in the absence of Article 17 they would have been rendered useless to the untouchables. However, all the other Fundamental Rights that are not dealt with here are also equally applicable or available to the Scheduled Castes as they are other citizens.

Legislative Measures Taken by Various States on the Issue of Untouchability During 1950 to 1955

The Constituent Assembly called in 1946 was to frame a new Constitution for independent India. Almost all the people were preparing themselves to welcome the dawn of a new social order based on a new political order which was to be incorporated in the Constitution. The anti-untouchability movement led by Dr. B.R. Ambedkar and Mahatma Gandhi also built a conducive atmosphere for the removal of untouchability. It was this situation which impelled many States and provinces to pass the laws to abolish untouchability in their respective States and implement them.

Our Constitution empowered the Parliament alone to make a uniform law prescribing punishment for the offences of untouchability, but the Parliament failed to do so till 1955. Therefore, all those laws passed by different States for the removal of untouchability in the pre-Constitution era were in force in their respective states till 30th May 1955 by virtue of Article 372 of the Constitution.

Table 2.1 shows which law was prevailing in which State during 1950 to 1955.

TABLE 2.1

Sr. No.	*State/Union Territories*	*Temple Entry Act*	*Anti-Disabilities Act*
1.	Assam	Nil	Nil
2.	Bihar	Nil	The Bihar Harijan (Removal of Civil Disabilities) Act, 1946
3.	Bombay	The Bombay Harijan Temple Entry Act, 1947	The Bombay Harijan (Removal of Social Disabilities) Act, 1946
4.	Madhya Pradesh	—	The Central Pr. and Berar S.C. (Rem. of Civil Dis. Act, 1947)
5.	Madras	—	The Madras Removal of Civil Disabilities Act, 1938. The Madras Temple Entry Authorisation Act, 1947
6.	Orissa	The Orissa Temple Entry Authorisation Act, 1948	The Orissa Removal of Civil Disabilities Act, 1946
7.	Punjab	The East Punjab (Removal of Reli. and Social Disabilities)	The East Punjab (Removal of Religious and Social Disabilities) Act, 1948
8.	Uttar Pradesh	—	The United Provinces Removal of Social Disabilities Act, 1947
9.	West Bengal	—	The West Bengal Hindu Social Disabilities Removal Act, 1948

Contd.

Sr. No.	State/Union Territories	Temple Entry Act	Anti-Disabilities Act
10.	Hyderabad	The Hyderabad Harijan Temple Entry Regulation 1358 F	The Hyderabad Harijan (Removal of Social Disabilities Regulation) 1358 F.
11.	Madhya Bharat	–	The Madhya Bharat Harijan Ayo Nivaran Vishan, 1949
12.	Mysore	The Mysore Temple Entry Authorisation Act, 1948	The Removal of Civil Disabilities Act, 1943
13.	Pepsu	–	–
14.	Rajasthan	–	–
15.	Saurashtra	–	The Saurashtra Harijan (Removal of Social Disabilities) Ordinance Act, 1948
16.	Travancore Cochin	The Travancore Temple Entry (Removal of disabilities Act, 1950)	The Travancore Cochin Removal of Social Disabilities Act, 1125 K
17.	Ajmer	–	–
18.	Bhopal	–	–
19.	Bilaspur	–	–
20.	Coorg	The Coorg Temple Entry Authorisation Act, 1949	The Coorg S.C. (Removal of Civil & Social Disabilities Act, 1949)
21.	Delhi	–	–
22.	Himachal Pradesh	–	–
23.	Kachh	–	–
24.	Manipur	–	–
25.	Tripura	–	–
26.	Vindhya Pradesh	–	–

Hence, out of 26 States/UTs the Temple Entry Acts were in operation only in seven States and the Anti-Disabilities Acts were in operation in fourteen States only. No Anti-Untouchability law was in force in twelve States/UTs.

(2) Under almost all the State Acts every offence under them was punishable with imprisonment which would extend to six months or with fine which would extend to Rs. 500.00 or with both. For every subsequent conviction, the convict was punishable with both imprisonment and fine. Under some Acts every offence was cognizable and it was compoundable with the permission of the Court. There was no provision of "Presumption" by the courts in favour of the complainant in any Act. The offences committed by the individuals only were governed by those Acts and not the offences committed by some company or corporate body.

(3) There were certain challenges to those Acts alleging that they were vires of the Constitutional Provisions. The first ground of the challenge was that, the Parliament only was empowered to make law for providing punishment for the offence under Article 17 and under Article 35 of the Constitution and not the State Legislatures. Hence the laws passed by the State legislatures would be *ultra vires* of the Constitution. In this respect the Indore Bench of the High Court laid down significant principle in *State v. Kishan* (1955), that "the Powers of State Legislatures to make laws prescribing punishment for those acts which were declared to be offences under Article 17 are withdrawn by Article 35 of the Constitution and are vested in the Central Parliament. The provision has a prospective application and laws in force in the state before the commencement of the Constitution, are specifically saved and are to continue until altered, repealed or modified or amended by the Parliament."

On the occasion of there being a challenge to the U.P. Removal of Social Disabilities Act, 1947, on the ground of religious freedom under Article 25(1) and Article 26 in *Swami Hariharanand Saraswati alias Karpatriji and 25 others v. the Jailor I/c of District Jail (Banaras)* (1954). It was held that according to Article 25(2) "the law authorising temple entry could appropriately come with in the definition of 'existing law' contained in Article 366(10) as such the law authorising the temple entry was protected inasmuch as this law only provided for the removal of those distinctions which caste Hindus enforced on the Dalits in respect of among other matters, entry of Dalits in temple on the same footing as caste Hindus."

In *Venkatraman Devaru v. State of Mysore* (1958) that the Madras Temple Entry Authorisation Act (1947) was not it was held *ultra vires* of the Constitution as the validity of the impugned Act was on Article 25(b) of the Constitution. Article 25 (2) (b) confers right on all classes and sections of Hindus to enter into public temple; on the unqualified terms that Article, that right must be available, whether it is sought to be exercised against an individual under Article 25(1) or against a denomination under Article 26(b). As a matter of fact though Article 25(1) deals with rights of the individuals, Article 25(2) is much wider in its contents and has reference to the rights of communities and controls both Article 25(1) and Article 26(b). It was held that the Act authorising temple entry would be a valid one under Article 25(2)(b). Thus the anti-disabilities laws were saved from any kind of constitutional challenges.

All the 21 Acts which were "laws in force" since their formation to 1955 till the formation of PCRA in their respective states ceased to be so as they repealed under Section 17 of the Protection of Civil Rights Act, 1955. Thereafter a new law i.e., the Protection of Civil Rights Act, 1955 which is uniform in its application all over India came into existence on 1st June 1955.

Protection of Civil Rights Act, 1955

The Parliament of India empowered under Article 35(a)(ii) to pass a law prescribing punishment for the 'offence' of "untouchability" under Article 17 of the Constitution passed—"The Protection of Civil Rights Act, 1955."

1. *Preamble* : The Preamble of any Act is the key to the interpretation of that statute.

It has been noted by the Nagpur High Court (1954) that, "the Preamble is conclusive as to the facts which operated on the mind of the legislature. It indicates the occasion and the reason for the enactment. But if the enacting part is clear and unequivocal, the Preamble can neither restrict nor enlarge the scope of the enacting provision."

According to Sarjoo Prasad C.J. (1955) of the Assam High Court "the Preamble to an Act discloses the primary intention of the legislature, but it cannot override the provisions of the Act, if in fact these provisions are in conflict with the Preamble itself and lead to some result not warranted by the Preamble."

The Preamble of the present Act should be seen in this context. Previously in 1955 it was designed as "An Act to prescribe punishment for the practice of 'untouchability', for the enforcement of any disability arising out of and for matters connected therewith.

Be it enacted by Parliament in the sixth year of the Republic of India as follows." This has been amended subsequently in the year 1976 by Act, 106 of 1976.

Now it stands as given below:

"An Act to prescribe punishment for the preaching and practice of untouchability, for the enforcement of any disability arising therefrom and for matters connected with it.

Be it enacted by Parliament in the sixth year of the Republic of India as follows:"

The Preamble of this Act shows the object of the Act which prescribes punishment for the "offence" of untouchability, which may presumably be in the form of (a) preaching of untouchability, (b) practice of untouchability, and (c) the enforcement of any disability arising therefrom.

1. *Title, extent and commencement:* The title of the Act is a significant aid in the interpretation of the statute, inasmuch as it reveals the intent and design of the legislature in passing the Act, "It is only in cases where the meaning of the legislation is not clear recourse may be had to the title of statute or to the Preamble." In course of ambiguity or an expression capable of more than one meaning, it is permissible to the court to look at the title of an Act for ascertaining the aim of the Act or the mischief which the legislature was out to rectify.

Concerning the Act in question, the title is of great significance. Previously, it was "the Untouchability (Offences) Act, 1955" but later on it has been amended as "the Protection of Civil Rights Act, 1955" by the Act of 106 of 1976.

During discussion on the untouchability (offences) Bill in Rajya Sabha on 16th September 1954 Dr. B.R. Ambedkar expressed that, "I think that is a very important matter, and I think that a good law ought to have a good and succinct name. What is the name of this Bill? A Bill to provide punishment for the practice of untouchability or the enforcement of any disability arising therefrom. I personally think that is a very clumsy name and very mouthful. What really should be the name of the Bill may be a matter of disability but I personally think that it ought to have been called, "The Civil Rights (Untouchables) Protection Act."

Emphasis ought to have been therefore on civil rights. I venture to tell my friend in charge of the Bill that if he had referred to the case of Negroes in the United States or to the civil war, he would have found that the Bill that he is now proposing to be passed by Parliament has had its predecessor in the United States and that Bill, if he will refer to it he will find a simply styled Civil Rights Protection Bill. Even the word 'Negro' is not used in it, I don't know why he should keep on repeating untouchability and untouchables all the time. In the body of the Bill he is generally speaking of the Scheduled Castes. The Constitution speaks of the Scheduled Castes and I don't know why he should feel shy of using the word "Scheduled Castes" in the title of the Bill itself, Personally for myself. I would be quite happy with the name untouchables Civil Rights Protection Bill or Scheduled Castes Civil Rights Protection Bill. However, this proposal did not come into reality and the name of the Act remained the same.

When the Government attempted to amend the existing Act and introduce the Bill in *1972 to that effect,* the Parliament referred the Bill to the Joint Committee of the Parliament headed by R.D. Bhandare and later on with effect from 27th February 1973, S.M. Siddayya. The said Joint Committee was of the view that "By reason of the abolition of 'untouchability' certain rights are conferred on those who are subjected to the disability of untouchability and, therefore, the law should mainly concern itself to Protect those rights. Hence, more stress should be laid in order to protect those rights rather than punishing the offenders who preach or practice untouchability in any form. Therefore, the committee feel that the short title of the Principle Act should be changed to the Protection of Civil Rights Act." Parliament finally stamped the said title. The present title of the Act seems to be more meaningful and appropriate as it reveals the positive pledge of the Parliament to protect the "Civil Rights" of the ex-untouchables which they accrued by reason of the abolition of untouchability. Of course, "the intention of the Act is not to give any more or better rights to the untouchables than caste Hindus. It is intended to bring untouchables at par with other Hindus."

(2) It extends to the whole of India. This Act is enforceable in all the courts of law throughout India. According to Article 1 (1) of the Constitution of India, "India that is Bharat shall be a union of States, (2) The States and the territories thereof shall be as specified in the first scheduled. (3) The territory of India shall comprise (a) the territories of the States, (b) the union territories specified in the first schedule and (c) such other territories as may be acquired".

The first scheduled contains the names of twenty two states and nine union territories. Of course, the present law is applicable throughout India.

(3) "It shall come into force on such date as the Central Government may by notification in the official Gazette appoint."

The Government brought the present Act into implementation from 1st June, 1955, *vide* notification No. Ś.R.O. 1109, dated the 23rd May 1955, published in the *Gazette of India,* 1955 (Extra Ordinary, Part II, Section 3, Page 0971). The said Act in its amended form came in to existence with effect from 19-11-1976 *vide* S. No. 734 (E) New Delhi, dated 16-11-1976, published in the *Gazette of India* [Extra Ordinary Part II, Section 3 (ii) page 491].

(4) In this Act, unless the context otherwise needs (a) "Civil Rights" means "any rights" means any right accruing to a person by reason of the abolition of 'untouchability' by Article 17 of the Constitution". This clause has been added in the original Act, by Act of 106 of 1976. It became necessary to define the term "Civil Rights" as it appears in the title of the Act w.e.f. 1976.

Here 'Civil Rights' have somewhat restricted meaning as Civil Rights means any right accruing to a person by reason of the abolition of "untouchability". Such rights are mentioned in the Act itself in various sections, viz. 3, 4, 5, 6, 7 and 7A. It is expected that those rights may help in raising the status of the ex-untouchables to that of others. Those 'Civil Rights' are not the privileges but the rights with the objective of attaining social equality.

It appears that such rights do not exhaust with sections 3, 4, 5, 6, 7 and 7A, as the term includes "any right" accruing to a person by reason of the abolition of "untouchability". As untouchability" is taken in its historical perspective, such rights would be available to those "persons" who were considered as "untouchables" in the course of history. The act chanalizes the restricted flow of all the Civil Rights in favour of the ex-untouchables.

(a)(a) "Hotel" includes a refreshment room, a boarding house, a lodging house, a coffee house and a Cafe". These terms would cover a canteen as also hotel in the sense in which a hotel is commonly understood in India as including a wayside hut where tea, coffee, etc., are sold. It appears that the place or location of the hotel is not significant here, but the activity of the 'hotel' is important in ascertaining such place.

(b) "Place" includes a house, building and other structure and premises, and also includes a tent, vehicle and vessel. In the

Original Act (1955) the "place" was to include "a house, a building, a tent and a vessel". The words "other structure, premises and vehicle" are included by the Amending Act of 1976.

(c) "Place of public entertainment" includes any place to which the public are admitted and in which an entertainment provided or held."

Explanation : "Entertainment includes any exhibition, performance, game, sport and any other form of amusement." The definition of public entertainment is not exhaustive. It involves "any place" to which the public are admitted and in which an entertainment is provided or held. Entertainment is also an inclusive term, which includes "any" exhibition, performance, game, sport and "other forms of amusement" like theatres, shows, "funfairs", music houses, or any such forms of amusement.

(d) "Place of public worship" means a place, by whatever name known, which is used as a place of public religious worship or which is dedicated normally to, or is used generally by, persons professing any religion or belonging to any religious denomination or any section thereof for the performance of any religious service, or for offering prayers therein and includes.

(i) all lands and subsidiary shrines appurtenant or attached to any such place;

(ii) a privately owned place of worship which is, in fact, allowed by the owner thereof to be used as a place of public worship, and

(iii) such land or subsidiary shrine appurtenant to such privately owned place of worship as is allowed by the owner thereof to be used as a "place of public religious worship".

The last two sub-clause, i.e., (ii) and (iii) are added by the Act, 106 of 1976 so as to include the privately owned place of worship in the definition of "place of public worship". There is no definition of "worship" as such in this clause. However, it seens under Travancore Cochin Temple Entry (Removal of Disabilities) Act, 1950, Section 2, that "worship" means such religious service as the bulk of the worshippers may take part or offer in a temple and includes the right to bathe in tanks appurtenant to the temple subject to such rules and regulations as may be made under this Act." Thus, according to Section 2(d) "place of public worship" means a place which is used as a place of "religious worship" or for performance of any "religious service" or for offering "prayers" therein.

These places include all lands and subsidiary shrines appurtenant or attached to any such place. For becoming such place as a place of "public religious worship" it must be "used" as a place of "public religious worship" or such place must be "dedicated" normally to the public, or is used normally by the public professing "any" religion or belonging to "any" religious denomination or "any" section thereof. Such place of public religious worship includes all lands and subsidiary shrines appurtenant or attached to any such place.

Also, such place of public religious worship includes a privately owned place of worship which is, in fact, allowed by the owner thereof to be used as a place of public worship, and such land or subsidiary shrine appurtenant to such privately owned place of worship as is allowed by the owner thereof to be used as a place of public religious worship. The name by which it is known does not matter.

(da) "Prescribed" means prescribed by rules made under this Act. Under Section 16(B) of this Act the Central Government is empowered to make rules to carry out the provisions of this Act.

(db) "Scheduled Castes" has the meaning assigned to it in clause (24) of Article 366 of the Constitution.

This clause has been included by the Act, 106 of 1976. According to Article 366(24). "Scheduled Castes" means races or tribes as or parts of or groups within such castes, races, or tribes as are regarded under Article 341 to be Scheduled Castes for purpose of this Constitution. Under Article 341 the President of India is to specify by public notification such castes or sub-castes as Scheduled Castes. The Parliament is empowered to amend such notification. The notification issued by the President under Article 341 is known as "the Constitution (Scheduled Caste) Order 1950."

(e) "Shop" means any premises where goods are sold either wholesale or retail or both wholesale and by retail, and includes (i) any place from where goods are sold by hawker or vendor or from a mobile van or cart, (ii) a laundry and a hair cutting saloon; (iii) any other place where services are rendered to customers.

Sub-clause (i) has been later added by the Act, 106 of 1976.

Shop, therefore, means any place where goods are sold and

includes any place where goods are sold by a hawker, vendor or from a mobile van or cart; laundry, hair cutting saloons and any other place where such services are provided to the customers, such as the "premises" where carpenter, blacksmith, jewellers, and tailor perform their job or services and sell the goods to the customers. Canteen is a shop within the meaning of this clause. Thus any place where goods are sold or services are provided to the customers is a "shop" within the meaning of this clause. Thus, the Act itself provides the meaning of certain words or terms that are used in the Act. "Unless the context otherwise requires" the meaning provided under this section would be constructed accordingly throughout the Act. However, when the Act itself provides a dictionary for the words used, the court must look into that dictionary first for the interpretation of the words employed in the statute.

Provision of Punishment for Enforcing Religious Disabilities

3. Whoever on the ground and of 'untouchability' prevents any person.

- (a) from entering any place of public worship which is open to other persons professing the same religion, or any section thereof as such person, or
- (b) from worshipping or offering prayers of performing any religious services in any place of public worship, or bathing in, or using the waters of, any sacred tank, well, spring or water-course river or lake or bathing at any ghat of such tank, water-course, river or lake in the same manner and to the same extent as is permissible other persons professing the same religion or any section thereof, as such person, shall be punishable with imprisonment for a term of not less than one month and not more than six months and also with fine which shall be not less than one hundred rupees and not more than five hundred rupees.

Explanation: "For the purposes of this section and section persons professing the Buddhist, Sikh or Jaina religion or persons professing the Hindu religion in any of its forms or developments including *Virashaivas, Lingayat, Adivasis,* followers of *Brahmo, Prarthana, Aryasamaj* and the *Swaminarayan Sampradaya* shall be deemed to be Hindus."

It is required to take into account the amendments made by Act 106 of 1976 while construing. The Act 106 of 1976 has made some additions and deletions. Under clause (A) "belonging to the same religious denomination" after the same religion is omitted. Under clause (B) "river or lake or bathing at any ghat or such tank, water course, river or lake" after water course is added; and "belonging to the same religious denomination" after the same religion is omitted. The provision of punishment is wholly readjusted, providing minimum punishment and providing both imprisonment as well as fine.

Further, it is needed to take into account that there are two parts in this section. (i) Entry in the place of public worship, and (ii) worship and exercise of religious rites in such places. Explanation part of this section is very significant in construction of this section, which reveals the scope of the right bestowed on the ex-untouchables.

The aim of this section is to abolish the religious disabilities which were put in place by the Caste Hindus on the so called untouchables. This section provides punishment for enforcing religious disabilities regarding entry as well as worship in the temple. It seems this section has its origin in the constitutional provisions contained under Article 17 and Article 25(2)(b).

The offence would become complete once any person "prevents" another from enjoying his religious right "on the ground of untouchability." Prevention need not be by use of force or threat of physical force. It *State v. Kanu Dharma,* (1955) the Bombay High Court observed that even loud shouting so as to deter any ex-untouchable from entering a temple would constitute to preventions. Any action or design which results in prevention may be 'prevention' according to this section.

Such prevention must be 'on the ground of untouchability'. However, neither "untouchability" is defined nor "on the ground of untouchability" under this Act or elsewhere. It is the general rule that an act constituting an offence must be done with guilty mind or evil intention or 'Mens rea'. "Mens rea means an intention to do the forbidden act."

During the course of *mens rea* or criminal intention is a design to do an act forbidden by the criminal law without reasonable cause or excuse. It reveals the mental attitude of the criminal while committing any criminal act.

Intention is the purpose or design with which an act is done.

Although intention is linked to knowledge of act, intention is not knowledge. Knowledge is the awareness of consequence of an act, whereas intention is a desire to do the act in question. Criminal intention is a mental attitude to do some act which is wrong under the criminal law. Negligence and compulsion or force reveal a different type of mental attitude than the intention. Motive differs slightly from intention.

Motive mean some ulterior purpose behind the intention. The international discrimination prejudicial to the ex-untouchables may accordingly be based on motive of avoiding the pollution or defilement, although based on wrong notion or superstition from touch of such person. This motive is a purpose which becomes the reason of intention to do some act, constituting offence under this Act.

Phrase "On the ground of untouchability" means the mental element or criminal intention of an offender. Of course "untouchability" has originated in the criminal intention of hatred, contempt, vengeance and suppression of a section of people, as stated in the preceding chapter. Therefore, the need of 'mens rea' under the offence of untouchability is quite reasonable and it is very much implied in the practice of untouchability itself. However, under this Act it is not required of complainant to prove that the defendant had discriminated him 'on the ground of untouchability' only and not on 'any other ground'. By virtue of Section 12 of this Act, the court shall presume unless otherwise proved, that the act constituting and offence under this act was committed 'on the ground of untouchability' if it is committed against a scheduled caste.

In a case where ex-untouchables other than Scheduled Castes are involved they have to prove the "act" or "offence" of untouchability was perpetrated on the ground of "untouchability" and nothing more because untouchability itself is inclusive of mens rea. Under this section the ex-untouchables are empowered to enter any "place of public worship', worship or offer prayers or perform any religious service therein and they are authorised to take bath or use the sacred waters of any tank, spring or water course, river or lake. Such place of worship must be a public place or dedicated to the public or if it is privately owned place must be open to the public for worship. If such place is not 'public' then any prevention to enter or worship therein would not constitute an offence.

Cuttack High Court has noted in a case that "where the

function was a private one and it was not a place of public worship and the prevention of the complainant was not on the basis of his being an untouchable as people of caste were allowed to take part in the function the case did not come under Section 3." It is decided that "Thidappally is a kitchen of the temple where Nivedyam is prepared and where admittedly no worship takes place. "Hence denial of entry such place which is not used for worship would not constitute an offence under this section. However, this right is subjected to "the same manner and to the same extent as is permissible to other persons professing the same religion or any section thereof." It is pointed out in a case by the Madhya Pradesh High Court that, "the object of Section 3 is not to create any new rights in favour of untouchables but it is intended only to put them at par with other caste Hindus."

In the same vein, the Kerala High Court also noted that, "All that Section 3 means is that no person should be refused admittance to a place of public worship where other persons professing the same religion or belonging to the same denomination are admitted on the ground that such person is an untouchable. The section cannot be deemed to have conferred an unfettered right to every Hindu to perform rituals which according to the principles and tenets of the religion must be conducted only by the priests or to enter such places where such ceremonies are being performed. It is clear from the main part of Section 3 that if a person is stopped from entering any place of public worship on the ground that he is untouchable the act of prevention is penal on the part of the person who does it only if the place be one of public worship and either allowed to other persons professing the same religion as the person prevented or belongs to persons of the same religions denomination as that person. It therefore, follows that the section means "to preserve the distinction between the places of public worship not only belonging to different religions but even between such places as belonging to different denominations or sections included in one religion."

The Supreme Court in *Commissioner Hindu Religious Endowments Board versus L.T. Swamiyar* (1954) held that, "there could be no such thing as an unregulated and unrestricted right of entry in a public temple or other religious institution, for persons who are not connected with the spiritual functions thereof. It is a traditional custom universally observed not to provide access to any outsider to the particularly sacred parts of the temple as for example, the place where the deity is located. There are also fixed hours of worship and rest for the idol when no disturbance by any member of public is allowed."

The same principle as stated above has been applied in *Venkatraman Devaru v. State of Mysore (1958)* by the Supreme Court that "the right protected by Article 25(2)(b) is a right to enter into a temple for purposes of worship, and that further it should be construed liberally in favour of the public. But it does not follow from this that right is absolute and unlimited in character. No member of the Hindu Public could, for instance, claim as part of the rights protected by Article 25(2)(b) that a temple must be kept open for worship at all hours of the day and night, or that he should personally perform those services, which the Archakas alone could perform.

A well-known practice is that of a religious institutions of all denominations to limit some of its services to persons who have been specially initiated though at other times, the public in general are free to take part in the worship." Thus, the right of temple entry to which the ex-untouchables are entitled is extensive with the other persons of the same religion. They are entitled to enter, worship in the temples and offer religious services in the same manner and to the same extent as others professing the same religion. Explanation to this section provides that, "persons professing the Buddhist, Sikh or Jaina religion or persons professing the Hindu religion in any of its forms or development including *Virashaivas, Lingayats, Adivasis,* followers of *Brahmo, Prarthana, Arya Samaj* and the *Swaminarayan Sampradaya* shall be deemed to be Hindus;" and of the one and "the same religion." Of course, a Scheduled Caste convert to Buddhism is regarded to be Hindu under this explanation but he is not deemed so under sub-section (db) of Section 2 of this Act.

The aim of explanation to Section 3 appears to bring the Act within the ambit of Article 25(2) and Explanation II of the Constitution.

As such Hinduism includes "any of its forms", "any of its developments" including *Virashaivas, Lingayats, Adivasis, Brahmo Samaj, Prarthana Samaj, Arya Samaj* and *Swaminarayan Sampradaya;* as well as "any" such "forms and developments", e.g., *Shaivaism, Mahanubhav Panth, Warkaripanth, Vaishnava, Shakta, Kabir Panth* or any sect or sub-sect under them. For the purpose of this section even Buddhism, Sikhism or Jaina religions are also expected to be treated as 'Hindu'.

However, in *State v. Puranchand* (1958) and *State of Kerala v. Venkateswara Prabhu* (1961) the Madhya Pradesh High Court and Kerala High Court respectively observed that Section 3 preserves the "distinction" between the places of worship not only belonging to separate religions but even between the places of different denominations or sections also. In the *Venkatraman Devaru* (1958) the Supreme Court held that the denominations exclusion of outsiders from temple services was a matter of religion regarding which they had all the freedom to manage their religious affairs.

Ultimately, the Parliament by Act 106 of 1976 has omitted the words, "belonging to the same religious denomination" from this Section. However, the word "sections thereof" are still retained. Does it mean that the section intends to leave out denominational difference and retain sectional difference? According to Shri R.G. Karmarkar, J., the rules laid down by Kerala and Madhya Pradesh High Courts "are still good law." According to K.D. Gangrade, "the amended Act (PCRA) continues to put the rights of untouchables on par only with the right of "others of the same religion" and does not clarify the meaning of the explanation.

On the basis of this one could very well conclude that the legal position under the new Act will probably be as held in the above case of *State v. Puranchand.* According to Vishnu Swarup "the Section preserves the distinction between the places of Public Worship belongings to different religious as well as to different Sections of one religion only." Of course, the Joint-Committee constituted by the Parliament to submit its report after due deliberation on the Bill, stated in its report that, "subject to the provisions of Article 26 of the Constitution, places of public worship of any particular religion should be open to all persons belonging to the same religion". Prevention of Temple Entry on the basis of untouchability of a person should be punishable even if the person concerned does not belong to the same denomination as the person prevented. Based on this report, the Parliament has deliberately dropped the word "belonging to any denomination" from this section, but retained the word "Section" thereof. Therefore, it seems that the Parliament to desires to recognize "Sectional" rights but not the "denominational" rights.

Even places of public worship which are privately owned as well as such lands and subsidiary shrines appurtenant to such privately owned place of public worship as are thrown open by the owner to be used as places of public worship have been brought under the purview of this Act.

Here, it is necessary to bear in mind that the Protection of Civil Rights Act not only abolition of untouchability among the Hindus, but it equally aims to abolish it among the other religions also. "Whoever" commits any act which is an offence under the present section of under any other section of the PCRA would be liable to punishment on conviction. While speaking on the untouchability (offences) Bill in the Lok Sabha, the then Home Minister G.B. Pant had categorically state that, "this Bill does not apply to Hindus alone. It applies to all—we have, however, enlarged the scope of this Act. It will apply not only to Scheduled Castes, but probably to Christians in the South who are not allowed to enter Churches by those who regard themselves as belonging to higher classes. There are certain Muslims who are treated in the same manner by the followers of Islam. They will have the benefit of the Provision". Thus the aim of the PCR Act is to abolish the inhuman institution of untouchability from the Indian Society as a whole. Therefore, "whoever" commits any act contemplated under the Act on the ground of untouchability in respect of "any person" belonging to the so-called low caste or status in punishable on conviction according to the Provisions of this Act.

As mentioned in this section, punishment on conviction as mention this section is imprisonment for a term of not less than one month and note more than six months and fine which shall not be less than one hundred rupees and not more than five hundred rupees.

Provisions for Punishment for Enforcing Social Disabilities

"Whoever on the ground of "untouchability" enforces against any person any disability with regard to

(i) Access to any shop, public restaurant, hotel or place of public entertainment; or

(ii) The use of any utensils, and other articles kept in any public restaurant, hotel, *dharamshala, sarai* or *musafirkhana* for the use of the general public or of any section thereof; or

(iii) The practice of any profession or the carrying on of any occupation, trade or business or employment in any job; or

(iv) The use of, or access to, any river, stream, spring, well, tank, cistern, water tap or other watering place, or any bathing ghat, burial or cremation ground, any sanitary convenience, any road or passage, or any other place of public resort which other members of the public, or any section thereof have a right to use or have access to; or

(v) The use of, or access to, any place used for a charitable or a public purpose maintained wholly or partly out of state funds or dedicated to the use of the general public; or any section thereof; or

(vi) The enjoyment of any benefit under a charitable Trust created for the benefit of the general public or any section thereof; or

(vii) The use of, or access to, any public conveyance; or

(viii) The construction, acquisition or occupation of any residential premises in any locality, whatsoever; or

(ix) The use of any *dharmashala, sarai* or *musafirkhan* a which is open to the general public or to any section thereof; or

(x) The observance of any social or religious custom, usage or ceremony or taking part in, or taking out, any religious, social or cultural procession or

(xi) The use of jewellery and finery.

shall be punishable with imprisonment for a term of not less than one month and not more than six months and also with fine which shall not less than one hundred rupees and not more than five hundred rupees."

Explanation: For the purposes of this section, "enforcement of any disability" includes any discrimination on the ground of "untouchability."

Explanation: For the purpose of this section "persons professing the Buddhist, Sikh or Jaina religion or persons professing the Hindu religion in any of its forms of developments including *Virashaivas, Lingayats, Adivasis,* followers of *Brahmo, Prarthana, Arya Samaj* and the *Swaminarayan Sampradaya* shall be deemed to be Hindus."

The object of this section is to end untouchability in certain areas as stated under this section. It appears that this section is arranged in such a way so as to give effect to Articles 17 and 15(2) as well as Articles 16(2), 19(1)(b), (e) (g), 21, 25(1) and 26(c) of the Constitution. Thus it intends to root out untouchability from the social sphere. This section also has undergone some changes under Act 106 of 1976. It has added "any section thereof" in clause (ii); "employment in any job" in clause (iii), "any section thereof" in clause (iv), (v), (vi) and (ix); "taking part in, or taking out, any religious, social and cultural procession" in clause (x). Provision of punishment, has been redrafted. Explanation of the word "enforcement" has been included.

According to this section states that whoever 'on the ground of untouchability' enforces against any person any disability regarding certain social rights is punishable in accordance with this section. "Enforcement of any disability" includes any "discrimination on the ground of untouchability." This definition is inclusive one as it includes any prevention, obstruction, deprivation, prohibition, objection or discrimination on the ground of 'untouchability' so as to make the complainant incapable of or disqualify from enjoying any right stated under this section. In other words, depriving any person from enjoying certain civil rights on the ground of untouchability amounts to 'enforcement of disability.' 'Enforcement of disability' has been used here as it has been used under Article 17 of the Constitution. Hence it leads us to the same meaning.

Clause (i): The words shop, hotel and public entertainment have been defined under Section (2) clause (e); (aa) and (c). "Public restaurant means a place where meals and other refreshments may be obtained or consumed. Public restaurant actually means a hotel where meals or refreshments are served and is open to the public." The words "access to" implies "actual entry" into such places and "means or ways of approach, an opportunity, right of approach," into such places equally with other customers.

Clause (ii): Any discrimination with regard to the use of any utensils, and other articles kept in any public restaurant, hotel, *dharamshala, sarai* or *musafirkhana* would be offence.

Clause (iii): Enforcement of any disability or discrimination regarding the practice of any profession, occupation, trade or business or employment in any job on the ground of untouchability is an offence.

Clause (iv): Every person is equally entitled to use and not misuse any place of public resort which is open for the public or any section of the public; including river, well, water-tap or any watering place, bathing ghat, burial or cremation ground, sanitary convenience or roads or passages. However, Section 4(iv) of this Act is not applicable to private wells. "The owner of a private well being free to regulate the use of his well by co-villagers, the fact that such owner permitted other people in the village to draw water from the well, would not be a proof of the fact that every villager has a right of access to or right to use the well. The prosecution must affirmatively establish that the public had a right of access to or use of the well in question before the offence Section 4(iv) can be said to have been established."

Clause (v): Any place used for a charitable or public purpose either maintained out of state fund or if it is a private one, dedicated to the use of public or any section thereof is the subject of this clause. Any discrimination with regard to use of such places would be an offence.

Clause (vi): A charitable trust created for the benefit of the general public cannot discriminate the beneficiaries on the ground of untouchability. Trust is a fudiciary relationship in which the Trustee holds the title to the property for the benefit of the beneficiaries.

Clause (vii): The enforcement of any disability with regard to the use of or access to any public conveyance on payment on the ground to untouchability is an offence.

Clause (viii): Any objection with regard to the construction or occupation of any residential premises in any locality on the ground of untouchability is an offence.

Clause (ix): *Dharamshala, Sarai* or *Musafirkhana* which is open to the public or any section thereof should be open to the untouchables.

Clause (x): Any discrimination on the ground of untouchability with regard to the observance on any social or religious function or ceremony or festival or religious, social or cultural procession is an offence. "Taking part in or taking out, any religious, social or cultural procession" has been added by Act 106 of 1976. Any prevention or objection to the untouchables in the caste Hindus function etc., or to the function etc., organised by untouchables on the ground of untouchability would be an offence.

Clause (xi): Any obstruction or prevention on the ground of untouchability with regard to the use of jewellery, finery of fine clothes, turban or footwears would constitute an offence.

Concerning any religious functions, ceremonies or places of public resort etc., the Buddhist, Sikh, or Jaina religion or Hindu religion in any of its forms or developments including *Virashaivas, Lingayats, Adivasis,* followers of *Brahmo, Prarthana, Arya Samaj* and *Swaminarayan Sampradaya* are regarded to be Hindus.

Under this section, any offence shall be punishable with imprisonment for a term of not less than one month and not more than six months and also with fine which shall be not less than one hundred rupees and not more than five hundred rupees.

Provision for Refusing to Admission in Hospitals etc.

"Whoever on the ground of 'untouchability':

(a) refuses admission to any person to any hospital, dispensary, educational institution or any hostel, if such hospital, dispensary, education institution or hostel is established or maintained for the benefit of the general public or any section thereof; or

(b) does any act which discriminates against any such person after admission to any of the aforesaid institutions.

shall be punishable with imprisonment for a term of not less than one month and not more than six months and also with fine which shall not less than one hundred rupees and not more than five hundred rupees."

The aim of this section is to being an end to untouchability in the hospitals and educational institutions. It appears that this section is based on Articles 17, 15(1), 29(2) and 46 of the Constitution.

The Amending Act 106 of 1976 has omitted the words "attached thereto" after "any hostel". Any hostel now need not be attached to the educational institution for bringing guilt for its discrimination on the ground of untouchability. The punishment part of this section is same as under Sections 3 and 4 of the Act.

The hospital, dispensary, educational institution or hostel for coming within ambit of this section must be set up or maintained for the benefit of the general public or any section thereof. Refusal to admit any person to such 'public' institutions as well as any discrimination against any such person after admission to such institutions on the ground of untouchability would be an offence.

According to Section 5 of the Act even if the discrimination is not solely or only on the ground of untouchability and if untouchability is only one of the bases of discrimination the person practising such discrimination would be guilty of the offence. So if one of the reasons for the segregation of the Harijan students is on the ground of untouchability the offence is made out." Any refusal or discrimination on the ground of merit, discipline or paying capacity will not form any offence under this section.

The place of such institution appears to be immaterial. It may be a private owned place or owned by the local authority or the State Government, or even such institutions may being the temples in the villages.

Punishment for Refusing to Selling Goods or to Render Services

"Whoever on the ground of 'untouchability' denies to sell any goods or refuses to provide any service to any person at the same time and place and on the same terms and conditions at or on which such goods are sold or services are rendered to other persons in the ordinary course of business shall be punishable with imprisonment for a term of not less than one month and not more than six months and also with fine which shall be not less than one hundred rupees and not more than five hundred rupees."

Not allowing the sale of goods to untouchables or refusing to provide any service would be an offence. Further, refusing to sell includes refusing to sell the goods or render the services at the same time and place and on the same terms and conditions at or on which such goods are sold or services are rendered to other persons in the "ordinary course of business." Any delay, discrimination and changing of the terms and conditions while selling goods on the ground of untouchability would be an offence, the convict would be liable to same punishment which is mentioned in the earlier sections.

Provisions for Punishment for other Offences Emanating from "Untouchability"

(a) Prevents any person from exercising any right accruing to him by reason of the abolition of 'untouchability' under Article 17 of the Constitution; or

(b) Molests, injures, annoys, obstructs or causes or attempts to cause obstruction to any person in the exercise of any such right or molests, injures, annoys or boycotts any person by reason of his having exercised any such right; or

(c) By words, either spoken or written, or by signs or by visible representations or otherwise incites or encourages any person or class of persons or the public generally to practice 'untouchability' in any form whatsoever; or

(d) Insults or attempts to insult, on the ground of 'untouchability' a member of Scheduled Caste.

shall be punishable with imprisonment for a term of not less than one month and not more than six months and also with fine which shall not less than one hundred rupees and not more than five hundred rupees."

Explanation I : A person shall be deemed to boycott another person who:

(a) refuses to let to such other person or refuses to permit such other person to use or occupy any house or land or refuses to deal with, work for hire for, or do business with, such other person or to render to him or receive from him any customery service, or refuses to do any of the said things on the terms on which such things would be commonly done in the ordinary course of business; or

(b) abstains from such social, professional or business relations as he would ordinarily maintain with such other person.

Explanation II: For the purpose of clause (c) a person shall be deemed to incite or encourage the practice of "untouchability":

(i) If he, directly or indirectly preaches "untouchability" or its practice in any form, or

(ii) If he justified, whether on historical, philosophical or religious grounds or on the ground of any tradition of the caste system or on any other ground, the practice of untouchability in any form.

(1)(A) Whoever commits any offence against the person or property of any individual as a reprisal or revenge for his having exercised any right accruing to him by reason of the abolition of 'untouchability' under Article 17 of the Constitution, shall where the offence is punishable with imprisonment for a term exceeding two years, be punish with imprisonment for a term whch shall not be less than two years and also with fine.

(2) "Whoever:

(i) denies to any person belonging to his community or any section thereof any right or privilege to which such person would be entitled as a member of such community or section; or

(ii) takes any part in the ex-communication of such person on the ground that such person has refused to practice 'untouchability' or that such person has done, any act in furtherance of the objects of this Act.

shall be punishable with imprisonment for a term of not less than one month and not more than six months, and also with fine which shall not less than one hundred rupees and not more than five hundred rupees."

Objective of this section is to give full effect to Article 17 of the Constitution. According to R.G. Karmarkar, "the legislature has taken note of the tensions such conferment of rights was bound to generate in a community ridden with centuries old orthodoxy and prejudice, with the untouchables attempting to exercise the newly accrued rights and with well meaning persons helping them exercise the same. The section is aimed at protecting effectively the rights granted to Harijans as well as the persons exercising them or helping their exercise from diverse forms of opposition that they may be subjected to, from insults to individual Harijans and physical violence towards them to reprisals against them out of vengeful attitudes."

Clause (d), Explanation II and Clause 1A are newly added by Act, 106 of 1976.

Clause (a): The abolition of the stigma of untouchability under Article 17 of the Constitution has resulted in bringing up the social status of the ex-untouchables to that of others and as such they become eligible to exercise all the civil rights made available under the Protection of Civil Rights Act, 1955. Probably this would be a junk to the feelings of the orthodox or obscurantists caste Hindus. After taking into account the probable future consequences, the Act under this clause states that whoever prevents the ex-untouchables from exercising any right accruing to them by reason of the abolition of 'untouchability' is punishable. 'Prevents' would have the same meaning as under section 1.

Clause (b): Whoever molests, injures annoys obstructs or causes to obstruct or attempts to cause obstruction while exercising any Civil Right would be an offence. Even "attempt" to cause obstruction is also an offence. In other words, the act of obstruction need not be complete for bringing the guilt. "Molests" means any interference or indecent behaviour. "Injure" means any harm or damage or any harm to his feeling and self-pride. "Annoy" means trouble which irritates such person for his no fault. "Obstruct" means prevent. Thus whoever molests, injures, annoys or obstructs any ex-touchable in his exercise of Civil Rights would be offence under this clause. After exercise of Civil Rights by an untouchable if he is molested, injured annoyed or boycotted only because such person has exercised his Civil Rights would be constitute an offence.

This clause *inter alia* provides punishment on account of boycott. It categorically states that whoever boycotts any person by reason of his having exercised any Civil Right is committing an offence.

According to Explanation I, boycott means:

(i) refusal to let or refusal to permit to use or occupy any house or land.

(ii) refusal to deal with such persons.

(iii) refusal to work for hire or dismissal from such work.

(iv) refusal to do any business with or severe such contacts.

(v) refusal to render to him or receive from him any customary service.

(vi) refusal to do the said things on the terms on which such things would be commonly done in the ordinary course of business, and

(vii) abstaining from such social, professional or business relations as he would ordinarily maintain with such other person.

As per the Randon House Dictionary boycott means "to combine in abstaining from or preventings with a person or organization as a means of coercion."According to Dr. B.R. Ambedkar, "...in legal terms, social boycott is nothing else than a conspiracy, which is an offence recognized by the Indian Penal Code. If two people engage themselves in doing wrong to a third person, well, that is conspiracy. The social boycott is brought about by the concurrence of the majority of the people and is also a conspiracy and could be recognized as an offence." Thus the boycott is a means of coercion, segregation and suppression, which is often used by the caste Hindus in respect of ex-untouchables, especially in the villages. Under this clause it is a punishable offence.

One has to bear in mind that for bringing the guilt under clause (a) and (b) it is not necessary to state that the offence was committed "on the ground of untouchability". For these two clauses it is enough to state the incident which is an offence under the Act has happened in respect of an ex-untouchable.The words "on the ground of untouchability is not used in both the clauses. As well as the heading of this section states that "punishment for other offences" arising out of "untouchability" and not "on the ground of untouchability". The prosecution has to show relationship of the incident to the untouchable which arises or springs out of untouchability. It is easier to prove arising out of untouchability "than on the ground of untouchability."

Clause (e): Whoever incites or encourages to the public or any section thereof to "practise" 'untouchability' in any form, either by written or spoken words or by signs or visible representations commits an offence under the clause. This is one of the significant features of this Act to provide punishment for preaching 'untouchability'.

Explanation II: It is added to this clause so as to explain the meaning of 'incite or encourage' the practice of untouchability by Act, 106 of 1976. Accordingly a person shall be deemed to incite or encourage the practice of untouchability—

(i) if he directly or indirectly preaches "untouchability" or its practice in any form, or

(ii) if he justifies the practice of untouchability on historical, philosophical or religious grounds, or

(iii) if he justifies it on the ground of any tradition of the caste system, or

(iv) if he justifies on any other ground the practice of untouchability in any form.

Any such incitement or encouragement may be provided either by words, either spoken or written, or by signs or by visible representation, or even by any other way. Here the 'intention' of the accused is significant and not the means that he uses for the expression or manifestation of the intention. The words "or otherwise" include a number of ways and means of inciting and encouraging others to observe and enforce untouchability in respect of untouchables, e.g., brow-beating, nodding the head etc.

Clause (d) : This has been added by Act, 106 of 1976. "Insult" means an intentional use of abusive filthy language which is capable of provoking breach of peace on the part of the complainant. Whoever insults or even tries to insult on the ground of untouchability would be an offence. It is, however, not necessary that the act of insult must be total. Whoever attempts to insult a member of Scheduled Caste commits an offence under this clause. For both an effort to insult or insult the punishment is same.

The ingredients of the offence under this clause are (i) There should be insult or attempt to insult, (ii) Such insult must be on the ground of untouchability, and (iii) It should be liked to a member of a Scheduled Caste. It appears that for other offences under this Act the complainant need not be a member of Scheduled Caste. What is required there is the complainant must prove that he or she is an ex-untouchable. But so far as this clause is concerned the complainant will have to prove that he belongs to Scheduled Caste. In other words if it is alleged that a member of Scheduled Caste has been insulted by the non-Scheduled Caste, the court shall *prima facie* presume that such insult was based on the ground of untouchability.

Insult is punishable as well as under IPC Section 504. Under PCRA Section 7(1) clause (d) also. But "attempt" to insult is punishable only under PCRA Section 7(1) clause (d). The present section should be read with Section 12 of PCRA, which reads "where any act constituting an offence under this Act is committed in relation to a member of "Scheduled Caste, the court shall presume, unless otherwise proved that such act was committed on the ground of "untouchability". Accordingly, those who were 'untouchables' but now who are ceased to be member of Scheduled Castes due to their conversion to Buddhism or any other religion do not get benefit of presumption under Section 12. The Scheduled Castes converted to Buddhism will get remedy under IPC Section 504 for their insult equally with others. Thus this clause is applicable only to the concerning Scheduled Castes.

In *Laxman Jayaram Shant v. State of Maharashtra,* (1980) the Bombay High Court noted that, "Every insult or attempt to insult of a member of Scheduled Caste, would not fall within the mischief of the said clause (d) of Section 7(1) of the Act unless such insult or attempt to insult is on the ground of 'untouchability'. There must be specific intention of person to insult. He must have means rea to that effect. Such insult must be referrable to practising and preaching of untouchability."

But the same court took a different stand in *Shantabai v. State of Maharastra,* (1982). Their Lordship stated, "when the offence under Section 7(1)(d) stands proved – Prosecution need not further prove that such act was committed on ground of 'untouchability'. If the act of insult is committed with reference to a member of Scheduled Caste was defined in Section 2(db) then presumption under Section 12 of the Act safely be raised."

"The word 'Mahardya' *prima facie* amounts to an insult. It is indicative of offensive disrespect and indignity. It is normally used to hurt the feelings and self-respect of the person whom it is addressed, such a person is treated with insolence and contempt."

Here, the convict would be liable to the same punishment which is mention for the preceding offences.

7 (1A): *Clause*: This clause has been added by Act, 106 of 1976 to deal with any offence against the person or property of any person committed as a reprisal or revenge for his having exercised any right accruing to him by reason of abolition of untouchability under Article 17 of the Constitution. The clause contemplates offences against person as well as property – of the ex-untouchables by the touchables as a matter of reprisal or revenge against them. Nowadays they are termed as 'atrocities' on the ex-untouchables.

The offences committed against the person or property are generally punishable under relevent sections of Indian Penal Code. This clause categorically states that where the offence is punishable with imprisonment for a term exceeding two years, be punishable with imprisonment for a term which shall not be less than two years and also with fine.

Punishment for the offences against the human body have been mentioned under Chapter XVI of the Indian Penal Code, from Sections 302 to 377 and punishments for the offences against the property have been provided under Chapter XVII of the Indian Penal Code, from Sections 379 to 462. The punishment part of this clause lays down the principles of punishment for the offences against person or property on the ground of untouchability and it does not elaborate the punishment. It lays down that the minimum punishment would be two years where it is provided exceeding two years and fine prescribed for that offence, whatever it may be. Thus it takes away the discretionary power of the court regarding award of minimum punishment is concerned. But it is not a bar on the court to award more than the minimum punishment in such cases as it is provided under IPC.

Clause (2): The object of this clause is to protect the persons belonging to touchable castes, in case of their ex-communication, owing to their refusal to practice untouchability in any form.

Whoever hinders any right or privilege to which a person is entitled as a member of his community, or takes any part in the 'ex-communication' of such person due to his refusal to practice 'untouchability' or such person has done any act in furtherance of the object of the Act, commits an offence under Clause 2(ii). The ex-communicate means, "to cut from communion or membership, especially from the sacraments and fellowship of the church by ecclesiastical sentence." It is a powerful weapon in the hands of the members of any community to ex-communicate any of its members so as to make him bend before them. The prosecution has to prove that the ex-communication was the direct result of his "denial" to practise "untouchability" or it was based on "any act" done by such person in furtherance of the objects of this Act. The scope of "any act done in furtherance of the object of this Act" is very wide. Any assistance or co-operation to the ex-untouchables also would come under its scope.

It is not necessary that one should take a major or active part in the 'ex-communication' of such person for bringing the guilt. It would be enough if it is proved that the accused has taken "any part" in the ex-communication for constituting the offence under this clause. It means that one cannot take a plea in defence that he was compelled to do contrary to the objects of this Act only on the ground of fear of 'ex-communication' by this community or the village. There being a legal remedy on the 'ex-communication' one has to go for that and not to be swayed by the compulsion of majority to do any act contrary to the objectives of this Act. Under this clause also the convict is punishable with imprisonment for a term of not less than one month and not more than six months, and also with fine which shall be not less than one hundred rupees and not more than five hundred rupees.

Unlawful Compulsory Labour and Practice of Untouchability

7A(1) "Whoever compels any person, on the ground of 'untouchability' to do any scavenging or sweeping or to remove any carcass or to flay any animal or to remove the umbilical cord or to do any other job of a similar nature shall be deemed to have enforced a disability arising out of 'untouchability'.

(2) Whoever is deemed under sub-section (1) to have enforced a disability arising out of 'untouchability' shall be punishable with imprisonment for a term which shall not be less than three months and not more than six months and also with fine which shall not be less than one hundred rupees and not more than five hundred rupees.

Explanation: For the purpose of this section, 'compulsion' includes a threat of social or economic boycott."

The so called untouchables were forced to do compulsory labour of different kinds in the past as a form and practice of "untouchability". The labour or services which they were asked to do or perform were of filthy nature, as they were to lower down the social status of untouchables in the eyes of the others, e.g., the removal of carcases, scavenging, sweeping etc. Such services or occupations worked to consolidate the institution of untouchability. Even after the abolition of untouchability also such services were being imposed to the ex-untouchables in some parts of the country. Therefore, the Parliament took note of this custom and provided punishment for the same by the Act 106 of 1976. This section is however, based on Article 17 and Article 23(1) of the Constitution of India. The objective of this section is to free such untouchables from the compulsion of such occupation.

It is stated under the section that, whoever compels the ex-untouchables to do any scavenging, sweeping or to remove any carcass or to flay away animal or to remove the umbilical cord or to do "any other job of a similar nature" on the ground of untouchability commits an offence. The scope of "any other job of a similar nature" is quite wide; and involves each and every filthy occupation or service.

The objective of this section is to forbid the age old practice of getting the unclean jobs done through the untouchables. The familiar forms of such filthy jobs are:

(1) scavenging,
(2) sweeping,
(3) removing carcases,
(4) to flay any animal, and
(5) removing the umbilical cord.

While deciding what comes under "any other job of a similar nature", one has to consider the nature of such jobs and identify them by reference to their "similar" nature as such. Thus,

(i) beating of drums,
(ii) cutting of woods,
(iii) conveying message of death,
(iv) digging the grave,
(v) working as attender in certain celebration,
(vi) carrying luggage,
(vii) cleaning the animal shed,
(viii) carrying petromax with the procession,
(ix) performing certain services or worshipping the village goddess in epidemics and such other customary services, are unclean and humiliating, as such they are "similar" to the jobs or services mentioned in the section.

Another important feature of this offence is "compulsion" of services on the part of untouchables by the touchables. Compulsion means committing or threatening to commit any act forbidden by the Indian Penal Code, or the unlawful detaining or threatening to detain any property and putting fear of social or economic boycott against the ex-untouchables with the intention to get the things done through them which are by nature unclean and which lower down the status of those persons. Of course, inducement and undue influence also exercise psychological compulsion, if not physical, as such it would form an offence. When such compulsion is on the basis of untouchability, the convict is punishable with imprisonment for a term which shall not be less than three months and not more than six months and also with fine which shall not be less than one hundred and not more than five hundred rupees. However, under Indian Penal Code, Section 374 is provided that whoever unlawfully compels any person to labour against his desire is liable to be punished with imprisonment for one year or fine or both.

Cancellation or Suspension of Licence

Any person who is convicted of an offence under Section 6 holds any licence under any law for the time being in force in respect of any profession, trade, selling or employment relating to which the offence is committed, the court conducting the offence may, without prejudice to any other penalty to which such person may be liable under that section, direct that the licence shall stand cancelled or be suspended for such period as the court may deem fit, and every order of the court so cancelling or suspending a licence shall have effect as if it had been passed by the competent authority to cancel or suspend the licence under any such provision of the law.

Explanation: In this section "licence" includes a permit or a permission.

Accordingly under this section the court has powers to direct the convict under Section 6, that the licence which he holds stands cancelled or suspended for a certain specified time. Thus the court has got the discretion whether or not to in addition to the punishment awarded under Section 6 of this Act, to cancel the licence or permit.

Resumption or Suspension of Grants

"Where the Manager of Trustee of a place of Public Worship or any educational institution or hostel which is in receipt of a grant or money from the government is convicted of an offence under the act and such conviction is not reversed or quashed in any appeal or revision, the Government may, if in its opinion the circumstances of the case warrants such a course direct the suspension or resumption of the whole or any part of such grant."

Words 'or any educational institution or hostel' are added by Act 106 or 1976. The aim of this section is to maintain a check on the places of public worship, educational institutions and hostels that they should not observe untouchability. If they are convicted of any offence under this Act, the Government holds power to direct the suspension or resumption of grant if such institution is in receipt of grant. It is an enabling section to the government to do so if "the circumstances of the case warrants such a course" and whether or not such circumstances arised in a particular case is to be assessed by the government.

Abetment of Offence

"Whoever abets any offence under this Act shall be punishable with the punishment provided for the offence.

Explanation: A public servant who wilfully ignores the investigation of any offence punishable under this Act shall be considered to have abetted an offence punishable under this Act."

This section provides punishment for abetment of any offence under this Act. Explanation to this section has been added by Act, 106 of 1976. The word 'to abet' means "encourage, support or countenance by aid or approval, usually in wrong doing." Thus one who encourages, supports or approves any wrong contemplated under this Act is doing an abetment punishable accordingly.

The Indian Penal Code, under Section 107 defines the offence of abetment as under:

Section 107: A person abets the doing of a thing who

(1) *Instigates* any person to do that thing. A person (instigates the doing of a thing who by (i) wilful misrepresentation, or (ii) wilful concealment of a material (which he is bound to disclose voluntarily) (i) causes of procures, or (ii) attempts to cause or procure the things to be done (Explanation).

(2) Engages: (with one more person) is a conspiracy (i) for the doing of that thing, if act or illegal omission takes place in pursuance of that conspiracy and (ii) in order to the doing of that thing.

(3) Intentionally aids (by any of illegal omission) the doing of that thing. A person is said to aid the doing of an act who facilitates the omission of the act."

Thus 'abetment' consists of three act :

(i) abetment by instigation,
(ii) abetment by conspiracy, and
(iii) abetment by aid.

The offence is complete as soon as the abettor has incited or instigated another to commit the offence, whether the latter consents or not, or whether, having consented, he commits the offence, or not is not material.

What is said under Section 107 of IPC is applicable by analogy to the 'abetment' under Section 10 of the PCRA. The definition of abetment as given under IPC has been adopted by the General Clauses Act, 1897 under sub-section 3(1).

The offender under this section or an abettor would be liable to the same punishment which is given for any offence under this Act. Thus the quantum of punishment is same to the abettor as also to the principle offender.

The explanation to this section states categorically that "A public servant who wilfully ignores the investigation of any offence punishable under this Act shall be regarded to have abetted of offence punishable under this Act."

According to Section 2(4) of the Code of Criminal Procedure "Investigation" includes "all the proceedings under this code for the collection of evidence conducted by a police officer or by any person (other than a Magistrate) authorized by a Magistrate in this behalf." When a police officer or any person authorised in this behalf, "wilfully neglects the investigation" of any offence punishable under this Act "shall" be deemed to have "abetted" an offence punishable under this Act. Thus one who wilfully or intentionally neglects the investigation or gives very little attention to investigation or fails to carry out the investigation as per procedure provided under Chapter XII of the Code of Criminal Procedure, 1973 amounts to "abetment" under PCRA and punishable according to the Penal Provisions of the said act.

The reason behind such enumeration is the Act intends those concerned police officer must complete thorough investigation of the offences as and when information to that effect is received by him so that no offender escapes. Therefore, it becomes incumbent on the part of the police officer to undertake the investigation as provided so as to fulfil the objective of this Act.

Whether 'wilfully neglects the investigation of an offence' includes "wilfully neglects the registration of an offence"? Apparently the reason and spirit of the Explanation, connotes that even wilful neglect of the registration of the alleged offence itself is an "abetment", of an offence under this section.

It is, however, necessary to bear in mind that "notwithstanding anything contained in the Code of Criminal

Procedure, 1973, when any public servant is alleged to have committed the offence of abetment of an offence punishable under this Act, while acting or purporting to act in the discharge of his official duty, no court shall take cognizance of such offence of abetment except with the previous section (a) of the Central Government in the case of person employed in relation to the affairs of the union, and (b) of the State Government, in the case of a person employed in relation to the affairs of a State."

At times it may be difficult to get such consent from the concerned Government. This situation is often described as a "catch."

State Government to Impose Collective Fine

10(A)(1) If, after conducting an "inquiry in the prescribed manner, the government is satisfied that the inhabitants of an area concerned, is or abetting the commission of, any offence punishable under this Act, or harbouring persons concerned in the Commission of such offence or failing to render all the help in their power to discover or apprehend the offender or suppressing material evidence of the commission of such offence, the State Government may, by notification in the official Gazette, impose a collective fine on such inhabitants and apportion such fine amongst the inhabitants who are liable to collectively pay it, and such apportionment shall be made according to the State Government's judgement of the respective means of such inhabitants and in making any such apportionment the State Government may assign a portion of such fine to a Hindu Undivided Family.

Given that the fine apportioned to an inhabitant shall not be realized until the petition, if any filed by him under sub-section (3) is disposed of.

(2) The notification made under sub-section (1) shall be proclaimed in the area by beat of drum or in such other manner as the State Government may think best in the circumstances to bring the imposition of the collective fine to the notice of the inhabitants of the said area.

(3)(a) Any person aggrieved by the imposition of the collective fine under sub-section (1) or by the order of apportionment may, within the prescribed period, file a petition before the state government or such other authority as that government may specify in this behalf for being exempted from such fine or for modification of the order of apportionment.

Given that no fee shall be charged for filing such petition.

(b) The State Government or the authority specified by it shall, after giving to the petitioner a reasonable opportunity of being heard, pass such order as it may think fit.

Given that the amount of the fine exempted or reduced under this section shall not be realisable from any person, and the total fine imposed on the inhabitants of an area under sub-section (1) shall be deemed to have been reduced to that extent.

(4) Notwithstanding anything contained in sub-section (3) the State Government may exempt the victims of any offence punishable under this Act or any person who does not, in its opinion, fall within the category of persons specified in sub-section (1), from the liability to pay the collective fine 'imposed under sub-section (1) or any portion thereof.

(5) The portion of collective fine payable by any person (including a Hindu undivided family) may be recovered in the manner provided by the Code of Criminal Procedure 1973, for the recovery of fines imposed by a Court as if such portion were a fine imposed by a Magistrate."

Therefore, it is stated under Section 10A(1) that if after initiating an inquiry in the prescribed manner the State Government is satisfied that inhabitants of an area are—

(1) concerned in the commission of any offence under this Act,
(2) abetting the commission of an offence,
(3) harbouring persons concerned in the commission of such offences,
(4) failing to render all the assistance in their power to discover or apprehend the offender, and
(5) suppressing material evidence of the commission of such offence.

The State Government is empowered to impose collective fine on such inhabitants by the notification in the Official Gazette, subject to the Protection of Civil Rights Rules, 1977 the State Government may appoint on officer of the rank of a Sub-Divisional Magistrate for holding an inquiry under the section. The Inquiry Officer will follow the procedure for Summary Trials as prescribed in Chapter XXI of the Cr. P.C. and complete such inquiry and submit his report to the State Government within a period not exceeding six weeks. Thereupon the State Government may impose collective fine on inhabitants of the area through notification in the Official Gazette. Any person aggrieved by the imposition of such collective fine may file a petition before the State Government seeking exemption from such fine within a period of thirty days from the date of proclamation of the notification. The State Government after giving him reasonable opportunity of being heard may pass such an order as it deems fit.

The State Government may exempt payment to the collective fine to the victims of any offence punishable under this Act or any other persons. The fine may be recovered in the manner provided by the Code of Criminal Procedure 1973, Sections 421, 422, and 424.

There appear to be some flaws in this provision.

(i) It is not certain that all the inhabitants occupying a particular area involve in the commission of the offence under this Act. It is not defined as to who are inhabitants. Inhabitants are persons having permanent residence in a particular area. Those persons may belong to different religion, believing in different philosophies, habituated to different manners and customs, following a different styles of life, they may either believe in untouchability or may not. Thus without taking into account the complex nature of the inhabitants, merely on the ground that they belong to a particular area where the offenders under this Act reside may not be a reasonable ground on which they should be subjected to punishments.

(ii) It is, however, stated that the State Government may exempt any person who does not, in its view, fall within the category of persons liable to pay the fine; under this Act. But it is not clear on what ground the State Government may exempt some persons, whether the human element would not reflect in such identification of persons.

(iii) Any aggrieved person by the imposition of the collective fine may within the prescribed period, file a petition before the State Government for being exempted from such fine. If such person happens to be innocent why he should be made to undergo such a lengthy procedure unnecessarily.

(iv) Whether it is imposed on all inhabitants or the Hindu Undivided Families? When it is imposed on Hindu Undivided Family? What is a Hindu Undivided Family? Whether Hindu Includes, Hindu, Buddhist, Sikh, Jaina or Hindu religion in any of its forms or developments including *Vaishnavas, Lingayat, Adivasis,* followers of *Brahmo, Prarthana, Arya Samaj* and the *Swaminarayan Sampradaya*? If such a liberal construction is applied, then so many persons believers in untouchability as well as non-believers, may be subjected to a collective fine. Moreover, if the whole Hindu undivided family is subjected to collective fine, probably innocent family members are likely to suffer.

(v) It is stated that the state government may take into consideration the "respective means of such inhabitants" for levying collective fine. Then whether it is 'collective fine' or 'individual fine'. Moreover, it is difficult to ascertain the "income" or "paying" capacity only by the "means" livelihood, without taking into consideration actual net income.

(vi) The imposition of collective fine may be justifiable in case of those persons who are engaged in :

(i) harbouring persons concerned in the commission of offence, and
(ii) failing to render all the assistance in their power in discovering or apprehending the offender.

But it is difficult to be justifiable in case of persons :

(i) concerned in the commission
(ii) concerned in abetting the commission of such offence
(iii) concerned in suppressing material evidence of the commission of such offence.

If the main culprits are subjected only to a percentage of collective fine, it would be wrong, which would further encourage them to act contrary to the objects of this Act.

All such persons, described above, fall under the offence of "abetment", as such liable to imprisonment for a term which may not be less than one month and not more than six months, and also with fine which shall not less than one hundred rupees and not more than five hundred rupees.

(vii) When a single person or a few persons commit an offence under the PCRA such person or persons would be subjected to comparatively heavy punishment of imprisonment as also fine. But, if they commit the offence collectively they would be subjected to collective fine only. Offenders know this fact would prefer to commit the offence collectively.

(viii) This provision may create an impression in the minds of ex-untouchables that the State Government in going to do something very concrete and bold. But the touchables or caste Hindus may feel that such provision is very harsh and teasing one. This may widen the gap between the two communities. The fact is that this provision has hardly come into implementations so far. If at all it is applied in future it would cause disharmony and disintegrity between the touchable and untouchable communities as a whole. Therefore, the very aim of the Act would be in jeopardy.

More Penalty on Repeated Convictions

"Whoever having convicted of an offence under this Act or of an abetment of such offence is again convicted of any such offence or abetment shall, on conviction be punishable—

(a) for the second offence, with imprisonment for a term of not less than six months and not more than one year and also with fine which shall be not less than two hundred rupees and not more than five hundred rupees;

(b) for the third offence or any subsequent to the third offence, with imprisonment for a term of not less than one year and not more than two years, and also with fine which shall be not less than five hundred rupees and not more than one thousand rupees." Of 1976 added clauses (a) and (b) to this section.

According to this section the offenders subsequent to their first offence are faced with enhanced punishment. It is obligatory on the part of the courts to award the punishment as stated under this section. This section intends to suppress the criminal mentality of the habitual offenders. However, the quantum of punishment under PCRA seems to be less than under IPC for the offences more or less similar nature. The Table 2.2 shows the difference between quantum of punishment under IPC and PCRA.

Presumption by Courts

"Where any act constituting an offence under this Act is committed regarding member of a Scheduled Caste. The Court shall presume, unless otherwise proved that such act was committed on the ground of 'untouchability'."

This section gives "as special rule of evidence." The most essential ingredient for constituting an offence under PCRA is that it should be committed "on the ground of untouchability." It is,

TABLE 3.2

Sections	3, 4, 5, 6, 7(1) Religion, Social Educ. Eco. Disabilities insult & boycott		7(A) Compulsory Labour		11 Enhanced Punishment				8	9	10	7(1) A offences against person/property		Rep. People's Act 1951
					Second offence		Third offence subsequent offence							
Punishment	Imprisonment	Fine (Rs.)	Imprisonment	Fine (Rs.)	Imprisonment	Fine	Imprisonment	Fine	Cancellation of Licence	Suspension of giants	Collective Fine	Imprisonment	Fine	Disqualification to contest election
Minimum	One month	100	Three months	100	Six months	200	One year	500	Cancellation of Licence	Suspension of resumption of grants	Collective	Two years	Fine	to any legislatrative body for six years
Maximum	Six months	500	Six months	500	One year	500	Two years	1000	—	—	—	As prescribed under IPC		

TABLE 3.3

IPC					PCRA				
Section	*Offence*	*Cognizable or Non-cognizable*	*Bailable or Non-bailable*	*Punishment*	*Section*	*Offence*	*Cognizable or Non-cognizable*	*Bailable or Non-bailable*	*Punishment*
153 A 1(b)	Promoting enmity between classes	Cognizable	Non-bailable	Imprison-ment for 3 years/Fine/ both	3	enfrang religious disabiliti-es	Cognizable	Bailable	Min. 1 month Max. 6 months plus fine (100 to 500)
153 A (2)	Promoting enmity in place of religious worship	Cognizable	Non-bailable	Imprison-ment for 3 years/fine/ both	3,4 (×)	enfacing obstruct-ion to processi-on 4(×)	Cognizable	Bailable	Min. 1 month Max. 6 months plus fine (100 to 500)
217	Public Servant disobeying the Law	Non-cognizable	Bailable	Imprison-ment for 2 years/fine/ both	10 (Ex)	abetme-nt	Cognizable	Bailable	Min. 1 month Max. 6 months plus fine

(Contd.)

(Contd.)

IPC					PCRA				
Section	*Offence*	*Cognizable or Non-cognizable*	*Bailable or Non-bailable*	*Punishment*	*Section*	*Offence*	*Cognizable or Non-cognizable*	*Bailable or Non-bailable*	*Punishment*
355	Assault intended to dis-honour	Non-cognizable	Bailable	Imprisonm-ent for 2 years/fine/ both	7(1) (b)	molest-ing in juning	Cognizable	Bailable	Min. 1 month Max. 6 months plus fine (100 to 500)
374	Unlawful comp. Labour	Cognizable	Bailable	Imprisonm-ent for 1 year/fine/ both	7(A)	Unlawful comp. Labour	Cognizable	Bailable	Min. 3 months Max. 6 months plus fine (100 to 500)
504	Insult	Non-cognizable	Bailable	Imprisonm-ent for 2 years/fine or both	7(1) (d)	Insult	Cognizable	Bailable	Min. 1 month Max. 6 months plus fine (100 to 500)

however, difficult to prove, and it is felt that for a Scheduled Caste it is very difficult to prove beyond reasonable doubt that the offence was committed on the ground of "untouchability." It may be due to his poor economic condition, inability to collect evidence and poor legal knowledge. Therefore, the Parliament taking into account these difficulties, has provided this section in the Act. Thus any act constituting an offence under this Act is committed relating to a member of Scheduled Caste offence, the Court shall presume, unless otherwise proved that such offence was committed on the ground of "untouchability."

The Amending Act 106 of 1976 has defected the words "as defined in Clause (24) of Article 366 of the Constitution" after "a Scheduled Caste" this might have been done as the term "Scheduled Caste" has already been defined under Section 2(db) of this Act.

"A presumption means a rule of law that courts and judges shall draw a particular inference from a particular fact or from a particular evidence, unless and until the truth of such inference is disproved."

In case there is a wording that "the court shall presume" the court "shall" consider such fact as proved, unless otherwise proved. The ordinary rule of law is that "the accused is presumed to be innocent." But when there is specific 'directive' in the Act itself, that the court shall presume. The ordinary rule of law in this respect is not applicable. The court shall presume in such cases unless and until it is proved contrary.

In *Ramachandran Pillai v. State of Kerala* (1964), it is held, that, when an effort of the accused to prove to the contrary has failed, the presumption arises and the court would be justified in holding that the alleged act was committed on the basis of untouchability. In *Laxman Jayaram Shant v. Maharashtra State* (1980), Kanade, J. observed that "the initial burden was on prosecution to prove that accused has insulted complainant of a species and then burden of proof would shift on accused, that insult was not on ground of untouchability and said on us accused not be so heavy to prove his case beyond reasonable doubt." Further, it is held that *mens rea* should be proved in such cases.

But Dharmadhikari J. of the same High Court observed in a similar case that "the decision in 1980 Mah. L.J. 833 has unduly restricted the scope of presumption contemplated by Section 12 of this Act. Assuming that the question of *mens rea* is relevant once it is established by the prosecution that the act constituting the offence viz., the insult or attempt to insult was quo a member of Scheduled Caste then in light of the provisions of Section 12 of the Act, it is necessary for the prosecution to further prove that such act was committed on the ground of untouchability. By Section 12 of the Act, unless the contrary is proved, it is presumed that such act was actually committed on the ground of untouchability. The said presumption is rebuttable one. If for proving an offence under Section 7(d) of the Act, the prosecution is also needed to prove the fact that the act constituting the offence was committed on the ground of untouchability, then the presumption contemplated by Section 12 will be meaningless and the entire Section 12 will become redundant or surplus-age."

According to R.G. Karmarkar, "The opening clause of Section 12 reads, 'Where any act constituting an offence under this Act is committed'. An argument can be advanced that the act was committed on the ground of untouchability, because nothing is an offence under this Act unless it is done on the ground of untouchability. If this argument be accepted, it would mean that the presumption permitted to be realised under this section would be still born and the entire section would be a nullity. It is submitted that such an interpretation cannot be accepted because it is hardly possible that the legislature intended to enact a mere nullity. The proper meaning of the clause 'where any act constituting an offence under this Act' would be the physical act constituting an offence under the Act only and would not include the ingredient 'on the ground of untouchability'."

There are three ingredients in the section: (i) the act alleged must have been committed, (ii) such act must be related to a member of Scheduled Caste, and (iii) unless the contrary is proved. If the contrary is proved then the presumption would not arise. Thus it is essential to prove that the "act" was committed, if it is proved finally will constitute an offence under this Act. Such act must be related to a member of Scheduled Caste only. Of course Scheduled Caste is a constitutional nomenclature used for the ex-untouchables and it involves certain castes, sub-castes, etc., as stated under Article 341 of the Constitution. However, no criteria has been laid down as to the determination of Scheduled Castes. But in order to belong to a Scheduled Caste, a person must profess either Hindu or a Sikh religion, according to the order of President of India. As soon as he converts to Buddhism he ceases to be a Scheduled Caste. The Civil Rights of all the "ex-untouchables", are protected throughout the Act, but concerning the benefit of presumption, only the Scheduled Castes, not the ex-untouchables who have converted, are entitled to that benefit under Section 12.

However, this may be rebutted, if the accused is able to prove. "But the degree and the character of the burden of proof which this section casts on an accused person to rebut the presumption raised thereunder, cannot be equated with the degree and character of proof which under Section 101 of the evidence Act rests on the prosecution. In other words, the accused may rebut the presumption by showing a mere preponderance of probability in his favour, it is not necessary for him to establish his case beyond a reasonable doubt."

Jurisdiction of Civil Courts

(1) No Civil Court shall entertain or continue any suit or proceeding or shall pass any decree or order or execute wholly or partially any decree or order if the claim involved in such suit or proceeding or if the passing of such decree or order of if such execution would in any way be contrary to the provision of this Act.

(2) No court shall, in adjudicating any matter or executing any decree or order, recognise any custom or usage imposing any disability on any person on the ground of "untouchability".

The aim of this section is to withdraw the custom as a source and sanction of untouchability. It appears that this provision is based on Article 13 of the Constitution which does not allow any custom or law opposite to the Fundamental Rights of the Citizens.

According to this section no custom or usage which is contrary to the object of the Act is valid. Therefore, the Act directs all the courts not to recognise any custom or usage imposing any disability on any person on the ground of 'untouchability' and not to recognise any right or duty under any such custom.

A suit by Hindus for declaration that they and their representatives alone were exclusively entitled to use the suit property for burial and cremation purpose being opposed to the provisions of this Act cannot be maintained.

Thus any hotel, place of public entertainment, place of public worship, shop, burial or cremation ground, road, rest house, etc., cannot be maintained for the exclusive use of caste Hindus. All such places would be open for all the ex-untouchables equally with others.

Offences by Companies

If the person committing an offence under this Act is a company, every person who at the time the offence was committed was in charge of and was responsible to, the company for the conduct of the business of the company shall be deemed to be guilty of the offence and shall be liable to be proceeded against and punished accordingly.

Given that nothing contained in this sub-section shall render any such person liable to any punishment, if he proves that the offence was committed without his knowledge or that he exercised all due diligence to avoid the commission of such offence.

(2) Notwithstanding anything contained in sub-section (1) where an offence under this Act has been committed with the consent of any director or manager, secretary or other officer of the company, such director, manager, secretary or other officer shall be deemed to be guilty of that offence and shall be liable to be proceeded against and punished accordingly.

Explanation: For the purpose of this section

(a) "Company" means any body corporate and includes a firm or other association of individuals; and

(b) "Director" in relation to a firm means a partner in the firm.

'Companies' also come within the ambit of this Act, under this section. Thus all natural and legal persons are equally made subject of this Act. The company, however, cannot be punished physically as it does not constitute an organic body, as such the "incharge" of such company is liable for punishment if an offence is committed under this Act by such company. However, he will not be held liable for the act of the company when he proves to the satisfaction of the court that any act constituting an offence committed with his knowledge or he exercised all the diligence to stop the commission of such offence.

Company is an inclusive term which includes a corporate body, firm and "other association of individuals". 'Other association of individuals' comprises the co-operative societies,

societies registered under the Societies Registration Act, statutory corporations, all local boards, unions, associations, clubs, etc.

Punishment for such offence would be same as it is provided under the relevant section of this Act.

Action Taken in Good Faith

(1) No suit, prosecution or other legal proceedings shall lie against the Central Government or a State Government for anything which is in good faith done or intends to be done under this Act.

(2) No suit or other legal proceedings shall lie against the Central Government or a State Government for any damage caused or likely to be caused by anything which is in good faith done or intended to be done under this Act.

The object of this section is to protect the Central and State Governments from any such liability as may arise while implementing this Act. This section is added by Act 106 of 1976.

Thus no suit or any legal proceedings shall be instituted against the Central and State Governments by any person for having suffered any loss owing to the action that has been taken by any such government in the fulfillment of the object of this Act, given that such action is taken in good faith.

Cognizable Offence and Summar Trial

15(1) Notwithstanding anything contained in the Code of Criminal Procedure, 1973, every offence punishable under this Act shall be cognizable and every such offence, except where it is punishable with imprisonment for a minimum term exceeding three months, may be summarily tried by a Judicial Magistrate of the first class or in a Metropolitan area by a Metropolitan Magistrate in accordance with the procedure specified in the said code.

(2) Notwithstanding anything contained in the Code of Criminal Procedure, 1973, when any public servant is alleged to have committed the offence of abetment of an offence punishable under this Act, while acting or purporting to act in the discharge of his official duty, no court shall take cognizance of such offence of abetment except with the previous sanction.

(a) of the Central Government in the case of a person employed in connection with the affairs of the union, and
(b) of the State Government in the case of a person employed in connection with the affairs of a state.

This section intends to deter and detract the orthodox touchable from practising untouchability. The present section which stands as amended in 1976 provides that all the offences under this section are cognizable. It remove purposely the word "compoundable" from the original Act, denoting that the offences under PCRA would be non-compoundable.

All the offences under this Act are cognizable. "Cognizable offence" means an offence for which and cognizable case means a case in which, a police officer may according to the first Scheduled or under any other law for the time being in force, arrest without warrants. This section gives the police officer powers to arrest the offender even without warrant.

When any public servant is alleged to have committed the offence of abetment of an offence punishable under this Act, while acting or purporting to act in the discharge of his official duty, no court shall "take cognizance" of such offence without the prior permission of the Government concerned.

The court "may" take cognizance of any offence (a) upon receiving a complaint of facts which constitute such offence, (b) upon a Police Report of such facts, and (c) upon information received from any person or upon his own knowledge that such offence has been committed. It is observed in *State v. Shanker Bhaurao Khirode* (1959) by the Bombay High Court that, "the Criminal Procedure Code has not defined the expression "take cognizance". But taking of cognizance is a thing separate from initiation of proceedings. The Magistrate may apply his mind and consider a report submitted to him by the Police Officer under Section 173 Cr. P.C., but before it can be said that he has taken cognizance under Section 190, Cr. P.C., it is not enough that he should have applied his mind to the report, but he must do something for proceeding under the subsequent provisions of the code, for example, under Section 200 under which the Magistrate has to examine the complainant on taking cognizance of an offence".

"Taking cognizance is a mental act. It is also a judicial act. Taking cognizance ordinarily means that the concerned Magistrate has come to the conclusion that there is a case to be enquired into." When any public servant is alleged to have committed the offence of abetment, the court shall "take cognizance" of that cognizable offence only after receiving prior sanction by the government concerned.

"In order to avoid", as R.G. Karmarker observes, "frivolous and vexations prosecutions against the officers, provision is made requiring the sanction of the Central Government or the State Government as the case may be before such prosecution is launched against the officers concerned."

The significant part of this clause is, every offence punishable under this Act may be tried summarily by a first class, Judicial Magistrate or in a Metropolitan area by a Metropolitan Magistrate in accordance with the procedure specified in the Code of Criminal Procedure, 1973. This rule will not apply where the offence is punishable with imprisonment for a minimum term exceeding three months. Summary trials are prescribed for minor offences. According to summary trials the cases are disposed of quickly not following a lengthy procedure as it happens in regular trial. In summary trials, on conviction no sentence of imprisonment for a term exceeding three months can be passed by the court. It is necessary to take into consideration that the minimum punishment which is to be awarded under this Act is one month and maximum six months in addition to fine, except under Sections 7(1A), 7A(1), 11(a) and (b) in which comes still it is higner.

In case where the trial for the offences under Sections 3, 4, 5, 6, 7(1), 8, 9, 10, 14 of this Act is held summarily, the trial Court will have to award only that punishment ranging from one month to three months only; whereas all the said offences are subjected to one month to six months' imprisonment. Thus on record the punishment appears to be more but actually it cannot be awarded more than three months if the trial takes place summarily. On the one hand the Act empowers the court to award one to six months' imprisonment, whereas the other hand, it restrains the court not to award more than three months' imprisonment by prescribing summary trial under Section 15(1). It is submitted that these two provisions are anomalous and contradictory to each other. Of course, "may be tried" does not mean 'must be tried' but why the Act itself empowers the court to resort to summary trial and award less punishment, is the valid objection.

Measures to Ensure Civil Rights

(A)(1): Subject to such rules as the Central Government may make in this behalf, the State government shall take such steps as may be necessary for ensuring that the rights arising from the abolition of "untouchability" are made available to and are availed of by the persons subjected to any disability arising out of "untouchability".

(2) In particular and without prejudice to the generality of the provisions of sub-section (1) such steps may include—

(i) The provision of adequate facilities, including legal aid to the persons subjected to any disability arising out of "untouchability" to enable them to avail themselves of such rights.

(ii) The appointment of officers for initiating or exercising supervision over prosecutions for the contravention of the provisions of this Act.

(iii) The setting up of Special Courts for the trial of offences under this Act.

(iv) The setting up of committees at such appropriate levels as the State Government may think fit to assist the State Government in formulating or implementing such measures.

(v) Provisions for a periodic survey of the working of the provisions of this Act with a view to suggesting measures for the better implementation of the provisions of this Act.

(vi) The identification of the areas where persons are under any disability arising out of "untouchability" and adoption of such measures as would ensure the removal of such disability from such areas.

(3) The Central Government shall take such steps as may be necessary to coordinate the measures taken by the State Government under sub-section (1).

(4) The Central Government shall, every year, place on the table of each House of Parliament, a report on the steps taken by itself and by the State Governments in pursuance of the provisions of this section.

This new section is added by Act 106 of 1976. The aim of this section is to ensure that the Civil Rights accruing to an ex-untouchable by reason of abolition of "untouchability" are "made available" and are "availed of" by such persons. Accordingly it is the responsibility of the State Governments to make sure that the rights arising from abolition of untouchability are not only made available to, but are availed of by the persons subjected to untouchability. The Constitution is, however, not sure on the matter of responsibility. So far as the making of law is concerned, the Central Government is responsible. But it is not enumerated in the Seventh Schedule whether the eradication of untouchability is the subject of the Central or State Government or it comes under concurrent list. The state list contains *inter alia* the subject of public health, burial or cremation places, communications, roads, etc., markets and fairs and inns. The concurrent list bears *inter alia* the subject of criminal law, criminal procedure, trust or trustees, education, charitable institutions and religious institutions and the Central list bears *inter alia* the subject of professional education and research. The Protection of Civil Rights Act touches all those subjects concerning removal of untouchability. But there is no direct reference as to "untouchability". However, the PCRA under the present section enumerates that, the State Government "shall" take such step as may be required for ensuring the Civil Rights.

The responsibility to take measures is on the State Governments, but the State Government would decide such measures, as may be necessary at their own. So far as 'rule' making is concerned in this behalf, the responsibility lies with the Central Government. Thus subject to such rules as the Central Government may make in this behalf, the State Government "shall" take such steps as may be needed for ensuring such rights.

Clause (2): This clause states what measures in particular the State Government may adopt for ensuring Civil Rights under this Art. "Such measures may include", legal and to the persons subjected to untouchability, appointment of officers for initiating or exercising supervision over prosecutions, setting up of special courts, setting up of committees, taking periodic survey and identification of the area where untouchability is prevailing to a greater extent.

Clause (3) states that the Central Government "shall" take "such steps as may be necessary" to co-ordinate the measures taken by the State Government under Sub-section (1).

Clause (4) enumerates that the Central Government "shall" every year submit to the Parliament a report on the measures taken by itself and by the State Governments under this section.

Act Overriding Other Laws

"Save as otherwise expressly provided in the Act, the provisions of this Act shall have effect notwithstanding anything inconsistent therewith contained in any other law for the time being in force or any custom or usage or any instrument having effect by virtue of any such law or any decree or order of any court or other authority." Thus, the Provision of this Act has an overriding effect notwithstanding anything inconsistent therewith contained in any other law for the time being in force or any custom or usage or instrument having the force of law.

Probation of Offenders

"The Provision of the probation of the offenders Act,1958 shall not apply to any person above the age of fourteen years who is found guilty of having committed any offence punishable under this Act."

This section was included through the Act 106 of 1976 so as to make the convict punishable under this Act who has completed his fourteen years. The probation of Offenders Act, 1958 provides that, when any person who is below the age of 21 years convicted of any offence, he cannot be sentenced to imprisonment. The concerned Magistrate has to give due consideration to the report of the Probation Officer and has to release such persons, on probation. But according to this Act any person, who completes his fourteen years cannot escape unpunished. It also to override other laws which go against the spirit of this section.

Powers to Form Rules

16(B)1 : "The Central Government may by notification in the official Gazette make rules to carry out the provisions of this Act.

(2) Every rule made by the Central Government under this Act shall be laid, as soon as may be after it is made, before each House of Parliament while it is in session for a total period of thirty days which may be comprised in one session or in two or more successive sessions, and if, before the expiry of the session immediately following the session or the successive sessions aforesaid; both Houses agree in making any modification in the rule or both Houses agree that the rule should not be made, the

rule shall thereafter have effect only in such modified from or be of on effect, as the case may be; so, however, that any such modification or annulment shall be without prejudice to the validity of anything previously done under the rule."

This section has been included by Amendment Act 106 of 1976. This section states that the Central Government may make rules to conduct the provision of this Act, subject to the approval of the Parliament. The Central Government, having powers under this section framed "the Protection of Civil Rights Rules, 1977 specifying the manner in which an inquiry under sub-section (1) of Section 10A of the Act—for imposing collective fine should be conducted and the manner in which the State Government should submit their reports to the Central Government regarding the steps they have taken under the PCRA.

Repealment of Other Enactments

"The enactments specified in the Schedule are hereby repealed to the extent to which they or any of the provisions contained therein correspond or are repugnant to this Act or to any of the provisions contained therein."

The Parliament having the power to make law for prescribing punishment for the offences of "untouchability" under the Constitution has passed, "The Protection of Civil Rights Act, 1955". Therefore, all the previous enactments existing in their respective states are repealed under the present section of this Act.

Indian Penal Code, and Protection of Civil Rights Act

Protection of Civil Rights Act, 1955 is a special law whereas Indian Penal Code, is general penal law dealing specifically with the offences of untouchability. Therefore, there is no provision under IPC having direct impact upon the removal of untouchability.

However, Section 7(1A) of PCRA states that "whoever commits any offence against the person or property of any individual as a reprisal or revenge for his having exercised any right accruing to him by reason of the abolition of "untouchability" under Article 17 of the Constitution, shall, where the offence is punishable with imprisonment for a term in excess of two years, be punishable with imprisonment for a term which shall not be less than two years and also with fine."

Therefore, one who commits any offence against the person

or property of any individual as a reprisal or revenge for his having exercised Civil Rights available to him by reason of abolition of 'untouchability' is punishable under IPC. It is specifically stated that the offence is punishable with imprisonment for a term exceeding two years, be punishable with imprisonment for a term which shall not be less than two years and also with fine. Most of the offences affecting the human body and property are punishable under IPC with imprisonment for a term exceeding two years. In all such cases the punishment would be for a minimum term of two years or more than that. Punishments for the offences against the person or property are provided under Sections 302 to 462 of IPC. This apart, all other sections are also equally applicable regarding offences against the untouchables.

Criminal Procedure Code, 1973

The Criminal Procedure Code is also a general Code providing general procedure for the institution and trial of any criminal case. Regarding removal of untouchability the said code provides under Section 110.

"When a Judicial Magistrate of the First Class receives that there is within his local jurisdiction a person who

(f) habitually commits, or attempts to commit, or abets the commission of

(i) any offence under one or more of the following Acts namely—

(f) the Untouchability (Offences) Act, 1955 (22 of 1955)

Such a Magistrate may, in the manner hereinafter provided need such person to show cause why he should not be ordered to execute a bond, will sureties, for his good behaviour for such period, not exceeding three years, as the Magistrate deeming fit."

This section is meant for dealing with ex-convicts or habitual offenders only. It has the objective of protecting the society from dangerous persons against perpetration of crimes by a placing them under security. When the Magistrate receives information regarding any habitual offenders who commits, tries to commit or abets the commission of offences under the Protection of Civil Rights Act, 1955 may inquire as to the truth of information under Section 116 or Cr. P.C. and if upon such inquiry he feels that it is necessary to order to execute a bond of good behaviour, may order to that effect. Any misbehaviour by the habitual offender would be treated as breach of bond. The person who is in breach would be arrested and detained in prison until the expiry of the period of the bond and such order shall be without prejudice to any other punishment or forfeiture to which the said person may be liable in accordance with law.

The People's Representation Act, 1951

The Untouchability (Offences) Amendment and Miscellaneous Provisions Act, 1973, No. 106 of 1976 has provided for an amendment in the Representation of the People Act, 1951.

Section 21 of the said Amendment Act states that "In Section 8 of the Representation of the People Act, 1951, in sub-section (1); after the words "The Indian Penal Code, 'the words and figures' or under the Protection of Civil Rights Act, 1955" shall be inserted.

Section 8 of the Representation of the People Act, 1951 stands as quoted below:

Disqualification on Conviction under some Offences

(1) A person convicted of an offence punishable under Section 153A or Section 171E or Section 171 for sub-section (2) or sub-section (3) of Section 505 of the Indian Penal Code or under the *Protection of Civil Rights Act, 1955,* or under Section 125 or Section 135 or clause (a) of sub-section (2) of Section 136 of this Act shall be disqualified for a period of six years from the date of such conviction.

(2) ...

(3) Notwithstanding anything in sub-section (1) and sub-section (2) a disqualification under either sub-section shall not in the case of a person who on the date of the conviction is a member of Parliament or the Legislature of a state, take effect until three months have elapsed from the date or; if within that period an appeal or application for revision is brought in respect of the conviction or the sentence until that appeal or application is disposed of by the court.

Accordingly, any person convicted for any offence under the Protection of Civil Rights Act, 1955 cannot fight the election for both the Houses of Parliament as well as for both the Houses of any State legislatures for a period of six years from the date of such conviction. It is of course reasonable that no person who commits the contempt of the Constitution should be allowed to be a member of the Parliament or state legislature formed under the Constitution.

Laws Made by the State Governments

The Constitution has empowered Parliament under Article 35(a)(ii) to make laws for prescribing punishment for those acts which are declared to be offences under Part III=Fundamental Rights. "Untouchability" being an offence under Article 17, Parliament has got special power to make law for prescribing punishment for the same offence. Therefore, the State Governments are no more entitled to enact laws to deal with the offences of untouchability. Thus the Constitution recognizes "untouchability" as a national problem for which it intends to have a uniform and comprehensive law to be passed by the Parliament alone. The Parliament has truly fulfilled its responsibility of passing such law in 1955, in the shape of "The Protection of Civil Rights Act, 1955".

The State Governments still have retained their power to make laws for 'removing religious disabilities and authorising the untouchables to enter temples in their respective states, under Article 25(2)(b) of the Constitution.

(i) It is provided under the said Article that, nothing in this Article "shall" prevent the state from making any law for throwing open of Hindu religious institution of a public character to all classes and sections of Hindus, including Sikh, Jaina or Buddhists. "The State" includes Central as well as the State Governments.

(ii) Moreover, the subject of "religious endowments and institutions" appears on the concurrent list.

(iii) Article 25(2) is applicable to all the Hindus in general, whereas Article 17 is applicable only to the ex-untouchables. "Untouchability" according to Marc Galanter, "does not include every exclusionary practice contained within the caste system, but only those concerned with certain defined groups. The exclusionary rights in temples enforceable prior to independence included rights to exclude not only untouchables but also other groups whose presence in the circumstances would amount to a pollution, e.g., *Palshe* Brahmins and Lingayats. The Temple Entry provision of Article 25 extends to all classes of Hindus, not merely to "untouchables". "The practice of 'untouchability' includes exclusion from temples, but the entire temple entry field is not pre-empted by Article 35." Thus, the state governments are constitutionally empowered to make laws for throwing open of Hindu Temples for all the Hindus, including Sikhs, Jainas and Buddhists.

The Temple Entry Acts are in force at present in the State of Tamil Nadu, Andhra Pradesh, Maharashtra, Gujarat, Uttar Pradesh and Kerala. They are as given below :

1. The Madras Temple Entry Authorisation Act, 1947 (5 of 1947) was passed by the Madras Government in order to remove the disabilities imposed by custom or usage on some excluded classes of Hindus concerning entry into Hindu Temples which were open to the general Hindu Public. The Act provides definition of the Temple. Accordingly a Temple is "a place, by whatever name known, which is dedicated to, or for the benefit of, or used as of right by the Hindu community or any section thereof as a place of public religious worship." According to Section 3(1) of the Act all the persons who were deprived of entering such Temples and worship therein were entitled to enter any Hindu Temple and offer worship therein much in the same manner and to the same extent as Hindus in general. Whoever stops any such person due to his so called low caste from entering any Hindu Temple or from worshipping therein would be punishable, in the case of first offence with fine which may extend to rupees one hundred and in the case of second and subsequent offence with imprisonment which would extend to six months, or with fine up to rupees five hundred, or with both. All the offences under this Act were cognizable.

2. The Uttar Pradesh Temple Entry (Declaration of Rights) Act, 1956 declares that all the sections of Hindus are equally entitled to religious rights and it bars the court from recognizing any custom, usage or practice to the contrary. But it has not provided punishment for those who disobey the 'declaration' under the Act. It is merely declaratory and not penal.

3. The Bombay Hindu places of public worship (Entry authorization) Act, 1956 came into operation on 1st July 1958. By virtue of the Maharashtra Adoption of Laws Order, 1960, it extends throughout Maharashtra. Previously it was extended to the State of Bombay, comprising Gujarat part of Bombay State. Now by virtue of the Gujarat Adoption of Laws Order, 1960, it extends to the whole State of Gujarat.

Under Section 3 it is stated that every place of public

worship which is open to Hindus in general or to any section or class thereof shall be open to all the sections and classes of all Hindus, and no Hindu of whatsoever section or class, shall in any manner be stopped, obstructed or discouraged from entering such place of public worship or from worshipping or offering prayers thereat, or performing any religious service therein in the like manner and to like extent as any other Hindu or whatsoever, section or class may so enter, worship, pray or perform." This Act does not recognize any distinction among the Hindus on the basis of any denomination or section as such. It has thrown open all Hindus Temples for all the H:ndus without any discrimination.

This, however, does not prescribed minimum punishment and it gives discretion to the Court either to punish the convict with imprisonment which may extend to six months or with fine which may extend to five hundred rupees or with both. Although the offences under the Act are "cognizable", but they are "compoundable". Therefore, it can be observed that this Act is not so severe to the Protection of Civil Rights Act, 1955.

4. Kerala Hindu Places of Public Worship (Authorization of Entry) Act, 1965 Section 3 of this Act states that "every place of public worship which is open to Hindus generally or to any section or class thereof, shall be open to all sections and class of Hindus, and no Hindu of whatsoever section or class shall, in any manner, be prevented, obstructed or discouraged from such place of public worship or from worshipping or offering prayers thereat or performing any religious service therein, in the like manner and to the like extent as any other Hindu of whatsoever section or class may so enter, worship, pray or perform." But it recognizes the identify of the religious denomination or section thereof. Therefore, the religious right under this Act are "subject to the right of that religious denomination or section as the case may be, to manage its own affairs in matters of religion."

However, it does not prescribe minimum punishment. It gives discretionary power to the courts to punish the convict with imprisonment which may extend to six months, or with fine which may extend to rupees five hundred or with both... the offences under the Act are cognizable and compoundable.

Encouraged Inter-Caste Marriages

Besides, some State Governments have adopted to measure of giving certain amount as incentive to those couples who perform inter-caste marriage in the matter of eradication of untouchability. Those states are, Andhra Pradesh, Bihar, Gujarat, Karnataka, Kerala, Madhya Pradesh, Maharashtra, Orissa, Tamil Nadu, Tripura and Uttar Pradesh and the Union Territory of Goa, Daman and Diu and Pondichery.

Disqualification from Effected Bodies

It appears on the Report of the Commission for SC and ST for the year 1978-79 that the State Governments were requested to amend the concerned laws to disqualify a person convicted of an offence under the PCR Act from contesting elections to Municipal Bodies and the *Panchayat Raj* Institutions of Representation of People's Act, 1951. It is found that the Gujarat State maintains a separate list of persons convicted under the PCR Act and they are not appointed in any Committee, Board or Corporation which may be constituted at the District and State level. The Government of Andhra Pradesh has amended the *Grampanchayat* Act, *Panchayat Samiti* and *Zilla Parishad* Act and Municipalities Act according to which a person convicted under the PCR Act is disqualified to contest election to all such bodies during the sentence and for a period of five years from the date of expiry of such sentence. The Government of Maharashtra also has made similar provisions in the Bombay Village Panchayats Act, 1958 [Section 14(ii)] and in the *Maharashtra Zilla Parishads* and *Panchayat Samitis* Act, 1961 [Section 16(ii) and 58 (1)A].

Conclusion

(i) The Constitution, so far as the provisions regarding abolition of untouchability and advancement of the ex-untouchables are concerned, is ambiguous one.

(a) It declares untouchability an offence punishable by law, but fails to define the very offence itself. Unless the offence is defined, it is difficult to determine whether the offence was committed or not.

(b) It contemplates advancement of the backward classes, but neither it defines backward class or the Scheduled

Castes not it provides any specific criteria for such classification.

(c) The provisions which enable the State for making any special provision for the advancement of the backward classes are ambiguous and most of them are not mandatory.

(d) "The State" is a ambiguous term giving rise to confusion and uncertainty. It becomes difficult to locate the responsibility of the advancement of the Scheduled Castes, there is no reference to the advancement of the ex-untouchables in either of the three lists.

(2) The Protection of Civil Rights Act is equally ambiguous and defective as the Constitution. The amending Act 106 of 1976 made it more appropriate but still it contains certain flaws.

(a) Like the Constitution, the PCR Act also fails to provide the definition of "untouchability". It does not define "on the ground of untouchability" phrase. This has, however, added to ambiguity and created a dilemma whether *mens rea* be viewed as an important ingredient of the offence or not.

(b) The word 'denomination' has been deleted in 1976, but still there appears "section" in Section 3 of the Act. It gives rise to confusion whether it maintains *status quo* in respect of sectional rights.

(c) 'The place' under Section 4 of PCR Act is qualified by "Public resort," as such it is exclusive of private place, whether the meaning given to "the place" under Sections 2 and 4 of the Act is not similar?

(d) The punishment provided under the Act seems to be inadequate to deter the prospective offenders. Moreover it fails to state specifically whether the punishment shall be rigorous or simple one.

(e) It contemplets "insult" in respect of Scheduled Castes, but not of the Scheduled Castes converts to Christianity or Buddhism.

(f) The principle of 'presumption' is applicable only to Scheduled Caste complainant and not to the converts to other religions.

(g) The provision of 'Collective Fine' is undesirable and unreasonable.

(h) The provision of summary trial, if applied would be an obstacle in the way of judges in awarding punishment for a period more than three months.

3. It is but admirable that the Representation of People's Act, 1951, as amended by Act 106 of 1976 renders the convict under PCR Act ineligible to contest the election for six years from the date of conviction.

Thus, there are plenty of laws with objective of abolition of untouchability, but they suffer from flaws.

4

Democratic Rights of the Dalits

Specific forms of violence are committed by a collectivity or individuals on the weaker sections in general and the Scheduled Castes are known as atrocities. Such violence manifests itself both in the social and physical forms. From the psychological angle, it may be part of an aggressive personality and behaviour patterns of a group or of an individual. But sociologically, this may have its roots in an unequally organised social structure which may be concretely visible in the different forms of social inequality. Since there are unequal institutional arrangements of both material and non-material goods and services of social interactions and relations between the people in such social structures. There are cases of violence and conflicts of one type or the other over having more access to the available resources and opportunities which, of course, are in short supply. This does not rule out completely the possibility of a smooth acceleration of competition among the various sections of people.

Owing to the unequal opportunity structure violence and conflicts are inevitable at certain stage between a few privileged and the much larger number of underprivileged or non-privileged ones where former try to retain their privileges by stressing on maintaining the *status quo* and the letter strive for having a place therein. Further, there are some kinds of social violence such as humiliation, insult, making disparaging remarks, etc. committed collectively or by individuals which are not cognisable and, therefore, are not taken note especially by the governmental agencies. Nevertheless, these are also significant kinds of atrocities committed more at individual and less at collectivity levels on those who are socially conscious but are placed at the bottom in the existing social hierarchy. In the given background, atrocities are to be regarded as social and physical violence committed collectively or individually by those groups, castes and communities or their members who try to have more control over the existing resources and monopolise their status-superiority over others.

Such atrocities are targetted against those who have traditionally been degraded and deprived and who try to find a place other than that prescribed to them in the social structure. Their such efforts are likely to disturb the *status quo* and intercept the unlimited chances of the privileged ones. Hence, violence and atrocities against them. There has been phenomenal rise in the number and intensity of both social and physical forms of atrocities inflicted on the Scheduled Castes and other weaker sections in rural and urban areas in the recent times (Ram 1983; 1986: 91-113). Due to their most downgraded social status and economic poverty and exploitation they have been subjected to the atrocious attitudes and behaviour of the people drawn from the various castes and communities, religions, regions, age and sex (both males and females), etc.

After independence, the State on its own has evolved some mechanisms to protect them from atrocities or physical violence and facilitate their social and economic progress. In course of time this has certainly facilitated, on one hand, their limited social progress and has led to a considerable amount of social awareness among them and, on the other side, it has antagonised the upper castes and communities. This together has contributed to the phenomenal rise in the cases of atrocities and violence inflicted on them as mentioned above. However, as there are changes in their social and economic progress, there are also variations in the nature and degree of roles of several factors causing perpetration of atrocities on them both in rural and urban areas. We shall examine some of the above mentioned variations. More specially, we shall examine atrocities and violence inflicted over a certain time-span on the Scheduled Castes in terms of the caste and communal affiliations, age and sex (gender) background of both the inflictors of atrocities and their victims located in various regions in rural and urban areas. We shall look into their literacy and educational levels, occupational and income positions, and growing awareness and socio-political consciousness. We shall explain further how different protective and developmental measures adopted by the State for betterment of the Scheduled Castes have antagonised, in varying degrees, the asymmetrical social relationship between the Scheduled and non-Scheduled Castes and have caused the infliction of more atrocities on the former in various parts of the country. And finally, we shall analyse the effectiveness of some internal and external mechanisms evolved to deal with the cases of atrocities committed in the forms of both physical and social violence.

Atrocity as a Concept: Some Clarifications

Atrocity, as a term, has not gained much currency in the academic language and so also in the sociological analysis unlike tension, conflict, antagonism, violence, etc; and this last one is considered as a psychological trait of an aggressive personality as mentioned above, which are used with specific connotations. Both tension and conflict may be closely related in which the former may function as an antecedent or complement to the latter though it is sometimes an essential condition for the rise of a conflict situation. Tension may be released without resulting into conflict and it may prevail even after the conflict or social conflict is resolved (Ram 1977: 112). On the other hand, conflict may exist as a means and an end in itself. Nevertheless, both are property of the inter-group or inter-community rivalry and are located in the nature of social interaction between two or more groups or communities. Both may also prevail over access to different kinds of privileges which are specific and are in short supply as stated at the very outset. More precisely, tension and conflict may occur between individuals and/or groups or even communities if they uncompromisingly make identical claims over the same object. On the other hand, antagonism refers to negative interaction and is said to be often associated with class in the Marxian sense of the term. Atrocity is conceptually closer to conflict and more so to violence. Generally speaking, conflict is a game of fight (not always physical fight) between two individuals, groups or communities of equal or almost equal standing. It may also happen between two unequals especially when the relatively weak in the game wishes to be socially equal with the relatively strong one or when the weak resists and tries to oppose the injustices and exploitation of the stronger individual.

Power is required to accomplish the objects of the conflicting parties. "The paradox derives from the fact that conflicts, as distinct from other forms of interaction, always involve power and that is tough to appraise the relative power of the contenders before a conflict has settled the issue" (Coser 1966: 134). Violence, on the contrary, is the mob action in which the physical and numerical strengths of the parties (the rival sides) are involved. The party inflicting violence on others may be socially, economically and politically more powerful and it may presume the other party or persons as the most dispensable in event of disowning its traditional privileges and dominance. Violence or social violence is connected with physical or social harm wherein the person looks to achieve his or her goals by injuring or completely eliminating others or their interests. Finally, atrocity is the net result of violence of the strong over the weak. "'Atrocity' has not been defined in any law and, therefore, the Government have been using the expression 'crimes against the Scheduled Castes and Scheduled Tribes'. However, since 1974 the Ministry of Home Affairs (Government of India) began collecting statistics of such crimes and indicated that 'atrocities' on SCs and STs might be classified into four categories, viz. murder, grievous hurt, arson and rape. Later, the collection of these statistics encompassed all IPC (Indian Penal Code) offences in which the Dalits were victims" (Sharma 1988: 228). This means, only those crimes against the SCs/STs have been treated atrocities which are cognisable offences and are physical in nature.

A large number of crimes against these people which have social-psychological dimensions were not regarded atrocities till recently. Only in 1989 the Government adopted an Act known as the Scheduled Castes and Scheduled Tribes (Prevention of Atrocities) Act which widely covers the socio-psychological dimensions, besides the physical or physiological one, of crimes against the SCs/STs (for details, see Clause 3(1)-i-XV and 3(2)-i-VII of the Act). It usually happens that atrocities are committed even due to little resistance shown initially by the weaks but in the situation of violence even such resistance is totally absent and the weaks become vulnerable to the most gruesome violence. Such explanations become receptive to the examination of atrocities inflicted on the Scheduled Castes though both conflicts and violence (both physical and social) may be called atrocities only if the other party (namely the Scheduled Castes in the present analysis) is weak and looser in the game. The atrocities may, thus, be committed collectively or by individuals in various kinds.

Atrocities, at the social level, may range from calling the name of a Scheduled Caste person by the caste, making taunts or disparaging remarks against him, discriminating or practising untouchability against him, calling him a 'government Brahman' or government's relative, asking him to compulsorily extend respect to the person of a high caste, insulting him without no fault of his own and social boycott on account of his showing resistance or disrespect to the persons of high castes. Elaborating the tyranny of social and economic boycott of the Scheduled Castes by the caste Hindus in villages in the 1920s. Ambedkar (1979: 416–17) quotes, "This (kind of) boycott is generally planned on such an extensive scale as to include the prevention of the Depressed Classes from using the commonly used paths and the stoppage of sale of the necessities of life by the village Bania. According to the evidence, sometimes small causes suffice for the proclamation of a social boycott against the Depressed Classes." Thus, the social boycott seems to be the severest form of atrocities committed collectively on the Dalits in the rural areas.

Increase in Atrocities

Different kinds of atrocities have been committed on the Scheduled Castes in all times in the history of India. Whenever these castes attempted to assert for their rights and improve their lots, these met with the atrocious behaviour of those who were socially and materially better-off. For example, during the period of *Smritis* and *Dharma Shastras* (between the fourth and the eleventh centuries AD) numerous forms of social and religious disabilities were imposed on the various untouchables castes usually known at that time as the unclean or *Ati*-Shudras. Even during the Gupta period (around 400 AD), the so-called golden era in the Indian history, these castes were considered as unseeable, unapproachable and untouchable depicting the three different types of severe punishment imposed on them if they tried to crossover (and in some cases they even crossed) the social and ritual boundaries of their caste.

At the start of the previous century, atrocities both in social and physical forms were inflicted on these castes which were then considered as the Depressed Classes or 'Harijans' or the Scheduled Castes (though their past parochial nomenclature remained the same) in some parts of Bihar, Gujarat, Maharashtra, Punjab, etc. (Omvedt 1980: 142–70). Ambedkar also had mentioned a number of cases of atrocities committed on the Scheduled Castes in various parts of the country during the 1930s and the 1940s. However, the cases of atrocities have gone multiplied in the recent times and have been known to the people at large through the media though these have not always played a fair role in this connection. These are the cases which have been committed collectively and are widely known to the people in those regions or areas where these have occurred. Also, these are those cases which have been registered with the local police and most of these have also been recorded in reports of the various governmental and non-governmental agencies. But not much is known about a large number of cases of atrocities and violence which have been committed and have neither been reported nor heeded to by any formal agencies due to the obvious reasons well known to every one. Even the cases of atrocities having socio-psychological dimensions committed against the SCs/STs specially after the 1989 Act are unknown.

The present examination is about only those cases which have been reported to the formal agencies and have been treated as cognisable offences. Without indulging in the political cliche of commission of more atrocities during the rule of a particular political party either at the Centre or in the States when we look at the number of cases of atrocities inflicted on Scheduled Castes in the country during several decades specially after independence, we find a multiple rise as mentioned above. There was a rise of 86.3 per cent in the cases of atrocities committed during 1951-61 in the entire country. In the following decades (1961-71 and 1971-81) the percentage increase remained 69.4 and 63.9 respectively though the total number of cases committed during these periods was much more especially in the previous decade. This is also supported, in a way, by the statistics collected at the government level according to which there was a rise of 75.5 per cent in the cases of atrocities committed during 1977 over those in the year of 1976 (Report 1978: 138). In the first half of the decade 1981-1991 the percentage rise of atrocities was 84.3 and the total number of cases committed during this period were 91,097.

This simply shows that a large number of atrocities were committed against these people. Finally, second half of the previous decade had witnessed again a sprawling increase in the cases of atrocities inflicted in various parts of the country.

TABLE 4.1
Total Cases of Atrocities Committed on the Scheduled Castes During 1955–92

Period	*Total registered cases**	*Increase (+)/ decrease (–) of cases over preceding period*	*Percentage increase (+)/ decrease (–) over preceding period*
1955–60	2911	–	–
1961–65	4693	(+) 1782	(+) 61.2
1966–70	5113	(+) 420	(+) 8.9
1971–75	10426	(+) 5313	(+) 103.9
1976–80	20115	(+) 9689	(+) 92.9
1981–85	75681	(+) 55566	(+) 276.2
1986–90	48950	(–) 26731	(–) 35.3
1991–92	28796+	(–) 20154	(–) 41.2
1995–96	36589	(–) 26295	(–) 42.2
Total	196685	(+) 25885	(+) 13.2

* Include cases registered under UOA 1955; PCR Act, 1976; and SC/ST (PA) Act 1989.

\+ Including 13393 cases committed in few months in 1992.

Sources: Computed from the Reports of the Commissioner for the Scheduled Castes and Tribes for 1955 to 1986; Reports of the National Commission for the Scheduled Castes and Scheduled Tribes for 1987 and 1990; Annual Report of Ministry of Welfare, Govt. of India for 1992–93.

During the period before 1960's there were more cases of atrocities of socio-psychological in nature. This was because of the fact that the Dalits or the Scheduled Castes were so much subdued under the socio-economic, political and religious dominance of the upper castes that they did not openly defy their unbridled dictates and protest against their injustices committed on them. The upper castes used to control them by keeping ritual and social distance with them, hurling abuses on them, intimidating them by threatening to eject from their dwellings and putting them to starvation. The individual resentment and protest were firmly dealt with. But one thing is clear that the number of physical violence or atrocities on the Dalits was less because of rare cases of their collective protests or group rebellions against that. Even such protests or rebellions were not recorded by administrators or social scientists. Contrary to all this, the cases of physical violence or atrocities on them in the present time are much more due to their collective consciousness and protests against injustices done on them. That means, the more the collectiveness and united protests of the Dalits, the more are the cases of physical atrocities on them by the caste Hindus.

Three main causes have been identified for committing atrocities on the Dalits. These are: dispute over possession of surplus land allotted to the Dalits by the Government, nonpayment or under payment of prescribed agricultural wages to them, and resentment against growing socio-political awareness and consciousness among them. In addition, many other factors have also contributed to the increase and decrease in the number of cases of atrocities inflicted on the Dalits during the past decades. For instance, the number of cases of physical atrocities reported upto 1950 was less because of the historical legacy of the struggle for the national freedom. In other words, since there was largely an extension of the emotional integration among the Indian during the freedom movement, the cases of atrocities committed against the Scheduled Castes and reported to the media and also to the governmental agencies were less in number and intensity.

The situation cropped up because of the socio-political roles by Ambedkar during the pre- and post-independence periods was also responsible for less number of atrocities committed on the Scheduled Castes. Moreover, the partition of the country diverted the hatred and anger of the caste Hindus towards the Muslims whose agitation and prowess caused to be a hindrance in the 'smooth' transfer of power from the British rule in India. The other reason for less number of atrocities committed on the Scheduled Castes could be minimal reporting and registering the cases during this period. Prior to adoption of the Untouchability (Offences) Act in June 1955, the cases of exploitation, harassment, untouchability and other forms of discriminations practised against the Scheduled Castes and atrocities perpetrated on them were dealt with under the general laws of the Indian Penal Code (IPC). In absence of any specific legal provisions for the purpose most of the cases of atrocities were not registered with the police as the police were often indifferent and biased against the Scheduled Caste victims.

Even if a few cases were registered under the various legal provisions these were easily dismissed and the offenders acquitted both by the police and the courts of law either on purely technical ground or in absence of adequate proofs and witnesses supporting the case. The victims themselves were not much conscious and aware of the then existing legal provisions. They were also not organised against their exploitation. A large number of cases were pending with different courts of law (this trend continues even today) as the courts were overburdened in dealing with cases of land disputes often resulted from adoption of the Land Reforms Act in 1956 and many other cases of different nature. Most of the cases relating to untouchability, harassment and atrocities against the Scheduled Castes were resolved amicably at the instance of either local influential persons, politicians or the judiciary.

The Untouchability (Offences) Act which was amended as the Protection of Civil Rights Act in 1976 had also failed to resolve most of the cases of atrocities, untouchability, exploitation, etc. practised against the Scheduled Castes in various parts of the country. Similar is the fate of the Scheduled Castes and Scheduled Tribes (Prevention of Atrocities) Act 1989 as is clear from the table given on the next page. This, however, cannot be denied that a large number of policies and schemes devised under the Protective Discrimination Policy were initiated soon after the independence for betterment of the Scheduled Castes. These policies had certainly contributed to some socio-economic improvements of the people of these castes but, more than that, had raised very high hopes and expectations among them in which the liberal attitudes and tall assurances given by the caste Hindu leaders specially of the Congress and Socialist parties also contributed a lot. But very soon particularly after the first decade of working of the policy of reservation for the Scheduled Castes, like several other castes and communities, became disillusioned about falsity of the situation of no likelihood improvement in their socio-economic conditions and no achievement of social quality in absence of their self assertion. The non-Scheduled Castes also became intolerant of the decennial extensions of the reservation policy (since its inception in 1950 the policy has been extended five times upto year 2000 after every ten years). In the current times this is coupled with effectiveness of a number of new institutions, growing aspirations and unemployment and the resultant unrest among the people at large. Hence, a very large number of cases of atrocities perpetrated took place during

TABLE 4.2
Disposal of Cases of Atrocities during 1955–1990

Period	Total cases registered*	Not challaned	Challaned	Acquitted	Convicted	Compounded or compromised	Pending	Remarks
		Disposal of cases						
1955–60	2911	379	2532	336	566	522	1108	–
1961–65	4693	816	3877	882	498	349	2148	Disposal of 366 cases registered in 1965 unvailable.
1966–70	5113	79	1053	190	262	82	466	Disposal of 2981 cases registered in 1966 unavailable
1971–75	10426	2039	8387	1388	3534	1658	1807	–
1976–80	20115	9417	10698	3194	561	155	6561	–
1981–85	75681	4802	12559	6649	1363	–	4547	Compounded cases included in acquitted for 1981–90, disposal of rest cases unavailable.
1986–90	48950	1950	5520	2369	538	–	2613	Figures available for 1986, 1989 and 1990 only. Disposal of rest cases unavailable.
Total	167889	19482	44626	15008	7322	2766	19240	–

*Includes cases registered under UOA 1955, PAR Act, 1976, and SC/ST (PA) Act 1989.

Sources: Computed from the Reports of the Commissioner for the Scheduled Castes/Scheduled Tribes for 1955 to 1986; and Reports of the National Commission for SC/ST for 1987 and 1990.

the following decades (1961–71 and 1971–81). This trend continued even during 1981–91 as is evident from the figures given in the earlier Tables 4.1 and 4.2.

It is not out of context to mention here that there has been sprawling rise in the nature and intensity or severity of atrocities committed on the Scheduled Castes during all these years over the earlier ones. For example, earlier there were more cases of untouchability and similar other forms of discretion like hurling abuses or calling names, taking *begar* (forced labour without payment) or making one bonded labour in lieu of non-payment of conspicuous loans, taming to accept astute of subordination to the upper castes and so forth.

There were also few cases of physical violence, killing and sexual exploitation of their womenfolks. Such kinds of atrocities broadly demonstrated the acts of feudal minds and colonial hangovers of the upper castes in villages. In a way, one may say that these were milder forms of atrocities though for the perspective from the below these were as harsh as murder, arson, gang-rape, etc. Yet, during the recent decades the cases of murder, grievous hurt, rape and arson have gone up. "It may be observed that there was a steady rise in the number of cases of murder of the Scheduled Caste persons from 1981 to 1986 except during 1985 when there was a slight fall. Similarly, there was a progressive rise in the number of cases of rape throughout this period".

A point is worth mentioning here that out of the three main causes identified by the government mentioned above—the possession of surplus land allotted to the landless Scheduled Caste persons, the growing tensions and bitterness arising out of non-payment of prescribed wages, and resentment against the manifestation of their socio-political awareness about their rights and privileges perhaps the last one is the overriding reason of commission of atrocities and the former two are inclusive in that as these are resultants of their awareness and consciousness. In other words, this last one may be termed proximate cause and the earlier two immediate causes of commission of atrocities. More so, the atrocities were committed in the past largely by the upper caste people on account of issues linked to their interests and dominance but now the collectivity—groups of individuals and members of the upper and middle caste(s) and community(ies)—as a whole attack on the Dalits in a particular village or region to terrorise the

TABLE 4.3

Types of Atrocities Committed on the Scheduled Castes during 1975-92

Period	*Types of Atrocities*							
	Murder	*Grievous Hurt*	*Rape*	*Arson*	*Others*	*Total*	*Increase (+) decrease (–) over the preceding period*	*Percentage*
1975–80	1795	1932	3519	6651	37841	51738*	–	–
1981–86	3139	8501	3998	6278	69181	91097	(+)39359	(+) 56.8
1987–92	2201	5491	3458	2230	48920	62330**	(–) 28767	(–) 46.2
Total	7135	15924	10975	15159	155942	205165	(+) 10592	(+) 5.2

* Figures for 1980 are unavailable.

** Figures for 1987 and 1988 are unavailable.

Sources : Computed from *Reports of the Commissioner for the Scheduled Castes/Scheduled Tribes* for 1975 to 1981; *Reports of the National Commission for the Scheduled Castes/Scheduled Tribes* for 1990; and *Annual Report* of the Ministry of Welfare, Govt. of India, 1992-93.

victims from raising their heads and claiming their rights and privileges in future.

Causes Behind Atrocities

A general trend may be noticed where both victims and inflictors of atrocities come from all ages and sexes though the majority of them are males who inflict physical violence against the victims. In fact, children and women are the worst sufferers though the targets may be the adult males.

The apparent cause of atrocities may not be total elimination of the victims but to intimidate them to accept the unconditional subordination to offenders.

However, it is true that in a number of cases the victims especially the children have to lose their life and women their chastity, honour and life. In some places they are ill-treated and ejected from their human dignity in the eyes of the offenders and of their own people. Here, the aim is to analyse the atrocities committed on the Scheduled Castes in various States/Union Territories in terms of a number of demographic features like size (both total and castes and community-wise) of population, age and sex of that found there. In other words, it is our intention to analyse whether atrocities are committed in more populous States/Union Territories. What are age and sex background of the persons or group(s) of persons who are involved, in one way or the other, in such acts? Our such examination is guided by the fact that atrocities are committed more in those States/Union Territories which are densely populated. Similarly, the persons—both males and females—of mature age are involved more in such acts than those who are either under- or over-age.

In event of limitations of the data collected through the secondary sources—either at the government end or at the end of the media—we may not be able to find any specific correlations between the two sets of variables. However, we may perhaps draw certain inferences in this connection from the data available at this stage. The Scheduled Castes represent about sixteen per cent of the total population of India. In certain States like Uttar Pradesh, West Bengal, Punjab, Haryana, Himachal Pradesh, Tamil Nadu, etc. they exceed whereas in States like Andhra Pradesh, Bihar, Gujarat, Jammu and Kashmir, Kerala, Madhya Pradesh, Maharashtra, etc. they are less than the average percentage of their

TABLE 4.4

Population-size and Atrocities Committed on the Scheduled Castes in 1981 and 1991

Sl. No.	State/UT	Population (percentage) to total population in the country in				Population percentage of SCs to total population in States in		Atrocities (%) committed in				Rank in committing atrocities in	
		1981		1991		1981	1991	1981		1991		1981	1991
		Total	SC	Total	SC			Total	%	Total	%		
1.	Andhra Pradesh	8.12	7.64	8.15	7.76	14.87	8.93	206	1.4	477	3.0	9	9
2.	Arunachal Pradesh	0.10	0.46	0.11	0.47	0.46	0.47	—	—	—	—	—	—
3.	Assam	x	x	2.66	1.20	x	7.40	—	—	14	0.1	—	14
4.	Bihar	10.60	9.73	19.58	9.21	14.51	14.56	2033	14.2	568	3.6	3	7
5.	Goa	0.15	0.02	0.14	0.02	2.05	2.08	—	—	05	0.1	—	16
6.	Gujarat	7.17	2.34	5.06	2.24	7.15	7.41	654	4.8	1355	8.6	6	4
7.	Haryana	1.96	2.36	2.02	2.38	19.07	19.16	74	0.6	65	0.4	11	11
8.	Himachal Pradesh	0.65	1.01	0.63	0.96	24.62	25.34	69	0.5	39	0.2	12	13
9.	Jammu and Kashmir	x	x	x	x	x	x	124	0.9	42	0.3	10	12
10.	Karnataka	5.63	5.37	5.51	5.54	15.7	16.38	397	2.8	591	3.7	7	6
11.	Kerala	3.86	2.44	3.57	2.41	10.01	9.92	260	1.8	660	4.2	8	5

(Contd.)

(Contd.)

Sl. No.	State/UT	Population (percentage) to total population in the country in				Population percentage of SCs to total population in States in		Atrocities (%) committed in				Rank in committing atrocities in	
		1981		1991		1981	1991	1981		1991		1981	1991
		Total	SC	Total	SC			Total	%	Total	%		
12.	Madhya Pradesh	7.91	7.06	8.11	7.05	14.10	14.54	4033	28.2	5380	34.1	1	1
13.	Maharashtra	9.52	4.30	9.67	6.41	7.14	11.10	695	4.9	573	3.6	5	7
14.	Manipur	0.22	0.02	0.23	0.03	1.25	2.20	–	–	–	–	–	–
15.	Meghalaya	0.20	+	0.22	0.01	0.41	0.51	–	–	–	–	–	–
16.	Mizoram	0.07	+	0.08	+	0.03	0.10	–	–	–	–	–	–
17.	Nagaland	0.12	–	0.15	–	–	–	–	–	–	–	–	–
18.	Orissa	4.00	3.71	3.88	3.76	14.66	16.20	80	0.6	372	2.4	11	10
19.	Punjab	2.55	4.33	2.49	4.20	26.87	28.31	51	0.4	37	0.2	13	13
20.	Rajasthan	5.20	5.60	5.39	5.57	17.04	17.29	1562	10.9	2098	13.3	4	3
21.	Sikkim	0.05	0.02	0.05	0.02	5.78	5.93	–	–	27	0.2	–	13
22.	Tamil Nadu	7.34	8.52	6.84	7.84	18.35	19.18	199	1.4	551	3.5	9	8

(Contd.)

(Contd.)

Sl. No.	State/UT	Population (percentage) to total population in the country in				Population percentage of SCs to total population in States in		Atrocities (%) committed in				Rank in committing atrocities in	
		1981		1991		1981	1991	1981		1991		1981	1991
		Total	SC	Total	SC			Total	%	Total	%		
24.	Uttar Pradesh	16.82	22.49	17.04	21.44	21.16	21.04	3825	26.7	4804	30.4	2	2
25.	West Bengal	8.28	11.51	8.34	11.77	21.22	23.62	23	0.2	10	0.17	14	15
Union Territories													
26.	Andaman and Nicobar Islands	0.03	–	0.03	–	–	–	–	–	–	–	–	–
27.	Chandigarh	0.07	0.06	0.08	0.08	14.09	16.51	–	–	–	–	–	–
28.	Dadra and Nagar Haveli	0.02	+	0.02	+	1.97	1.97	–	–	–	–	–	–
29.	Daman and Diu	0.01	+	0.01	+	3.56	3.83	1	–	–	–	–	–
30.	Delhi	0.94	1.08	1.15	1.31	18.03	19.05	6	0.1	4	0.17	16	17
33.	Lakshadweep	0.01	–	0.01	–	–	–	–	–	–	–	–	–
32.	Pondicherry	0.99	0.09	0.10	0.10	11.99	16.25	8	0.1	5	0.12	16	16

– Nil + Negligible

X Population enumeration not done

Sources: Computed from *Censuses of India*, 1981 and 1991; *Report of the Commissioner for the Scheduled Castes and Tribes*, 1986–87; and *Annual Report* of the Ministry for Welfare, Govt. of India, 1992–93

population in the country. In fact, the phenomenon of atrocities committed on the Scheduled Castes does not always go along the population size of these States. For instance, States like Himachal Pradesh, Punjab, Tamil Nadu and West Bengal are smaller in terms of population size but they accommodate larger percentage of the total Scheduled Castes in the country.

Similarly, representation of the Scheduled Castes both in rural and urban areas is proportionately much below than that of the non-Scheduled Castes though the former are found in majority (eighty-four per cent) in villages except in Union Territories like Delhi and Chandigarh where about ninety per cent of them live in urban areas. Almost in every village in the country the Scheduled Castes are in minority. They are economically dependent on others and are subjected to different kinds of atrocities and harassment. It was observed by Ambedkar as early as in the late 1930s that since the Scheduled Castes were found in minority in every village (and also in city) in India. They were subjected to social boycotts and different kinds of harassments and atrocities of upper caste Hindus and others if they raised voice against their degraded status and asserted for their own rights. The same continues even today wherein they are isolated and made target of attacks by the entire village, if they deny their continued association with old customs and practices. On such occasions even members of other Scheduled Castes are opposed to people of a specific Scheduled Caste who refuse to perform the traditional customs and practices in villages. In fact, the former ally with non-Scheduled Castes and reinforced crusades against the latter as their interests also get adversely affected by such denial. The old persons of the Scheduled Castes in different types of disadvantages and subordination of others specially the upper and middle level castes and classes without raising any voice. This may be so because of their economic dependence, low or the lowest level structural placement in the caste hierarchy, and different kinds of disabilities, i.e. social or religious imposed on them.

Their economic dependence, social neglect, lack of outside contacts, and social and political awareness aggravate their misery. Contrary to that, younger people of the Scheduled Castes is literate, exposed to outside experience, and are socially and politically conscious of their rights and privileges. Hence, they find uneasy to accept their placement at the lowest level in the village society.

A number of social reforms and changes among the Scheduled Castes have been started by them. In most of the cases they have persuaded and reinforced the old generation to assert for their rights and better status in society. Thus, they easily become target of atrocities (both physical and social) as they are more conscious about their exploitation and degraded social status though in providing them certain stimuli the old people also face different types of atrocities in villages. In some cases even the old people openly protest against their exploitation and harassment and face one type of atrocities or the other.

Contrary to this, both young and old persons belonging to caste Hindus and others behave atrociously against Scheduled Castes and other weaker sections of society. It has been a common practice in villages that even old persons of the Scheduled Castes have to bow, obey and pay maximum respect to children and women of the upper castes. The atrocities and harassment in several cases are initiated and multiplied by the youth of the upper and middle level castes in which the old people sometimes play diplomatically and at times openly and, thus, provide reinforcement to atrocious and conflict situations. In fact, the old persons of upper castes are intolerant to literacy, social and political awareness, a little economic improvement and claim for social equality of the Scheduled Castes. Upper Caste youth are jealous and tyrannical to the plausible beneficiaries of the much publicised Policy of the Protective Discrimination enacted for the upliftment of the Scheduled Castes and Scheduled Tribes. Thus, there exists a "developmental cycle" of atrocities in the cases of both their victims and inflictors. In the former case, old generation of the Scheduled Castes face atrocities in preparing their young generation to become socially and politically conscious and, also in certain cases, in raising voice against their downgraded social position and legitimacy of the *status quo*. Their younger generation is target of more severe attacks as they increasingly pull out of their age-old psychology of subordination. They strongly protest against atrocities and harassment and stimulate the old people for the same. Similarly, the old persons of non-Scheduled Castes have traditionally behaved with the Scheduled Castes in the atrocious manner as mentioned above.

In the initiating and intensifying atrocities by their youth they provide reinforcement either by encouraging them, or actively joining their hands, or pacifying and fissiling out the conflict situation afterwards.

Apparently, the Scheduled Castes men are the prime target of atrocities. They are stated earlier but it is also a fact that most of the times atrocities are perpetrated indiscriminately in which men, women and children are equally suffering. However, it is empirically true that the Scheduled Castes women are more subjected to atrocities and harassment of caste Hindus and others. The reason may be that women as a social category have always been considered physically weak and subjected to atrocities and harassment of men. Unlike women of the upper castes and classes, the Scheduled Caste women are generally illiterate, tradition-ridden and economically insecure as are their men in villages.

As a consequence, they are unable to socially organise and unitedly face atrocities and harassment of caste Hindus both men and women since on such occasions the non-Scheduled Caste women are always governed by acts of their men, their caste prejudices and class positions and not by their position of being women. The Scheduled Caste men also, owing to their economic insecurity and traditional subordination to the upper and landowning castes, are unable to provide full protection to their womenfolk. This is not to deny the fact that in certain parts of the country both the Scheduled Caste men and women have fought unitedly against the atrocities and harassment perpetrated on them in spite of their poor social and economic standings.

Post-Independence Atrocities and Dominant Castes

The dominant caste is a post-independent phenomenon and includes those castes which have been considered as Shudra castes, or the backward castes or classes in the traditional caste hierarchy. These are more appropriately known today as the Other Backward Castes or Classes though there appears to be no unanimity among the social scientists on their definition nor the Constitution of India makes any definite specifications of these castes or classes. These castes have now become economically and politically dominant snatching away such dominance enjoyed by the upper castes in the past. There are two main responsible factors for their acquisition of both economic and political powers of dominance specially in villages. These are: benefits of the *Jamindari* abolition including land reforms and their numerical strength. After independence, the *Jamindari* system was abolished. As a result, the legal possession of land in most of the cases got transferred from upper caste landlords to the tenants or the actual tillers of the land who were mainly the middle level castes people known today as backward castes. They also got land ownership due to enactment of Land Reforms Act and Tenancy Act. Even in the recent decades the upper castes in various regions have migrated to the urban areas after disposing-off their lands to the backward castes. Thus the dominant peasants, apart from the middle and small farmers, are mostly from these castes. Their economic dominance is also result of their traditional peasant family background in which all members of their family worked (and work even today) on the fields saving wages to be paid to the farm labourers. In democracy numbers or numerical strengths count a lot. Population of the backward castes is estimated to be fifty-two of the total population in the country. It is true that the political mobilisation of people in the electoral politics is based, in principle, on policies and programmes of a political party and charismatic personality of its leader(s). But in practice it is not free from its traditional connections with caste or religious community besides with money and muscle powers. Caste and community are largely used both by the politicians and the people at the local, State and Central level politics.

The numerical strength of a caste or community plays a significant role in emotional mobilisation of its members on some specific occasions even in villages. Thus, the backward castes largely their numerical strength both at macro (district, State, and Centre) and micro (village) levels. Besides their economic and political dominance, they also enjoy the benefits of modern education and occupation. They fulfil if not all then most of the elements of a dominance mentioned by Srinivas according to which "Numerical strength, economic and political power, ritual status, and Western education and occupations are the most significant elements of dominance.

Usually various elements of dominance are distributed among different castes in a village. When a caste enjoys all or most of the elements of dominance, it may be said to have decisive dominance" (Srinivas 1987: 114). But generally speaking, all members of a caste or for that matter of a backward caste may not be economically and politically relevant. Rather, there are poor and rich or powerful and powerless in every caste. Then, a caste is dominant in the sense of its numerical strength only in a village or a region though emotional ties of caste members have weakened to a great extent in the recent decades even in the rural areas. In 1977 the Janata Party captured political power and formed its governments at the Centre and in some States. This gave tremendous moral boost to the backward castes as the Chief Ministers in various States were from these castes. They not only consolidated their political power at different levels but also used it, along with their economic dominance, for enhancing their social status in the caste hierarchy in villages. For this they adopted twin processes of resenting against the traditional dictates of the upper castes whose earlier economic and political dominances were declining and subjugating the landless agricultural labourers majority of whom was constituted by the Dalits.

Contrary to adopting the conventional principle of upward social mobility in which the upwardly mobile person or group subordinates to the subsequently higher group or strata by emulating its social values, culture and lifestyles and distancing from the immediately lower group or strata, they neglected the socio-religious supremacy of the former and tried to tame the latter through terrorising them. "The existing relations among higher castes, the backward castes and the Scheduled Castes in the villages underwent a sea change."

The abolition of landlordism, the introduction to *Panchayat Raj* and of adult suffrage in the elections coupled with land reforms and agricultural development led to a decline in the power of the higher castes and a consequent increase in the power of backward castes at the village level. The backward castes had also improved their political clout by getting elected to the legislatures in larger numbers, on account of their larger population" (Sachchidanand 1988: 64). The Dalits on their part did not easily accept economic and political dominance and they claimed higher status of the backward castes precisely on four grounds. One, the backward castes too were subordinates of the upper castes and these castes were subjected to different types of ignominies in the past. Two, in spite of their economic and political dominance there was not much difference in their lifestyles from that of the Dalits as the women and children of the former were very much engaged in the manual activities on the field like that of the latter. But the difference between the two was that whereas former were engaged in such activities mostly on their own fields, the latter worked as labourers on the fields of upper castes. Third, the backward castes in general and their dominant peasants in particular tried to extract the maximum social respect from the Dalits without extending their patronage to them like that of the upper castes in the past. Finally, the Dalits had acquired by that time a good degree of socio-political consciousness about their socio-economic exploitation and social degradation.

Hence, they were organising for achieving social justice and equality with others in society. "This increase political consciousness led to a feeling of resentment and hostility in their hearts against their oppressors. They were no longer prepared to take things lying down. Thus, a psychological climate had been created for a confrontation between the Scheduled Castes and the upper castes" (*ibid:* 65). This also led confrontations between the Scheduled Castes and the Backward Castes. In fact, the same scenario exists even today with greater degree of socio-political consciousness among the Scheduled Castes and hostility and confrontation between them and the upper and the backward castes in villages. We have stated earlier that from 1977 onwards there has been dramatic increase in the cases of atrocities on the Dalits. We have also mentioned that on certain specific issues concerning the Dalits' opposition to carry out their customary practices the people of entire castes in a village become awry and furious against them. They commit both physical and social atrocities on them. This fact is quite evident by now that in majority of the cases of atrocities it is the backward castes people like Yadavs, Kurmis and Koeris in Bihar; Yadavs, Kurmis and Jats in U.P.: Reddis and Kammas in Andhra Pradesh; Patels and Kanbis in Gujarat; Patils and Kanbis in Maharashtra, etc. who have committed physical and social violence against the Dalits since 1977. Their economic and political dominances have reinforced them in committing different types of atrocities on the Dalits and getting easy sway from these because of their connivance with the civil and police administrations. In fact, the recent efforts to politically unite the Dalits and the backward castes have not yielded any positive results regarding curbing the atrocities and lessening arrogance of these castes towards the Dalits.

Imbalanced Growth and its Impact on Atrocities

Atrocities are the result of protest, tension and conflict between the Scheduled Castes and non-Scheduled Castes. "In fact,

TABLE 4.5
Socio-economic Development and Atrocities Committed on the Scheduled Castes During 1981–91

Sl. No.	*State/UT*	*Socio-economic Development*										*Atrocities in per cent*	
		Literacy Rate in				*Workers (%) in*				*Per capita income (Rs.) in*			
		1981		*1991*		*1981*		*1991*		*1974–75*	*1982–83*	*1981*	*1991*
		Total	*SC*	*Total*	*SC*	*Total*	*SC*	*Total*	*SC*				
1.	Andhra Pradesh	35.7	20.92	44.1	31.59	42.26	54.26	37.46	51.08	877	1955	1.4	3.0
2.	Arunachal Pradesh	26.6	45.85	41.6	57.27	*	45.74	46.24	44.27	*	*	*	*
3.	Assam	+	+	52.89	53.94	+	+	39.09	34.40	776	1762	*	0.1
4.	Bihar	32.1	12.84	38.5	19.49	29.68	39.45	32.16	37.40	718	1174	14.2	3.6
5.	Goa	65.7	42.69	75.5	58.73	30.59	40.0	35.28	38.07	*	*	*	0.03
6.	Gujarat	52.2	48.04	61.3	61.07	32.22	36.05	40.23	37.61	1036	2795	4.6	8.6
7.	Haryana	43.9	25.01	55.8	39.22	28.35	32.51	31.0	30.97	*	3647	0.6	0.4
8.	Himachal Pradesh	51.2	38.26	63.9	53.20	34.36	43.62	42.83	43.44	1037	2230	0.5	0.2
9.	Jammu and Kashmir	26.67	27.97	+	+	30.37	45.02	+	+	708	1820	0.9	0.2
10.	Karnataka	46.2	25.11	56.0	38.06	36.76	44.90	41.99	44.66	786	1957	2.8	3.7

11.	Kerala	81.6	64.78	89.8	79.66	26.68	42.10	31.43	41.21	785	1761	1.8	4.2
12.	Madhya Pradesh	34.2	23.43	44.2	35.08	38.41	45.04	42.82	43.42	794	1636	28.2	34.1
13.	Maharashtra	55.8	42.47	64.9	56.46	38.71	44.41	42.97	42.82	1251	*	4.9	3.6
14.	Manipur	49.7	40.97	59.9	56.44	40.35	45.53	42.18	48.96	*	1673	*	*
15.	Meghalaya	42.0	31.0	49.1	44.27	43.44	34.80	42.67	35.71	*	1483	*	*
16.	Mizoram	74.3	89.76	82.3	77.92	*	82.22	48.91	79.16	*	*	*	*
17.	Nagaland	50.3	—	61.5	—	47.53	—	42.68	—	*	*	—	—
18.	Orissa	41.0	26.76	49.1	36.78	32.75	42.02	37.53	39.26	690	*	0.6	2.4
19.	Punjab	48.2	29.0	58.5	41.09	29.35	32.39	30.88	30.71	1386	3691	0.4	0.2
20.	Rajasthan	30.1	17.52	38.6	26.29	30.48	43.98	38.27	39.26	819	1881	10.9	13.3
21.	Sikkim	41.6	34.78	56.9	51.03	46.60	43.95	41.51	38.55	*	1300	*	0.2
22.	Tamil Nadu	54.4	34.23	62.7	46.74	39.30	49.09	43.31	48.43	942	1827	1.4	3.5
23.	Tripura	50.1	40.80	60.4	56.66	29.60	29.84	31.14	28.69	*	*	0.1	*
24.	Uttar Pradesh	33.4	18.48	41.6	26.85	29.22	33.67	32.20	35.29	812	1567	26.7	30.4
25.	West Bengal	48.6	29.68	57.7	42.21	28.26	31.64	32.19	33.31	1065	2237	0.2	0.1
Union Territories													
26.	Andaman and Nicobar Islands	63.2	—	73.0	—	*	—	35.24	—	*	*	—	—
27.	Chandigarh	74.8	44.89	77.8	55.44	34.65	34.21	34.94	32.33	*	*	x	x

Contd.

Contd.

Sl. No.	State/UT	Socio-economic Development										Atrocities in per cent	
		Literacy Rate in				Workers (%) in				Per capita income (Rs.) in			
		1981		1991		1981		1991		1974–75	1982–83	1981	1991
		Total	SC	Total	SC	Total	SC	Total	SC				
28.	Dadra and Nagar Haveli	32.7	62.81	40.7	77.64	*	41.79	53.25	38.94	*	*	x	x
29.	Daman and Diu	59.9	66.42	71.2	79.18	30.59	40.0	37.63	29.43	*	*	x	x
30.	Delhi	71.9	47.85	75.3	57.60	31.93	40.0	31.64	29.25	*	*	0.1	0.1
31.	Lakshadweep	68.4	–	81.8	–	*	–	26.43	–	*	*	–	–
32.	Pondicherry	65.1	37.82	74.7	56.26	28.66	42.86	33.08	40.85	*	*	0.1	0.1
	India	43.7	25.83	52.2	37.41	36.70	36.13	37.46	39.25	343	2201	100.0	100.0

– No Scheduled Caste population in the State/Union Territory.
+ Census enumeration was not done.
* Figures are unavailable.
x No atrocities were committed.

Sources: Literary Trends in the 1980's in India – occasional paper No. 4 of 1993, p. 20; *Census of India*, 1991-*Union Primary Census Abstract for SC/ST.* Paper I of 1993, pp. 14–15; *Census of India*, 1981, Part II–B (ii) – *Primary Census Abstract – Scheduled Castes*, pp. xxix-xxxii.

conflicts or social conflicts have been considered as characteristics of the modern industrial society" (Beteille 1975) rather than of an agrarian society. After independence, India has achieved industrialisation and economic development but more in urban than in rural areas. As a whole, country has progressed in the recent times but such progress is not uniform as some regions are still socially and economically backward. These are part of Bihar and eastern Uttar Pradesh; some parts of Orissa and Madhya Pradesh; parts of Maharashtra, Gujarat, Rajasthan; and parts of the southern States. This is evident from the fact that the per capita income (barring their overall economic and industrial growth) in some of these States is less than in other States. For instance, Andhra Pradesh, Bihar, Madhya Pradesh, Orissa, Rajasthan and Uttar Pradesh had per capita income of less than one thousand rupees during the year 1974–75 whereas it was more than that in Gujarat and Maharashtra during the said period. Such trends are exist, with some differences, even today. This has resulted from the industrial and agricultural development in these States in the recent years. Then, atrocities *vis-a-vis* conflict between the Scheduled Castes and non-Scheduled Castes should have occurred more in those States where per capita income is high. But contrary to that, atrocities have been committed on the Scheduled Castes in various States irrespective of their social and economic development.

The cases of atrocities are more in the States of Madhya Pradesh, Maharashtra, Gujarat, Uttar Pradesh, Karnataka, Bihar, Rajasthan and Tamil Nadu than in other States. It can, however, be pointed out here that in the States or regions which have experienced more economic and industrial development the traditional relationships between the Scheduled Castes and non-Scheduled Castes have undergone a number of changes though not very substantive in nature.

As the landowning classes in the countryside have found cultivation more gainful in the recent times, the agricultural labourers drawn mostly from the Scheduled Castes have began asserting for their rights of possession and cultivation of land. They demand increase in wages particularly the approved one. This has resulted into tension and conflict between them and the landowning castes and classes.

Hence, atrocities on them by these castes and classes. The socio-economic conditions of the Dalits have not changed even in those areas where the Green Revolution in agriculture has taken place. The case of notorious killings of 44 Dalit men, women and children by the landlords and their henchmen in Kilvenmanai village in Thanjore district of Tamil Nadu in 1968 was a glaring example. Even in the backward regions and States they have started, with their bare subsistence living, with certain amount of their consciousness and mobilisation, with knowledge of happenings elsewhere, etc. to protest against the social and economic exploitations.

As a result, they are victims of atrocities committed on them by caste Hindus and others. This does not mean that the Scheduled Castes are safe in urban areas. In fact, they have been attacked, on one pretext or the other, in some towns and cities also in various parts of the country. For example, Jatavs' procession of the birth centenary celebration of Dr. B.R. Ambedkar was attacked on April 14, 1978 by both caste Hindus and later by the police in the name of maintaining the law and order. A number of Jatavs lost their lives, houses and properties were ransacked, looted and destroyed.

Likewise, the Scheduled Castes and the neo-Buddhists were brutally assaulted, some were killed and their houses and properties were destroyed by caste Hindus in Aurangabad city in 1981 because of agitation for renaming the Marathwada University after Dr. Ambedkar (which now is renamed). The cases of atrocities committed in 1981 on the Scheduled Castes by the Patels and the police in Ahmedabad, Surat, Baroda and several other cities (and villages) in Gujarat on the issue of reservation are still present in our memory. Thus, the atrocities are committed on the Scheduled Castes both in urban and rural areas where the caste Hindus and the police get relatively free hands in mounting assault on them. The cases of atrocities committed on the Dalits in urban areas are relatively less in number because soon these highlighted by the media, police get alert and take charge of the situation, and the nation's attentions are immediately drawn towards them.

Changing Social Structure and its Impact

Social structure in India particularly in the countryside has been based on the caste system and other primordial categories of relations. Of course, the country has experienced a number of changes in the recent times as stated above. Consequently, the social structure has also changed to some extent but its basic ethos has not been changed. In other words, social structure more in rural than in urban areas still continues with certain amount of closeness, segregation and traditionality. In such situation, changes especially at the aspirational level and relatively less at material level go along with certain basic contradictions in social arrangements and relationships among the people of various castes and communities.

These contradictions are rooted primarily in continuation, with some forms of the traditional social structure and the adaptive form of changes introduced in recent times in the country. People at large in the country are still accustomed of perceiving and accepting changes in the horizontal and not in the vertical direction though these changes have also been used by the Dalits and the Backward Castes to enhance their social status in vertical direction in the caste hierarchy wherein they generally confront with those who have traditionally remained at the higher ranks and who desperately strive for maintaining the *status quo.* Then, their personality formation and as a result their social interaction and social relations with others are also part of the in-built social contradictions.

The changes taking place or intending to take place among the Scheduled Castes and other weaker sections are, therefore, not easily acceptable to the caste Hindus and upper and middle classes in urban and more in rural areas. Atrocities are often seen regarding deprivations of one type or the other specially in event of scarcity of material goods or social positions. "The greater the deprivation felt by a social category, the more is its responsiveness to radical ideologies and militant mechanisms for redressing their grievances once they are emancipated from the traditional clutches of society".

Those Scheduled Castes who are socially mobile and who assert for their rights and respectable status in the society than on those compromise with the *status quo,* are more prone to atrocity. For example, the Chamars in Bihar and Uttar Pradesh, Malas and Madigas in Andhra Pradesh, Mahars in Maharashtra, Vankars in Gujarat, etc. are more victims of atrocities than other Scheduled Castes in these States. Yet, one thing is clear that those members of such castes who are better educated, employed in bureaucratic jobs and have improved their political and economic positions are comparatively less victims of physical violence than those who lag behind. Nevertheless, certain more subtle forms of atrocities-discriminations such as making disparaging remarks, taunting, etc. are inflicted on them. Not only that but they are made, to some extent, to look as alienated from the problems of majority of the Scheduled Castes though the reality may be something different. Another in-built contradictions are found in the socio-demographic composition of the parties (rival groups) involved in the cases of atrocities.

Traditionally, the lower castes people had been considered as subordinate to the upper castes irrespective of their age and sex. This continues to some extent even today as an aged lower caste person is subjected his subordination to a child or a woman of the upper castes. The Scheduled Caste educated youth resent to such customary practices and act of behaviour whereas the upper caste youth, like their elders, expect and insist for the traditionally pattern of behaviour and respect from the lower castes. Hence, a growing amount of tension is increasing atrocities in which the elder lower castes try to restrain whereas the caste Hindu elders in villages incite the cases of atrocities against the Dalits for continuing their traditional dominance and unconditional access to the resources available in the present time as stated ealier.

In recent times another significant development has taken place in the cases of atrocities committed on the Scheduled Castes. In the traditional social structure not only the lower castes but the middle castes had been subjected to subordination of the upper castes irrespective of their economic standing. But after the *Jamindari* abolition, enactment of land reforms and imposition of ceilings on the excess land owned by the big landlords the middle level castes, who were connected with cultivation earlier as small and middle level castes, peasants or share croppers, got most benefited. They have also succeeded in having their better share in political power, bureaucracy and education as stated above. In other words, they have successively improved their socio-economic conditions and power position. This has also helped them claim better social status, command more respect and assert their dominance especially over the lower castes people.

In fact, they demand the same amount of respect from the Scheduled Castes as the upper castes used to enjoy. The Scheduled Castes, on their part, are reminded of the earlier subordination of the backward castes to the upper castes and they find a contradiction in their (backward castes) traditional and newly achieved social statuses. Consequently, the clash of their interests and in-built contradictions result into different kinds of atrocities inflicted by the middle level castes on the Scheduled Castes. It does not, however, mean that other castes support the cause of the Scheduled Castes and do not inflict atrocities on them. In fact, all the castes together or separately commit atrocities depending upon the issues and contexts involved in the cases. There are certain elements (duties) concerning the basic structure of rural society which have traditionally bound all the castes together. Some of these are removal of dead cattle, traditional midwifery, paying *begar*, extending unconditional respects, etc. The Scheduled Castes have customarily been performing these 'duties' in favour of the upper and the middle level castes in villages. In the changed circumstances when the Scheduled Castes have started to discard them, they are subjected to atrocities of all castes and communities in the countryside as mentioned above though these customary practices have loosened their significance in the recent times.

Yet, these continue to work as the underneath reasons along with the economic and political ones in commission of atrocities on the Scheduled Castes in various parts of the country. The atrocities—a form of collective violence—have been inflicted on the weaker sections in general and the Scheduled Castes in particular in all the times but have consistently risen in recent years more in rural than in urban areas in the country. There are a number of factors which contribute to the occurrence and recurrence of the atrocities on the Scheduled Castes but most of these are located in the uneven socio-economic development and manifold social contradictions rooted in the social structure in the country.

The atrocities have also been contributed negatively even by the limited benefits of the reservation policy adopted for the betterment of the Scheduled Castes. In such situation, those castes and communities which have become socially and economically mobile in the recent years are more involved in social conflicts, atrocities and collective violence than those who are otherwise. In other words, the forms and magnitudes of atrocities are more subtle in cases of those Scheduled Castes who have successfully improved upon their socio-economic positions but more crude and naked in those cases where they are backward and yet, with some amount of social consciousness and mobilisation, they try to improve their lots.

5

The Protection of Civil Rights Act, 1995

(Act No. 22 of 1995)
(As amended by Act No. 106 of 1976)

An Act to prescribe punishment for the preaching and practice of "untouchability", for the enforcement of any disability arising therefrom and for matters connected therewith.

Be it enacted by Parliament in the Sixth Year of the Republic of India as follows:

1. ***Short title, extent and commencement.*** 1. This Act may be called the Protection of Civil Rights Act, 1955.

2. It extends to the whole of India.

3. It shall come into force on such date as the Central Government may, by notification in the official Gazette, appoint.

2. ***Definitions.*** In this Act, unless the context otherwise requires:

(a) "civil rights" mean any right accruing to a person by reason of the abolition of untouchability by Article 17 of the Constitution;

(aa) "hotel' includes a refreshment room, a boarding house, a lodging house, a coffee house and a cafe;

(b) 'place" includes a house, building and other structure and premises, and also includes a tent, vehicle and vessel;

(c) "place of public entertainment" includes any place to which the public are admitted and in which an entertainment is provided or held;

Explanation. "Entertainment" includes any exhibition, performance game, sport and any other form of amusement;

(d) "place of public worship" means a place by whatever name known, which is used as a place of public religious worship or which is dedicated generally to, or is used generally by persons professing any religion or belonging to any religious denomination or any section thereof, for the performance of any religious service or for offering prayers therein and includes –

(i) all lands and subsidiary shrines appurtenant or attached to any such place,

(ii) convately owned place of worship which is, in fact allowed by the owner thereof to be used as a place of public worship, and

(iii) such land or subsidiary shrine appurtenant to such privately owned place of worship as is allowed by the owner thereof to be used as a place of public religious worship];

[(da) "Prescribed" means prescribed by rules made under this Act;

(db) "Scheduled Castes" has the meaning assigned to it in Clause (24) of Art. 166 of the Constitution];

(e) "show" means any premises where goods are sold either wholesale or by retail or both wholesale and by retail and includes –

(i) any place from where goods are sold by a hawker or vendor or from a mobile van or cart;

(ii) a laundry and a hair-cutting saloon,

(iii) any other place where services are rendered to customers;]

3. ***Punishment for enforcing religious disabilities.*** Whoever on the ground of "untouchability" prevents any person –

(a) from entering any place of public worship which is open to other persons professing the same religion or any section thereof as such person; or

(b) from worshipping or offering prayers or performing any religious service in any place of public worship, or bathing in, or using the waters of, any sacred tank, well, spring or water-course, river or lake or bathing at any *ghat* of such tank, water course, river or lake in the same manner and to the same manner and to the same extent as is permissible to the other person professing the same religion or any section thereof, as such person.

shall be punishable with imprisonment for a term of not less than one month and not more than six months and also with fine which shall be not less than one hundred rupees and not more than five hundred rupees.

Explanation: For the purposes of this Section and Section 4 persons professing the Buddhist, Sikh and Jaina religion or persons professing the Hindu religion in any of its forms or developments including Virashaivas, Lingayats, Adivasis, followers of Brahmo, Prarthana, Arya Samaj and the Swaminarayana Smoradaya shall be deemed to be Hindus.

4. ***Punishment for enforcing social disabilities.*** Whoever on the ground of "untouchability" enforces against any person any disability with regard to—

(i) access to any shop, public restaurant, hotel or place of public entertainment, or

(ii) the use of any utensils, and other Articles kept in any public restaurant, hotel, *dharmasala, sarai* or *musafirkhana* for the use of the general public or of any section thereof; or

(iii) the practice of any profession or the carrying on of any occupation, trade or business or employment in any job; or

(iv) the use of or access to, any river, stream, spring, well, tank, cistern, water-tap or other watering place, or any bathing *ghat,* burial or cremation ground, any sanitary convenience, any road, or passage, or any other place of public resort which other members of the public, or any section thereof, have a right to use or have access to; or

(v) the use of or access to, any place used for a charitable or a public purpose maintained wholly or partly out of State funds or dedicated to the use of the general public or any section thereof; or

(vi) the enjoyment of the benefit under a charitable trust created for the benefit of the general public or of any section thereof; or

(vii) the use of, or access to, any public conveyance; or

(viii) the construction, acquisition, or occupation of any residential premises in any locality, whatsoever, or

(ix) the use of any *dharamsala, sarai,* or *musafirkhana* which is open to general public, or to any section thereof; or

(x) the observance of any social or religious custom, usage or ceremony or taking part in, or taking out, any religious, social or cultural processing; or

(xi) the use of jewellery and finery.

shall be punishable with imprisonment for a term of not less than one month and not more than six months and also with fine which shall be not less than one hundred rupees and not more than five hundred rupees.

Explanation. For the purposes of this Section, enforcement of any disability includes any discrimination on the ground of "untouchability".

5. *Punishment for refusing to admit persons to hospitals, etc.: Whoever on the ground of "untouchability".*

(a) refuses admission to any person to any hospital, dispensary, educational institution or any hotel [x x x] if such hospital, dispensary, educational institution or hotel is established or maintained for the benefit of the general public or any section thereof; or

(b) does any action which discriminates against any such person after admission to any of aforesaid institution;

shall be punishable with imprisonment for a term of not less than one month and not more than six months and also with fine which shall be not less than one hundred rupees and not more than five hundred rupees.

6. *Punishment for refusing to sell goods or render services.* Whoever on the ground of "untouchability" refuses to sell any goods or refuses to render any service to any person at the same time and place and on the same terms and conditions at/on which such goods are sold or services are rendered to other persons in the ordinary course of business shall be punishable with imprisonment for a term of not less than one month and not more than six months and also fine which shall be not less than one hundred rupees and not more than five hundred rupees.

7. *Punishment for other offences arising out of "untouchability".* Whoever:

(a) prevents any person from exercising any rights accruing to him by reason of the abolition of "untouchability" under Article 17 of the Constitution; or

(b) molests, injuries, annoys, obstructs or causes or attempts to cause obstruction to any person in the exercise of any such right or molest, injuries, annoys or boycotts any person by reason of his having exercised any such rights; or

(c) by words, either spoken or written, or by signs or by visible representation or otherwise, incites or encourages any person or class of persons or the public generally to practice "untouchability" in any form whatsoever; or

(d) insults or attempts to insult on the ground of "untouchability" a member of a Scheduled Caste;

shall be punishable with imprisonment for a term of not less than one month and not more than six months, and also with fine which shall be not less than one hundred rupees and not more than five hundred rupees.

***Explanation* 1.** A person shall be deemed to boycott another person who—

(a) refuses to such other person or refuses to permit such other person, to use or occupy any house or land or refuses to deal with, work for hire for, or do business with, such other person or to render to him, receive from him any customary service, or refuses to do any of the said things on the terms on which such things would be commonly done in the ordinary course of business; or

(b) abstains from such social, professional or business relations as he would ordinarily maintain with other person.

***Explanation* 2.** For the purpose of clause (c) a person shall be deemed to incite or encourage the practice of "untouchability"—

(i) if he directly or indirectly, preaches "untouchability" or it practices in any form; or

(ii) if he justifies whether on historical, philosophical or religious grounds or on the ground of any trading of the caste system or on any other ground, the practice of "untouchability" in any form.

1-A. Whoever commits any offence against the person or property of any individual as a reprisal or revenge for his having exercised any right accruing to him by reason of the abolition of "untouchability" under Article 17 of the constitution, shall, where the offence is punishable with imprisonment for a term proceeding two years, be punishable with imprisonment for a term which shall be of less than two years and also with fine.

2. Whoever:

(i) demise to any person belonging to his community or any section thereof any right or privilege to which such person would be entitled as a member of such community or section; or

(ii) takes any part in the ex-communication of such person, on the ground that such person has refused to practice "untouchability" that such person has done any act in furtherance of the objects of this Act;

shall be punishable with imprisonment for a term of not less than one month and not more than six months, and also with fine which shall be not less than one hundred rupees and not more than five hundred rupees.

7. (a) ***Unlawful compulsory labour when to be deemed to be a practice of "untouchability".*** 1. Whoever compels any person, on the ground of "untouchability" to do any scavenging or sweeping or to remove any carcass or a flay any animal, or to remove the umbilical cord or to do any other job of a similar nature shall be deemed to have enforced a disability arising out of "untouchability".

2. Whoever is deemed under sub-section (1) to have enforced a disability arising out of "untouchability" shall be punishable with imprisonment for a term which shall be not less than three months and not more than six months and also with fine which shall be not less than one hundred rupees and not more than five hundred rupees.

Explanation. For the purposes of the section "compulsion" includes a threat of social or economic boycott.

8. Cancellation or suspension of licences in certain cases. When a person who is convicted of an offence under Section 6, holds any licence under any law for the time being in force in respect of any profession, trade, calling or employment in relation to which the offence is committed to court trying the offence may, without prejudice to any other penalty to which such person may be liable under that section, direct that the licence shall stand cancelled or to be suspended for such period, as the Court may deem fit, and every order of the Court to cancelling or suspending a licence shall have effect as if it had been passed by the authority competent to cancel or suspend the licence under any such law.

Explanation. In this section, "licence" includes a permit or permission.

9. Resumption or suspension of grants made by Government. Where the manager or trustee of a place of public worship or any educational institution or hostel which is in respect of a grant of land or money from the Government is convicted of an offence under this Act and such conviction is not reversed or quashed in any appeal or revision, the Government may, if in its opinion the circumstances of the case warrant such a course, direct the suspension or resumption of the whole or any part of such grant.

10. Abatement of offence. Whoever abets any offence under this Act shall be punishable with the punishment provided for the offence.

Explanation. A public servant who willfully neglects the investigation of any offence punishable under this Act shall be deemed to have abetted an offence punishable under this Act.

10.A. Power to State Government to impose collective fine. 1. If after an inquiry in the prescribed manner the State Government is satisfied that the inhabitants of an area are concerned in, or abetting the commission of, any offence punishable under this Act, or labouring persons concerned in the commission of such offence or failing to render all the assistance in their power to discover or apprehend the offender or offenders or suppressing material evidence of the commission of such offence, the State Government may, by notification in the Official Gazette, impose a collective fine on such inhabitants and apportion such fine amongst the inhabitants who are able collectively to pay it, and such apportionment shall be made according to the State Government's judgment of the respective means of such inhabitants and in making any such apportionment the Government may assign a portion of such fine to a Hindu undivided family to be payable by it:

Provided that the fine apportioned to an inhabitant shall not be realized until the petition, if any, filed by him under sub-section (3) is disposed of.

2. The notification made under sub-section (1) shall be proclaimed in the area by beat of drum or in such other manner as the State Government may think best in the circumstances to bring the imposition of the collective fine to the notice of the inhabitants of the said area.

3. (a) Any person aggrieved by the imposition of the collective fine under sub-section (1) or by the order of apportionment, may

within the prescribed period file a petition before the State Government or such other authority as that Government may specify in this behalf for being exempted from such fine or for modification of the order of apportionment:

Provided that no fee shall be charged for filing such petition.

(b) The State Government or the authority specified by it shall, after giving to the petitioner a reasonable opportunity of being heard, pass such order as it may think fit:

Provided that the amount of the fine exempted or reduced under this section shall not be realizable from any person, and the total fine imposed on the inhabitants of an area under sub-section (1) shall be deemed to have been reduced to that extent.

4. Notwithstanding anything contained in sub-section (4), the State Government may exempt the victims of any offence punishable under this Act or any person who does not, in its opinion, fall within the category of persons specified in sub-section (1), or any portion thereof.

5. The portion of collective fine payable by any person (including a Hindu undivided family) may be recovered in the manner provided by the Code of Criminal Procedure, 1973 (2 of 1974), for the recovery of fines imposed by a Court as if such portion were a fine imposed by a Magistrate.

11. Enhanced penalty on subsequent conviction. Whoever having already been convicted of an offence under this Act or of an abatement of such offence is again convicted of any such offence or abatement shall, on conviction, be punishable:

(a) for the second offence, with imprisonment for a term of not less than six months and not more than one year, and also with fine which shall be not less than two hundred rupees and not more than five hundred rupees;

(b) for the third offence subsequent to the third offence with imprisonment for a term of not less than one year and not more than two years, and also with fine which shall be not less than five hundred rupees and not more than one thousand rupees.

12. Presumption by Courts in certain cases. Where any act constituting an offence under this Act is committed in relation to a member of a Scheduled Caste [xx], the Court shall presume, unless the contrary is proved, that such Act was committed on the ground of "untouchability".

13. Limitation of Jurisdiction of Civil Courts. 1. No Civil Court shall entertain or continue any suit or proceeding or shall pass any decree or order or executive wholly or partially any decree or order if the claim involved in such suit or proceeding or if the passing of such decree or order or if such execution would, in any way, be contrary to the provisions of this Act.

2. No Court shall, in adjudicating any matter or executing any decree or order, recognize any custom or usage imposing any disability on any person on the ground of "untouchability".

14. Offences by companies. 1. If the person committing an offence under this Act is a company, every person who at the time the offence was committed was in-charge of and was responsible to, the company for the conduct of the business of the company, shall be deemed to be guilty of the offences and shall be liable to be proceeded against and punished accordingly:

Provided that nothing contained in this sub-section shall render any such person liable to any punishment, if he proves that the offence was committed without his knowledge or that he exercised all due diligence to prevent the commission of such offence.

2. Notwithstanding anything contained in sub-section (1) where an offence under this Act has been committed with consent of any director or manager, secretary or other officer of the company such director, manager, secretary or other officer shall also be deemed to be guilty of that offence and shall be liable to be proceeded against and punished accordingly.

Explanation. For the purposes of this section—

(a) "company" means any body corporate and includes a firm or other association of individuals; and

(b) "director" in relation to a firm means a partner in the firm.

14-A. Protection of action taken in good faith. 1. No suit, prosecution or other legal proceeding shall lie against the Central Government or a State Government for anything which in good faith done or intended to be done under this Act.

2. No suit or other legal proceeding shall lie against the Central Government or a State Government for any damage cause or likely to be caused by anything which is in good faith done or intended to be done under this Act.

15. ***Offences to be cognizable and triable summarily.***

1. notwithstanding anything contained in the Code of Criminal Procedure, 1973 (2 of 1974) every offence punishable under this Act shall be cognizable and every such offence except where it is a punishable with imprisonment for a minimum term exceeding three months may be tried summarily by a Judicial Magistrate of the first class or in a Metropolitan area by a Metropolitan Magistrate in accordance with the procedure specified in the said code.

2. Notwithstanding anything contained in the Code of Criminal Procedure, 1973 (2 of 1974) when any public servant is alleged to have committed the offence of abatement of an offence punishable under this Act while acting or purporting to act in the discharge of his official duty, no court shall take cognizance of such offence of abatement except with the previous sanction—

(a) of the Central Government, in the case of a person employed in connection with the affairs of the Union; and

(b) of the State Government, in the case of a person employed in connection with the affairs of a State.

15-A. *Duty of State Government to ensure that the rights accruing from the abolition of "untouchability" may be availed of by the concerned persons:* 1. Subject to such rules as the Central Government may make in this behalf, the State Government shall take such measures as may be necessary for ensuring that the rights from the abolition of "untouchability" or made available to and are availed of by, the persons subjected to any disability arising out of "untouchability".

2. In particular, and without prejudice to the generality of the provisions of sub-section (1) such measures include—

(i) the provision of adequate facilities including legal aid, to the persons subjected to any disability arising out of "untouchability" to enable them to avail themselves of such rights;

(ii) the appointment of officer for initiating exercising supervision over prosecution for the contravention of the provision of this Act;

(iii) the setting up of Special Courts for the trial of offences under this Act;

(iv) the setting up of Committees at such appropriate levels as the State Government may think fit to assist the State

Government in formulating or implementing such measures;

(v) provision for periodic survey of the working of the provisions of this Act with a view to suggesting measures for the better implementation of the provisions of this Act; and

(vi) the identification of the areas where persons are under any disability arising out of "untouchability" and adoption of such disability from such areas.

3. The Central Government shall take such steps as may be necessary to co-ordinate the measures taken by the State Government under sub-Section (1).

4. The Central Government shall, every year, place on the Table of each House of Parliament, report on the measures taken by itself and by the State Governments in pursuance of the provisions of this section.

16. Act to override other laws. Save as otherwise expressly provided in this Act, the provisions of this Act shall have effect notwithstanding anything inconsistent therewith contained in any other law for the time being in force, or any custom or usage or any instrument having effect by virtue of any such law or any decree or order of any Court or other authority.

16-A. Probation of Offenders Act, 1958, not to apply to persons above the age of fourteen years. The provisions of the probation of Offenders Act, 1958, (20 of 1958) shall not apply to any person above the age of fourteen years who is found guilty of having committed any offence punishable under this Act.

16-B. Power to make rules. 1. The Central Government may by notification in the Official Gazette, make rules to carry out the provisions of this Act.

2. Every rule made by the Central Government under this Act shall be laid as soon as may be after it is made, before each House of Parliament while it is in session for a total period of thirty days which may be comprised in one session or in two or more successive sessions, and if, before the expiry of the session immediately following the session or the successive session aforesaid, both Houses agree in making any modification in the rule or both Houses agree that the rule should be made, the rule shall thereafter have effect only in such modified form or to be of no effect, as the case may be, so however, that any such modification

or annulment shall be without prejudice to the validity of anything previously done under that rule.

17. Repeal. The enactments specified in the Schedule are hereby repealed to the extent to which they or any of the provisions contained therein correspond or are repugnant to this Act or to any of the provisions contained therein.

6

The Scheduled Castes and The Scheduled Tribes (Prevention of Atrocities) Act, 1989

(No. 33 of 1989)
(11th September, 1989)

Received the assent of the President on September 11, 1989 and published in the Gazette of India, Extra, Part II, Section 1, Dt. 12th September, 1989, Sl. No. 39.

An act to prevent the commission of offences of atrocities against the members of the Scheduled Castes and the Scheduled Tribes, to provide for Special Courts for the trial of such offences and for the relief and rehabilitation of the victims of such offences and for matters connected therewith or incidental thereto.

Be it enacted by Parliament in the Fortieth Year of the Republic of India as follows:

The Scheduled Castes and the Scheduled Tribes (Prevention of Atrocities) Act, 1989 is an Act to prevent the Commission of offences of atrocities against the member of the Scheduled Castes and the Scheduled Tribes and to provide for special courts for the trial of such offences.

CHAPTER I

PRELIMINARY

1. *Short title, extent and commencement.* 1. This Act may be called the Scheduled Castes and the Scheduled Tribes (Prevention of Atrocities) Act, 1989.

2. It extends to the whole of India except the State of Jammu and Kashmir.

It shall come into force on such date as the Central Government may by notification in the Official Gazette, appoint.

2. *Definitions.* 1. In this Act unless the context otherwise requires—

(a) "Atrocity" means an offence punishable under Section 3;
(b) "Code" means the Code of Criminal Procedure 1973 (2 of 1974);
(c) "Scheduled Castes and Scheduled Tribes" shall have the meanings assigned to them respectively under Clause (24) and Clause (25) of Article 366 of the Constitution;
(d) "Special Court" means a Court of Session specified as a Special Court in Section 14;
(e) "Special Public Prosecutor" means a Public Prosecutor specified as Special Public Prosecutor or an advocate referred to in Section 15;
(f) Words and expressions used but not defined in this Act, and defined in the Code or the Indian Penal Code (45 of 1860) shall have the meanings assigned to them respectively in the Code, or as the case may be, in the Indian Penal Code.

2. Any reference in this Act to any enactment or any provision thereof shall, in relation to an area in which such enactment or such provision is not in force, be construed as a reference to the corresponding law, if any, in force in that area.

CHAPTER II

OFFENCES OF ATROCITIES

3. ***Punishment for offences of atrocities.*** 1. Whoever, not being a member of a Scheduled Caste or a Scheduled Tribe

(i) forces a member of a Scheduled Caste or a Scheduled Tribe to drink or eat any inedible or obnoxious substance;
(ii) acts with intent to cause injury, insult or annoyance to any member of a Scheduled Caste or a Scheduled Tribe by dumping excreta, waste matter, carcasses or any other obnoxious substance in his premises or neighbourhood;
(iii) forcibly removes clothes from the person of a member of a Scheduled Caste or a Scheduled Tribe or parades him naked or with painted face or body or commits any similar act which is derogatory to Human Dignity;
(iv) wrongfully occupies or cultivates any land owned by, or allotted to, or notified by any competent authority to be allotted to, a member of a Scheduled Caste or

Scheduled Tribe or gets the land allotted to him transferred;

(v) wrongfully dispossesses a member of a Scheduled Caste or a Scheduled Tribe from his land or premises or interferes with the enjoyment of his rights any land, premises or water;

(vi) compels or entices a member of a Scheduled Caste or Scheduled Tribe to do 'begging' or other similar forms of forced or bonded labour other than any, compulsory service for public purpose imposed by Government;

(vii) forces or intimidates a member of a Scheduled Caste or a Scheduled Tribe not to vote or to vote to a particular candidate or to vote in a manner other than that provided by law;

(viii) institutes false, malicious or vexatious suit or criminal or other legal proceedings against a member of a Scheduled Caste or a Scheduled Tribe;

(ix) gives any false or frivolous information to any public servant and thereby causes such public servant to use his lawful power to the injury or annoyance of a member of a Scheduled Caste or a Scheduled Tribe;

(x) internationally insults or intimidates with extent to humiliate a member of a Scheduled Caste or a Scheduled Tribe in any place within public view;

(xi) assaults or uses force to any woman belonging to a Scheduled Caste or a Scheduled Tribe with intent to dishonour or outrage her modesty;

(xii) being in a position to dominate the will of a woman belonging to Scheduled Caste or a Scheduled Tribe and uses that position to exploit her sexually to which she would not have otherwise agreed;

(xiii) corrupts or fouls the water of any spring reservoir or any other source ordinarily used by members of the Scheduled Castes or the Scheduled Tribes so as to render it less fit for the purpose for which it is ordinarily used;

(xiv) denies a member of a Scheduled Caste or a Scheduled Tribe any customary right to passage to place of public resort or obstructs such member so as to prevent him from using or having access to a place of public resort to which other members of public or any section thereof have a right to use or access to;

(xv) forces or causes a member cf a Scheduled Caste of Scheduled Tribe to leave his house, village, or other place or residence;

shall be punishable with imprisonment for a term which shall not be less that six months but which may extend to five years and with fine.

2 Whoever, not being a member of a Scheduled Caste or a Scheduled Tribe:

(i) gives or fabricates false evidence intending thereby to cause, or knowing it to be likely that he will thereby causes any member of a Scheduled Caste or a Scheduled Tribe to be convicted of an offence which is capital by the law for the time being in force shall be punished with imprisonment for life and with fine and if an innocent member of a Scheduled Caste or a Scheduled Tribe be convicted and executed in consequence of such false or fabricated evidence the person who gives or fabricates such false evidence shall be punished with death.

(ii) gives fabricated false evidence intending thereby to cause, or knowing it to be likely that he will thereby cause, any member of a Scheduled Caste or a Scheduled Tribe to be convicted of an offence which is not capital but punishable with imprisonment for a term of seven years or upwards, shall be punishable with imprisonment for a term which shall not be less than six months but which may extend to seven years or upwards and with fine;

(iii) commits mischief by fire or any explosive substance intending to cause or knowing it to be likely that he will thereby cause damage to any property belonging to a member of a Scheduled Castes or a Scheduled Tribes, shall be punishable with imprisonment for a term which shall not be less than six months but which may extend to seven years and with fine;

(iv) commits mischief by fire or any explosive substance intending to cause or knowing it to be likely that he will thereby cause destruction of any building which is ordinarily used as a place of worship or as a place for human dwelling or as a place for custody of the property by a member of a Scheduled Caste or a Scheduled Tribe, shall be punishable with imprisonment for life and with fine;

(v) Commits any offence under the Indian Penal Code (45 of 1860) punishable with imprisonment for a term of 10 years or more against a person or property on the ground that such person is a member of a Scheduled Caste or a Scheduled Tribe, or such propert belongs to such member, shall be punishable with imprisonment for life and with fine;

(vi) Knowingly or having reason to believe that an offence has been committed under this Chapter, causes any evidence of the commission of that offence to disappear with the intention of screening the offender from legal punishment, or with the intention gives any information respecting the offence which he knows or believes to be false, shall be punishable with the punishment provided for that offence; or

(vii) being a public servant, commits any offence under this section shall be punishable with imprisonment for a term which shall not be less than one year but which may extend to the punishment provided for their offence.

4. ***Punishment for neglect of duties.*** Whoever, being public servant but not being a member of a Scheduled Caste or a Scheduled Tribe, willfully neglects his duties required to be performed by him under this Act, shall be punishable with imprisonment for a term which shall not be less than six months but which may extend to one year.

5. ***Enhanced punishment for subsequent conviction.*** Whoever, having already been convicted of an offence under this Chapter is convicted for the second offence or any offence subsequent to the second offence, shall be punishable with imprisonment for a term which shall not be less than one year which may extend to the punishment provided for that offence.

6. ***Application of certain provisions of the Indian Penal Code.*** Subject to the other provisions of this Act, the provisions of Sec. 34, Chapter III, Chapter IV, Chapter V, Chapter V-A, Section 149

and Chapter XXIII of the Indian Penal Code (45 of 1860), shall, so far as may be, apply for the purposes of this Act as they apply for the purposes of the Indian Penal Code.

7. Forfeiture of property of certain persons. 1. Where a person has been convicted any offence punishable under this Chapter, the Special Court may, in addition to awarding any punishment, by order in writing, declare that any property, movable or immovable or both belonging to the person, which has been sued for the commission of that offence, shall stand forfeited to Government.

2. Where any person is accused of any offence under this Chapter, it shall be open to the Special Court trying him to pass an order that all or any of the period of such trial, be attached, and where such trial ends in conviction, the property so attached shall be liable to forfeiture to the extent it is required for the purpose of realization of any fine imposed under this Chapter.

8. Presumption as to Offences. In a prosecution for an offence under this Chapter, if it is proved that—

(a) the accused rendered any financial assistance to a person accused of, or reasonably suspected of committing an offence under this Chapter, the special Court shall presume, unless the contrary proved, that such person had abetted the offence;

(b) a group of persons committed an offence under this Chapter and if it is proved that the offence committed was a sequel to any existing dispute regarding land or any other matter, it shall be presumed that the offence was committed in furtherance of the common intention or in prosecution of the common object.

9. Conferment of powers. 1. Notwithstanding anything contained in the Code or in any other provision of this Act, the State Government may, if it considers it necessary or expedient so to do—

(a) for the prevention of and for copying with any offence under this Act, or

(b) for any case or class or group of cases this Act, on any district or part thereof, confer by notification in the Official Gazette, on any district or part thereof, as the case may be, for such case or class or group of cases, and in particular, the powers of arrest, investigation and prosecution of persons before any Special Court.

2. All officers of police and all other officers of Government shall assist the officer referred to in sub-section (1) in the execution of the provisions of this Act or any rule, scheme or order made hereunder.

3. The provisions of the Code shall, so far as may be apply to the exercise of the powers by an officer under sub-section (1).

CHAPTER III
EXTERNMENT

10. Removal of person likely to commit offence. 1. Where the Special Court is satisfied, upon a complaint or a police report that a person is likely to commit an offence under Chapter II of this Act in any area included in 'Scheduled Area' or 'tribal areas', as referred to in Article 244 of the Constitution, it may by order in writing, direct such person to remove himself beyond the limits of such area, by such route and within such time as may be specified in the order, and not to return to that area from which he was directed to remove himself for such period, not exceeding two years, as may be specified in the order;

2. The Special Court shall, along with the order under sub-section (1), communicate to the persons directed under that sub-section the grounds on which such order has been made.

3. The Special Court may revoke or modify the order made under sub-section (1) for the reasons to be recorded in writing, on the representation made by the person against whom such order has been made or by any other person on his behalf within thirty days from the date of the order.

11. Procedure and failure of person to remove himself from area and enter thereon after removal. 1. If a person to whom direction has been issued under Section 10 to remove himself from any area—

(a) fails to remove himself as directed; or

(b) having so removed himself enters such area within the period specified in the order.

Otherwise than with the permission in writing of the Special Court under sub-section (2) the Special Court may cause him to be arrested and removed in police custody to such place outside such area as the Special Court may specify.

2. The Special Court may, by order in writing, permit any

person in respect of whom an order under Section 10 has been made, to return to the area from which he was directed to remove himself for such temporary period and subject to such conditions as may be specified in such order and may require him to execute a bond with or without surety for the due observation of the conditions imposed.

3. The Special Court may at any time revoke any such permission.

4. Any person who, with such permission returns to the area from which he was directed to remove himself shall observe the conditions imposed and at the expiry of the temporary period for which he was permitted to return or on the revocation of such permission before the expiry of such temporary period, shall remove himself outside such area and shall not return thereto within the unexpired portion specified under Section 10 without a fresh permission.

5. If a person fails to observe any of the conditions imposed or to remove himself accordingly having so removed himself enters or returns to such area without fresh permission the Special Court may cause him to be arrested and removed in police custody to such place outside area as the Special Court may specify.

12. Taking measurements and photographs, etc. of persons against whom order under Section 10 is made. 1. Every person against whom an order has been made under Section 10 shall, if so required by the Special Court, allow, his measurement and photographs to be taken by a police officer.

2. If any person referred to in sub-section (1), when required to his measurements or photographs to be taken resists or refuses to allow his taking of such measurements or photographs, it shall be lawful to use all necessary means to secure the taking thereof.

3. Resistance to or refusal to allow the taking of measurements or photographs under sub-section (2) shall be deemed to an offence under Section 186 of the Indian Penal Code (45 of 1860).

4. Where an order under Section 10 is revoked, all measurements and photographs (including negatives) taken under sub-section (2) shall be destroyed or made over to the person against whom such order is made.

13. Penalty for non-compliance with order under Section 10. Any person contravening an order of the Special Court made under

Section 10 shall be punishable with imprisonment for a term which may extend to one year and with fine.

CHAPTER IV

SPECIAL COURTS

14. Special Court. For the purpose of providing for speedy trial, the State Government shall, with the concurrence of the Chief Justice of the High Court, by notification in the Official Gazette, specify for each district a Court of Session to be a Special Court to try the offences under this Act.

15. Special Public Prosecutor. For every Special Court, the State Government shall, by notification in the Official Gazette, specify a Public Prosecutor or appoint an advocate who has been in practice as an advocate for not less than seven years, as a Special Public Prosecutor for the purpose of conducting cases in that Court.

CHAPTER V

MISCELLANEOUS

16. Power of State Government to impose collective fine. The provision of Section 10-A of the Protection of Civil Rights, Act, `1955 (22 of 1955) shall so far as may, apply for the purpose of imposition and realization of collective fine and for all other matters connected therewith under this Act.

17. Preventive action to be taken by the law and order machinery. 1. A District Magistrate or a Sub-Divisional Magistrate or any other Executive Magistrate or any Police Officer not below the rank of a Deputy Superintendent of Police may on receiving information and after such inquiry as he may think necessary has reason to believe that a person or a group of persons not belonging to the Scheduled Castes or the Scheduled Tribes, residing in or frequenting any place within the local limits of his jurisdiction is likely to commit an offence or has threatened to commit any offence under this Act and is of the opinion that there are sufficient grounds for proceeding declare such an area to be an area prone to atrocities and take necessary action for keeping the peace and good behaviour and maintenance of public order and tranquility and may take preventive action.

2. The provisions of Chapter VII, X and XI of the Code shall, so far as may be apply for the purposes of sub-section (1).

3. The State Government may, by notification, in the Official Gazette, make one or more schemes specifying the manner in which the officers referred to sub-section (1) shall take appropriate action specified in such scheme or schemes to prevent atrocities and to restore the feeling of security amongst the members of the Scheduled Castes and the Scheduled Tribes.

18. Section 438 of the Code not to apply to person committing an offence under the Act. Nothing in Section 438 of the Code shall apply in relation to any case involving the arrest of any person on an accusation of having committed an offence under this Act.

19. Section 360 of the Code or the provision of the Probation of Offenders Act not apply to persons guilty of an offence under the Act. The provisions of Section 360 of the Code and the provisions of the Probation of Offenders Act, 1958 (20 of 1958) shall apply to any person above the age of eighteen years who is found guilty having committed an offence under this Act.

20. Act to override other laws. Save as otherwise provided in this Act, the provisions of this Act shall have effect notwithstanding anything inconsistent therein contained in any other law for the time being in force or any custom or usage or any instrument having effect by virtue of any such law.

21. Duty of Government to ensure effective implementation of the Act. 1. Subject to such rules as the Central Government may make in this behalf, the State Government shall take such measures as may be necessary for the effective implementation of this Act.

2. In particular, and without prejudice to the generally of the foregoing provisions, such measures may include—

(i) the provision for adequate facilities, including legal aid, to the persons subjected to atrocities to enable them to avail themselves of justice;

(ii) the provisions for travelling and maintenance expenses to witness, including the victims of atrocities, during investigation and trial of offences under this Act;

(iii) the provision for the economic and social rehabilitation or the victims of the atrocities;

(iv) the appointment of officers of initiating or exercising supervision over prosecution for the contravention of the provisions of this Act;

(v) the setting up of committees at such appropriate levels as the State Government may think fit to assist that

Government in formulation or implementation of such measures;

(vi) provision for a periodic survey of the working of the provisions this Act with a view to suggesting measures for the better implementation of the provisions of this Act;

(vii) the identification of the areas where the members of the Scheduled Castes and the Scheduled Tribes are likely to be subjected to atrocities and adoption of such measures so as to ensure safety for such members.

3. The Central Government shall take such steps as may be necessary to co-ordinate the measures taken by the State Government under sub-section (1)

4. The Central Government shall, every year, place on the table of each House of Parliament a report on the measures taken by itself and by the State Governments in pursuance of the provisions of this section.

22. ***Protection of action taken in good faith.*** No suit, prosecution of other legal proceedings shall lie against the Central Government or against the State Government or any officer or authority of Government or any other person for anything which is in good faith done or intended to be done under this Act.

23. ***Power to make rules.*** 1. The Central Government may, by notification in the Official Gazette, make rules for carrying out the purposes of this Act.

2. Every rule made under this Act shall be laid, as soon as may be after it is made, before each House of Parliament, while it is in session for a total period of thirty days which may be comprised in one session or in two or more successive sessions and if, before the expiry of the session immediately following the session of successive sessions aforesaid, both Houses agree in making any modification in the rule or both Houses agree that the rule should not be made, the rule shall thereafter have effect only in such modified form or be of no effect, as the case may be; so however, that any such modification or annulment shall be without prejudice to be validity of any thing previously done under that rule.

SCHEDULED CASTES AND THE SCHEDULED TRIBES (PREVENTION OF ATROCITIES) RULES, 1995

Ministry of Welfare, G.S.R. No. 316 (E), New Delhi, the 31st March 1995

Notification. In exercise of the power conferred by sub-section (1) of Section 23 of the Scheduled Castes and the Scheduled Tribes (Prevention of Atrocities) Act, 1989 (33 of 1989), the Central Government hereby makes the following rules, namely—

1. Short title and commencement. 1. These rules may be called the Scheduled Castes and the Scheduled Tribes (Prevention of Atrocities) Rules, 1995.

2. They shall come into force on the date of their publication in the Official Gazette.

2. *Definitions.* In these rules unless the context otherwise requires—

(a) Act means the Scheduled Castes and the Scheduled Tribes (Prevention of Atrocities) Act, 1989 (33 of 1989).

(b) dependent with its grammatical variations and cognate expressions, includes wife, children, whether married or unmarried, dependent parents, widowed sister, widow and children of pre-deceased son of a victim of atrocity;

(c) 'identified area' means such area where State Government has reason to believe that atrocity may take place or there is an apprehension of reoccurrence of an offence under the Act or an area prone to victim of atrocity;

(d) 'Non-Government Organisation' means a voluntary organisation engaged in the welfare activities relating to the Scheduled Castes and the Scheduled Tribes and registered under the Societies Registration Act, 1860 (2 of 1860) or under any law for the registration of documents or such organisation for the time being in force;

(e) 'Schedule' means the Schedule annexed to these rules;

(f) 'Section' means section of the Act.

(g) 'State Government' in relation to a Union Territory means the Administrator of that Union Territory appointed by the President under Article 239 of the Constitution;

(h) words and expressions used herein and not defined but in the Act shall have the meanings respectively assigned to them in the Act.

3. ***Precautionary and Preventive Measures.*** 1. With a view to prevent atrocities on the Scheduled Castes and the Scheduled Tribes, the State Government shall

(i) identify the area where it has reason to believe that atrocity may take place or there is an apprehension of reoccurrence of an offence under the Act;

(ii) order the District Magistrate and Superintendent of Police or any other officer to visit the identified area and review the law and order situation;

(iii) if deem necessary, in the identified area cancel the arms licences of the persons, not being member of the Scheduled Castes and Scheduled Tribes, their near relations, servants or employees and family friends and get such arms deposited in the Government Armory;

(iv) seize all illegal fire arms and prohibit any illegal manufacture of fire arms;

(v) with a view to ensure the safety of person and property, if deem necessary, provide arms licences to the members of the Scheduled Castes and the Scheduled Tribes;

(vi) Constitute a high power State-level committee, district and divisional level committees or such number of other committees as deem proper and necessary for assisting the Government in implementation of the provisions of the Act;

(vii) set-up a vigilance and monitoring committee to suggest effective measures to implement the provisions of the Act;

(viii) set-up Awareness Centres and organize workshops in the identified area or at some other place to educate the persons belonging to the Scheduled Castes and the Scheduled Tribes about their rights and the protection available to them under the provisions of various Central and State enactments or rules, regulations and schemes framed thereunder;

(ix) encourage Non-Government Organizations for establishing and maintaining Awareness Centres and organizing workshops and provide them necessary financial and other sort of assistance;

(x) deploy special police force in the identified area;

(xi) by the end of every quarter, review the law and order situation, functioning of different committees, performance of Special Public Prosecutors, Investigating Officers and other Officers responsible for implementing the provisions of the Act and the cases registered under the Act.

4. ***Supervision of prosecution and Submission of Report.*** 1. The State Government on the recommendation of the District Magistrate shall prepare for each District a panel of such number of eminent senior advocates who have been in practice for not less than seven years, as it may deem necessary for conducting cases in the Special Courts, Similarly, in consultation with the Director of Prosecution, officer-in-charge of the prosecution, a panel of such number of Public Prosecutors as it may deem necessary for conducting cases in the Special Courts, shall also be specified. Both these panels shall be notified in the Official Gazette of the State and shall remain in force for a period of three years.

2. The District Magistrate and the Director of prosecution, officer-in-charge of the prosecution shall review at least twice in a calender year, in the month of January and July the performance of Special Public prosecutors so specified or appointed and submit a report to the State Government.

3. If the State Government is satisfied or has reason to believe that a Special Public Prosecutor so appointed or specified has not conducted the case to the best of his ability and with due care and caution, his name may be, for reasons to be recorded in writing denotified.

4. The District Magistrate and the officer-in-charge of the prosecution at the District level, shall review the position of cases registered under the Act and submit a monthly report on or before 20th day of each subsequent month to the Director of Prosecution and the State Government. This report shall specify the actions taken—proposed to be taken in respect of investigation and prosecution of each case.

5. Notwithstanding anything contained in sub-rule (1) the District Magistrate or the Sub-Divisional Magistrate may, if deem necessary or if so desired by the victims of atrocity engage an eminent Senior Advocate for conducting cases in the Special Courts on such payment of fees as he may consider appropriate.

6. Payment of fee to the Special Public Prosecutor shall be fixed by the State Government on a scale higher than the other panel advocates in the State.

5. ***Information to Police Officer-in-charge of a Police Station.***

1. Every Information relating to the commission of an offence under the Act, or given orally to an officer-in-charge or a police station shall be reduced to writing by him or under his direction, and be read over to the informant, and every such information, whether given in writing or reduced to writing as aforesaid, shall be signed by the persons giving it, and the substance thereof shall be entered in a book to be maintained by that police station.

2. A copy of the information as so recorded under sub-rule (1) above shall be given forthwith, fee of cost, to the informant.

3. Any person aggrieved by a refusal on the part of an officer-in-charge of a police station to record the information referred to in sub-rule (1) may send the substance of such information, in writing and by post, to the Superintendent of Police concerned who after investigation either by himself or by a police officer not below the rank of Deputy Superintendent of Police, shall make an order in writing to the officer-in-charge of the concerned police station to enter the substance of that information in the book to be maintained by that police station.

6. Spot inspection by officers. 1. Whenever the District Magistrate or the Sub-Divisional Magistrate or any other executive Magistrate or any police officer not below the rank of Deputy Superintendent of Police receives an information from any person or upon his own knowledge that an atrocity has been committed on the members of the Scheduled Castes or the Scheduled Tribes within his jurisdiction he shall immediately himself visit the place of occurrence to assess the extent of atrocity, loss of life, loss and damage to the property and submit a report forthwith to the State Government.

2. The District Magistrate or to Sub-Divisional Magistrate or any other executive Magistrate and the Superintendent of Police, Deputy Superintendent of Police after inspecting the place or area shall on the spot—

(i) draw a list of victims, their family members and dependents settled for relief;
(ii) prepare a detailed report of the extent of atrocity, loss and damage to the property of the victims;
(iii) order for intensive police patrolling in the area;
(iv) take effective and necessary steps to provide protection to the witness and other sympathizers of the victims; and
(v) provide immediate relief to the victims.

7. *Investigating Officer.* 1. An offence committed under the Act shall be investigated by a police officer not below the rank of a Deputy Superintendent of Police. The investigating officer shall be appointed by the State Government, Director General of Police, Superintendent of Police after taking into account his past experience, sense of ability and justice to perceive the implication of the case and investigate it being with right lines within the shortest possible time.

2. The investigating officer so appointed under sub-rule (1) shall complete the investigation on top priority within thirty days and submit the report to the Superintendent of Police who in turn will immediately forward the report to the Director General of Police or the State Government.

3. The Home Secretary and the Social Welfare Secretary to the State Government, Director of Prosecution, the officer-in-charge of Prosecution and the Director General of Police shall review by the end of every quarter the condition of all investigation done by the investigating officer.

8. *Setting up of the Scheduled Castes and the Scheduled Tribes Protection Cell.* 1. The State Government shall set up a Scheduled Castes and the Scheduled Tribes Protection Cell at the State headquarters under the charge of Director of Police, Inspector General of Police. These cell shall be responsible for.

(i) conducting survey of the identified area;

(ii) maintaining public order and tranquillity in the identified area;

(iii) recommending to the State Government for deployment of special police force or establishment of special police post in the identified area;

(iv) making investigations about the probable causes leading to an offence under the Act;

(v) restoring the feeling of security amongst the members of the Scheduled Castes and the Scheduled Tribes;

(vi) informing the nodal officer and special officer about the law and order situation in the identified area;

(vii) making inquiries about the investigation and spot inspections conducted by various officers.

(viii) making inquiries about the action taken by the Superintendent of Police in the cases where an officer-in-charge of the police station has refused enter an information in a book to be maintained by that police station under sub-rule (3) of Rule 5;

(ix) making inquiries about the willful negligence by a public servant;

(x) reviewing the position of cases registered under the Act; and

(xi) submitting a monthly report on or before 20th day of each subsequent month to the State Government nodal officer about the action taken, proposed to be taken in respect of the above.

9. Notification of Nodal Officer. The State Government shall nominate a nodal officer of the level of a Secretary to the Government preferably belonging to the Scheduled Castes or Scheduled Tribes, for coordinating the functioning of the District Magistrates and Superintendent of Police or other officers authorized by them as investigating officer and other officers responsible for implementing the provisions of the Act. By the end of the every quarter, the nodal officer shall review:

(i) the reports received by the State Government under sub-rules (2) and (4) of Rule 4, Rule 6, Clause (xi) of rule 8;

(ii) the position of cases registered under the act;

(iii) law and order situation in the identified area;

(iv) various kinds of measures adopted for providing immediate relief in cash or kind or both to the victims of atrocity on his or her dependent;

(v) adequacy of immediate facilities like rationing, clothing, shelter, legal and travelling allowance, daily allowance and transport facilities provided to the victim of atrocity on his or her dependents;

(vi) performance of non-Governmental organizations, the Scheduled Castes and the Scheduled Tribes Protection Cell, various committees and the public servants responsible for implementing the provisions of the Act.

10. Appointment of a Special Officer. In the identified area a Special Officer not below the rank of an Additional District Magistrate shall be appointed to co-ordinate with the District Magistrate, Superintendent of Police or other officers responsible for implementing the provisions of the Act under various committees and the Scheduled Castes and the Scheduled Tribes

Protection Cell.

The Special Officer shall be responsible for:

(i) providing immediate relief and other facilities to the victims of atrocity and initiate necessary measures to prevent or avoid re-occurrence of atrocity;

(ii) setting up an awareness centre and organizing workshop in the identified area or at the district headquarters to educate the persons belonging to the Scheduled Castes and the Scheduled Tribes about their rights and the protection available to them under the provisions of various Central and State enactments or rules and schemes, etc. framed therein; and

(iii) coordinating with the Non-Government Organizations and providing necessary facilities and financial and other type of assistance to Non-Government Organisation for maintaining centres or organizing workshops.

11. ***Travelling Allowance, Daily Allowance, Maintenance Expenses and Transport Facility to the Victim of Atrocity, his or her Dependents and Witnesses.*** 1. Every victim of atrocity on his/her dependents and witnesses shall be paid to and from fare by second class in express/mail/passenger train or actual bus or taxi fare from his/her place of residence or actual bus or taxi fare from his/her place of residence or place of stay to the place of investigation or hearing of trial of an offence under the Act.

2. The District Magistrate or the Sub-Divisional Magistrate or any other Executive Magistrate shall make necessary arrangements for providing transport facilities or reimbursement of full payment thereof to the victims of atrocity and witnesses for visiting the investigating officer, Superintendent of Police/Deputy Superintendent of Police, District Magistrate or any other Executive Magistrate.

3. Every woman witness the victim of atrocity or her dependent being a woman or a minor, a person more than sixty years of age and a person having 40 per cent or more disability shall be entitled to be accompanied by an attendant of her/his choice. The attendant shall also be paid travelling and maintenance expenses as applicable to the witness or the victim of atrocity when called upon during hearing investigation and trial of an offence under the Act.

4. The witness, the victim of atrocity or his/her dependent

and the attendant shall be paid daily maintenance expenses for the days he/she is away from the place of his/her residence or stay during investigation hearing and trial of an offence, at such rates but not less than the minimum wages, as may be fixed by the State Government for the agricultural labourers.

5. In addition to daily maintenance expenses the witness, the victim of atrocity (or his/her dependent) and the attendant shall also be paid diet expenses at such rates as may be fixed by the State Government from time to time.

6. The payment of travelling allowance, daily allowance, maintenance expenses and reimbursement of transport facilities shall be made immediately or not later than three days by the District Magistrate or the Sub-Divisional Magistrate or any other Executive Magistrate to the victims, their dependents/attendants and witnesses for the days they visit the investigating officer or in-charge of police station or hospital authorities or Superintendent of Police, Deputy Superintendent of Police or District Magistrate or any other concerned or the Special Court.

7. When an offence has been committed under Section 3 of the Act, the District Magistrate or the Sub-Divisional Magistrate or any other Executive Magistrate shall reimburse the payment of medicines, special medical consultation, blood transfusion, replacement of essential clothing, meals and fruits provided to the victim(s) of atrocity.

12. Measures to be taken by the District Administration. 1. The District magistrate and the Superintendent of Police shall visit the place or area where the atrocity has been committed to assess the loss of life and damage to the property and draw a list of victims, their family members and dependents entitled for relief.

2. Superintendent of Police shall ensure that the First Information Report is registered in the book of the concerned police station and effective measures for apprehending the accused are taken.

3. The Superintendent of Police, after spot inspection, shall immediately approach investigation officer and deploy such police force in the area and take such other preventive measures as he may deem proper and necessary.

4. The District Magistrate or the Sub-Divisional Magistrate or any other Executive Magistrate shall make arrangements for providing immediate relief in cash or in kind or both to the victims of atrocity, their family members and dependents according to the

scale as in the schedule annexed to these Rules (Annexure I read with Annexure II). Such immediate relief shall also include food, water, clothing, shelter, medicine aid, transport facilities and other essential items necessary for human beings.

5. The relief provided to the victim of the atrocity or his/her dependent under sub-rule (4) in respect of death, or injury to, or damage to property shall be in addition to any other right to claim competition in respect thereof under any other law for the time being in force.

6. The relief and rehabilitation facilities mentioned in sub-rule (4) above shall be provided by the District Magistrate or the Sub-Magistrate or the Sub-Divisional Magistrate or any other Executive Magistrate in accordance with the scales provided in the Scheduled annexed to these rules.

7. A report of the relief and rehabilitation facilities provided to the victims shall also be forwarded to the Special Court by the District Magistrate or the Sub-Divisional Magistrate or the Executive Magistrate or Superintendent of Police. In case the Special Court is satisfied that the payment of relief was not made to the victim or his/her dependent in time or the amount of relief of compensation was not sufficient or only a part payment of relief or compensation was made, it may order for making in full or part payment of relief or any other kind of assistance.

13. Selection of Officer and other State Members for Completing the work Relating to Atrocity. 1. The State Government shall ensure that the administrative officers and other staff members to be appointed in an area prone to atrocity shall have the right aptitude and understanding of the problems of the Scheduled Castes and Scheduled Tribes.

2. It shall also be ensured by the State Government that persons from the Scheduled Castes and the Scheduled Tribes are adequately represented in the administration and in the police force at all levels particularly at the level of police posts and police station.

14. Specific Responsibility of the State Government. The State Government shall make necessary provisions in its annual budget for providing relief and rehabilitation facilities to the victims of atrocity. It shall review at least twice in a calendar year, in the month of January and July the performance of the Special Public Prosecutor specified or appointed under Section 15 of the Act, various reports received, investigation made and preventive steps taken by the District Magistrate, Sub-Divisional Magistrate and Superintendent of Police, relief and rehabilitation facilities provided to the victims and the reports in respect of lapses on behalf of the concerned officers.

15. Contingency Plan by the State Government. 1. State Government shall prepare a model contingency plan for implementing the provisions of the Act and notify the same in the Official Gazette of the State Government. It would specify the role and responsibility of various departments and their officers at different levels, the role and responsibility of Rural/Urban Local Bodies and Non-Government organizations. *Inter alia* this plan shall contain a package of relief measures including the following:

(a) scheme to provide immediate relief in cash or in kind or both;
(b) allotment of agricultural land and house-sites;
(c) the rehabilitation packages;
(d) scheme for employment in Government or Government undertaking to the dependent or one of the family members of the victim;
(e) pension scheme for widows, dependent children of the deceased handicapped or old age victims of atrocity;
(f) mandatory compensation for the victims;
(g) scheme for strengthening the socio-economic condition of the victim;
(h) provisions for providing brick/stone masonry house to the victims; and
(i) such other elements as health care, supply of essential commodities, electrification, adequate drinking water facility, burial/cremation ground and link roads to the Scheduled Castes and the Scheduled Tribes rehabilitates.

2. The State Government shall forward a copy of the contingency plan or a summary thereof and a copy of the scheme, as soon as may been to the Central Government in the Ministry of Welfare and to all the District Magistrates, Sub-Divisional Magistrates, Inspector Generals of Police and Superintendents of Police.

16. Constitution of State-Level Vigilance and Monitoring Committee. 1. The State Government shall constitute a high power vigilance and monitoring committee of not more than 25 members consisting of the following:

(i) Chief Minister/Administrator-Chairman (in case of a State under President's Rule Governor—Chairman).
(ii) Home Minister, Finance Minister and Welfare Minister—

Members (in case of a State under the President's Rule Advisors-Members).

(iii) All elected Members of Parliament and State Legislative Assembly and Legislative Council from the State belonging to the Scheduled Castes and the Scheduled Tribes Members.

(iv) Chief Secretary, the Home Secretary, the Director General of Police, Director/Deputy Director of National Commission for the Scheduled Castes and the Scheduled Tribes—Members.

(v) The Secretary, in-charge of the welfare and development of the Scheduled Castes and the Scheduled Tribes—Convenor.

2. The high power vigilance and monitoring committee shall meet at least twice in a calendar year, in the months of January and July to review the implementation of the provisions of the Act, relief and rehabilitation facilities provided to the victims and other matters connected therewith, prosecution of cases under the Act, rule of different officer/agencies responsible for implementing the provisions of the Act and various reports received by the State Government.

17. Constitution of District Level Vigilance and Monitoring Committee. 1. In each district within the State, the District Magistrate shall set up a vigilance and monitoring committee in his district to review the implementation of the provisions of the Act, relief and rehabilitation facilities provided to the victims and other matters connected therewith, prosecution of cases under the Act, role of different officers/agencies responsible for implementing the provisions of the Act and various reports received by the District Administration.

2. The District-level vigilance and monitoring committee shall consist of the elected Members of the Parliament and State Legislative Assembly and Legislative Council, Superintendent of Police, three group 'A' Officers, Gazetted Officers of the State Government belonging to the Scheduled Castes and the Scheduled Tribes not more than one official members belonging to the Scheduled Castes and the Scheduled Tribes and not more than 3 members from the categories other than the Scheduled Castes and the Scheduled Tribes having association with Non-Government Organizations. The District Magistrate and District Social Welfare Officer shall be Chairman and Member-Secretary respectively.

3. The District-level Committee shall meet at least once in

three months.

18. Material for Annual Report. The State Government shall before every 31st March, forward the report to the Central Government about the measures taken for implementing provisions of the Act and various schemes/plans framed by it during the previous calendar year.

RULES OF PROCEDURE OF THE NATIONAL COMMISSION FOR SCHEDULED CASTES AND SCHEDULED TRIBES

CHAPTER I

GENERAL

1. *Constitution of the Commission.* The National Commission for Scheduled Castes and Scheduled Tribes (hereinafter called the Commission) has been constituted under Article 338 of the Constitution of India as amended by the Constitution (Sixty-fifth Amendment) Act, 1990. The Commission shall consist of a Chairperson, a Vice-Chairperson and five other Members.

2. *Headquarters of the Commission.* The Headquarters of the Commission shall be located at New Delhi.

3. *State Offices of the Commission.* The Commission shall have under its control the following State Offices:

	Location	**Jurisdiction**
1.	Agartala	Tripura
2.	Ahmedabad	Gujarat, and UT of Dadra and Nagar Haveli
3.	Bangalore	Karnataka
4.	Bhopal	Madhya Pradesh
5.	Bhuvneshwar	Orrisa
6.	Kolkata	West Bengal, Sikkim and UT Andaman and Nicobar Islands
7.	Chandigarh	Punjab, Haryana, Himachal Predesh, J&K and UT of Chandigarh
8.	Guwahati	Assam, Arunachal Pradesh, Manipur and Nagaland
9.	Hyderabad	Andhra Pradesh
10.	Jaipur	Rajasthan
11.	Lucknow	Uttar Pradesh and Uttaranchal

12. Madras	Tamil Nadu and UT of Pondicherry
13. Patna	Bihar
14. Pune	Maharashtra, Goa, and UT of Daman and Diu
15. Shillong	Meghalaya and Mizoram
16. Thiruvananthapuram	Kerala and UT of Lakshadweep and Minicoy Islands

4. The Commission may, if considered necessary, open new offices and sub-offices and upgrade or downgrade the status and change the jurisdiction of any of its State Offices.

5. The function and responsibilities of the Commission as laid down in the Constitution are:

(a) to investigate and monitor all matters relating to the safeguards provided for the Scheduled Castes and Scheduled Tribes under the Constitution or under any other law for the time being in force or under any order of the Government and to evaluate the working of such safeguards;

(b) to inquire into specific complaints with respect to the deprivation of rights and safeguards of the Scheduled Castes and Scheduled Tribes;

(c) to participate and advise on the planning process of socio-economic development of the Scheduled Castes and Scheduled Tribes and to evaluate the progress of their development under the Union and any State;

(d) to present to the President, annually and at such other times as the Commission may deem fit, reports upon the working of those safeguards;

(e) to make in such reports recommendation as to the measures that should be taken by the union or any State for the effective implementation of those safeguards and other measures for the protection, welfare and socio-economic development of the Scheduled Castes and Scheduled Tribes; and

(f) to discharge such other functions in relation to the protection, welfare and development and advancement of the Scheduled Castes and Scheduled Tribes as the President may, subject to the provisions of any law made by Parliament, by rule specify.

6. The Commission shall function by holding 'sittings' and 'meetings' at any place within the country and also through its officers at the Headquarters and in the State Offices. The Members

of the Commission including the Chairperson and the Vice-Chairperson shall function in accordance with the procedure prescribed under these rules.

CHAPTER II

DIVISION OF RESPONSIBILITIES AND ALLOCATION OF WORK

Chairperson. *7.* The Chairperson shall be the head of the Commission and shall have the residuary powers to decide on all questions and matters arising in the Commission excepting such matters where specific provision has been made in these rules.

8. The Chairperson shall allocate subject and responsibilities among the Members of the Commission. The Order allocating the subjects and responsibilities shall be circulated to all concerned by the Secretariat of the Commission.

9. The Chairperson shall be the authority to sanction leave and approve tours of the Members.

10. The Chairperson shall preside over the meetings of the Commission.

11. All important decisions in the Commission pertaining to the subjects allotted to the Members shall be taken with the approval of the Chairperson.

12. The Chairperson may call for any records on any matter which he considers important any may take a decision on it himself or, if necessary, place it at the meeting of the Commission.

13. ***Vice-Chairperson.*** The Vice-Chairperson shall preside over the meetings of the Commission in the absence of the Chairperson.

14. The Vice-Chairperson shall perform such functions as are entrusted to him by the Chairperson.

15. ***Members.*** The Members of the Commission shall have collective responsibility and shall function by participating in the 'meetings' and 'sittings' of the Commission and looking after the subjects allocated to them. Important actions and decisions of a Member may be brought at a meeting of the Commission which may review for same.

16. Any Members may suggest items for inclusion in the agenda of a meeting of the Commission and the same shall be so included after obtaining the consent of the Chairperson.

17. Each member shall have overall responsibility of subjects and/or regions or State(s) as may be allocated to him.

18. The Members shall play the role of advising the State Governments under their jurisdiction on matters of planning and development relating to the welfare of Scheduled Castes and Scheduled Tribes. The Commission's Secretariat at Headquarters and the State Offices shall assist the Members in keeping them fully informed of the problems and activities of the States and subjects under their respective charge.

19. One or more Members may, in accordance with the procedure specified in the rules elsewhere, hold sittings of the Commission to give hearing to the cases or to collect evidence or information on any matter, issue or case under investigation or inquiry by the Commission.

20. The Members shall communicate their tour programmes well in advance to the State Offices indicating in detail the purpose of the visit and to the State Government Department and others concerned for discussions/inquiry, etc., during the tour/visit. The Members will observe the norms laid down by the State Governments regarding security/travel/accommodation etc., during such tours.

21. Secretary. The Secretary shall be the administrative head of the Commission and shall assist the Commission in the discharge of its functions with the assistance of the officers of the Commission.

22. All important administrative matters shall be placed before the Secretary who may pass general or specific orders on such matters.

23. The Secretary shall be responsible for having the agenda prepared for the meetings of the Commission and for circulating the minutes.

24. The Secretary shall assist the Commission in finalising the Reports.

25. The Secretary may, in his discretion, delegate any of the functions or authority to a subordinate officer of the Secretariat.

CHAPTER III

INVESTIGATION AND INQUIRY BY THE COMMISSION

26. Methods of investigation and inquiry. The Commission may adopt any one or more of the following methods for investigating or inquiring into the matters falling within its authority:

(a) by the Commission directly;
(b) by an Investigating Team Constituted at the Headquarters of the Commission; and
(c) through its State Offices.

27. Investigation and Inquiry by the Commission directly. The Commission may hold sittings for investigation into matters relating to safeguards, protection, welfare and development of the Scheduled Castes and Scheduled Tribes or for inquiring into specific complaints for which the Commission decides to take up investigation or inquiry directly. Such sittings may be held either at the headquarters of the Commission or at any other place within the country.

28. The sitting(s) of the Commission would be held after giving due notice to the parties intended to be heard and also due publicity notice to the general public. Care will be taken to see that the members of the Scheduled Castes or Scheduled Tribes who are affected in the matter under investigation or inquiry are given due information through notice or publicity.

29. When a decision for direct investigation is taken, an officer not below the rank of Research Officer/Section Officer along with necessary staff may be attached to the Member(s) entrusted with such sittings.

30. During the course of the investigation or inquiry the Commission, acting through such a sitting, may make evidence on oath or receive affidavits. When considered necessary, the Commission, for the purpose of taking evidence in the investigation or inquiry, require the presence of any person and may issue summons to him. The summons shall provide at least fifteen days' notice to the person directed to be present before the Commission from the date of receipt of the summons.

31. Where the property, service/employment of SCs and STs and other related matters are under immediate threat and prompt attention of the Commission is required, the matter shall be taken cognizance by issue of telex/fax to the concerned authority for making it known to them that the Commission is seized of the issue. Urgent reply by telegram or fax shall be called from the concerned authority. In case no letter is received within a week, the authority concerned shall be summoned at a short notice for enquiry.

32. The Commission may issue Commission to take evidence in any matter under investigation or inquiry and for this purpose appoint any person by an order in writing. The Commission may make further rules for payment of fee and travelling and other allowances to persons appointed to take evidence on commission.

33. After holding the required sittings, the Member(s) who conducted the investigation shall make a report which shall be sent to the Secretary or any other officer authorised to receive the report. After examination, action may be initiated on the report with the approval of the Chairperson.

34. Investigation or Inquiry by an Investigation Team Constituted at the Headquarters of the Commission. The Commission may decide about the matter that is to be investigated or enquired into by an Investigating Team of officials of the Commission, provided that in case the matter is urgent, the decision for such investigation or inquiry may be taken by the Chairperson.

35. The Investigating Team shall hold the investigation or inquiry, as the case may be, promptly and for this purpose may initiate necessary correspondence including issuance of notices for production of documents in Form I.

36. The Investigating Team may visit the area concerned after observing due formalities for obtaining approval of tours and other administrative requirements and after giving information to the concerned local authorities regarding the matter, purpose, scope and procedure of the investigation or inquiry. The Investigating Team may enlist the help of the officers and staff of the concerned State Office but the responsibility of preparing and presenting the report shall rest with the head of the Investigating Team.

37. The Investigating Team shall submit the report of the investigation or enquiry, as the case may be, to the Secretary or a subordinate officer of the Commission as may be directed by general or specific orders within the stipulated time, if any. If the time limit stipulated is likely to be exceeded the head of the Investigating Team shall obtain the orders of the Secretary through the Officer-in-Charge of the matter. The report shall be examined and put up to the competent authority for decision regarding the action to be taken on the report.

38. The report shall be placed before the Chairperson of the Commission who will take appropriate action in the matter.

39. Investigation and inquiry through the State Offices. The Chairperson, the Vice-Chairperson, the Members having jurisdiction over the subject or the Secretary of the Commission may decide about an investigation or inquiry that may be carried out through the State Offices of the Commission. The decision will be conveyed to the Officer-in-Charge of the concerned State Office who will be asked to get the matter investigated or inquired into within a stipulated time and send the report. The State Office shall conduct the investigation or inquiry through interrogation, on the spot visit, discussions and correspondence and examination of documents as may be necessary in the case and shall follow any special or general instructions issued in the matter by the Secretariat of the Commission from time to time.

40. If the investigation or inquiry cannot be completed within the stipulated time the Officer-in-Charge of the State Office may send a communication to the Secretariat of the Commission before the expiry of the stipulated time and explain the circumstances and reasons for non-completion of the investigation or inquiry, as the case may be, within the stipulated time. The Secretary to the Commission or an officer acting under delegated functions may consider the request and communicate a revised date for the completion of the investigation or inquiry.

41. If during the course of investigation or inquiry the head of the State Office feels that it is necessary to invoke the powers of the Commission to require the production of any document or compelling the attendance of a person, he may make a special report with full facts to the Secretariat of the Commission. On receipt of such special report the matter shall be placed before the Secretary/ Member-in-Charge of the subject/State/UT who may make an order that necessary legal processes to compel attendance or to require production of any document may be issued. The summons and warrants issued for the purpose may be served on the person concerned either directly or through the Officer-in-Charge of the State Office as may be directed by the Secretary/Member authorising issue of such legal process.

42. After completion of the investigation or inquiry, as the case may be, the head of the State Office shall submit the report to the Secretary of the Commission suggesting the course of action that could be followed in the matter. The gist or findings of the report may be placed before the Secretary who may decide about further action in the matter.

43. Confidentiality of certain reports. The Commission may, through a decision at a meeting or otherwise, direct that the contents of any report made on any matter shall be kept confidential and shall not be revealed to any person other than those who have been authorised access to such report.

44. Legal Processes. All summons and warrants that are required to be issued in pursuance of the exercise of the powers of a Civil Court by the Commission shall be written in the prescribed from the shall bear the seal of the Commission. The legal process shall be issued from the Legal Cell of the Commission and shall bear its seal. The provisions of the Code of Civil Procedure applicable for the service of the legal processes shall be followed by the Commission.

45. Issue of letters and notices. Letters and notices requiring production of documents which are issued without exercising the powers of the Civil Court by the Commission may be signed by an officer not below the rank of Research Officer/Section Officer.

46. Form of summons and warrants. The summons and warrants shall be as provided in Forms II and III respectively, appended to these rules.

CHAPTER IV

MEETINGS OF THE COMMISSION

47. Frequency of meetings. The Commission shall meet at least once in two months. The notice for a meeting shall normally be issued two weeks in advance. Emergent meetings may also be called by the Chairperson either on his own or on the request of a Member or the Secretary for disposing of important matters requiring urgent consideration by the Commission.

48. Quorum. The Chairperson or the vice-Chairperson and two other Members shall form the quorum for holding a meeting of the Commission.

49. Matters requiring decisions by the Commission at its meetings. The following matters shall be brought up before the Commission at a meeting for consideration and decision;

(i) any amendment to these Rules of Procedure;
(ii) matters to be investigated by the Commission directly;
(iii) all the reports that are required to be considered by the Commission as provided in these rules;
(iv) any matters that a Member may like to bring to the meeting, with the approval of the Chairperson;

(v) importing matters relating to planning and development for the welfare and advancement of the Scheduled Castes and Scheduled Tribes and specially references received under Article 338(9) of the Constitution; and

(vi) any matter that the Chairperson may direct to be placed at a meeting of the Commission.

50. ***Agenda for the meeting.*** The agenda will normally be circulated to all the Members at least seven days before the date of the meeting, provided that for an Emergent meeting this time limit may not apply.

51. The minutes of a meeting shall be circulated as soon as possible to all the Members.

52. ***Place of meeting of the Commission.*** Normally the place of meeting of the Commission shall be the Headquarters of the Commission at New Delhi. The Commission may, however, decide to hold a meeting at any other place in India.

53. ***Fee.*** The Chairperson, the Vice-Chairperson and the Members shall not be entitled to any fee for sitting in the meeting of the Commission. However, the entitlement of Part-time Members, if any, may be determined by the terms of appointment of such Members.

CHAPTER V

SITTINGS OF THE COMMISSION

54. ***Need for Sittings.*** Whenever a matter is to be investigated into directly by the Commission it may do so by holding sittings of the Commission. In the case of such sittings the presence of all the Members may not be necessary.

55. ***Officers to be Present.*** Whenever a Member(s) is holding a sitting, an Officer of the Commission, not below the rank of Research Officer/Section Officer, duly deputed for the purpose shall be present to assist the Member(s) holding the sitting to discharge the functions properly and promptly. It shall be the duty of the officer to assist the Member(s) in preparing the report if called upon to do so by the Member(s). The Officer shall also be responsible for assisting the Member(s) in following the prescribed procedure.

56. ***Frequency of Sitting(s).*** Sittings of the Commission may be held as and when necessary. The Commission may hold more than one sitting simultaneously in different parts of the country with different Members functioning separately.

57. Programme of the Sittings. The programme of the sittings, both at the Headquarters and at other places, would normally be worked out each month in advance and duly circulated.

58. Defraying Expenses to Witnesses. The Commission may defray travelling expenses to persons who have been called through summons to appear before the Commission in a sitting, provided that the place of residence of one person is more than 8 kms, from the place of the sittings of the Commission. The amount so defrayed shall be limited to the actual travelling expenses plus Daily Allowance for the number of days that the person has appeared before the Commission in its sitting, provided that the person is not entitled to travelling and daily allowance from any other source, Persons who are employees of the Government/Public Sector Undertaking shall be deemed to be on duty if they are summoned to depose before the Commission or produce documents. The limit of travelling expenses shall be determined on the basis of the rail fare and road mileage calculated on the basis of the rates that may be prescribed by the Commission. In the case of any doubt regarding the entitlement of the person the decision of the Secretary of the Commission shall be final.

59. The officer attached to the Member for the purposes of the sitting shall take steps to ensure that sufficient cash amount is carried if the sitting is held at a place other than the Headquarters of the Commission. The Secretariat of the Commission may devise a suitable procedure to ensure that such claims as above are paid on the spot and in cash to the person(s) so appearing.

60. The claim for travelling expenses as above shall not be admissible in the case of a person who appears before the Commission during any investigation or enquiry on his own accord or in response to a communication or notice which is not a summon issued by the Commission.

CHAPTER VI

DUTIES OF THE STATE OFFICES OF THE COMMISSION

61. It shall be the duty of the State Offices of the Commission:

(i) To act as the "eyes and ears" of the Commission in the State(s) of their jurisdiction.

(ii) To maintain effective interaction and liaison with State Government/UT administrations on behalf of the Commission.

(iii) To serve on State Level Advisory Council/Committees/Corporations, etc. on behalf of the Commission.

(iv) To provide information and documentation about the policies and programmes of the Union Government for the welfare and advancement of SCs and STs to the States, NGOs, Media in their respective jurisdiction. Obtain similar information and documentation from such organisation and provide to the Headquarters of the Commission information/documentation about important development, social movements, policy changes, etc. in the State affecting the interest of SCs and STs.

(v) To monitor and assist the working of voluntary and other non-governmental organisations receiving grant-in-aid from the Ministry of Social Justice and Empowerment as also other Ministries/Departments of the Central Government and the concerned State Governments, Foreign Aid Agencies, etc., for Research Studies and any other development work relating to SCs and STs.

(vi) To conduct Research Studies, Seminars, Conferences, Surveys, etc. either on their own or as entrusted to them by headquarters from time to time.

(vii) To conduct on the spot inquiries into cases of atrocities on SCs and STs either on their own or as entrusted to them by Headquarters and interact with the concerned Administrative/Police authorities having jurisdiction and report to the Headquarters.

(viii) To deal with complaints/representations from individuals, SC/ST Welfare Associations, etc. on various matters.

(ix) To participate and advise in the planning process for socio-economic development of the SCs/STs as envisaged under Clause 5 of Article 338 of the Constitution of India.

(x) To collect, compile, analyse and monitor issues pertaining to development of SCs and STs in the States especially with reference to SCP, TSP and SCA, and prepare drafts of Reports pertaining to the State/UT under their jurisdiction.

(xi) To prepare and maintain a comprehensive and uptodate data base of SC/ST population, education, development, etc. in the State/UT; and

(xii) To perform any other duty specifically assigned/entrusted to the State Office(s) by the Commission or the Secretary or any other officer empowered in this regard.

CHAPTER VII

ADVISORY ROLE OF THE COMMISSION

62. ***Interaction of the Commission with the State Government.*** The Commission shall interact with the State Governments through its Members, Secretariat and the State Offices.

63. The Member in charge of the State/UT would interact with the State Government/UT Administration through meetings, personal contacts, visits and correspondence. The information in this regard may be sent to the concerned Department/Organisations well in advance and the State Offices should also be informed about the same. For this purpose, detailed guidelines may be formulated by the Commission. The Secretariat of the Commission through its concerned Wing(s) would provide necessary assistance and information to the Member for enabling him to discharge his functions effectively. The State Government should provide facilities for transport, security, accommodation etc., to the Member as per his entitlement.

64. ***Interaction with the Planning Commission.*** The Commission shall interact with the Planning Commission at appropriate levels through representation in the various Committees, Working Groups or other such bodies set up by the Planning Commission. The Commission shall indicate this requirement through general or specific communication to the Planning Commission.

65. The Commission may request the Planning Commission to forward copies of all the documents concerning the process of planning and development and evaluation of all programmes and schemes touching upon the Scheduled Castes and Scheduled Tribes.

66. The Commission may decide about the manner of interaction between the Chairperson/Members of the Commission and the Deputy Chairman/Members of the Planning Commission.

67. Interaction of the State Office with the State Government. The State Offices of the Commission shall work in a manner so as to provide a regular and effective link between the State

Governments concerned and the Commission. For this purpose the Commission may send communication to the State Government suggesting that the officers-in-charge of the State Offices of the Commission may be taken on important Planning, Evaluation and Advisory Bodies including Corporations concerned with the welfare protection and development of the Scheduled Castes and Scheduled Tribes.

68. The officer-in-charge of the State Offices may be directed or authorised by the Commission to convey to any State Authority the formal view, opinion or approach of the Commission on any specific or general matter or issue arising at any meeting or deliberation.

69. Research/Studies/Surveys/Evaluation. The Commission may undertake studies to evaluate the impact of the development schemes on the socio-economic development of the Scheduled Castes and Scheduled Tribes taken up by the Union or State Governments. For this purpose the Commission may constitute Study Teams either at the Headquarters or at the State Offices. The Study Teams may undertake investigations, survey or studies either in collaboration with the Central or State Government authorities or Universities or Research Bodies, as the case may be, or may do so independently.

70. The Commission may entrust surveys or evaluation studies to any professional body or person considered suitable and competent to undertake such work and for this purpose may make any reasonable payment to such body or person towards the cost of the study by way of fee or grant.

71. The studies so undertaken or their gists may form part of the Annual or Special Report of the Commission to be presented to the President or may be published separately by the Commission.

72. The Commission may forward a copy of such a study report to the Union or the State Government concerned, as the case may be, asking for their comments, if any. The comments or action taken reports by the Union/State Government may also form part of the Annual Report of the Commission.

CHAPTER VIII

MONITORING FUNCTIONS OF THE COMMISSION

73. The Commission to Determine Subjects for Monitoring. The Commission may determine from time to time the subjects or matters and areas that it would monitor relating to safeguards and other socio-economic development measures provided for the Scheduled Castes and Scheduled Tribes under the Constitution or under any other law for the time being in force or under any order of the Government.

74. Prescribing Returns and Reports. The Commission may prescribe periodical returns or reports to be furnished by any authority responsible for or having control of the subject-matter of which monitoring is being done by the Commission.

75. The Commission may from time to time issue instructions to its State Offices to collect information and data on any particular subject or matter from the State Governments. Local Bodies, Corporate Bodies or any other authorities which is charged with the implementation of the safeguards provided for the Scheduled Castes and Scheduled Tribes.

76. The Commission may direct its State Offices to process the information or data in the State Offices with a view to arriving at conclusion with regard to the deficiencies or shortcoming discovered through such processing or analysis of the data and to bring these to the notice of the concerned authority for comments and rectification, where necessary.

77. The Commission may have data, relating to the subject monitored collected to the headquarters and may prescribe returns and reports for the purpose to be sent directly to its Headquarters by the Ministries/Departments of the Central Government or a State Government or Public Sector Undertaking or any other body or authority which is charged with the responsibility of implementing safeguards relating to the Scheduled Castes and Scheduled Tribes.

78. Follow-up Action. In order to ensure that monitoring is done effectively the Commission, after getting the information as prescribed in the above rules and after reaching conclusions, may as earıy as possible send out communication to the concerned authority describing the shortcomings that have been noticed in the implementation of the safeguards and suggesting corrective steps. Decisions on sending out such a communication may be taken at a level not lower than that of Joint Secretary/Secretary at Headquarters. Directors-in-Charge of State Offices may take decisions on routine matter whereas they will seek approval of the Secretary and the concerned Member on complex and important matters effecting the interest of SCs and STs, as a group.

79. The Commission may ask for the comments of the concerned authority on the action taken in pursuance of the communication sent under the provisions of Rule 78.

80. The Commission may include in its Annual Report or any Special Report findings and conclusions arrived at through the process of monitoring of the subjects relating to the safeguards and socio-economic development measures provided for the Scheduled Castes and Scheduled Tribes under the Constitution or under any other law for the time being in force or under any order of the Union/State Government.

CHAPTER IX

NON-FORMAL ACTIONS BY THE COMMISSION

81. The Commission may initiate correspondence in special cases in matters or cases which are not strictly covered under the law if the matter is such that the welfare of an individual person belonging to the Scheduled Castes and Scheduled Tribes or that of a group of such persons is involved and it is necessary for the Commission in its inherent capacity as the protector of the interests of these classes of persons, to take action. The decision for correspondence on such matter shall be taken at the level of Director or above.

82. All routine formal communications from the Commission shall be issued under the signatures of an Officer not below the rank of Research Officer/Section Officer.

83. The Commission can sue or be sued through its Secretary.

84. The Scheduled Castes and Scheduled Tribes in these rules will have the same connotation as is given in Clause 10 of Article 338 of the Constitution.

85. ***Applicability of Rules, etc., of the Central Government.*** All rules, regulations and orders issued by the Central Government and applicable in the Ministries/Departments will also apply in the Commission.

86. The provisions relating to the delegation of financial powers in the Government of India shall apply to the corresponding officers in the Commission.

87. ***Use of Staff Cars.*** The Staff Car Rules of the Government of India shall apply for the purposes of utilisation of staff cars in the Commission.

88. Decision on Matters not Specified in these Rules. If a question arises regarding any such matter for which no provision exists in these rules, the decision of the Chairperson shall be sought. The Chairperson may, if deems fit, direct that the matter may be considered at a meeting of the Commission.

FORM I

NATIONAL COMMISSION FOR SCHEDULED CASTES AND SCHEDULED TRIBES

(A Constitutional body under Article 338 of the Constitution of India)

5th Floor, Loknayak Bhawan
New Delhi – 110 003

(Notice for collecting basic facts)

To

Whereas a Petition/complaint/information has been received by the National Commission for Scheduled Castes and Scheduled Tribes from .... press news under caption ....appearing in................dated................as enclosed and the Commission has decided to investigate/inquire into the matter in pursuance of the powers conferred upon it under Article 338 of the Constitution of India, you are hereby requested to submit the facts and information on the action taken on the allegations/matters to the undersigned within 30 days of receipt of this notice either by post or in person or by any other means of communication.

Please take notice that in case of the Commission does not receive reply from you within the stipulated time, the Commission may exercise the powers of Civil Courts conferred on it under Article 338 of the Constitution of India and issue summons for your appearance in person or by a representative before the Commission.

Signature
Director/Under Secretary/Dy. Director/Assistant
Director/Research Officer/Section Officer
National Commission for Scheduled Castes
and Scheduled Tribes

Dated:

FORM II

BEFORE THE NATIONAL COMMISSION FOR SCHEDULED CASTES AND SCHEDULED TRIBES

(A Constitutional body exercising powers of Civil Court under Article 338 of the Constitution of India)

SUMMONS

File No.

5th Floor, Loknayak Bhawan
New Delhi—110 003

To

Whereas the National Commission has decided to investigate into the following matter in pursuance of powers conferred upon it under Article 338 of the Constitution of India, your attendance is hereby required in person to appear before the National Commission on the .... of ....19...............at...............hours at...............

You are required to bring with you the connected documents for examination by the National Commission.

Case reference

If you fail to comply with this order without lawful excuse, you shall be subjected to the consequences of non-attendance laid down in Rule 12 of Order XVI of Code of Civil Procedure, 1908.

Given under my hand and seal of the National Commission for SCs & STs exercising powers of Civil Courts this...............of...............200...............

Seal **Court Officer**

FORM III

(WARRANT OF ARREST OF WITNESS)

National Commission for Scheduled Castes and Scheduled Tribes

(A Constitutional body exercising powers of Civil Court under Article 338 of the Constitution of India)

Loknayak Bhawan (Floor V)
New Delhi—110 003

To,

Whereas............................r/o............................has been duly served with a summons but has failed to attend (absconds and keeps out of the way for the purpose of avoiding service of a summons), the National Commission for Scheduled Castes and Scheduled Tribes exercising powers of a Civil Court under Article 338(8) of the Constitution of India hereby order you to arrest and bring the said....................before the National Commission at New Delhi.

You are further ordered to return this warrant on or before the ....day of...................200....................with an endorsement certifying the day and the manner in which it has been executed, or the reason why it has not been executed.

Given under my hands and the seal of the National Commission exercising powers of Civil Courts, this ....day of...................200....................

Seal Signature

THE NATIONAL COMMISSION FOR BACKWARD CLASSES ACT, 1993[2]
(Act 27 of 1993)

[2 April, 1993]

An Act to constitute a National Commission for Backward Classes other than the Scheduled Castes and Scheduled Tribes and to provide for matters connected therewith or incidental thereto.

Be it enacted by Parliament in the Forty-fourth Year of the Republic of India as follows—

Statement of Objects and Reasons. In its judgment dated 16th November, 1992 on matter arising out of Government Orders on reservation of appointments or posts under the Government of India in favour of Backward Classes of citizens under Article 16(4) of the Constitution, the Supreme Court, *inter alia* directed the Government of India to constitute a permanent body within four months from the date of judgment, i.e. by 15th March, 1993 for entertaining and examining and for recommending upon request made to it for, inclusion and complaints of over-inclusion and under-inclusion in the lists of Backward Classes of citizens. The Supreme Court observed that the body so created can also be consulted by the Government in the matter of periodic revision of lists of backward classes. The Supreme Court has also observed that the permanent body must be empowered to examine complaints relating to such matters and pass appropriate orders. Its advice/opinion should ordinarily be binding upon the Government.

As Parliament was not in session, and as the Government was required to comply with the direction of the Supreme Court within the time-frame stipulated in the judgment, the President promulgated the National Commission for Backward Classes Ordinance, 1993 on the 1st day of February, 1993.

The Bill seeks to replace the said Ordinance.

CHAPTER I

PRELIMINARY

1. *Short title, extent and commencement.* 1. This Act may be called the National Commission for Backward Classes Act, 1993.

2. It extends to the whole of India except the State of Jammu and Kashmir.

3. It shall be deemed to have come into force on the 1st day of February, 1993.

2. ***Definitions.*** In this Act, unless the context otherwise requires—

(a) "backward classes" means such backward classes of citizens other than the Scheduled Castes and the Scheduled Tribes as may be specified by the Central Government in the lists;

(b) "Commission" means the National Commission for Backward Classes constituted under Section 3;

(c) "lists" means lists prepared by the Government of India from time to time for purposes of making provision for the reservation of appointments or posts in favour of backward classes of citizens which, in the opinion of that Government, are not adequately represented in the services under the Government of India and any local or other authority within the territory of India or under the control of the Government of India;

(d) "Member" means a Member of the Commission and includes the Chairperson;

(e) "prescribed" means prescribed by rules made under this Act.

CHAPTER II

THE NATIONAL COMMISSION FOR BACKWARD CLASSES

3. Constitution of National Commission for Backward Classes. 1. The Central Government shall constitute a body to be known as the National Commission for Backward Classes to exercise the powers conferred on, and to perform the functions assigned to, it under this Act.

2. The Commission, shall consist of the following Members nominated by the Central Government:

(a) a Chairperson, who is or has been a Judge of the Supreme Court or of a High Court;
(b) a social scientist;
(c) two persons, who have special knowledge in matters relating to backward classes; and
(d) a Member-Secretary, who is or has been an officer of the Central Government in the rank of a Secretary to the Government of India.

4. Term of Office and Conditions of Service of Chairperson and Members. 1. Every Member shall hold office for a term of three years from the date he assumes office.

2. A Member may, by writing under his hand addressed to the Central Government, resign from the office of Chairperson or as the case may be, of Member at any time.

3. The Central Government shall remove a person from the office of Member if that person—

(a) becomes as undischarged insolvent:
(b) is convicted and sentenced to imprisonment for an offence which, in the opinion of the Central Government, involves moral turpitude;
(c) becomes of unsound mind and stands so declared by a competent Court;
(d) refuses to act or becomes incapable of acting;
(e) is, without obtaining leave of absence from the Commission, absent from three consecutive meetings of the Commission; or
(f) has, in the opinion of the Central Government, so abused the position of Chairperson or Member as to render that person's

continuance in office detrimental to the interests of backward classes or the public interest:

Provided that, no person shall be removed under this clause until that person has been given an opportunity of being heard in the matter.

4. A vacancy caused under sub-section (2) or otherwise shall be filled by fresh nomination.

5. The salaries and allowances payable to, and the other terms and conditions of service of, the Chairperson and Members shall be such as may be prescribed.

5. *Officers and Other Employees of the Commission.* 1. The Central Government shall provide the Commission with such officers and employees as may be necessary for the efficient performance of the functions of the Commission.

2. The salaries and allowances payable to, and the other terms and conditions of service of, the officers and other employee appointed for the purpose of the Commission shall be such as may be prescribed.

6. *Salaries and Allowances to be Paid out of Grants.* The salaries and allowances payable to the Chairperson and Members and the administrative expenses, including salaries, allowances and pension payable to the officers and other employees referred to in Section 5, shall be paid out of the grants referred to in sub-section (1) of Section 12.

7. *Vacancies, etc. not to Invalidate Proceedings of the Commission.* No act or proceedings of the Commission shall be invalid on the ground merely of the existence of any vacancy or defect in the constitution of the Commission.

8. *Procedure to be Regulated by the Commission.* 1. The Commission shall meet as and when necessary at such time and place as the Chairperson may think fit.

2. The Commission shall regulate its own procedure.

3. All orders and decisions of the Commission shall be authenticated by the Member-Secretary or any other officer of the Commission duly authorised by the Members-Secretary in this behalf.

CHAPTER III

FUNCTIONS AND POWERS OF THE COMMISSION

9. Functions of the Commission. 1. The Commission shall examine requests for inclusion of any class of citizens as a backward class in such lists and hear complaints of over-inclusion or under-inclusion of any backward class in such lists and tender such advice to the Central Government as it deems appropriate.

2. The advice of the Commission shall ordinarily be binding upon the Central Government.

10. Powers of the Commission. The Commission shall, while performing its functions under sub-section (1) of Section 9, have all the power of a Civil Court trying a suit and in particular, in respect of the following matters, namely:

(a) summoning and enforcing the attendance of any person from any part of India and examining him on oath;
(b) requiring the discovery and production of any document;
(c) receiving evidence on affidavits;
(d) requisitioning any public record or copy thereof from any court or office;
(e) issuing commissions for the examination of witnesses and documents; and
(f) any other matter which may be prescribed.

11. Periodic Revision of Lists by the Central Government. 1. The Central Government may at any time, and shall, at the expiration of ten years from the coming into force of this Act and every succeeding period of ten years thereafter, undertake revision of the lists with a view to excluding from such lists those classes who have ceased to be backward classes or for including in such lists new backward classes.

2. The Central Government shall, while undertaking any revision referred to in sub-section (1), consult the Commission.

CHAPTER IV

FINANCE, ACCOUNTS AND AUDIT

12. Grants by the Central Government. 1. The Central Government shall, after due appropriation made by Parliament by law in this behalf, pay to the Commission by way of grants such sums of money as the Central Government may think fit for being utilised for the purposes of this Act.

2. The Commission may spend such sums as it thinks fit for performing the functions under this Act, and sums shall be treated as expenditure payable out of the grants referred to in sub-section (1).

13. ***Accounts and Audit.*** 1. The Commission shall maintain proper accounts and order relevant records and prepare an annual statement of accounts in such form as may be prescribed by the Central Government in consultation with the Comptroller and Auditor-General.

2. The accounts of the Commission shall be audited by the Comptroller and Auditor-General at such intervals as may be specified by him and any expenditure incurred in connection with such audit shall be payable by the Commission to the Comptroller and Auditor-General.

3. The Comptroller and Auditor-General and any person appointed by him in connection with the audit of the accounts of the Commission under this Act shall have the same rights and privileges and the authority in connection with such audit as the Comptroller and Auditor-General generally has in connection with the audit of Government accounts and, in particular, shall have the right to demand the production of books, accounts, connected vouchers and other documents and papers and to inspect any of the offices of the Commission.

14. ***Annual Report.*** The Commission shall prepare, in such form and at such time, for each financial year, as may be prescribed its annual report, giving a full account of its activities during the previous financial year and forward a copy thereof, to the Central Government.

15. ***Annual Report and Audit Report to be Laid before Parliament.*** The Central Government shall cause the annual report, together with memorandum of action taken on the advice tendered by the Commission under Section 9 and the reasons for the non-acceptance, if any, of any such advice, and the audit report to be laid as soon as may be after they are received before each House of Parliament.

CHAPTER V

MISCELLANEOUS

16. Chairperson, Members and Employees of the Commissio to be Public Servants. The Chairperson, Members and Employee of the Commission shall be deemed to be public servants withi the meaning of Section 21 of the Indian Penal Code (45 of 1860).

17. Power to Make Rules. 1. The Central Government may by notification in the Official Gazette, make rules for carrying ou the provisions of the Act.

2. In particular, and without prejudice to the generality o the foregoing powers, such rules may provide for all or any of the following matters, namely:

(a) salaries and allowances payable to, and the other terms and conditions of service of, the Chairperson and Members under sub-section (5) of Section 4 and the officers and other employees under sub-section (2) of Section 5;

(b) the form in which the annual statement of accounts shall be prepared under sub-section (1) of Section 13;

(c) the form in, and the time at, which the annual report shall be prepared under Section 14;

Any other matter which is required to be, or may be, prescribed.

3. Every rule made under this Act, shall be laid, as soon as may be after it is made, before each House of Parliament, while it is in session, for a total period of a month which may be comprised in one session or in two or more successive sessions, and if, before the expiry of the session immediately following the session or the successive session aforesaid, both houses agree in making any modification in the rule or both Houses agree that the rule should not be made, the rule shall thereafter have effect only in such modified form or be of no effect, as the case may be; so, however, that any such modification or annulment shall be without prejudice to the validity of anything previously done under that rule.

18. Power to Remove Difficulties. 1. If any difficulty arises in giving effect to the provisions of this Act, the Central Government may, by order published in the Official Gazette, make provisions, not inconsistent with the provisions of this Act as appear to it to be necessary or expedient, for removing the difficulty:

Provided that no such order shall be made after the expiry of a period of two years from the date of commencement of this Act.

2. Every order made under this section shall, as soon as may be after it is made, be laid before each House of Parliament.

19. Repeal and Saving. 1. The National Commission for Backward Classes Ordinance, 1993 (Ordinance 23 of 1993) is hereby repealed.

2. Notwithstanding such repeal, anything done or any action taken under the said Ordinance, shall be deemed to have been done or taken under the corresponding provisions of this Act.

7

Post-Partition Violation of Democratic Rights

The theme of caste and communal violence in the post-partition Indian Union has acquired crucial significance in contemporary Indian society for various reasons which are described below:

1. The Indian National Congress (INC) and all those who bargained for Independence on the basis of the partition of India on communal lines, felt that such a measure would root out the chief causes of communal violence in the Indian Union and therefore, the Indian society to be reshaped under the Constitution and plans would be liberated from this cancer which had corroded the National Liberation Struggle against British Rule.

2. It was also propagated that the INC, permeated with the spirit of Gandhism, Nehruism and a philosophy which negated the spirit of discriminatory caste hierarchy, including its most heinous form untouchability, by framing a Constitution and taking affirmative action in the form of special facilities to the Scheduled Castes and Scheduled Tribes, would be able to eliminate the age-old problem of untouchability, that cancerous growth of Indian society, and would usher in a society founded on harmonious existence, the equality of all citizens, free from caste, class, communal, sex and race discrimination.

3. Though it was recognised that this task was difficult, there was hope that the party which led to the transfer of power from the British, which was wedded to active intervention through newly acquired political power, by enacting a Constitution and evolving a conscious pattern of planning which included not just economic growth but also a programme of social justice based on equalitarian, "secular socio-political and normative legal institutional measures rooted in the notion of equality of all citizens, would eliminate the cancer of communalism and class and caste violence. It was also propagated that the economic policies to be adumbrated by the rulers, would augment wealth, in a manner would eliminate basic poverty, generate growth with

justice and would augment prosperity founded on the redistribution of income from the richer sections to the poorer sections, thereby paving the way for a "socialist pattern of Society" of a unique Indian variety.

4. It was also presumed that the state wedded to secularism and the welfare of all its citizens would actively spread norms and values, and elaborate institutional and the media mechanisms which would create a humane, equalitarian, scientific, rationalist and anti-superstitious climate and would elaborate economic, political and social institutional framework which would cut at the roots of the disease of caste, communal, sexist and class exploitative relationships among citizens of Secular Democratic India.

Wrongs done by the Ruler. But what has been the real development in the country after more than half a century of Independence? What has been the impact of the path of development pursued by the rulers, through their Five-Year Plans, comprised of industrial, agrarian, educational and socio-cultural policies? All the rosy pictures painted by our dream merchant rulers have not only turned out to be moonshine but in fact an opposite night-marish, social situation is emerging in the country for the majority of citizens.

Both urban and rural life today is inflamed by growing caste, communal, class and sexist violence. Since 1960, the eruption of these types of violence has been rampant and has acquired an almost explosive intensity. The upper castes, classes and sections of the dominant and minority religious communities, and the male upper sections of the society, have increased their violent offensive and have been systematising this attack with almost calculated precision. We will describe the extent as well as main characteristics of the caste and communal violence that has been taking place in the country post-independence.

Severity of Atrocities. As observed in a number of studies, violent attacks on the Dalits by upper and intermediate caste Hindus who constitute land owning, trading and politically and socially dominant groups in rural areas are acquiring meaning proportions.

1. According to one observer, during Indira Gandhi's rule between 1966 and 1976 alone, 40,000 clear cases of atrocities on the Dalits were recorded.

2. According to the National Integration Committee sponsored by the Central Government, the cases of atrocities against Harijans rose during 1977.

3. A pamphlet entitled "Atrocities on Harijans and Weaker Sections" by P.K. Kodian published in 1978 indicated that between 1977 and 1978, during the Janata regime, more than one thousand Harijans were killed, hundreds of Harijan women were raped and tortured, thousands of houses were burnt, the lands allocated to Harijans were grabbed back, the institution of social boycott was used in hundreds of villages to deprive the Harijans of jobs, occupation, the payment of minimum wages, access to water and other necessities.

4. In March 1978, Dhaniklal Mandal presented in the Lok Sabha the figures of atrocities as 40,000 between 1973 and 1977.

5. On September 3, 1981, the Minister of State in the Central Cabinet stated that in 1980 alone, 13,745 cases of atrocities had been recorded, and in the first few months of 1981 as many as 5,124 had already been registered.

6. The atrocities and attacks on the Dalits were perpetrated with an accelerating tempo even in 1981 and 1982 as revealed in the cruel offensive against Harijans in Jetalpur and other places in Gujarat, in villages in Patna district in Bihar, in Deoli and Sadhupur in Uttar Pradesh and in the rural areas of Durg now in Chhattisgarh.

Cast Offensive. The rising offensive against Harijans exhibits certain characteristics which need proper attention.

1. The rise in the scale of atrocities and violence is taking place in a setting, in which the plans have had distinct bearings. They have strengthened the process of class differentiations both in urban and rural areas. At one end, certain sections of the upper and intermediate castes are being strengthened politically and economically and these are influencing social institutional and cultural networks which are being evolved systematically by the State, through its economic, political and socio-cultural policies. At the other end the plans have resulted in the process of pauperisation and proletarianisation taking place at an accelerated rate with the passage of decades. Today a big part of our population is depending on agriculture has been reduced to the state of agricultural landlessness. Of the remaining land owing groups nearly eighty per cent have been reduced by a gradual process of pauperisation, to poor sub-marginal or marginal farmers

descending further and further down the ladder. The overwhelming majority of the Dalits and tribals are reduced to landless labourers or to pauperised landholders on the way to landlessness. Further regarding growing monetisation, agrarian production acquires the character of production for marketing and profit and the poor sections of the rural areas are deprived of the traditional securities in the form of customary payments, however meagre and inequitious they may have been. This process is taking place without creating conducive conditions for generating purchasing power, or the security of getting the goods and services these sections require. The growing awakening among the poorer strata, and their efforts to prevent further deterioration of their living conditions and their sense of dignity as human beings and citizens of this country is prompting them to protest and evolve struggles against the old caste and other forms of indignities hurled at them.

2. The intermediate and upper castes who are rising as new dominant and land-owners and trading classes and as the administrative strata in emerging bureaucratic and other political institutions, in the context of the surplus labour available in India, are utilising caste sentiments and caste ideology and practices, to augment their surplus value by forcing the untouchables and other lower castes to work under semi-feudal conditions. They attempt to deprive them of their legitimate, and even legally recognised share and terrorise them with more ruthlessness to carry on in their old helpless lower caste oppressive situations. In the new competitive and economically deteriorating situation, the Harijans unable to work as of old and not ready to suffer the old form of oppression and humiliation, are slowly protesting, are unwilling to accept the humiliations hurled at them in the form of caste-disabilities, are demanding rights as citizens, and are also asking for better conditions of work and terms of pay in the emerging bourgeois economy. The logic of hectic profit-chase by the emerging land-owning prosperous farmers and traders, moneylenders, comprising mostly of upper and intermediate castes, in the context of abundant labour supply, creates favourable conditions for these classes to utilise pre-capitalist feudal or semi-feudal, casteist modes of exploitation and oppression to accelerate their profit-hunt.

These pre-capitalist forms prove functional to the new rising prospering classes in rural areas to extract surplus value more intensively, to divide the pauperising and proletarianising sections of rural populace belonging to different castes and to divert the anger of the poorer sections of upper and intermediate castes, from the chief enemy, i.e., their own prospering sections, who are the root cause of their present situation, to the Dalits and other backward castes and tribes who are also equal victims of the same groups and classes. These multiple functions of caste-violence against the Dalits have to be recognised.

3. The growing caste violence has also be properly comprehended. It is taking place in the background of growing violence against the entire poor, exploited, oppressed masses in the country. There is a growing alround rise of violence. There is growing violence against the exploited and oppressed poor, against working class, ordinary consumers, footpath and slum dwellers, against *adivasi* landless or land hungry people, against women and against the oppressed nationalities whose exploitation and oppression has increased and who are falling in the race of limited development that is taking place unevenly in the country. In the view of the capitalist path of development pursued by the Indian rulers, the classes comprised of rich farmers and landlords as well as traders and businessmen are made the lynchpin of the development.

The rulers have elaborated an economic policy in which the State is providing enormous facilities, resources and legal and normative values favouring these classes. The State is also undertaking its own economic activities in a manner which would strengthen these classes in various ways. Within the background of India's ex-colonial labour surplus matrix, the rulers' policies which look to benefit these classes have led to limited economic growth. Simultaneously, the policies have been generating the phenomena of massive unemployment, underemployment, pauperisation, proletarianisation and a growing lack of purchasing power among the majority of the population. The State, pretending to be a Welfare State cannot find the resources to serve all. It cannot generate purchasing power, or provide securities to the poverty stricken mass of people. Basically wedded to a policy of not tapping resources from the proprietary classes of the country, and even further of directing the limited resources mobilised by the State, from indirect taxation, deficit financing, borrowings both from within and outside or from rising prices of the services provided by the State to the public, the State strengthens these proprietory classes and therefore, finds it difficult to generate resources for assisting the poor, except for some token gestures. In fact, from the mid-sixties even the limited economic growth is characterised by jolts, zig-zags, stagflation and even halts.

To prevent the economy from further recession and breakdown, the State has to drastically rationalise its economic policy, withdraw the limited services and protection which it has granted to the poor; retrench large sections of the workers employed both in the public and private sectors; streamline the efficiency of the productive processes—which means making them more capital intensive and labour replacing—and thereby augment further unemployment or underemployment; and withdraw the perquisite made available to the masses. From the start of the seventies, this has process continuously accelerated. The exploited and oppressed poor are facing more and more hardships and finding conditions of work and life more and more unbearable. They have started various forms of opposition against such policies. These struggles take on many forms, acquire a wider base, greater intensity and even militancy in various parts of the country. They take on the form of strikes and other appropriate actions by the industrial working class and the class of salaried workers in private and public sectors, of struggles of tribals against non-tribal exploiters and oppressors of struggles of the masses of consumers against the traders and Government. It also reveals itself in the form of struggle of workers, students, teachers of oppressed sections of the nation, of agrarian labour, poor farmers, ruined artisans and other sections of the countryside and of women against the growing oppression and violence launched against them at their places of work, at home, and in public places. From the mid-sixties, the State has become hard towards these poor citizens, has taken to more repressive and brutal forms of suppression, has been buttressing, conniving and colluding with the upper classes and even inviting them to adopt ruthless and violent means to crush the struggles of different classes and strata of Indian population comprising of poorer toiling people. The growing atrocities against Harijans have to be seen in this wider context because the root causes of this growing violence against the Dalits have to be located in this larger framework.

4. The atrocities on the Dalits occur predominantly in rural areas. Though not absent in some of the urban areas, their spread and growing frequency, intensity and ferocity are to be found in rural areas. Further, such violence is found relatively more in those rural areas where, under the impact of land reforms and other measures, a class of landowners, actively interested in land and agricultural processes and coming predominantly from intermediate castes has grown powerful. This class of prosperous farmers and landlords, have acquired control over land, inputs, associations and institutions evolved in the countryside, and command over administrative apparatus, including those linked to the provision of welfare and input services.

This class has become extremely adept in extracting surplus value at an enchanced rate from labourers as well as in the operations of the market situation, input-output calculations, and ways of augmenting profits by cheapening the cost of production, particularly the cost of labour. It also is astute and adopts various devices cunningly to take advantage of the situation arising out of the large labour surplus and the lack of alternative opportunities for that labour to get employment elsewhere. It uses many legal and illegal means to reduce the cost of labour, to divide the sections of job seeking labourers on caste, religious, regional and sex lines, to import labourers from other regions in order to subject the agrarian poor, particularly the Dalits, to humiliation, semi-serf-labour and other forms of exploitation and oppression, to utilise a chain of contractors, who huddle the job-hungry rural poor, particularly from lower castes and tribes, to semi-concentration camps like hovels and make them semi-bonded ill paid workers. They use different devices from social boycott to terrorisation and starvation. Rising atrocities on Harijans have to be seen in this context.

5. Dalit atrocities, are taking place in a cultural and moral climate of upper caste Hindu norms, very assiduously stimulated by the State, and financed, supported and powerfully backed up by proprietory classes which are benefitting from the path of capitalist development pursued in the country. After partition, the normative, cultural values regarded superior, tolerant, moral and spiritual in the Indian Union are basically upper caste Hindu norms and practices, generally described as the spiritual and moral ethos of Hinduism which are also being foisted as the essence of secular

values. While in economic activities, the bourgeois norms of private property as the means of production, production for profit and human labour as a commodity, are accepted as values. In the larger social and cultural field, the rulers have accepted norms based not on man as the supreme value and sanctions based on morality in this world, but man as an inferior being, created, guided and governed by supernatural forces, and sanctions of different types based on them as the true bond cementing human bonds.

The Government has defined secularism in a very pernicious and cunning manner. Secularism does not mean that religion is a private affair of the individual in a society where the morality is based on norms derived from the interests of citizens of this world solely on the criteria of regarding human being as the supreme value; secularism is equated to a positive respect for all religions, faiths and active involvement of the State in stimulating a climate, promoting morality founded on sacred and supernatural sanctions. The state and the ruling class both have never clearly the basis of morality which should permeate the cultural climate of the country.

It has nowhere been formulated how the State wedded to a respect for all religions should act if various religions and sects within religions prescribe diverse, contradictory, discriminatory and unequal and opposite prescriptions of beliefs and practices, and generate conflicting institutional forms and social rituals, rooted in injustice and discrimination against other groups and citizens. Should the State, in the name of respect for all religions, both in public and in private allow these contradictory, iniquitous, discriminatory and hostility-generating values and practices among the citizens? What is the position of citizens who do not believe in religion and are atheists, materialists and rationalists? It has also never been clearly stated whether the value systems and practices which are followed by atheists, materialists, agnostics or rationalists should be equally respected. If so, should the religious and moral practices and rituals which offend them be permitted to be publicly performed in the name of respect for all religions? In fact if different preachings and practices, various legal norms and social, institutional and cultural values and public practices of the State and the ruling classes in the country are carefully scrutinised, they clearly suggest that State and the ruling classes have systematically, both through enactments and through actual practices and propaganda, violated the principle of the equality of citizens based on the morality of the equal worth of human beings.

In fact they have hindered the fostering of values and institutions, practices and norms based on the worth of the human being in this world. For instance, a vast array of personal laws has been enacted in the form of Hindu Law, Muslim Law, etc., based on religious dogmas which are fundamentally discriminatory and humiliating to women and vast sections of citizens including even the believers in the faiths. It has in the name of tolerance and respect to all religions, enacted laws and stimulated public practices which offend, not only the religious faiths but also the moral susceptibilities of all who are believers and stand for humanism, who are atheists, materialists, in the philographical sense, and who consider man as supreme value. The State itself has involved the *Sadhu Samaj* and organised *Bhajan Mandals* for the spread of morality. It is initiating numerous public functions with distinctly religious rituals. It has through its chief mass media, viz., radio and TV, systematically inculcated upper caste-Hindu values in the name of the great spiritual and cultural traditions of India. It has also stimulated took part in, facilitated and, by spending enormous amounts of money, accelerated the spread of religious values, practices, rituals, festivals, sacrifices, *havans, kathas,* and musical recitals and other artistic and cultural activities which spread a religious climate in general and a Hindu upper caste cultural climate in particular. The State and the ruling class have actively encouraged the religious superstitions, discriminatory, iniquitous, creating hostility and contradictory cultural norms and practices by permitting, patronising, idolising and generating a specific messianic godman aura around proliferating salesman of religious and spiritual values, who are elaborating costly, contradictory and confusing practices and institutions.

The State and the ruling class are also helping to build a new holy aura around the heads of different traditional religious establishments in the form of Monestries and temples and sects belonging to different categories. It favours Hindu sacred values about the cow and others, which have been responsible for massive anti-Muslim Hindu communal revivalism in the country. The rulers of the state and the overwhelming majority of the ruling class in India are basically Hindus and are steeped in upper caste Hindu cultural practices even in their daily personal routine. They have very astutely built and strengthened the climate conducive upper caste Hindu cultural tradition as a dominant and superior national, spiritual, moral, cultural ethos and are spreading it as identical with secular ethos. This is being sedulously propagated through rituals, practices, festivals and religious scriptures which enhance this upper caste Hindu ethos.

The rulers not only tolerate these practices but even actively encourage them. The cultural revival of higher Hinduism and its different practices and rituals which are basically founded on contempt for lower caste and intolerance to other religious groups is proving an extremely suitable hurdle to subserve the interests of exploiting propertied classes, overwhelmingly Hindu, against the poor, exploited and oppressed of all religious faiths by hiding the real causes of exploitation from people including the poor Hindus. It also eminently serves the objective of helping to beat down the rival groups belonging to other religious faiths, by dubbing them as aliens, anti-national and foreign agents. It is unfortunate that scholars and activists belonging to various political parties, particularly of the left, have never systematically analysis the ideological and cultural functions performed by the State in India which is wedded to capitalist path of development, to buttress the exploitative system it is evolving. They have also not analysed how the INC and its subsequent fissure groups including several brands of socialists and Sarvodayaits claiming to espouse secularism are themselves basically Hindus and work consciously or unconsciously as a powerful vehicle to create a climate of upper caste Hindu ethos as the spiritual and moral ethos which alone, according to them can provide emotional cement for national integration. They have not examined its impact in generating the countryside a climate to launch offensives against the Dalits and a sort of hysterical zenophobia in favour of the dominant upper caste Hindu ethos, generating hostile approaches towards people belonging to other religious groups.

These functions form the emerging Hindu cultural ethos, need proper exploration, if the real foundations of upper caste violence against Harijans as also violence against other minority groups have to be properly analysed.

Atrocities on Weaker Sections

The atrocities and violence against Harijans and other weaker sections assumed alarming proportions under the Janata Party rule.

The violent offensive launched against the rural poor by the landlords and other rural vested interests following the victory of Janata Party in the March 1977 Lok Sabha elections and the installation of that party's government at the Centre continue almost unabated in several parts of the country. Harijans, the most downtrodden and exploited section of our society, were the main victims of this offensive. The continued suffering and agony of Harijans as a result of this unabated fury of the vested interests and caste and communal obscurantists have become a matter of grave concern to all right-thinking and well-meaning people throughout the country who believe in social justice and social equality.

Atrocities on Harijans have occurred in the past also. But what is new in the situation today is that now atrocities and violence against Harijans and other rural poor are carried out in an organised and concerted manner and almost with impunity.

The landlords believed that it was their own *raj* in the country. They regarded the victory of the Janata Party their victory and the Janata Party government as their own government and in many places they openly said this. The reluctance of the Janata Party government at the Centre and in the States took firm action against the perpetrators of atrocities really acts as a source of encouragement to them to carry their acts of violence and depredations against the village poor. During Janata Party rule innumerable incidents of atrocities took place in various parts of the country. More than a thousand Harijans had been murdered, hundreds of their womenfolk had been raped, thousands of houses had been burnt down and many places the lands distributed among them had been forcibly taken away. Harijan agricultural workers had been denied employment. Social boycott had been imposed on Harijans in hundreds of villages. Minimum wages laws had been frequently flouted everywhere.

Bonded labourers which were earlier freed had been forced to return to their former bondage in many places. A feeling of insecurity had gripped Harijans over a greater part of the country. Atrocities and violence against Harijans and other weaker sections were not confined to Janata Party ruled States alone. Harijans and other village poor were subjected to harassment, terror, intimidation, violence and social oppression in almost of all parts of the country. But the situation in some of the Janata Party ruled States and more particular in Bihar, Uttar Pradesh and Madhya

Pradesh is extremely serious. It was impossible and not needed to gave a catalogue of incidents of atrocities that had been taken place in the country in the recent past. We are here giving only a few of the most glaring instances of inhuman atrocities perpetrated against weaker sections in the country in the recent times.

The Bihar Scenario

The Belchhi Massacre. The first incident which strikes one's mind when we talk of atrocities is the Belchhi massacre. The Belchhi incident is too well-known to be detailed in full here. It happened on 27 May 1977. It was on this day that eight Harijans and three poor *sonars* were mercilessly shot by Kurmi landlords and were thrown into the burning fire. Some of them were still alive when they were thrown into the fire. The victim included a 12 years old Harijan boy who jumped out of the fire many a time, but each time he was pushed back into the fire by the human beasts surrounding him till he ultimately perished in the fire. The Belchhi massacre shocked the entire country. The barbarous act was universally condemned and wide protests were raised in many parts of the country. It was felt that the feeling of revulsion, resentment and protest expressed over the Belchhi massacre would put some sense of responsibility in the State administration and they would take steps to prevent a repetition of such cruelties in the future and the situation would improve. But no such thing has happened. On the contrary, many Belchhi-type incidents have been repeated in many parts of Bihar.

Pathadda

Belchhi was soon followed by Pathadda in Bhagalpur district (Bihar). There the Yadava landlords decided to punish Harijans who denied to work for them for pitiably low wages. They sent their boys with armed men to the Harijan colonies.

The entire area was surrounded and they began beating every one in the Harijan families including old men, women and children. After the first round of beating, thirty of them, including women were taken to the village school. There they were given another round of beating and then they were locked up in a small room and kept there the whole day without even water being given. In the evening they were let off. But three of the Harijans who were thought to be leaders were held back. Ropes were tied round their waist. All three of them were then paraded through the village streets, the landlord youth holding them at the other end of the rope. All through the parade the landlord youth and their men were jeering and abusing the unfortunate Harijans. In the end they were given the final round of beatings with *lathis* and sticks and left on the road. The district magistrate reached the village only after three days. He found many Harijans bleeding with multiple injuries, some with fractures in their legs and hands. They were all taken to the hospital. Thus for three days the injured Harijans wreathed in pain without any medical aid. This incident took place on 19 June 1977.

Dharampura

The Dharampura village in Bhojpur district of Bihar experienced yet another gruesome massacre. Four Harijans, including three educated youth, were shot dead by the local landlords led by a *mahant* of the village. One of the victims was Shiv Muni who had studied up to B.A. and was an independent candidate in the last election to state legislative assembly. The *mahant* was a tyrant of the village who used to harass the Harijans in various ways. The crime of the young Harijans was that they made efforts to organise the village poor against the oppression of the *mahant*. In December 1977 in Peona village of the same district two Harijan sisters Ramvati and Kumud were raped by the landlords. When Ramvati resisted, her left hand was chopped off.

In early February 1978 Vasisht Dusadh, a forty-five years old Harijan was assaulted, shot at and then burnt alive in Rupetha village in defence minister Jagjivan Ram's constituency of Sasaram.

Bishrampur

Yet another Belchhi was enacted at Bishrampur in Rohtas district on the day of holi revelry. The Kurmi landlords with their marauding gang descended on the village and set fire to Harijan houses and shot at Harijans indiscriminately. Many died on the spot. Some of the injured were burnt alive. The victims included the aged of local Harijan leader Bansorapan. Both were over seventy years old. They were dragged out of their house, shot and then thrown into the fire. During the panchayat elections in the State several Harijans were killed, including candidates contesting for *mukhiyaship*.

Parliament's panel on the Scheduled Castes and Scheduled Tribes which toured Bihar has stated that the attacks and violence on Harijans are still continuing in the state.

Situation in Uttar Pradesh

A freed Harijan bonded labourer Aniruddha was shot dead by his former landlord in Unchava village in Gorakhpur district when he refused to return to his old bondage. On 24 June 1977 a bonded drama was played in Dhakwa-Kamoli village in Barabanki district. Harijans refused to remove the dead animals from the village. This was the traditional job of low-caste people.

The landlords decided to teach the 'defiant' Harijans a lesson. They descended on the village fully armed. Badri, a 22 year-old youth, was shot at. His father Mulva rushed to save his son. He was also shot and injured. Baladeen, a brother of Mulva, who rushed was asked by the landlord to lift the injured Badri. When he bent to lift Badri, he too was shot at. He died on the spot and Badri, died on reaching the police station. The *thakurs* then told the frightened Harijans: "It is now our *raj*. You should carry out our orders without the frightened Harijans. UP is a state where the programme of forcibly taking away the lands of Harijans had been conducted in a big way.

According to the report, in UP alone, Harijans had lost about one lakh acres of land in this period. Meerut, the home district of former Home Minister Charan Singh, was one of the districts where this land-grabbing had been done in a systematic manner with the aid of the police and administration. Sampuranand's statue was 'purified' with *Gangajal* by some caste Hindus in Benares because it was inaugurated by Jagjivan Ram.

Land-grabbing Incidents

Hadipur Gamdi and the adjoining villages were the worst affected areas in the district in this respect. Baithu was a Harijan ex-serviceman with both his hands chopped off in a mine blast. He was living in Ram Raj village with his wife and five children. His source of living was his land. The entire harvest was destroyed under the wheels of a tractor by the village rich before the family was thrown out. All the Harijans of the village were relieved of their lands. The dispossessed Harijans pathetically told the pressman who visited them: "Daroga (policeman) does not listen to us. He does not take down our complaints. Big *sahebs* never meet us. We have no place to appeal to." What happened in Ramnagar village in Gorakhpur district was a typical example of how the Harijans were being deprived of their lands with the help of the police.

A jeepload of policemen came to the village on 10 July 1977 accompanied by a tractor driven by a local landlord. There were half a dozen *goondas* sitting on the tractor. In the presence of the police the tractor was taken to the standing crops of the Harijans. Meanwhile some ruffians set fire to a Harijan house. The Harijans then rushed to save the house from fire. But they were stopped by the police who fired in the air to scare them away. The frightened Harijans were then beaten with *lathis*. Eleven of the Harijans, including an eleven years old boy who had just then returned from school, were taken into custody. They were charged with rioting.

Near Hardwar, in Ruhalka village landlords attacked Harijans and removed them from the lands they were cultivating. This happened on 6 August 1977. Next day R.K. Garg, Supreme Court advocate and trade-union leader, along with some of his union workers from Hardwar went to the village to examine the incident. They were attacked by the landlords and three of them received bleeding injuries.

Mass Killings at Pantnagar

The Pantnagar massacre of farm workers took place on 14 April 1978. The farm workers of the Agricultural University at Pantnagar were peacefully marching to the administrative building to submit a memorandum to the authorities. It was then that PAC (Provincial Armed Constabulary) fired on them from close range. Several were killed. The PAC men then started a hunt for workers in their living quarters. Several of them were dragged out from their quarters and shot. All the dead and the injured were dragged to a sugarcane field and then burnt. A woman and her small boy who were witnessing this ghastly scene were also dragged and burnt in the same fire.

According to the UP government, sixteen workers were killed. Many people were missing. Nobody knew how many were actually killed. The number of killed was much more than the figure given by the government when we took into account that the PAC had fired 164 rounds. The university farm workers were mostly Harijans. They were given very low wages. So naturally they were agitating for wage increase which the university authorities consistency refused at the behest of the landlords in the Terai region. The landlords feard that any wage rise in the university farm would have its bearing in the surrounding areas in Terai and they would have to pay more.

The Agra Massacre

Then came the massacre of Jatavs (Harijans) in Agra city by the police and RSS Goondas and the orgy of violence indulged in by them on 1 May 1978 and subsequent days in the Harijan *mohallas.*

The Agra incident arose mainly out of the denial of fundamental civil right to the Harijans to took out a procession through the public thoroughfare on the birthday of Dr. Ambedkar.

The police imposed a ban on the procession going through a public road where upper castes were living. The *Jatavs* defied the ban. The police resorted to a severe lathicharge in which more than a thousand people were injured. Following this the *Jatavs* began a peaceful *satyagraha.* The satyagrahis were attacked by upper-caste hoodlums on the 1st of May. The *Jatavs* resisted. Following this, the Harijan *mohallas* were subjected to a combined siege by *goondas* for three-four days. Tear gas shells were fired into Harijan houses to force the inmates to come out and then smother them with bullets and lathis. Young Harijan girls were molested and then dumped in jail. Many Harijans were killed by the shots and some bayonets. According to Government only eight persons were killed. The number of those actually butchered was unknown.

Outrages in Madhya Pradesh

According to Madhya Pradesh Government's own statement, as many as 3,000 crimes of different kind were committed in the state within six months of Janata Party rule from June 1977 to November 1977. Of these 137 were rape cases, 102 related to loot, 1075 physical assaults, 85 to exploitation and 1061 to various other excesses. It was also admitted in the Vidhan Sabha that between April and November 1977 as many as 105 Harijans were murdered in the State. We are giving below only two of the most shocking outrages committed in the State.

Kannadia

The Harijans of Kannadia village in Ratlam district had been given some lands by the Government some years back which they were cultivating. The landlords did not like the Harijans cultivating their own lands. They thought it to be an insult to them. One day they assembled in the temple premises in the village and decided to take away the lands from the Harijans.

Armed with guns and other weapons they proceeded to the fields where the Harijans were working and began destroying their crops. Harijans protested. Then they were brutally attacked. Four Harijans died in the field and several were injured seriously. This happened on 5th August 1977. Another barbarous atrocity on 8 August in Sendhpa village in Chhattarpur district. There the landlords engaged dacoits to suppress the agricultural workers' movement.

Hardas was a young tribal agricultural worker who took the initiative in 1976 to free the bonded labourers in the Sendhpa village and surrounding areas. Thus forty bonded labourers were set free in the area. This had infuriated the local landlords. One day when he and another worker Punawa were working in the fields, the dacoits employed by the landlords suddenly sprang on them and beat them severely. Then they chopped off the noses of both Hardas and Punawa. The bleeding Hardas and Punawa were taken to the hospital by the villagers.

The landlords not only attacked and tortured the Harijans. They also enjoyed the suffering of the Harijans. In Ratlam district in one village the landlords led the cattle to the standing crops of the Harijans to the accompaniment of music and band. When the bullocks began destroying the crops, the landlords and their men sang, danced and shouted in merriment. This kind of cruel merrymaking was reported from some other districts also.

Punjab

In various villages *nakabandi* (social and economic boycott) was imposed on Harijans for their refusal to work for low wages. On 27 January 1978 of Jasian village in Ludhiana district a Harijan boy was chained with iron strings and a heavy stone was tied round his neck and he was forced to parade through the streets of the village at a gun-point. His mother tried to save him, but she was turned back. When she went to the police station to lodge a complaint, she was turned back there too. The Punjab Chief Minister admitted in the Vidhan Sabha that 45 Harijans were killed in the state during period between June 1977 and February 1978.

Violence in Andhra Pradesh

In June 1977 a 30 years old tribal youth Ramaiah was tortured to death in Chennur village in Nellore district by the local landlords. His wife was raped and two other women relatives were beaten up. What happened in Chinnaogirala in Krishna district on 23 July 1977 was a Kannadia-type attack on the Harijans while they were on the banjar lands allotted to them. One Harijan Subba Rao was speared to death and eighteen people were injured. A large number of cases of harassment, torture, killings, rape, forcible efforts took away lands belonging to Harijans and tribals were reported from other states also.

Poor Performance of the Police

We have seen how the police and the administration, especially at the lower level, were colluding with the landlords and the rural rich in committing atrocities against the Harijans and other rural poor in a number of cases of landgrabbing in UP and the Pantnagar massacre and in the Agra killings. This has been a common characteristic and is one of the most serious aspects of the Harijan problem.

If the police machinery had acted in time many of the sordid acts of killings and massacre in the villages could have been avoided. Reports of the gathering storms in Belchhi village reached the police well in advance. But the police proceeded to the trouble spot in a leisurely manner after having lost valuable time. They reached the village only after everything was over. The outrage at Bishrampur was perpetrated in the very presence of a police contingent who remained mere spectators. There have been a large number of cases where the police have arrested agricultural workers, Harijans and their leaders, taken them to the landlords' houses to be tortured and killed either by the landlords themselves or by the police in the lock-ups. The most typical example of this kind was that of the arrest and death of Gambhira Prasad Sah who was a fearless leader of the rural poor of East Champaran district of Bihar. He was arrested by the police and taken to the Darpamath. The *mahant* was also a local landlord. There he was beaten by the police and the Goondas of the landlord. Then he was taken to the police station and again beaten as a result of which he died in the station itself.

Strangely enough, the ASI who led the attack on Gambhira Prasad Sah was recommended for promotion later on by the DIG-Police on consideration of his "meritorious service."

Government Inaction

Rising violence on the Harijans was the subject matter of a discussion in both Houses of Parliament on many occasions. Many members including Harijan MPs belonging to the Janata Party; vehemently attacked by the government for its failure to take any deterrent action to put an end to atrocities. They said, there had been an alarming rise in the incidence of atrocities on Harijans. But the former Home Minister Charan Singh, who did not care to visit a single place where the Harijans had suffered, each time tried to belittle the gravity of situation with the help of statistical jugglery, he attempted to show that there has been no increase in the incidence of atrocities on Harijans since the Janata Party came to power. But truth cannot be suppressed for long however much one may try to conceal it.

In answer to a question in the Lok Sabha on 29 March 1978, Minister of State for Home Affairs Dhaniklal Mandal laid a statement on the table of the House concerning atrocities on the Scheduled Castes and Scheduled Tribes. The statement revealed that the number of violent incidents affecting the Scheduled Castes and the Scheduled Tribes in 1977 was the highest in comparison to the previous four years.

TABLE 7.1

	1973	*1974*	*1975*	*1976*	*1977*
Scheduled Castes	6186	8860	7781	5968	8872
Scheduled Tribes	362	397	884	1067	1138
Total	6548	9257	8665	7035	10010

The above table shows that the violent incidents affecting the Scheduled Castes and Scheduled Tribes crossed the ten thousand limit for the first time in 1977. The Minister's statement also revealed the fact that out of the 8872 violent incidents affecting the Scheduled Castes as many as 7528 or 84 per cent had taken place in three States alone, i.e., UP, Madhya Pradesh and Bihar. UP topping the list with 4974 cases. It also tops the list of murders of the Dalits in 1977. These figures cannot be taken as indicative of the real situation because there are several other incidents which are not reported at all either because of fear of the victims or because of the connivance of the offenders and the bureaucrats. Nonetheless these figures themselves are revealing.

The concern over gravity of the situation lies not merely in the number of incidents, but the ferocity and ruthlessness with which crimes are committed and the atmosphere of helplessness, insecurity and fear they create in the village. The violence and cruelties are being perpetrated on the Dalits on such a wide scale even five decades after independence is a matter of shame for the whole country.

Social Disabilities

The Dalits suffer from numerous social disabilities. For centuries they have been segregated from the mainstream of society. Evil practice of untouchability is still prevalent in various parts of the country and especially in the rural areas. Only recently a report appeared in the press that a Harijan in a village in Karnataka was whipped by caste Hindus for drawing water from the common village tank. Only a few years ago a Harijan was beaten by Brahmin youths in Benares for the crime of going on a bicycle in front of a Brahim's house.

In many teashops in the villages Harijans have no entry. Even if they are served they have to sit in a separate place and to wash the glasses after drinking. In some villages they are not allowed to take out marriage processions without permission from the caste Hindu landlords. There are a large number of places where the Harijans are not allowed to use certain public thoroughfares. They find themselves discriminated against in every sphere of life. Widespread violence and all-round discrimination against Harijans and the ruthless attempts to suppress them whenever they try to claim their rights pose the problem of denial of human rights to a substantial section of our population.

It is true the Constitution of our country has provided equality of all its citizens irrespective of their caste, religion and sex. Harijans and tribals have also been provided with special safeguards in the Constitution in order to protect their interests. Untouchability stands abolished under Article 17 of the Constitution. Besides there is also a law to prevent the practice of untouchability. But despite all these safeguards and laws, Harijans still continue to suffer. All kinds of social indignities are heaped on them. The real troubles began when they try to exercise these rights provided under law and the Constitution. Reality today is that Harijans are not allowed to enjoy these rights or rather they are prevented from exercising these rights. During the elections, they are prevented from voting in various villages, or if they exercise their franchise at their free will against the dictates of the landlords, they are being physically assaulted, their properties destroyed and they are even murdered in some places. This has happened even during the recent *panchayat* elections in Bihar. Whether it is a struggle for wages or for land, their movement is ruthlessly suppressed.

The State which is supposed to create the conducive conditions to enable the weaker sections to exercise their rights and protect them when they are attacked generally behave in a manner which helps only the oppressors and exploiters. Thus millions of poor people in the villages are faced with a helpless situation in which they are not allowed even to enjoy the rights guaranteed under law. Is this tantamount to denial of basic human rights? In these circumstances there is no other way left for the suffering people except to rally unitedly and fight and defend their rights. A sense of resistance to injustice and oppression should grow among the Harijans. Ultimately it is their united will and determination to fight and defend their rights which will help them in achieving their goal of social equality. But in this struggle, the Harijans will have to look for cooperation and help of other sections of our toiling masses. If anybody thinks that Harijans alone can fight and win their battle without the help of other democratic masses, it will be a wrong way of thinking which will only result in the isolation of the Harijan masses and thus help their oppressors.

All progressive forces in the country, left and democratic parties and organisations, and all those who believe in social justice and social equality should come to the help of the Harijans in their struggle against atrocities and social oppression. This is not just a humanitarian task, but the very interests of the country's development and national advance require such cooperation and help from all progressive and democratic sections. As long as large sections of our people are forced to live a life of utter misery and are denied even the basic civic rights, there cannot be any national progress in the real sense. Such a situation will act as a drag on the country's forward march.

Hence the struggle against atrocities and social oppression is really a national struggle in which all progressive sections of our people should take part. The Communist Party of India, as the party of the working class, has always fought against social oppression and atrocities. Innumerable number of its valuable members and cadres have sacrificed their lives in defending the Harijans and other downtrodden sections in various parts of the country.

Atrocities, violence and terror and intimidation against Harijans have assumed such alarming proportions as in recent times. That is why the party's leader in the Lok Sabha, M.N. Govindan Nair, has decided to undertake a fast on the issue of atrocities against them. The Communist Party of India does not believe in the theory which is being propagated by some that with the achievement of economic emancipation all other inequalities will automatically disappear and, therefore, the main stress should be laid on economic struggles. The Communist Party of India believes that while fighting for economic demands, it should also equally struggle for the elimination of social disabilities from which the weaker sections suffer.

Rising Crimes Against the Scheduled Castes and Scheduled Tribes

There is a public indignation over continuing atrocities on members of the Scheduled Castes and Scheduled Tribes in various parts of the country. In both Houses of Parliament questions have been raised on major cases. For example, recently questions were brought over the gruesome killing of 14 Scheduled Caste agricultural labourers by a mob of over 300 caste Hindu landlords and others in Pipra, about 20 km from Patna. This was one of the major outrages on members of the Scheduled Castes and Scheduled Tribes in the post-independence period. Occurring as it did shortly after the assumption of power by the Congress (I) at the Centre, it certainly indicated that change of fortunes among the ruling political parties is of no vital importance to the lives and the lot of the millions of members of the Scheduled Castes and Scheduled Tribes in the country and that in the context of sharpening contradictions in rural areas the path forward for them is bound to be one of bitter struggles in the face of brutal repression.

The figures of crimes given in the Parliament in response to questions reportedly consist of IPC cases in which members of Scheduled Castes become victims of offences at the hands of members of non-Scheduled Castes in the various States. These crimes are of the categories of 'murder', 'rape', 'arson', 'grievous hurt' and 'other IPC offences'. The offences which occur under the different provisions of the Protection of Civil Rights Act 1955, as amended in 1976, though large in number are not given in response to Parliament questions. Similarly, cases in which a few members of Scheduled Castes may join hands with a large number of members of non-Scheduled Castes in attacking members of other Scheduled Castes are also left out. Among the factors advanced for the rise in the incidence of these cases are the growing social and political awareness and consciousness on the part of the members of the Scheduled Castes coupled with the increased determination of the old elites and the emerging new ones to resist and put down such consciousness.

The state-wise figures of IPC crimes against members of the the Scheduled Castes given in Parliament reveal that other interesting characteristics. Over seventy per cent of all cases of such crimes are registered in Uttar Pradesh, Madhya Pradesh and Bihar. Among the other states in which a large number of such cases occurred were Rajasthan, Maharashtra, Kerala, Karnataka, and Gujarat and Tamil Nadu. In other words, the predominant areas of concern regarding such atrocities were largely confined to the north Indian states. Another feature was the large number of cases of major IPC crimes against members of the Scheduled Castes such as murder, grievous hurt, rape, arson and so on in all the major states but specially in Bihar, UP and MP. It is useful to remember that the figures given in Parliament relate only to registered cases and that too only IPC cases.

It is well known that a large number of cognisable IPC cases are simply not reported to the police for different reasons, including fear of rural vested interests and fear of police harassment. It is also known that not all the cases which are reported to the police are registered and investigated by them. In several cases, complaints are turned away on one ground or another are not conscious enough to insist on registration. In several other cases, there is also minimisation of offences on the part of the police when they register major IPC cases as minor ones.

Considering all this, it would be reasonable to conclude that the figures given in the Parliament are only indicative and do not reflect fully the actual situation on the ground. During the Janata regime some of the Chief Ministers who were under attack for the increasing number of cases of atrocities against Scheduled Castes in their states raised a point concerning the definition of the term 'atrocity'. They pointed out that the figures given by the Government of India in Parliament included all cases in which members of the Scheduled Castes were victims and members of non-Scheduled Castes were offenders irrespective of motivation and that the correct way to assess the situation regarding atrocities in their states would be to strictly define the term 'atrocity' and count only those cases in which caste considerations were the only factor in the commission of the offence. Their argument advanced was that a majority of these cases of 'atrocities' arose as a consequence of the operation of the socio-economic factors and therefore, cannot be counted as 'atrocities' in the strict definition of the term acceptable to them. Such a reasoning is artificial and unrealistic.

It is difficult to conceive of a situation in which a member of the Scheduled Caste becomes victim of an atrocity simply due to his caste status. Invariably, socio-economic factors enter into the picture in the light of the occupational and social position of the members of the Scheduled Castes as agricultural labourers, small and marginal farmers, bonded labourers and so on. In practice, therefore it is impossible to separate caste from other socio-economic aspects in the commission of crimes against members of the Scheduled Castes. In fact, caste itself is a socio-economic category. Another line of reasoning is that only major IPC offences such as murder, grievous hurt, rape etc., should be counted as atrocities and not other IPC offences. Here again one may note a preoccupation to minimise the gravity of the situation concerning crimes on members of the Scheduled Castes. Those who advance such arguments forget that a member of the Scheduled Caste might hold justifiably that even an abuse against him based on should be regarded as an 'atrocity' and that no 'logical' argument can be advanced against such a position. A third line of argument that is sometimes put forth is that the Scheduled Caste constitute fifteen per cent of the population of the country and that the crimes committed against them as a proportion of the total number of crimes is so small that no serious notice need be taken of them. This again is a spurious argument on the basis of a superficial statistical approach. What is need is to recognise that the members of the Scheduled Castes are in a peculiary vulnerable weak socio-economic position and that they have been victims of exploitation and social injustice over centuries and, therefore, stand in need of special protection.

Further the crimes against the rest of the population consist in a majority of cases of property offences while the propertyless masses of the Scheduled Castes are subjected to the most inhuman forms of offences against their person such as rape, murder, grievous hurt and so on. Therefore there can be no comparison such as rape, murder, grievous hurt and so on. Therefore there can be no comparison of the two kinds of offences against the Scheduled Caste and non-Scheduled Caste segments of the population in qualitative terms. While dealing with the administrative aspect of the problem of crimes against members of Scheduled Castes, it would be useful to take a look at the constitutional and legal position in regarding the handling of atrocity cases. Under the Constitution, law and order is a state subject and is within the exclusive jurisdiction of the State Governments. Although there are provisions in the Constitution which provide for special responsibility on the part of the Central Government for the welfare of Scheduled Castes, this cannot be stretched to cover law and order steps for the protection of the Scheduled Castes. The state police forces therefore are empowered to deal with crimes of all types including crimes against members of the Scheduled Castes. The Centre can, however, give general guidelines to the State Governments on this subject. As law and order is a state subject there an opinion that, in order to ensure and enforce effective measures of protection for the members of the Scheduled Castes, the Centre should be armed with more powers, say be entrusting some law and order functions to the Central Government by a suitable amendment of the Constitution. If however, there are any obstacles and problems in the State Governments rendering effective protection to the Scheduled Castes, the matter should be analysed carefully and steps taken to remove those obstacles and problems. In a vast country such as India, law and order can only be handled effectively at the level of the State Government. In fact, the major reforms that need to be undertaken in the sphere of law and order administration should be in the direction of decentralisation, democratisation and popular participation rather than in the opposite direction. This alone can ensure effective protection for the members of the Scheduled Castes as well as other sections of the population.

Any measure for centralisation of powers will be retrograde and wrong. Besides constitutional provisions, there are many measures that can and must be taken by the State Governments to improve the condition of members of Scheduled Castes and reduce if not eliminate the number of cases of crimes against them. Measures of an economic and developmental character as well as effective administrative steps can be taken. On the developmental front, speedy economic development of members of the Scheduled Castes is an essential prerequisite. Special programmes can and must be thought of and adequate flow of funds and their effective utilisation ensured. On the administrative front, similarly, a number of measures are possible. State Governments, particularly the more affected ones, can launch a comprehensive review of the measures of land reforms, tenancy reforms, payment of minimum agricultural wages, abolition of bonded labour and so on and takes steps for their effective implementation.

It is also possible to comprehensively analyse the figures of crimes in each state, district-wise and cause-wise, work out their regional and seasonal pattern and changes and adopt appropriate administrative, police and legal steps to effectively prevent the occurrence of these crimes, speedily investigate, and try the cases registered and punish offenders quickly and instil a sense of security and confidence among members of the Scheduled Castes and so on. The foregoing discussion makes clear the seriousness of the situation concerning crimes on members of the Scheduled Castes which are being committed in various parts of the country. The sharp rise in the figures of these crimes in the period after 1977 is a notable feature and has to be gone into in depth. Even if the increase in numbers is only the result of better registration and reporting of cases by the state police authorities, there is an urgent need for a deeper analysis by the State Governments concerned of the true magnitude and nature of the different offences and their socio-economic roots with a view to adopting effective and permanent remedial measures.

However, it would be well to bear in mind the overall socio-historical context and the emerging pressures and tensions of the Indian polity in the current phase while studying and understanding the phenomenon of increasing crimes against the members of the Scheduled Castes. These crimes have to be seen in the context of the anti-Scheduled Caste conflagrations that broke out some time ago in Agra and Muzaffarnagar (UP), Villupuram (Tamil Nadu) and Marathawada (Maharashtra). These emerging pressures and tensions of the polity are also well documented. One of the major points that emerge from a study of recent trends in the country appears to be that in the context of the sharpening class and caste polarisations in rural society, such anti-Scheduled Caste atrocities are likely to rise rather than fall with the state machinery performing a by no means impartial rose between the oppressed and the oppressor.

8

Prevention of Atrocities and Civil Rights of Dalits

The Hindu society in India finds itself stratified permanently. The caste has rigidly divided the Hindus into several birth-based categories. One has to remain confined to the caste in which one is born and accept its advantages and disadvantages. The untouchables live on the fringe of society. They are denied social and economic justice by the people from the so called "upper class". They suffer from a number of stigmas, both social and economic, which are birth based.

Provisions of Social Justice

To confront such a situation, the framers of the Indian Constitution have made certain provisions which appear to be inadequate to grant social and economic justice to the depressed and oppressed people. Let us study the nature of injustice done to the people in the villages with reference to some of the cases which took place in Karjat *Taluka* of Ahmednagar District, taking into account the implementation of Protection of Civil Rights Act of 1976 and Atrocities Act 1989. The cases selected here indicate whether the untouchables were able to get due justice or not. These cases show the discrimination meted out to the lower caste people by the caste Hindus. The study shows that the Hindu society is not a homogeneous society. It is due to this nature of society that the quarrels and conflicts take place.

1. An incident took place in Kombhali, Karjat Taluka, Ahmednagar District, in which a higher caste Hindu, who was a Sarpanch, abused a lower caste villager. The Sarpanch demanded Rs 300 for building a channel in the farm. The lower caste villager refused to pay the money. The quarrel led them to the court on the ground of abuse, in the name of caste.

The charges was made against the accused under Section 7 (1)(d)(c) of Protection of Civil Rights Act, 1976 and under Section 323, 504, 506 Indian Penal Code.

After going through legal formalities, the Judge (the Judicial Magistrate First Class Karjat) passed the order on May 6, 1991 with the effect that, the basic complaint was false and the higher caste person had never demanded the said amount from the lower caste person. Therefore, there was no question of his abusing the aggrieved party; his bail bond was cancelled and he was set free.

The Judge was of the view that the intention of the Sarpanch was not of abusing the lower caste villager. So after hearing the case, the accused Sarpanch was acquitted. This easy reveals that lower caste villagers resort to lodging false complaints if their interests are not protected. The Article that makes an implementation of non-discrimination of law, clearly states, "All are equal before law and entitled without any discrimination to equal protection of the law. The violation of the law will result in punishment as offered by the law." The Article further says that the law shall prohibit any discrimination and guarantee equal and effective protection against any injustice on any ground.

According to this provision every citizen can enjoy the rights given to him by the Constitution no one is superior or inferior. Hence every person is equal in the eyes of the law. With reference to this, the atrocities committed on the backward people in Karjat *Taluka* of Ahmednagar District make one aware of the opinions expressed by some of the scholars in the field and the senior members of the Parliament. They are worthwhile to be considered in view of the prevention of Atrocities Act. When the Bill was being introduced in the Parliament, there were mixed reactions amongst its members about the passing and implementing of this Act against the Indian social background. Parliament witnessed hot discussions when the Bill was being passed. The question was constantly being raised in the House that there was increase in such offences against members of Scheduled Castes, Scheduled Tribes. Sometimes, Hon. Members were also agitated on this point.

2. There was another case of vital notice which took place in the village called Alsunde. A lower caste person complained about the absence of the street lights in the Harijanwada, whereupon a high caste person abused him. As a result, the lower caste person lodged a complaint. This complaint was filed against the accused (a higher caste Hindu) under Section 7 (1) (d) of Protection of Civil Rights Act, 1976.

After going through the entire case, the Additional Session Judge, Ahmednagar, acquitted the higher caste person, for he found that there was no intention on the part of the higher caste person to insult the lower caste villager on the grounds of untouchability. It is quite evident that the above complaint was based on local level issue. The Judge also remarked that all complaints do not come within the ambit of law of untouchability. Constitutionally, racial and religious discrimination is prohibited by Article 19. Accordingly, every villager irrespective of his caste, creed or religion has a right to demand civil facilities in his village. But sometimes incidents take place because of and misunderstanding among villagers. These create problems and additional cases are lodged in the courts.

Objectives of the Bill are to give deterrent punishment to the accused persons who are involved in the case of atrocities on Scheduled Castes and Scheduled Tribes. There are general Acts like IPC and Civil Rights Act, but it appears that they have "not been properly implemented and that is why the present Bill had been brought. While the Bill was being brought, it was necessary to define atrocity. Here the word "atrocity" had not been defined exactly and fully and only certain offences have been quoted, i.e., taking possession of land forcibly, removing clothes of Scheduled Castes and Scheduled Tribes, etc. The Bill has provision to an enhanced punishment, i.e., more punishment to those who are habitual offenders and who committed offences more than just once. One of the senior parliamentrians said in his speech: "I think it is necessary to define the word "atrocity" here fully if not today at least after some time".

3. A similar and interesting incident like the above onces took place in the village called Nimbodi, Karjat Taluka, Ahmednagar District. The higher caste persons approached the lower caste persons for the share in the agricultural produce. But the party refuse to oblige the higher caste persons. Being provoked by this they turned down their request and indulged in abusing him. As a result was that the lower caste persons lodged a complaint against the higher caste persons at the police station. The chargesheet was filed against the accused under section 7 (1) (d) of Protection of Civil Rights Act, 1976, and under Section 506 Indian Penal Code. After hearing the case, witnesses and facts, the Judicial Magistrate, First Class Karjat passed the order on January 15, 1983. Accordingly,

the accused persons of higher caste were acquitted of the charges punishable under Section 7 (1) (d) of Protection of Civil Rights Act and Section 504 of Indian Penal Code and their bail bond was cancelled. The Judge decided that such an incident never occurred. In fact, the Judge inevitably acquitted the higher caste persons. The Judge expressed quite clearly that the case before the court, was concerned with a dispute on the share of crops and hence it was not concerned with the law of untouchability. The motive of the higher caste persons was purely pecuniary. Therefore, the question of untouchability was irrelevant and beyond consideration. The question of abusing the lower caste people is to be seen in the light of the UNESCO Declaration of Human Rights (Article 9). It clearly describes equality of opportunity to all, absence of any racial discrimination under all circumstances. and also a sense of human dignity. This will ensure an era of human brotherhood. The M.P. wanted to know from Dr. Rajendra Kumari Bajpayee, the then Law Minister, as to what would be the future of the passing of this Bill. In reply to the questions raised by the M.P. she said: "The Bill that is going to be passed by the House is a good step in this direction. I am hopeful that the Bill will be proved much helpful in future as well."

4. There was another interesting case which took place in the village called Babhulgaon in Karjat Taluka, Ahmednagar District where a lower caste person demanded some loan from the Chairman of the Co-operative Society who was a higher caste Hindu. The Chairman explained that a permission had to be taken from the District Co-operative Bank. A quarrel took place between them in which the higher caste person abused the lower caste villagers. Therefore, the villagers lodged a complaint against the Chairman and the peon of Co-operative Society. The charge was framed by Judicial Magistrate (First Class Karjat), against the accused on the ground of untouchability, punishable under Section 7(d) of Protection of Civil Rights Act.

The Judicial Magistrate giving his judgement observed that the bail bond was cancelled and the accused were set free because this case did not stand on the grounds of untouchability. Therefore, the complaint stood false. It was more a legal matter than the matter of untouchability. Therefore, it did not form an offence under Section 7(1)(d) of the Act on the grounds of untouchability. In this case also one can see that the Untouchability Act was misused by the person belonging to the lower caste people. However, the Chairman and the peon were acquitted. One has to look at this case in the light of the Universal Declaration of Human Rights (Article 9) which forbids any type of discriminatory measures and stresses on various democratic values. In several cases lower caste villagers are disallowed to enter a village temple. Complaints are lodged by the lower caste people. After recording the complaint, verification process was issued under Section 7 (d) of Protection of Civil Rights Act and Sections 323, 506 (2) of Indian Penal Code, a charge was lodged against the high caste Hindus. The Judge did not find the witness and acquitted upper caste accused. Declaration of Human Rights does not allow religious separation. This implies that everybody can worship according to the provisions of the constitution. The only precaution to be taken is observance of the prevailing local practices. In this regard, it is everywhere observed that every normal person can have access to religious temples.

A special provision has been incorporated in the Bill. The responsibilities imposed upon the people in the Bill and administrative setup is of much help in the implementation of the Atrocities Act. If they show no concern for doing their duties in this regard, they would be entitled to punishment. Clause 4 of the Bill very categorically says, "Punishment for neglect of duty". The Government had gone a step further and provided more protection to the victims of this act. In his speech the Minister says: "Whoever being a public servant but not being a member of Scheduled Castes or Scheduled Tribes wilfully neglects his duties required to be performed by him under the Act shall be punishable with imprisonment".

5. There is one peculiar case which took place on April 21, 1982, in the village Babhulgaon (Khalsa) Karjat Taluka, Ahmednagar District in which a higher caste Hindu abused a lower caste person and refused him an entry into the temple of God Bhairvanath in the village. The lower caste person was going to perform rituals in front of the God Bhairvanath. He, along with other villagers, went into the temple for worship. On seeing this person in the temple, a higher caste Hindu came there and made an attempt to drive him out of the temple. The quarrel which followed led a higher caste Hindu threating to kill the lower caste. He insulted the lower caste person in the name of his caste and also abused him. Thereupon the lower caste person lodged a

complaint at the police station. The matter went to the Court. After verification, the case was registered under Section 7 (A) (D) of Protection of Civil Rights Act and Section 323, 506 (2) Indian Penal code. After hearing the case, witnesses and facts the Judicial Magistrate, First Class Karjat, passed the following order:

"All the accused persons of Babhulgaon (Khalsa), who are higher caste, are acquitted of the offence punishable under Section 7(1)(D) of Protection of Civil Rights Act, and they are also acquitted of offence punishable under Sections 323, 506 (2) Indian Panel code. Their bail bond stands cancelled. They are set at liberty vide Section 428 of the Criminal Procedure Code.

Elaborating on the judgement, the Judge noted that no such incident had taken place in the village. The Judge further observed that the high caste Hindu person who was charged of abusing the lower caste person on the grounds of untouchability was seriously ill and was taking in hospital at the time of crime. Thirdly, the police head constable was present in the temple at the time of the village fair. The police had written in their daily notebook that no such incident had taken place in the said village. The village priest (Gurav) who was an eye witness to the incident, also strongly denied that no such incident had occurred. The village priest submitted that the entry into the temple was open to all, irrespective of caste, creed and religion.

After hearing all the witnesses, including the nephew of the lower caste person, the Judge was of the view that the entry to the temple was allowed to the lower caste people also. The nephew of the complainant submitted that before this caste took place, he used to recite the hymns of *Bhagwat Gita* and *Ramayana* in the temple of Lord Bhairvanath. It is significant to note that temple entry is allowed to all sections of society irrespective of caste and religion under Section 25 of the Indian Constitution.

The Constitution emphatically stresses that all are equal before law and Article 19 grants equal freedom to all citizens. Nowadays nobody refuses entry to the untouchables into public temples in the villages. If anybody obstructs this, it is a punishable crime according to the Indian Panel Code. It is acknowledged that the whole objective of this Bill is to focus on atrocities committed by persons other than SC/ST on members of Scheduled Castes and Scheduled Tribes. Such atrocities are perpetuated by a group against another or by an individual against another. We come to an understanding that there are some good provisions in the present Bill which need to be highlighted. Just passing of the Bill and making the Act is not enough to stop or prevent anyone from unleashing atrocities on backward classes. This is good Bill in so far as the prevention of atrocities are concerned. But some of the members showed their deep concern and lamented about the Act. One of the Hon. Members stated: "I feel extremely sorry that this type of Bill is necessary at the end of 20th century. It is very regrettable that the so-called high caste people and the land owners are the main culprits for committing the atrocities on Scheduled Castes and Scheduled Tribes." In order to arrive at a certain understanding, we should look into more cases.

Here is a similar case in which a lower caste person lodged a complaint against a person from a higher caste. The incident, in short, is as follows. In the same village (Babhulgaon), the villagers arranged a community meal for the teachers of the primary school. At the time of lunch higher caste persons abused lower caste villager. Thereupon, the lower caste villagers filed a case against the higher castes. The matter went to the police station. Both the parties arrived at a compromise after the higher caste persons apologized. The accused was really guilty but his intention was not to harm or insult the lower caste persons on the grounds of untouchability. It is noted that every insult of a lower caste is not on the grounds of untouchability.

For any offence, the intention behind the insult is to be followed. However, in this case the lower caste person was denied the opportunity to take his meal alongwith the higher caste Hindus. In connection with such type of cases, it is commonly noticed that the Harijans are discriminated on social occasions and at public places. The lower caste people are not allowed to enjoy equal status. It is a very sad and pitiable situation that in spite of the constitutional protection of SC and ST people, the country has been unable to prevent the atrocities on the backward class people. One of the MPs brought to the notice of the House that mostly atrocities on Harijans are committed in predominantly Hindu villages in Bihar. He opined that not a single case of atrocity on Harijans has been reported from any village in Bihar inhabited by Muslims. He said, "If the Government is not able to check atrocities on Harijans, they should be rehabilitated around the Muslim villages, so that they would feel safe and secure". Many laws have been enacted and forwarded to the States for implementation but before reaching the district level, these laws get crippled and weakened by certain forces.

The provisions to stop atrocities have been made in the Bill and they are good too. But if we look at the already existing provisions made in the Constitution or in the Indian Penal Code, the cases of atrocities are delayed and finally some cases are dismissed.

6. There was one more incident that took place in village Babhulgaon, Karjat Taluka, Ahmednagar District in which a lower caste villager secured a loan for construction of a well in his agricultural land. According to a custom prevalent in the village, the party concerned carried the water from the new well to the local deities, namely, Hanuman and Bhairvana as the offerings. But the higher caste people did not allow an entry to these temples, hence, the party decided to lodge a complaint at the police station. The aggrieved person approached different authorities including the Home Minister for seeking justice. The Head Constable visited the concerned village, convened a meeting of the villagers and later the complaint was presented at the villegers meeting and the complainant offered his apologies for what had happened; and therefore, the local police authorities close the case.

It is observed here in this case that the lower caste person misused the Protection of Civil Rights Act which says that no villager should be discriminated on the basis of caste and suffer injustice. In view of the above observations one of the MPs commented.

"I would like to state that the provision dealing with the production of chargesheet within ninety days should be strictly implemented. Besides, the Bill should also ensure that chargesheet relating to incidents of atrocities committed on the Harijans should be produced in the courts within a maximum period of 90 days."

It is absolutely essential to limit the period to minimum days so that justice may not be delayed. It is said that justice delayed is justice denied. Atrocities committed on the Scheduled Castes and Scheduled Tribes can be checked only by ensuring their economic development.

During the freedom struggle, it was Gandhiji who initiated a social revolution followed by Dr. B.R. Ambedkar to abolish the practice of untouchability. Practically, he gave them the status of

God. But what is the plight of the depressed classes today? Political awareness has been created by the Government as far as the Acts of prevention of atrocities are concerned. but it should be followed by economic development of the Scheduled Castes and Scheduled Tribes. Social and political justice is not adequate if it is not followed by economic justice. Economic factor is also responsible for the atrocities committed on the backward class people. Feudal elements continue to hold these people as bonded labourers. Economic opportunities could be provided by way of giving employment to the backward class people in the bureaucratic set up where the cases of the atrocities are being brought. There is a different case for the purpose of making it clear that discriminatory treatment is not given to the lower caste person not only on social occasions but in their daily life. It so happened that a lower caste person went to purchase oilcake at the shop of a higher caste person at Mirajgaon, Karjat Taluka, Ahmednagar District and inquired the rates of oilcake. The owner of the shop got annoyed and a quarrel took place. The lower caste person filed a complaint against the owner, who exploited the Untouchability Act.

In this case also the higher caste person got acquitted. In his remark the Judge declared that the complaint was false and the person who complained was a Buddhist and the provisions of the Untouchability Act are not applicable to such persons according to Section 12 of the Protection of Civil Rights Act. It seems that the case was filed by the lower caste person for the purpose of blackmail. Nobody dare commit atrocities on these people if they are given employment opportunities in various fields. It is being noted that educated people belonging to these ignored sections of society do have the opportunities of becoming doctors, teachers and engineers. But they are forbidden even to draw water from the well in their own native place. However, it is said that even the barbers of their areas do not meet them even if their economic condition has improved.

8. One more case took place in the village of Kolwadi, Karjat Taluka which appeared politically motivated. In this case one lower caste person went to attend a public meal. He was denied the use of leaf-dish by the higher caste person. A complaint was lodged by the lower caste person against the higher caste person. According to the provision the matter went to the Court. The Court gave the verdict that the incident took place because of political

rivalry between two groups in the village, and so the lower caste person was forced to lodge a complaint. Such incidents take place on account of political moves and the vested interest of the different political groups in the villages.

9. The above cases are concerned with the lower caste people. Now, we will study a case which is entirely different from the earlier ones and is connected with a woman from a village Nimgaon Gangarda, Karjat Taluka, Ahmednagar District. The lady lodged a complaint against a male neighbour for having abused her in the name of lower caste. The matter went to the Court according to the Protection of Civil Rights Act. The Judge passed an order saying that the lady did not belong to the lower caste because she had married a high caste Hindu and; thus the case did not come under the provisions of Protection of Civil Rights Act. It is essential to the debate which took place in the Lok Sabha as it aimed at pointing out the nature of intercaste marriages and the treatment given to the newly married couples by the family members in the society. A careful study of this case shows the nature of intercaste marriages in India.

It is strongly felt that improvement in the economic status does not bring the required changes in the minds of the upper caste Hindus. What is significant is that they should go in for intercaste marriages if they want to do away with the caste system.

Mahatma Gandhi had clearly stated that he would give his blessings to couples where one of the partners is a Harijan and other one is non-Harijan. But the fact today is that a person from a privileged class marrying a Harijan girl incurs the wrath of his family and does not get protection from any corner. To support the cause of intercaste marriages, the researchers fell that some provision should be made where the top priority is given to the intercaste marriage giving a specified protection to those who go in for intercaste marriages. The aim here is to abolish the stigma of untouchability. The aims and objects of the prevention of atrocities Bills are to give deterrent punishment to the accused persons who are involved in the cases of atrocities on Scheduled Castes and Scheduled Tribes. There are many general Acts like IPC, Civil Rights Act, but they are not enough to fulfil the objectives of the Bills prevention on atrocities.

10. On January 1, 1981, an incident place in the village Babulgaon, Karjat Taluka, Ahmednagar District in which a quarrel

took place between a lower caste and a higher caste person due to political differences, which led the lower caste person being abused in the name of caste by the higher caste person. The matter went to the court and the higher caste person was set free. Such cases happen due to the rival groups in the villages that instigate the complainant for some political gains.

11. There is another case in point which took place at Koregaon, Karjat Taluka, Ahmednagar District in which a lower caste milkman was not given proper treatment by the high caste Hindu while purchasing the milk. The lower caste person was abused and beaten. The case went to court and the Magistrate of Karjat, after analysing the witnesses and hearing the case and the facts, acquitted the higher caste person on the grounds of bogus filing of the case. From the above case, one can gather that false cases do not yield desired results in favour of the lower caste complainants.

12. Now let us examine the attitude of the higher caste people towards the lower caste people. An incident took place in Karjat Taluka, Ahmednagar District in which a lower caste person was abused by a higher caste person on account of some love affair. The girl whom the lower caste person loved belonged to the higher caste. The matter went to court and the Judge on hearing the case and witnesses, acquitted the higher caste person. Thus, it is noted that the lower caste people do not get enough proofs and witnesses in the rural areas.

13. One more case on a different issue is here for the purpose of study. An incident took place in Chilawadi, Karjat Taluka, Ahmednagar District in which a lower caste person was abused by the higher caste person when he asked for the correct decision of the wrestling match which was being held at the village fair. The case went to court. Because of the lack of insufficient eye witnesses, the higher caste person was acquitted by the Judge.

From this case it is learnt that the lower caste people in rural areas do not get eyewitnesses owing to the suppression from the higher caste Hindus.

14. A case from Mirajgaon, Karjat Taluka, Ahmednagar District shows the kind of relations the lower caste people and high caste Hindus have in the rural area. In this incident a lower caste person picked up a quarrel with a higher caste person because

the latter was constructing a house on the land owned by the lower caste person. The matter went to District Court and is still pending. This case suggests the delay in the decision of the Court because of some unknown reasons.

15. There is another case of land issue which took place in Bhairobawadi, Karjat Taluka, Ahmednagar District in 1984. In this case a lower caste person was abused and insulted in the name of caste by a higher caste Hindu farmer concerning the right of ownership over the land. The lower caste person tilled the land of the higher caste person on contract basis. But later on he refused to disclaim the ownership of the land. The matter went to court at Karjat and the higher caste person was acquitted and his bail bond was cancelled.

16. A similar case of land issue took place in Kopardi, Karjat Taluka, Ahmednagar District, on November 2, 1983, in which a lower caste person was abused and insulted in the name of caste over the nature of the boundary of the land they possessed. The matter went to the court and the higher caste person was acquitted due to lack of witnesses.

In both these cases, lack of eyewitnesses led to acquittal of higher caste person.

17. An incident took place in the village Babhulagon Dumala, Karjat Taluka, Ahmednagar District on October 28, 1987. In this case a lower caste person was forbidden to take the road which passed through the farm of a higher caste Hindu. The lower caste person was abused and insulted in the name of the caste by the higher caste person. The lower caste person filed a complaint and the matter went to court at Karjat. The Judge acquitted the higher caste Hindu after hearing the caste and witnesses.

18. There is another similar case in point in which a lower caste person from the village Therwadi, Karjat Taluka, Ahmednagar District, was abused by a Hindu in the name of the caste. This case took place in the year 1990. The quarrel took place over the rights of ownership of the land which was tilled by the lower caste person, and was owned by him on rent. The matter went to the Court and the higher caste Hindu was acquitted on the grounds that the case was admitted falsely.

19. There are some cases which concerned the Atrocity Act and which took place in the same taluka. An incident took place in the village Mirajgaon, Karjat Taluka, Ahmednagar District in the

year 1993, in which a lower caste person was abused and harassed by a higher caste person in the name of the caste. The quarrel took place during the Gram Panchayat meeting which led both the parties to the High Court. The decision still pending.

20. A similar incident is here for the purpose of study. The incident took place in Karjat Taluka, Ahmednagar District in 1994. A brother of an MLA who belonged to the lower caste was abused by the members of higher caste. Thereupon, a complaint was registered by the brother of the MLA. The matter went to the High Court and is still awaited.

21. One more case of atrocities was filed by a lower caste person of the village Shinde, Karjat Taluka, Ahmednagar District, on the grounds that the right to the post of Sarpanch was denied to a low caste person. In his complaint he made a mention that the high caste people stoned him in front of his house and beat him black and blue and also abused him in the name of his caste and even went to the context of threatening to murder him. The above said complaint was lodged at the Karjat police station on May 29, 1991. The result of the case is still pending.

22. There is yet another case for the purpose of study. It took place in Takali Khandeshwari, Karjat Takula, Ahmednagar District, in which a lower caste person lodged a case against a higher caste person on the ground that the latter did not allow him to send the copying material to his ward who was taking annual examination. The quarrel took place which led the lower caste person to file a false atrocity case under Sections 110, 107 (2) 143, 149 (3) 12A. The case remains pending in the High Court.

23. Let us study a similar case of lodging a complaint of atrocities in Patewadi, Karjat Taluka, Ahmednagar District, in which a lower caste person lodged a case against a higher caste person on the ground that the latter did not allow him to take the funeral procession through the temple gates of the village. The decision of the Court is pending till now.

24. There is another case of atrocities which took place in the village, Malthan, Karjat Taluka, Ahmednagar District, in which a lower caste person filed a case against a higher caste person over the dispute of possession of land. The decision on the case is pending in the court of law.

25. The final case took place in the village Khandvi, Karjat Taluka, Ahmednagar District. The complainant claimed that he

was abused and harassed in the name of caste by the upper caste person. In his complaint he said that the higher caste people had always insulted him in the name of caste and created problems for him in the village unnecessarily. The case is still pending in the court.

Ultimately, we reach to an understanding that serious crimes regarding to atrocities have been committed against the Scheduled Castes and Scheduled Tribes people for different historical, social and economical reasons. Some of the cases have taken place on the grounds of historical reasons. It is due to the political awareness created amongst the Scheduled Caste and Scheduled Tribes people through spread of literacy, that they are trying to assert their rights and this is not taken very kindly by others. It is found that when these suppressed people assert their rights against the practices of untouchability, the vested interests of the upper class people try to suppress them and create terrorism in the society to which they belong. When they attempt to preserve their self-respect or the honour of their women, they take revenge on the upper caste people and lodge false complaints of atrocities and bring the matter to the courts which lead to dismissal or withdrawal of cases. One point which emerges out of this and which should be taken into consideration is that the executive, the police or the bureaucrats are not really stand very sincere in implementing the preventive measures taken by the Government.

The cases do not really stand before the courts and the acquitted or the accused are set free. In this context one of the senior members of Parliament pointed out, "We have already enacted so many Acts but the question remains that why the Judiciary is silent in this respect. It takes years and years for a case to get settled". He further lamented and questioned, "Do you think these poor people can afford to pursue the cases for years and years?"

In the light of the above remarks we are led to think that it is a pity that despite various measures taken by the Government, all these provisions and facilities do not reach the rural areas where these people reside.

Therefore, it is the need of the hour to find out the real reasons and rediscover the process of the implementation of PCR Act and the Atrocities Act. The researcher feels that besides enacting this legislation we must also consider the effective implementation of steps taken for their upliftment. Dr. B.R. Ambedkar had also suggested the reservation for improving their social lot because these people are subjected to social discrimination and segregation for thousands of years. The reservation will provide them a base to create their own employment and to improve their economic condition. The Harijans and *Adivasis* are trying to assert their rights in getting their employments in different fields, i.e., education, agriculture, industry, administration, etc. But the question remains unanswered as to how we are going to prevent the atrocities committed on the Dalits in the remote, rural parts of the country where the economic status of these people is below poverty line and where people lead hand to mouth existence. Dr. B.R. Ambedkar was unhappy over the plight of the downtrodden and people living in poor conditions. Even today poverty exists in the society and the *Adivasis* still live in deplorable conditions as their forefather did thousands of years ago.

Of course, there are various reasons behind atrocities committed on Harijans and Tribals. It is because of the improvement in the social setup during these 50 years of Independence, that these people have arisen, awakened and have begun resisting oppression.

In urban areas, these people do not find it difficult in getting justice regarding cases of atrocities because they are well organized and united. But in the rural parts of the country we experience that the people are disorganized and they lack unity which prevents them from getting early justice. So far much has been said about the PCR Act and the Atrocities Act and how they are being implemented.

Now we shall turn to specific solutions which can be offered for the total eradication of untouchability and establishing an ideal society where there will be no scope for any type of opposition, depression or segregation. It is no doubt a very difficult task to be achieved. But we must not leave any stone unturned while marching towards a progressive, united India. After carefully examing the cases of PCR Acts and atrocities committed on some of the Scheduled Caste people in Karjat Taluka of Ahmednagar District; it has been found that the above Acts were misused by the upper caste people forcing the lower caste people to lodge false complaints. Sometimes, the lower caste people themselves are responsible for filing false cases against the higher caste people.

Here, one can notice that both the Acts were unsuccessful in fulfilling the intentions for which they were enacted.

The provisions of these Acts are for the protection of the civil rights of the downtrodden but the very purpose of implementing these Acts appears to have been unsolved. The present study shows that the Scheduled Castes and Scheduled tribes have not been benefitted by the steps taken by the government. One of the MPs remarked, "Our ideology is clear and the intention of our Government is also good, but the implementation of these laws is the responsibility of the State Governments and they do not fulfil it. We enact the laws, but they are rarely implemented effectively."

The above remarks make it quite clear that the laws are for uplifting the downtrodden people to the level of higher caste people. The rift between the lower caste and higher caste people is to be removed and measures should be taken to bring these classes together with common culture. India has a fine legacy of cultural values. But the question is that whether we should preserve these values or not. Therefore, it is essential to see that there is no misuse of the PCR and the Atrocities Act by the upper caste as well as the lower caste people. The State Governments should take strong measures for the successful and proper implementation of the Acts. Governmental machinery is not taking the Acts seriously and therefore the FIRs are not properly filed leading to the failure of the cases. The respective police stations do not give sufficient protection to the poor Scheduled Caste people in the rural parts of our country in general and Maharashtra in particular. After having studied the cases which took place in Karjat Taluka of Ahmednagar District, in the light of the PCR Act and the Atrocities Act, it is necessary to draw a conclusion notwithstanding the verdict passed by the respective judges after the hearing of each one of the cases selected for the purpose of the study.

It is keenly followed that the verdict passed by the judges in these cases is based on the facts, witnesses and the nature of the Acts applicable to the cases. The results of most of these cases reveal that the higher caste Hindus, who were the accused, were either acquitted by the court or the cases were withdrawn. The question remains as to why the untouchables or the Dalits tend to file complaints against the higher caste Hindus. Do they think that the higher caste Hindus are the most cruel and barbaric people in the world? Why do the Dalits feel alienated from the mainstream of Hindu society. Today, the Dalits, comprising twenty per cent of the country's population, refuse to be called Hindus. Why? The Hindu society has always deprived the Dalits of their rights, ill treated, segregated and ostracized them. According to *Varnashram dharma,* they are to be placed in the lowest strata of Hindu society. Because of these and other reasons they prefer to keep themselves in isolation from the Hindu society. The following conclusions can be drawn in the light of the above questions and relating to the use of the PCR Act and the Atrocities Act in Karjat Taluka:

1. In majority of the cases which have been studied so far, it is noted that the accused is because of by the Judge concerned. If we go to the root of the problem, we feel that because of enough evidence and eyewitnesses in the villages, the higher caste Hindu is benefitted. The untouchables or the Dalits involved in these cases do not produce evidences and witnesses before the court. Despite the crime committed by the upper caste Hindus, people in the villages are unable to open their mouths before the police and the Judge. The fear in their minds does not allow them to come out with the truth. The untouchables are afraid of the police. The people who witness the incident of a higher caste Hindus abusing a Dalit, do not come forward and stand in the witness box for the Judge to give the verdict. Therefore, most of the cases were either withdrawn or the accused were set free.

2. The second genuine reason is "poverty". The lower caste people are not economically well off. They have to toil from dawn to dusk for earning their livelihood. Most of their time is spent in collecting food and other needs. Therefore, the untouchables who complain against the higher caste persons are unable to handle the case. In fact, they are unable to produce evidence in the court of law. On the other hand the upper caste person who are accused are comparatively quite rich. The poor people fall a prey to the rich man's offer of bribe money and speak against the untouchables.

3. It is observed that some cases are politically motivated. There are so several people belonging to different political parties. The Dalits also join hands with these political parties. It is because of rivalry, that the upper caste Hindus or landlords, instigate the poor untouchables to lodge a complaint against their high caste Hindu using the PCR Act and the Atrocities Act with the intention of giving a lesson to the members of the rival political party. However, these cases are either withdrawn or remain pending for several years.

4. The untouchables or the Dalits do not have adequate knowledge of the Acts on the basis of which they lodge complaints. Several Dalit villagers are not educated enough to understand and realize the pros and cons of the situation. They only know that law is behind them. It is communicated to them that the Government is with them and they can file a complaint against a higher caste Hindu who abuses them in the name of their caste. They do not know how to lodge a complaint. They take the help of the upper caste person who knows how to register a complaint. Nobody gives them the knowledge of the said matter.

5. It has been categorically stated that there exists casteism within the castes in the villages, where the Dalits among the Dalits exercise superiority over the weaker backward caste people or show that they are superior to the people of upper caste. There is a common tendency to provoke the more backward among the backwards and to lodge a complaint of atrocities against the persons from upper class category.

6. One of the observations is that there have been some lower caste people or higher caste people who instigate some of the lower people and force them to register a complaint in the name of caste against the person from the so-called established class. The vested interest of these people can be of various kind. For instance, in order to take revenge on others these cases of atrocities are lodged. Some cases are being lodged on the grounds of establishing superiority over other's success. Earning money is also one of the objective of lodging the complaints which are false in nature.

After studying the cases, one is led to realize that some of them are lodged on the basis of rivalry between the groups in the villages, trying to pull down one another and drawing the attention of the entire village community. It also has been noticed that because of conflict or strife between two political parties, some cases of atrocities have taken place in the villages of Karjat Taluka of Ahmednagar District. The cases taken for the purpose of study also indicate that there has been a selfish motive behind each one of them and, therefore, all those cases were set free by the respective judges and the accused were set free. Some cases reveal that there has been a revenge motive in the social groups involved in them. Some people in the villages who are unemployed, unnecessarily try to create disturbances in the society causing disharmony, leading the backward class people to register a case of atrocities in the court. In other words, there has been a tendency in some of the villagers to provoke quarrels between the backward class and the upper caste persons.

The Scheduled Castes and Scheduled Tribes (Prevention of Atrocities) Bill: Debates in the Parliament)

The Minister of State of the Ministry of Welfare (Dr. Rajendra Kumari Bajpai). I beg to move:

"That the Bill to prevent the commission of offences of atrocities against the members of the Scheduled Castes and the Scheduled Tribes, to provide for Special Courts for the trial of such offences and for the relief and rehabilitation of the victims of such offences and for matters connected therewith or incidental thereto be taken into consideration."

Mr. Deputy-Speaker, Sir, this House is aware of the deep concern our Government has for the welfare of the Scheduled Castes and Scheduled Tribes. A separate Ministry was created in 1985, specially for the welfare of weaker section of the society. Many new initiatives have been taken, particularly in the last few years to improve the lots of Scheduled Castes and Scheduled Tribes in trying to discharge a mandate of the Constitution. Poverty alleviation programmes which provide a special attention to the Scheduled Castes and Scheduled Tribes have been expanded and intensified.

Somnath Rath (in the chair)

First the IRDP and other programmes were improved considerably and now these have been replaced by a bigger scheme of the Jawahar Rozgar Yojana. It is because we think if we have to improve the economic conditions of the weaker sections of the society, specially Scheduled Castes and Scheduled Tribes and those who are below the poverty line, they should be given employment. For that, Jawahar Rozgar Yojana has come to help in a big way. Drinking water wells and irrigation wells have been provided for this group.

The need of housing has been met by the Indira Awaș Yojana. The programme for liberation of scavengers has been given a greater impetus. I want to tell the House that though in the Constitution, we have abolished untouchability it also true that unless and until we remove this sort of work, i.e., scavenging, there will not be much impact. So, the liberation of scavenging programme is very important for removing untouchability from our society. The education of Scheduled Castes and Scheduled Tribes which is of crucial importance to their growth and development has received much greater attention. Education is very important to fight not only poverty but it gives them strength to fight social injustice as well. We want Scheduled Castes and Scheduled Tribes people to stand against social injustice and for that awareness should be created through education. So, education programme is very important and under the new education policy and under the 20-point programme, we have laid emphasis to this aspect. The number of students studying beyond the matriculation stage has gone up to 13 lakhs. This is an open-ended scheme where we are providing scholarships to our Scheduled Castes and Scheduled Tribes boys so that they can go for higher studies. Coaching centre are provided to them so that they can take the advantage or avail the opportunity of competing with other sections of the society.

A special drive is currently on for filling up the backlog which had arisen as a result of non-fulfillments of reserved seats for SC/ST. Efforts are also being made to free them from bonded labour and to find land for cultivation.

As we all know, about forty five per cent of the Scheduled Castes population are landless labourers and they are mostly living below poverty line. So, they have to be given these facilities and we have to give them opportunity and some of them are bonded labour too. We will free them through this Bonded Labour Act and they will be rehabilated by giving them land and money as well.

Today we are witnessing the signs of development reaching the Scheduled Castes and Scheduled Tribes. But it is not all. With greater spread of education and with the socio-economic condition are improving, the relations in society sometimes come under tension as a result of this change. As the situation is changing and the change is coming into the society, we see that in the countryside, in rural India specially, there is some kind of tension also and that is due to atrocities on Scheduled Castes and Scheduled Tribes in some parts of the country or the other. Higher caste groups sometimes do not like change in the socio-economic structure and tension develop. These are the causes of atrocities and the Bill is intended to prevent these atrocities and so I am dealing with that.

The demand for justice, for equality, for a human living standard, for knowledge, for education and freedom leads in some cases to a realisation by groups who are not enlightened enough to recognise the healthy signs of growth. People are still not going to tolerate the growth of the development of Scheduled Castes or of those people who were till now working under them. They can come up and demand their rights. Sometimes tension erupts in the locality. In such situations, atrocities or a variety of offences are committed on members of Scheduled Castes and Scheduled Tribes. These are the causes. I have had occasion to tell this House regarding the recent trend in the increase of such offence against members of the Scheduled Castes and Scheduled Tribes. I have answered such questions many times in the last four years about atrocities on Scheduled Castes and Scheduled Tribes. Last week I was saying that I will be coming with some Bill on atrocities. Sometimes there was heated discussion on this point. This question is constantly raised in this House that there is increase of such offences against members of Scheduled Castes and Scheduled Tribes. Sometimes Hon. Members are also agitated on this. During 1988, there were a little over 15,000 offences against Scheduled Castes and 3,300 cases in respect of Scheduled Tribes. Of these, heinous offences such as murder, arson, rape and grievous hurt accounted for about 3,300 cases in respect of Scheduled Castes and 783 in respect of Scheduled Tribes. There are other minor offences also. This shows the tendency, trend and thinking of the upper caste people. They do not want that Scheduled Castes and Scheduled Tribes people should be respected in the society like others. The nature of these offences in many States indicated that these were not isolated instances but represented a trend in the country. In cities and towns and areas where the society was generally aware of the need to bring about such changes, the upward socio-economic mobility of the Scheduled Castes and Scheduled Tribes was accepted and tensions did not arise. But in certain rural areas things are very bad. In rural areas, traditions seem to be difficult to dislodge. It is difficult to dislodge the prejudices and traditions there. Hence, the Government thought that certain special measures would be necessary at this point of time. So, we are bringing in the Scheduled Castes and the Scheduled Tribes (Prevention of Atrocities) Bill. In this Bill, we have also defined as to what are the atrocities and we will specifically deal with those things.

Sir, the causes of such incidences were related generally to land or to continued exploitation or enforcement of traditional demeaning practices. It is regrettable that such instances have been reported such as in Kerala where a member of Scheduled Castes was forced to eat Human excreta. There are reports of a bridal party being chased and houses of this community razed to the ground merely because the bridegroom had the temerity to ride on a horse through the village streets. That bridegroom was riding on a horse. He was going through the village streets. So, the upper-caste people felt as to how he could ride on a horse and to the houses of those poor Scheduled Castes people were razed to the ground. The efforts of the Government to provide land have been frustrated in many cases. This is another example of atrocities on such people. In some States where the land is allotted to Scheduled Castes people, forcible dispossession or illegal occupation. Caste people forcible dispossession or illegal occupation of such land is reported to government. This is due to the fact that the upper-caste people are strong people. They think that these poor Scheduled Castes people should have no right on such lands. They forcibly occupy the land. So, land is also a cause of such atrocities. In Madhya Pradesh, recently the Government launched a special programme to see that possession or effectively restoring land to members of Scheduled Castes and Scheduled Tribes who had been pattas for the land, is implemented. Such programmes are taking place as a special drive. That is our policy. That is the guideline from the Central Government. So, they are trying to implement the programmes. But still there are cases where things are not properly implemented or if pattas are given to Scheduled Castes or Scheduled Tribes people, the upper-caste people in the village or those who are in possession of such land still try to hold the possession of the land or they grab the land meant for weaker sections. They will not part with that land. So the Scheduled Caste is not able to occupy that though he has got pattas. It is the one point of under cause or the pattern of atrocity that is committed on womenfolk. In unfortunate incidents the women folk or Scheduled Castes and Scheduled Tribes sought to be dishonoured and assaulted with the object of teaching a lession to that community. This is a very ugly sort of thing and a very cruel mode of thing which is resorted to by certain people. And this is the worst type of atrocities committed on Scheduled Castes people in dishonouring women. In tribal areas sexual exploitation is now to occur and the willingness of the innocent tribal women is secured by exercise of authority or influence. The community is sometimes sought to be pressurised by denying them access to public places for easing themselves or for cremation or a water source, etc. Such type of things are still going on in some parts of India. Now in the 20th century, this is very shameful for the society. We have to not only create awareness but we have also to stop it with strong hand. We are going to take this strong measure.

Instances have occurred of fouling of water source or dumping carcass in the vicinity of their houses. It is to humiliate and tease the Scheduled Caste people. All these when taken together form a pattern which calls for more stringent legislative measures.

The Bill which is before this House seeks to classify most of such instances as Atrocities on Scheduled Castes and Scheduled Tribes. We have defined these atrocities and included all these atrocities in this Bill. Although many of these offences could probably be covered under normal law of the land, we are witnessing today a difference in degree which calls for a differentiation in kind in respect of these offences. It was necessary to bring this Bill. The Bill hence proposes to specify higher punishments as also laying down some minimum punishment for such offences. We have elaborately mentioned the various kinds of atrocities which we have included in this Bill.

I will only mention two or three points though there are so many other points which are the salient features of the new legislation. For the first time, we have defined this term in this Bill, that is, what will constitute atrocity. It says: "Forcing a member of Scheduled Caste or Scheduled Tribe to drink or eat any inedible or obnoxious substance as the human excreta or acting with as intention to cause injury, insulting or annoying by dumping excreta, carcasses and other similar items in the locality, taking off their clothes forcibly particularly of the women folk, forcibly dispossessing them of their land and keeping them as bonded labour and forcing them to do beggar, interfering in the rights guaranteed to them for representation in public bodies, through elections, utilising legal process for causing harassment and injury by instituting false, malicious or vexatious suits or legal proceedings against them and subjecting their women folk to assault and sexual exploitations by persons in a position to dominate their will".

Property is often the basis of atrocities on Scheduled Castes and Scheduled Tribes. Hence, wrongful dispossession of the property is made an atrocity under the Bill. The Bill also provides that upon conviction, in addition to a sentence to be passed, the movable and immovable property belonging to the convicted persons and used in the offences would be liable for forfeiture. This is very important and that is why it is made very stringent.

The Bill includes offences relating to property of persons and carrying punishments of ten years and above under the Indian Penal Code and committed by non-Scheduled Castes and non-Scheduled Tribes on the ground that the victims happen to be members of Scheduled Castes and Scheduled Tribes, as atrocities.

The Scheduled Tribes living in Scheduled Areas or Tribal Areas are harmed in many ways by vested elements. Article 19 (1) provides for the protection of the interests of the Scheduled Tribes. The Bill, therefore, provides for externment of a person who is likely to commit an atrocity as defined in the Act against a member of a Scheduled Tribe in a Scheduled or Tribal Area, from that area for a period extending to two years.

The Bill provides for minimum punishment of six months imprisonment and fine for the offences.

Some of the other features of the Bill are appointment of Special Courts and Special public prosecutors, conferment of powers exercisable by a police officer or any officer of the State Government and protective and preventive measures that are to be taken by the law and order machinery to check the atrocities. The Bill further contemplates arrangements for effective implementation of the Act, and among other things, provides for economic and social rehabilitation of the victims of atrocities. These are the salient features of the Bill.

We say that prevention is better than cure and the Bill also looks after the preventive measures. If an area is declared prone to atrocities it will become the bonded duty of the law and order machinery to take all possible measures for instilling a sense of safety and security. Schemes would be formulated under the general guidance of the Government of India to provide for such measures as also for providing prompt and adequate relief and rehabilitation in the unfortunate event of atrocities taking place. We have kept all these provisions not only on the preventive side, but at the same time to see the rehabilitation part also.

The Bill places a special responsibility on the public servants who are not members of Scheduled Castes or Scheduled Tribes to take action to protect the interests of Scheduled Castes and Scheduled Tribes against atrocities being committed or taking of protective and rehabilitative measures.

The Bill overall aims at ensuring this when the fruits of development and spread of education is now reaching the Scheduled Castes and Scheduled Tribes the benefits therefrom are not taken away or denied by vested interests. I am sure these measures will be welcomed by all and enlightened sections of society and that we shall in our country succeed in removing the stain of such inhuman treatment towards a section of our people by vested interests. The dream of Mahatma Gandhi for the uplift of these groups is being brought to reality by our government and I seek your cooperation in passing this Bill and taking message to that far corners of our country. I hope that after giving your comments, this Bill will help in creating a proper atmosphere in the whole of the country and this Bill is going to have effect all over.

With these few words, Sir, I beg to move the motion for consideration.

Mr. Chairman: Motion moved.

"That the Bill to prevent the commission of offences of atrocities against the members of the Scheduled Castes and the Scheduled Tribes to provide to special courts for the trial of such offences and for the relief and rehabilitation of the victims of such offences and for matters connected therewith of incidental there to be taken into consideration."

Mr. Ram Ratan Ram (Hajipur): Mr. Chairman, Sir, first of all, I would like to congratulate the Prime Minister and also the Welfare Minister Dr. Rajendra Kumari Bajpai, of going ahead with this very progressive Bill, after the lapse of forty years of our independence.

Just now, our respected Welfare Minister has mentioned about the dream of Mahatma Gandhi. No doubt, his dream of Mahatma Gandhi is going to be fulfilled after the lapse of fifty-four years of independence.

So far as the question of atrocities, tortures, land grabbing, rape and whatsoever is incorporated in this Bill, is concerned, it has been going on for centuries after centuries. It is not that it is just coming up today. It has been there for the last so many centuries.

I would like to congratulate the Prime Minister and also the Welfare Minister—who has got the motherly affection for the members of the Scheduled Castes and the Scheduled Tribes—for bringing forward this unique Bill. With this unique Bill, no doubt, the members of the Scheduled Castes and the Scheduled Tribes will have some relief. I would like to thank Dr. Rajendra Kumari Bajpai for this. Before I go ahead—as the Hon. Minister has said just now—I would like to read the Statement of Objects and Reasons, which says:

"Despite various measures to improve the socio-economic conditions of the Scheduled Castes and the Scheduled Tribes, they remain vulnerable. They are denied number of civil rights. They are subjected to various offences, indignities, humiliations and harassment. They have, in several brutal incidents, been deprived of their life and property. Serious crimes are committed against them for various historical, social and economic reasons.

Due to awareness created amongst the Scheduled Castes and the Scheduled Tribes through spread of education, etc. they are trying to assert their rights and this is not being taken very kindly by others. When they assert their rights and resist practices of untouchability against them or demand statutory minimum wages or refuse to do any bonded and forced labour, the vested interests try to cow them down and terrorise them. When the Scheduled Castes and Scheduled Tribes try to preserve their self-respect or honour of their women, they become irritants for the dominant and the mighty. Occupation and cultivation of even the Government allotted land by the Scheduled Castes and Scheduled Tribes is resented and more often these people become victims of attacks by the vested interests".

So, all these details are here. No doubt, this Bill is very unique. There is nothing left out in this Bill. Even a slightest point is not left out, so far as the question of prevention of the atrocities and the crime is concerned.

But what is that was not there is the Indian Penal Code by which action could not be taken but the main thing is one the civil side—the executive and the police are not really very sincere to implement these measures and go ahead with the very object and vision of the government. That is the whole question. We have already enacted so many Acts but the whole question is till today the judiciary is silent on this matter. It takes years and years for a case to get settled. Do you think these poor people can afford to pursue the cases for years and years? They cannot afford to do so with the result of offenders get scot free and thereby our people are put to a lot of harassment. No doubt, this Act will give some benefit and relief to our members but I want to touch the basic point. Whenever a crime, atrocity, torture etc. is committed against the members of the Scheduled Castes and Scheduled Tribes first of all they have to go to the police station to lodge an FIR. Here in this Act nothing has been mentioned about the police officers. Crimes, atrocities, tortures, etc. are there but when they go to the police station the police officers there refuse to record the FIR. What is the way out for this? What action do we propose to take against those police officers who are still silent on the matter? In that respect I would have been grateful to the Hon. Minister if some way had been found out to curb such police officers as well. Now no case can stand unless an FIR is there and the police report is there. Our people go to the police station. The police officers there refuse to register the FIR. On the other hand our people are put to difficulty by being accused that they are making a false statement. So our people are afraid of going to the police station. They rather prefer to tolerate the inhuman treatment.

Mr. Chairman: May I draw the Hon. Member's attention to Clause 4 of the Bill?

Mr. Ram Ratan Ram: Mr. Chairman, my point is, will my people go to the police to lodge the FIR and also will the police officers there be sincere enough to take note of that? There are provisions even in the IPC. My point is what action you propose to take against such police officers who refuse to record the FIR and on the other hand put our people to harassment and torture. They go to the police station. They are asked to sit there for one or two days. No action is taken. So, what action has been proposed to be taken against such police officers? There should be a remedy to tackle such a situation. A special court will no doubt be there. Our prosecutor will be there. A separate advocate will also be there.

Everything has been provided in this Bill. But there is no mention about action against such police officers. That is what I wanted to bring to the notice of the Hon. Minister.

Everything is mentioned in detail in this Bill. But so far as the question of externment is concerned, the option has been given to the offender. On page 6, it has been said:

"Where the Special Court is satisfied, upon a complaint or a police report that a person is likely to commit an offence under chapter II of this Act in any area included in 'Scheduled Areas' or 'Tribal areas', as referred to in Article 244 of the Constitution, it may, by order in writing, direct such person to remove himself beyond the limits of such area, by such route and within such time as may be specified in the order, and not to return to that area from which he was directed to remove himself for such period, not exceeding two years, as may be specified in the order."

My point is that option has been given to the man who is going to commit a crime of who has already committed a crime. Will the man, who has been asked by the court to remove himself, carry out the order or not? That question has to be considered. Why should an option be left to the criminal. Suppose such person does go from the areas as defined, what is the guarantee that he will not come again and commit the offences? Such lacunae are there.

I am very thankful to the Hon. Minister for having brought forward such a progressive Bill after 40 years of our independence for the welfare and protection of people belonging to the Scheduled Castes and Scheduled Tribes. Our people are getting education. It is a marvellous and unique. We are happy and satisfied. But still there are some lacunae. Some options have been given which should not be there.

So far as the question of casting of vote concerned, what is the remedy? Booth-capturing is still there. Our people are not allowed to cast their votes in favour of the candidates whom they like. Separate booths are there. Booths are also set up in the localities of the Scheduled Castes and Scheduled Tribes. Since I come from the tribal area. I know that the tribal population is concentrated much more than the Scheduled Castes. The Scheduled Castes are not that much concentrated as the tribals. And that is why, Government was kind enough to create booths for the Scheduled Castes in every locality so that people can exercise their franchise. In spite of the fact that there are booths in every locality and village, there are *goondas* persons who bribe and do not allow people to caste their votes. There is no doubt that remedy is there in this Bill. But I would like to point out to the Minister that remedy is also possible by appointing a police officer when the question of adult franchise comes. I would like to say that some police arrangement must be made. But at the same time, I have got an apprehension about he police officers. The police officers are there to create offences themselves. They train the criminals. They ask the criminals to commit crimes. So, more Scheduled Castes and Scheduled Tribes officers should be appointed and posted at the police stations and unless our people are posted at the police stations itself and made the officer-in-charge. I do not think that the objective of the Government will be fulfilled by the Act since the power is in their hands. At the very initial stage, people will have to go to the police station to report the crime. Unless this is done, nobody can go to the court, whether it is a special court or whatever court it may be. The question of going to court comes later on. First of all, one has to go to the police station to report. Somehow our people have gone to the police station to have FIRs lodged after the offences like murder, rape, etc. were committed, as mentioned in this Act. But whole question is about the witnesses. The court will have to proceed according to the witnesses. The court cannot hang anybody simply on my saying, as a member of a Scheduled Castes or a Scheduled Tribes, that my daughter has been raped or my son has been murdered by this man or that man. The court of law cannot convict a person like that. So, witness is necessary. Wherefrom will be witness come? That is my point. Some torture is going on by some persons who still cannot be influenced. They still terrorise the people by saying that if they go to the court as witnesses, none will be allowed to remain in the village, all of them will be burnt or murdered. No doubt, there is action taken. Even if there is any apprehension, our people will go to the court or the police station and report by saying that an apprehension is there. And action will be definitely taken by this Act. But a sort of fear is there in the minds of people. People are afraid. When my whole village gets burnt and when we will not survive, what will the court do? This sort of feeling is there among the people. We have to look into this aspect also. The Government cannot go into all these details. They cannot post a magistrate for every door or every village. We have to find some ways so that the minds of our people are free from such weaknesses and fear. All those people who come and frighten and threaten people will have to be set right. This aspect will have to be looked into. We cannot depend on the government all the time that they would do everything for us. We have to do something ourselves also. Of course, the Bill as brought forward by the Hon. Minister is very unique and marvellous and I would like to express my thanks for the same.

I would like to make one more point regarding the grabbing of land. The Government was very kind to allot land to our landless people. Most of our people are landless, and bonded labourers in the villages. Though the land had been allotted to these poor people, in many cases it has been grabbed from them and it is a very big problem to restore the possession to them. Though the Bill deals and takes care of the various problems relating to the bonded and landless labourers and grabbing of land by unauthorised people, yet it would require a lot of effort to put these provisions into practice. By this Central Act, we are going to give protection to these poor people throughout the country, but at the same time, in many matters we have to depend on the State administration. This legislation will be applicable throughout the country, and the State Government should be very sincere and honest in implementing it and particularly, they must take care of the Scheduled Castes and Scheduled Tribes so far as the land problem is concerned. We have given land to the landless people and most of these people have been dispossessed from the land, and the possession has not been restored to them. They have to go to the court of law. How many of our people have got enough money to go to the court of law? Of course, the provision is there that you will finance our people for this. In fact, these innocent people are afraid of going to the court. Though this problem has been definitely dealt with very nicely and adequately in this Bill, it is very difficult to restore the possession of the land, allotted to these people, once they are dispossessed of it. The law is there, the magistracy is there, the officers are there, yet we are not getting the required protection. I do not think the special courts will ever go to the spot to restore possession of the land to these people.

In this context, I would like to suggest that the cases relating to the land problem as also atrocities on these people should not take more than thirty days; these should be disposed of within that period. Only then, we can have faith and confidence that something is going to be done for us.

With these words, I conclude and would like to convey my heartiest thanks to the Prime Minister as also the Welfare Minister for bringing forwards this Bill, which would definitely provide relief to the poor people.

[*Translation*]

Mr. Ganga Ram (Firozabad): Mr. Chairman, Sir, the Scheduled Castes and Scheduled Tribes (Prevention of Atrocities) Bill, 1989 moved by the Hon. Minister of Social Welfare is the culmination of deep studies made on the problem process of which was started 4 to 5 years ago. During this period, the Hon. Minister had several rounds of discussion with the Hon. Members of Parliament and organised seminars and conventions of the representatives of the Scheduled Castes and the Scheduled Tribes to interact with them about the difficulties being faced by them. This is not only an exhaustive Bill but an improved one also as it contains all the good provisions for introducing this Bill.

After forty years of independence, a concrete step has been taken to prevent the atrocities on the people belonging to Scheduled Castes and Scheduled Tribes and constitute 25 crore of the total population of the country. It was Mahatma Gandhi who in 1932 had staked his life to make these castes as an integral part of the Indian society and he also did a lot for their betterment. Words falls short to describe the efforts of Pt. Jawaharlal Nehru and Dr. Baba Saheb Ambedkar in ameliorating the lot of these poor sections of our society and infusing the feeling of self-respect among them. I would like to quote what Pt. Jawaharlal Nehru said about Dr. Ambedkar.

"I imagine that the way he will be remembered most will be as a symbol of revolt against all the oppressive forces and features of Hindu society. He rebelled against something against which all should and ought to rebel and we have in face rebelled in various degrees."

[*Translation*]

After going through this Bill, it appears that the Hon. Minister and for that matter the Government of India brought this Bill with a view to giving a warning to the oppressors, and who exploit the poor in order to remove social inequality.

The Hon. Minister has explained in detail the objects of moving this Bill in the House. The Acts and laws made till date on the subject, mainly the Removal of Untouchability Act, 1955 and the Protection of Civil Rights Act, 1987 could not be proved effective. All of us agree that the implementation of these Acts have been very poor.

A number of schemes have been launched for upliftment and development of the people belonging to Scheduled Castes and Scheduled Tribes and weaker section of society which constitute twenty-five per cent of the total population of the country. The credit for the scheme such as 20-point programme, IRDP, NREP, Jawahar Rozgar Yojana, Special Component Plan and the Scheduled Castes and Scheduled Tribes Financial Corporation goes to none other than the Congress Party. During the stewardship of the Hon. Minister, Central Government has set up a separate Financial Development Corporation for these sections, whose jurisdiction runs throughout the country. Indira Awas Yojana and many other schemes were also launched, but unfortunately they could not be effectively implemented by the present machinery of the Government. This reminds me of a few lines of a couplet of a poet:-

Kitne Badal Baras Rahe Hain, Phir Bhi Paudhe Taras Rahe Hain,
Yahi Chaman Ko Acharaj Bhai, Pani Kahan Chala Jata Hai?

It is a pity that despite several measures taken by Government, all these facilities have not reached the rural areas at the grassroot level. We must find out the reasons, for this. Besides enacting this legislation we must also consider the effective implementation of measures taken for their upliftment because atrocities are closely inter-related to their upliftment.

I do remember that during the Janata Party rule, when I was in Lucknow, a decision was taken to withdraw reservation facility for SC/ST. However the Government of Janata Party was dismissed that very evening thereby saving the helpless poor. On coming to power, the Congress Party not only continued the policy of reservation, but also implemented it effectively. Recently, the young Hon. Prime Minister has tried his best to clear the backlog of reserved vacancies very earnestly. For this the Hon. Prime Minister and the Hon. Minister of Social Welfare both deserve to be congratulated. This created great fervour and enthusiasm among the poor all over the country, especially the constitutional amendment Bills of *Panchayati Raj* and the *Nagarpalika* have infused great confidence in the people.

Under *Panchayati Raj* system, reservation for them has been given upto the grassroot level only.

Many people do not understand the meaning of reservation. I would like to explain its meaning before the House. We keep on demanding reservation in appointment and promotion in services and in allotment of gas agencies etc. Explaining the meaning of reservation, Dr. Ambedkar had stated that the reservation had been made for social upliftment of the people who had been subjected to social discrimination for thousands of years and in order to achieve the goal, some sort of discrimination against some people would have to be done. That discrimination can be termed as reservation for which down from Mahatma Gandhi to all the leaders of the present generation trying to achieve in right earnest.

The opposition has done nothing in this direction except making hue and cry. The House is the witness to their behaviour and sincerity shown during the last fourty years when they raised the issue of Bofors only and nothing else. Opposition never discussed the issues pertaining to the poor and on the other hand wasted time of the House. They do not know against whom they are levelling charges. They are levelling charges against the person who is trying to anchor the ship of the country from the turbulent sea. To them I can-say, *Tum sahil wale kya jano, yeh tufan kaun uthata hai, yek kishti kaun dubota hai.* It is the opposition which is raising storms to drown the ship which is being anchored by our leader. Therefore, under the present conditions, neither we nor the people have any expectations from the opposition parties. The poor people are looking towards the Congress Party headed by the Hon. young Prime Minister only and the Hon. Minister of Social Welfare, who have political will and the determination to act upon. The present Bill to stop atrocities is bold and praiseworthy, though many programmes are already in progress.

A little time ago, Shri Ram Ratan Ram, who is a veteran Member of the House pointed out some shortcomings in the Bill. But before I go into them, I would like to refer to the last report of the Scheduled Castes and Scheduled Tribes Commission regarding atrocities. Commission has stated, which I quote.

[*English*]

"A review of the available atrocity data for the years 1982 to 1984 presents a somewhat disturbing trend. The overall number of cases of atrocity against the Scheduled Castes that had decline from 15,051 in 1981 to 14,8947 in 1983, recorded an increase to 16,586 in 1984. In 1987, the highest number of atrocity cases was reported from Madhya Pradesh (6128) followed by Uttar Pradesh (4200), Bihar (1845) and Rajasthan (1648). These States together with Tamilnadu (489), Gujarat (690) and Maharashtra (579) among themselves accounted for about ninety five per cent of the cases of atrocities reported during the year under review."

[*Translation*]

This has been stated by the Commission. The report of the Commissioner for Scheduled Castes and Scheduled Tribes for the year 1986 is also available now. At present Shri B.G. Sharma is the Commissioner. He has made an indepth studies of the problem throughout the country and his report is before us. As regards atrocities, total number of serious crimes committed in 1986 has been given in the report. Earlier, only serious crimes were treated as atrocities. Under the G.O. of the ministry of home affairs, serious crime includes murder under Section 302 of IPC, grievously hurt under Sections 324 and 376 IPC, rape under Section 376 IPC, arson under Section 436 IPC and some other serious crimes but in the present Bill, the Hon. Minister has made the definition of the serious crime more exhaustive. The Commissioner for the Scheduled Castes and the Scheduled Tribes in his report has stated that in 1986 alone, as many as 15,416 serious crimes, earlier used to known as atrocities, were committed. Out of them, as many as 3945 crimes were committed against the people belonging to the Scheduled Tribes. In our country, there are 1085 Scheduled Castes and 639 Scheduled Tribes. As regards their population in the country, population of Scheduled Castes and Scheduled Tribes are 15 crore and 10 crore respectively. Atrocities have also been committed in the same proportion against them. The causes of atrocities as pointed out by the Commissioner and the Hon. Minister are cent per cent correcr. In the objects and reasons of the bill, it has been correctly stated that the atrocities are committed on them because feudal elements in the society do not tolerate that the poor peope should live with honour and peace in the society. The poor the Scheduled Castes and Scheduled Tribes wish to lead a peaceful and happy life in this independent India, without being forced to bear insults. In the objects of Bill, it has been accepted that they are subjected to atrocities. This Bill has been brought forward with a view to stop atrocities on them so that they may lead a respectable life. This is the need of the hour. Even on moral ground, nobody has got any right to insult one. It can be observed from the statement of objects and reasons attached to the Bill that maximum atrocities are committed in Madhya Pradesh followed by Uttar Pradesh, Bihar and Rajasthan. After a deep study of the matter as to why Madhya Pradesh is on the top of the list, I came to conclusion that feudalism was the sole reason for it. This area has been under the control of feudal big *zamindars* and *nawabs* for a pretty long time. There were several small princely states who used to force the people to work. Their outlook was so feudal that in order to satisfy their false ego, these people did not allow common men to sit down on the cots before them. Mostly incidents of arocities have occurred mainly in North India, e.g., Jahangirabad, Deoli, Sadupur, etc. I would like to tell about Deoli incident which occurred in 1982 in which as many as 23 persons were massacred. Two main accused named Santosha and Radhe were not allowed to be arrested on behest of the then Chief Minister of Uttar Pradesh who is the leader of opposition today and is leading them. He helped those accused and made them surrender in the courts only. This ghastly crime was committed in 1980-81 and the case is still pending in the court. The case is being get delayed by big *zamindars* and feudal lords who have been helping them. Not only this, Santosha filed even nomination for the post of *Pradhan* from the Jail itself. They are providing protection to those criminals. People of Janta Dal are providing protection to persons having criminal record. I think that if such people come in power what benefit they will provide to Scheduled Castes and Scheduled Tribes. The future of the Harijans will become bleak if they come in power.

Hon. Minister has rightly said that bonded labour is one of causes of atrocities on them. An Act to abolish bonded labour system was passed in 1976 on the initiative of our leader late Shrimati Indira Gandhi but bonded labour still exists in our country in one form or the other. In a conference, a high police official had expressed his views that political awareness among weaker sections, Scheduled Castes and Scheduled Tribes, for which credit goes to our Party, was one of the reasons for atrocities on them. The Congress Party has infused a sense of self-respect among them. Now when their self-respect is hurt, conflicts arise and atrocities are committed. Their women are raped and entire village is burnt. I have seen in Uttar Pradesh that atrocities are committed merely for such reasons. Bihar Government faced a lot of difficulties in implementing provisions of Minimum Wages Act. People who commit atrocities do not give minimum wages to these poor people. The Commissioner for Scheduled Castes and Scheduled Tribes has mentioned in his report that farm labourers are given 5 kilograms of flour and some quantity of rice as daily wages or Rs. 8.50 in cash and it is also not known if it is actually paid or not, whereas an amount or less than Rs. 18.50 a day has been prescribed as the Minimum Wage under the Minimum Wages Act. Demand of minimum wages is one of the major causes of atrocities and harassment to Harijans.

Many aspects of the problem have been covered in this Bill. However, I would like to draw the attention of Hon. Minister towards some of points about which he has just made a mention. It is good that a provision has been made to setup special courts which has a long standing demand. In this regard, I would like to submit that cases of atrocities should be disposed of in summary trials, particularly in view of the fact that a number of years are wasted in investigation of the case and justice is not provided to them, as has been said by Ram Ratan Ram. More the delay, more the injustice is done to them. While drawing attention towards Section 4 of the Bill, the Hon. Minister has stated that if public servant is found involved in it, he will also be punished. I would like to say in this connection that police officers also commit atrocities on Scheduled Castes and Scheduled Tribes. The Hon. Minister should think as to how he will tackle this problem of involvement of police officials in commissioning atrocities on these classes.

[Mr. Deputy-Speaker *in the Chair*]

Their FIR will be written by the police officers. What provision has been made for this? The Government should make special arrangements for the areas from where a large number of cases of atrocities are reported. It is true that different State Government have appointed special IGs and DIGs for this purpose. But it would have been better if a provision is made specifically in this Bill itself. Of course, a provision has been made in Section 4 with regard to atrocities to be committed by the public servants, still there is a need to look into this matter.

I would like to say one thing about the onus of providing the crime. You should think about it. Under Section 5 of Prevention of Corruption Act and Section 161 of IPC onus of proving innocence lies on the accused. Similarly, onus of proving innocence should be laid on the accused under this Bill. In that case, he will have to prove that he has not committed atrocities or he has not abused or insulted the complaint, then it will be a great thing. People will get justice. I welcome and support this Bill provisions of which are well considered.

It would like to conclude my speech with recital of a few lines of a poem of Shri Rangji:-

Ab na sahan hogi bebasi ki yatna,
Ant swayam kar raha srijan ki sadhana,
Aadmi ka kal aaj aadmi bana,
Ek-dusare se aaj ho rahi ghrina,
Aadmi ko aadmi ka pyar chahiye
Aaj desh ko naye vichar chahiye

and

Vartman ka ore dekhta
Aaj bhavishya mahan,
Kya jane kis khyan ho jaye
Navyug ka Nirman

By moving this Bill, government has done a very good work. I hope that twenty five per cent people of this country will get relief from this Bill, their problems will be solved and their difficulties and troubles will be reduced.

With these words, I support the Bill.

Mr. Harish Rawat (Almora): Hon. Deputy-Speaker, Sir, I would like to thank the Minister for Welfare for moving this Bill. This Bill is a warning to the people who kept on commiting atrocities on the people belonging in Scheduled Castes and Scheduled Tribes by taking undue advantage of some lacunae in the law. I feel that the Hon. Minister has consolidated the various offences so as to include them in this Bill. This Bill has been drafted after indepth studies and careful consideration, I would like to extend my thanks to all those people who have assisted in drafting this Bill and consolidating the list of atrocities, etc.

Mr. Deputy-Speaker, Sir, laws were already there for giving protection to the people belonging to Scheduled Castes and Scheduled Tribes but the people who were entrusted responsibility to implement the law, belonged to the class who were aversed to it. That is why the law was not implemented properly. This is the reason why we have been raising this issue from time to time in this House.

I am in complete agreement with Mr Ganga Ram that with the awareness among Harijans, atrocities on Harijans have also increased. I would even like to add that whenever a Government comes into power which thinks about the welfare of the Harijans and wants to give protection to them either at the Centre or in the States, incidents of atrocities increase as Harijans and Tribals resist atrocities in the hope that the present Government is benefactor and protector of their rights.

A debate was held in 1982 in this House on atrocities on Harijans. At that time Members belonging to Janata Party expressed view that incidents of atrocities on Harijans had gone down during the period from 1977 to 1980 when they were in power at the Centre, whereas the fact was otherwise atrocities were committed in greater degree but they were not reported because the victims did not want to go to police stations to lodge reports. If at all some of them went to police stations to lodge reports, their reports were not lodged by the police. When Congress Government was formed in 1980, a new awareness was created among Harijans and Tribals who began to feel secure. They again began to resist atrocities perpetrated on them in the villages. I feel that the drawbacks and loopholes in IPC and criminal procedure code will be plugged to a great extent after enactment of this Bill. Now accused will not take undue advantage of the loopholes to escape punishment for the crime. These drawbacks have been removed.

Hon. Deputy Speaker, Sir, it has all along been the policy of our Government and the Congress Party that the weaker section should be protected. Even during the days of freedom struggle,

Congress Party was the champion of the cause of weaker sections. Removal of untouchability was a part of our national struggle. When Gandhiji talked about freedom from the British rule, he also talked about removal of untouchability and religious discrimination. The Congress Party has inherited these ideals as its legacy. Voice has always been raised against those who commit atrocities. It is the reason why our Government always thinks in this direction. So far as necessity of enactment of laws are concerned, necessary laws have been enacted to check arocities on Harijans and weaker sections, even then atrocities on them have not stopped due to economic base of the people belonging to weaker sections, Harijans and Tribals is very weak. No atrocity is committed on the person who is economically sound. He can go to the court and seek protection. He can even resist but the Harijans and Tribals who are landless and unable to go to the court for remedy are subjected to atrocities. Even police does not heed to their complaints. He has no time to register their complaints.

Government has taken several steps in this direction. Very recently, Jawahar Rozgar Yojana has been introduced and representation of Harijans and weaker sections has been provided in Panchayats. This been done because the Government wants to make these sections economically self-reliant and to provide representation to them at the grass-root level. In this way, they will be able to express their views and raise their voice freely without any fear. Unless the weaker sections will be given ownership right of land, they will not be able to resist the atrocities being committed on them. Therefore, I would like to request the Government through you that there is need to allot land to every Harijan under Land Reforms Act so that he is able to build his house on the land of his own and cultivate it for agricultural purposes. This is the primary duty of the Government. Those who do not own agricultural land should be provided other means of livelihood. The Government and the whole society should think in this direction so that the Harijans and the Tribals can become self-reliant. I think this will enable us to control the atrocities to a large extent and to solve the problem. With these words, I support this Bill and thank the Hon. Minister of State of the Ministry of Welfare, the Hon. Prime Minister and the Government in this regard.

Bapulal Malviya (Shajapur): Mr. Deputy Speaker, Sir, I support the Scheduled Castes and Scheduled Tribes (Prevention of Atrocities) Bill. Today, the Hon. Prime Minister has assured that all the reserved vacancies shall be filled up within a maximum period of three months and ceaseless efforts are being made to fulfil this pledge. This is a very significant step. It is for the first time since independence that the Hon. Prime Minister has taken the initiative of clearing the backlog of reserved vacancies. The Hon. Prime Minister has made a major contribution to the upliftment of the Scheduled Castes and Scheduled Tribes through the *Jawahar Rozgar Yojana.* The Bill under consideration will also go a long way in solving the problems of the Scheduled Castes and Scheduled Tribes as is evident from its provisions.

Two of the provisions of this Bill are very appropriate. I would like to submit the social problems of the Scheduled Castes and Scheduled Tribes in the rural areas and expect that the Hon. Prime Minister will provide assistance in solving them. Apart from these problems the primary problem is that of land. The 20-point Programme Coordination Committee was constituted during the tenure of Indira Gandhi. Lease deeds of land were given through these committees but they were not given actual possession of their land. What is the reason behind it. In this connection, the work of the Madhya Pradesh Government is laudable. The former Chief Minister of the State, Arjun Singh and the present Chief Minister Motilal Vora have done praiseworthy work. A committee by the name of *Adhikar Abhiyan Samittee* has been constituted there and I am also a member of this committee. This committee has been doing commendable work. Those persons who were given lease deeds for land 15 to 20 years ago have given actual possession of their land. The Collectors and Tehsildars in the State have been told that if the lease deed holders are not given possession of land, action will be taken against them. They were also told that if the Department of Revenue is incapable of carrying out this task the assistance of Police should be taken. The results have been very encouraging seventy-five per cent of the lease deed holders have not got possession of their land and only twenty-five per cent have still to get it. I think they will also get their possession shortly. Similar committees should be constituted all over the country. If a piece of land belonging to a Harijan happens to be located in between two plots of land is forcibly occupied and he is evicted with the result that he is compelled to sell it off. As per my experience, if a Harijan has a piece of land in the village and it is also fertile, the caste Hindus would entrap him by turning him into an alcohol addict and would provide money for purchasing the same and in this way, they would eventually rob his piece of land. As in the case of Adivasis, there should be restrictions on the sale of land belonging to the Harijans as well. There should be a law to the effect that the land cannot be occupied forcibly. The land belonging to the Harijans are not registered with the result that they are often evicted by those to whom they owe money. The Hon. Minister has stated that 3,000 cases of atrocities have come to their notice. Besides these cases, there are several cases which are not reported because the poor Harijans are prevented by the village musclemen from filing their complaints to the police in this regard. In this way many atrocities are committed on them, but the rich and influential people in the village do not allow them to report the matter to the police and even harm them physically. Some Harijans came to me with their complaints and they informed me that they had to take a separate and a longer route because they feared that the musclemen in their villages would prevent them from going to lodge the complaint. FIRs in this regard should be filed in the local police stations but they are unable to do so and they have to approach the SP for this purpose. These days the political leaders and even the police officers have little say with the result that cases are not registered. Only these influential people hold away and everybody is at their mercy. This is a very big problem. Presently, police stations have been set up exclusively for the Harijans. But in these police stations also, the situation is same. The policemen who register their complaints demand bribes and in this way atrocities are committed on the Harijans. It has also been observed that the Prevention of Untouchability Act has also not proved effective. It is necessary to make this law effective. During the Janata wave in 1977, a Harijan Congress worker was much harassed by the BJP workers. He was made to wear the clothes of a women and made to dance on the streets. Such atrocities should be checked by framing necessary legislation. So far as I think, social programmes are based on social perspectives....

Mr. Virdi Chander Jain (Barmer): Provisions have been made in this Bill.

Mr. Bapulal Malviya: I am putting forward one suggestion. You will observe that Harijans are discriminated against on social occasions and at public places. They are not allowed to sit at the same place with the caste Hindus. If the caste Hindus sit on the mats, the Harijans are told to sit somewhere else. If the Harijans sit on the mats, the caste Hindus sit on raised platform. This kind of discrimination which is practised everywhere should be removed. Atrocities are committed on women but they are prevented from reporting them. Much discrimination is practised in the rural areas. The Harijan children are not allowed to sit along with the children of other castes. In the tea-clubs of the teachers, the Harijan teachers are not included. The messengers also do not fetch tea for them nor do they wash their clothe. Consequently, the Harijan members of the staff refuse to become members of the staff tea-club. These are minor problems which should be removed. I think, the government should took into this aspect of practising discrimination even in places which are open to all. There are private temples in rural areas and the Harijans are not allowed to worship in these temples. The newly wed Harijan couples cannot enter into any temple and offer their prayers to the deity. Therefore, I would like to suggest that measures should be taken to build separate temples for Harijans in the Harijans colonies in order to avoid any confrontation. With these words, I thank the Hon. Minister for moving such magnificent Bill and I would like to offer my support to it.

[*English*]

Mr. Syed Shahabuddin (Kishanganj): Mr. Deputy Speaker, Sir, man's inhumanity to man has no limits. Indeed no species of life on this earth is as cruel to itself as the Homo sapiens. This morning we woke up to the horrifying news of Gohpur, which is the latest case orf atrocities. Bt my mind goes back to a few years ago when I visited a Harijan village in Andhra Pradesh, where everybody had been terrorised out of the village, except a lone woman, an old woman who had lost her mind and was loitering through the streets with a blank face and there was a dog following her. I could see the charred remains of rice in the granaries of various houses which had been turned into carbon. Madam, these atrocities are not only directed against a community, they are directed against the nation, they are directed against humanity, and it is with this sense and purpose that we have got to fight them out...(*Interfruptions*).

Mr. Bipin Pal Das (Tezpur): When did that incident take place in Andhra Pradesh?

Mr. Syed Shahabuddin: Around 1981 or 1982. I had a meeting of the National Executive of the Janata Party there at that time and then I visited that place.

Mr. Bipin Pal Das: What is the name of that village?

Mr. Syed Shahabuddin: I have forgotten the name. I will give it to the Madam Minister some time.

Sir, man does not live by bread alone. He essentially needs dignity, he essentially needs a social existence, social recognition, social respect as a human being. Therefore, I congratulate the Hon. Minister for bringing this Bill before us. It has been overdue. We have long contended ourselves with an illusion that by passing the Protection of Civil Right Act, we have done all that was needed, that by putting in beautiful phrases in the Constitution we have done all that was needed. I am happy that the Government has realised that atrocities need to be dealt with a firm hand, with all tshe power this is at the command of a civilised State, with all the feelings and emotions that we can bring to bear on this despicable situation as human beings and as citizens of a country which swears by Mahatma Gandhi. These atrocities cut across the political complexion of the State Governments and, therefore, one should not look at it as party question. It is a shame for the country. It is a national problem and we have got to look at it and deal with it as a national problem. The other day a case was referred to here in the House of a Harijan being forced to eat human waste. I came across the other day a case in which a citizen of free India...(*Interruption*)

An Hon. Member: It was a place in Karnataka where Janata regime was there.

Mr. Syed Shahabuddin: I also came across a similar case of a Harijan only recently, who had been forced to drink urine, in Uttar Pradesh in the very constituency of the Prime Minister and I have brought that case to the notice of the Prime Minister. Not that I am holding the Prime Minister responsible for that case of atrocity. Fa from it. But what I am trying to sayf is that this is a social and national malaise which cuts across political barriers and, therefore, we have got to unite here in this House to fight against this evil.

Here is a list of atrocities committed in 1987 and 1988. The figures are here. I do not know how far the figures represent the truth because many of these figures are only partial truth. It is only where a person finally gets across the many administrative, social and legal barriers to record his anguish and his pain and his shame that they appear here in the reply. But even as it is, they are rather revealing. I have got the figures for Bihar, Gujarat, Kerala, Madhya Pradesh, Rajasthan and Uttar Pradesh. I have chosen all those which have recorded more than 500 cases in a given year. There, six States alone account for eighty-five per cent of the cases of atrocities recorded. I think some special effort has to be made by the Central Government and I would request the Hon. Minister to draw the attention of the Chief Minister of these States to make a special study as to why is that these State are responsible for so many atrocities. Therefore some very special methods are necessary to fight this evil in those States. Mr. Deputy-Speaker, Sir, I would like to place a few suggestions before the Hon. Minister. It is absolutely necessary that the weaker sections like the 'Harijans' and the 'Adivasis' have due representation not only in the Police Force, but in the Intelligence machinery and in the Magistracy because the police does not act by itself. It is all these three agencies which together by their sins of omission and commission make such atrocities possible. Therefore, I would plead with the Hon. Minister to ensure that there is due representation in all these three branches and that not a single seat which is in the reserved/quota remains unfilled. What is more important is to have a composite pattern of deployment in the particular districts which are atrocities prone. For example, in every 'thana' is such areas, in every scheme of deployment of the magistrates in these areas, in these districts, you must ensure due representation of the weaker sections, I would suggest to Hon. Minister for her consideration that in every district let there be one *thana* specially for recording the cases of atrocities and it should be manned from top to bottom by the weaker sections only. Just have one *thana,* call it by whatever name you like because the poor illiterate Harijans and Adivasis and weaker sections are not permitted access to the normal *thana*. They are shoved away. They are treated as sub-humans and they are not permitted to record their anguish. Whereas in such a separate *thana* their pain and sufferings shall be shared by the people in power and they shall be humanly impelled to record these cases of atrocities and it is these *thanas* which should then be responsible for investigating these cases of atrocities. The *thana* alone will not do. The political parties casting aside all the differences, and other social organisations, all those who speak in the name Gandhiji and Nehru must organise themselves into committees for the protection of civil rights at district level, at the town level so that any Harijan, any Adivasi, any member of the weaker section who feels aggrieved can go to them and seek their learned assistance and seek their expert help. Let these voluntary institutions be given full support by the Government.

Sir, I would like to suggest one thing which is not there in the Bill. Any person who is convicted of an act of atrocity as has been defined in this Act, should be disenfranchised from voting, from standing as a candidate in any elections in this country. He has no right to commit an atrocity and then come up and demand a share in running the society. Total disenfranchisement of any person who has been convicted of any offence under this Act including public service should be applied. I would like to draw the attention of the Hon. Minister to historic judgement recently by the Madras High Court, by the Justice Khadar. Of course, it was given in a different context. But the basic situations remains the same. His argument was that the State's primary duty is to protect the life and property of the citizen and if for some reason the police system of the State fails, the State is morally bound to compensate the citizen for the loss that he has suffered. Here in this Bill you talk about some compensation, some relief and rehabilitation as a gesture of generosity. No. It should be taken as a matter of right, as a matter of State obligation for the failure of its machinery for the failure to perform the duty that it is supposed to exist for. Therefore, there must be full compensation for all losses suffered, and for loss of lives and injury you must have a prescribed scale as there is in the case of Industrial Accident Act. Depending upon the age of the person, the earning period ahead of him, his earning capacity, you work out a definite reasonable sum that he would have earned had he lived. Similarly in the case of loss of property, there should be a compensation on the basis of full substitution, not that you give a Harijan a paltry sum of Rs. 100/- to buy a few bamboos to re-erect his shelter. Whatever he has lost because of the negligence of the State, because of the failure of the machinery, must be fully compensated on the basis of substitution. Substitution cost should be the criterion for all losses of property. Of course, punitive line is mentioned there. But I would like to emphasize that the entire society is responsible for these atrocities, those who commit them and also those who remain silent spectators. Therefore, take the *mohalla* as a unit, take the *panchayat* as a unit or take the revenues village as a unit and let everybody contribute towards the punitive fine so that out of the punitive fine, you can pay the compensation that I have just demanded.

Sir, as far as the public servants are concerned, there is a lovely clause which I welcome fully. They are subject to prosecution, but they must be punished even administratively because sometimes it may not be possible to bring home the charge, to prove it in a court of law. Therefore, there must be administrative punishment for anybody who is negligent, who is found not to have acted in time, who is found to have looked the other way while the atrocities have been committed and at least there should be a black mark in his record. He should at least be subjected to suspension.

Sir, I fully support the view of Mr. Ganga Ram that there should be a summary trial. Merely a special court would not do. A special court must have a summary procedure and a time-bound activity in order that these atrocities can be controlled.

I am fully conscious of the fact that violence and atrocities will continue to mount in our society because we are passing through a state of transition. People are standing up and demanding their rights. People are asking for the minimum that are because of them under the law of the land. They do not want anything more and yet for that cry, they are punished. Even today, I have seen a report from Bihar where some Harijans merely for the sin of asking for minimum wages were fired upon one person was killed and 30 other injured. Therefore, you have to steel your nerves, if the State, is to exist as a civilised State, you have got to gird up your loins, you have to stand up this challenge and you have got to take a full measure of the situation of whatever power has been vested in you by the people of India and bring it to bear upon those mischievous elements who are bringing disgrace to the country until Gandhi's dream is realised, until justice dawns in our society, until we learn to treat each other as human beings and no as 'them' not as another group, but as human beings and as common citizens of a free India.

[*Translation*]

***Mr. Harihar Soren** (Keonjhar): Mr. Deputy Speaker, Sir, I rise to support the Scheduled Castes and Scheduled Tribes (Prevention of Atrocities) Bill. Sir, 40 years have passed since we achieved independence. The Government of India have taken a number of steps for the welfare of Scheduled Castes and Scheduled Tribes. But, it is a matter of great regret that these people are still neglected. They are still suppressed and oppressed by the upper caste people. So, this Bill will go a long way in protecting the Scheduled Castes and Scheduled Tribes from the atrocities. So, I welcome this Bill. The Honourable Minister, Smt. Bajpaiji is looking after his Ministry. She has studied the problems of the Scheduled Castes and Scheduled Tribes. Therefore, she has brought this Bill before the House. There are some good provisions in this Bill. But, mere passing of the Bill and making Act will not be able to stop atrocities on Scheduled Castes and Scheduled Tribes. We have to find out the root cause for the atrocities which are being perpetuated on them. If we make a proper analysis of it we will see that social, economical and educational backwardness are the main reasons as to why atrocities are being perpetuated on them. The entire Scheduled Caste and Scheduled Tribe population in the country is not educated. Because of their illiteracy, they are not able to know many things which are going on in the country. Since the economic condition of these people is not sound, they are not able to get respectable status in the society. Of course, our Government have launched several schemes for the upliftment of the Scheduled Castes and Scheduled Tribes. The Government want to enhance their status in the society by conferring many economic benefits on them through various schemes. But the duty of the Government will not be over by launching those schemes and by allocating funds under those schemes. The Government is to see to whether the schemes launched for the welfare of Scheduled Castes and Scheduled Tribes are effectively implemented or not, the government is to see as to whether funds earmarked under those schemes are properly utilised or not. So far as my information is concerned, the officials who are put in charge of implementing various schemes for the socio-economic development of Scheduled Castes and Scheduled Tribes are not doing their duties honestly and sincerely. They are not able to provide benefits to all the beneficiaries.

Similarly, the officials who are supposed to maintain law and order and to protect the lives and property of the Scheduled Castes and Scheduled Tribes are not able to give them due protection at the appropriate time. They are not able to check atrocities perpetrated on them (Scheduled Castes and Scheduled Tribes).

If we will not be able to give due protection to the SCs and STs, the situation will further aggravate in future and it will be beyond control. Sir, I would like to say a word about the Reservation Policy of the Government. I thank the Government for making reservation of posts of SCs and STs. In the past the posts reserved for SCs and STs were not being filled by SCs and STs, on the plea of the non-availability of suitable candidates from among them. I am grateful to the Government that drives have been launched to clear the backlog of employment of SC and ST candidates. This will protect the interest of the candidates. In this context I would like to say one thing. Sir, at some places we find that the SC and ST candidates are able to secure the marks supposed to be secured by general candidates. That means they are qualified to get the posts reserved for general candidates. But it is seen that whatever best may be their performance they are appointed only against the posts reserved for them. If we take this attitude then the upliftment of SCs and STs will not become possible.

[Mr. Sharad Dighe *in the Chair*]

Sir, you know the present situation in the country. At one place it is Uttarakhand, at another place it is Jharkhand, at some other place it is *Bahujan Samaj Vadi* and at some other place it is Bodo in the name of the movements are rising their ugly head. I do not support these movements. But we can not reject the issue simply by saying that the movements are unlawful. What are the root causes of their movements? Is it a fact that the people involved in those movements are being neglected since long, is it a fact that they are being suppressed by the upper caste people, if so, how will the Government protect them? How will the Government take action against the people who are exploiting them? All these factors should be studied very carefully. If we will be able to stop atrocities, if we will improve their economic conditions and if we will give them proper status in the society, they will never be involved in any kind of movement. At least I know that the tribals are simple and innocent and they are peace loving people. So, we must provide them protection and we must give them social justice. The Honourable Minister an experienced Minister. I request her to study the burning problems of SCs and STs. Then she should take immediate steps to tackle those problems. Otherwise you cannot cow down them. Because 40 years after independence now a kind of awareness is being created among them. They know that due justice has not been given to them in all these years. Therefore, please find out some ways to remove their problems and restore peace in the society. Sir, our Government have drawn up various schemes for the upliftment of SCs and STs. Most of those schemes are being implemented in the country. But it is regrettable that the State governments are not very sincere in the effective implementation of those schemes. Therefore, I would like to urge upon the Central Government to send necessary instructions to the state Governments to implement those schemes with right earnestness and sincerity. Because it involves the upliftment of SCs and STs.

Sir, my second request is with regard to the better administration in the tribal areas. Some provisions have been made in this regard in the 5th and 6th Schedules of our Constitution. These provisions have been made to tackle the problems of tribals. Separate administrative systems have been provided in some tribal populated areas under the provisions made by the 6th Schedule of the Constitution. It is seen that the people are living peacefully in those areas. They are not being exploited by the upper caste people. The development process is taking place in full swing in those areas. The people living in those areas are very much satisfied with the existing administration. But the situation in other tribal areas which are under 5th Schedule is different. The people have many grievances. In order to help them getting the full benefit of the various schemes which are being implemented by the Government and in order to give them due justice it is very necessary to bring all the tribal areas under the 6th Schedule and necessary administrative system should be introduced in those areas. With these suggestions I thank you very much and conclude my speech.

[English]

Mr. Digvijay Singh (Rajgarh): Sir, I rise to support the Bill and congratulate our Prime Minister Rajivji and our Welfare Minister Bajpaiji for bringing this Bill which, I hope, shall go a long way to curb the atrocities on Scheduled Castes and Scheduled Tribes.

Sir, it is unfortunate that in spite of giving Scheduled Castes and Scheduled Tribes the constitutional protection and protecting them under the Civil Rights Act 1955 and various provisions of Cr. P.C. and IPC, we have been unable to curb the atrocities on SC and ST. We must realise that it is the structure which is coming in the way. We find that the system is not responding to the needs of today and it is not solving the problem at the ground level and, that is why, whenever we find a situation like this, we again come back to bring in some kind of different law to make the penal provisions more stringent. What is needed is a political will at the state and district level so that the enforcing authority and the political masters take stringent action against those persons who are committing these atrocities on Scheduled Castes and Scheduled Tribes.

I welcome the penal provisions made against those officers who are negligent in their duty regarding the provisions made in this Bill. But I do not understand why the officers belonging to Scheduled Castes and Scheduled Tribes have been exempted from these penal provisions. I feel that officers and public servants belonging to this section of Scheduled Castes and the Scheduled Tribes have a greater responsibility to see that these penal provisions of this Bill and the provisions of this Bill are faithfully implemented because ultimately it is their kith who are to be helped. I request the Hon. Minister to consider and delete this provision.

I do not understand why, although after making the penal provisions, we are not monitoring the percentage of conviction in such cases. Simply booking them under the law and bringing them before the court is not the answer. We have to ensure, through a close monitoring to such cases, that conviction is to a higher level and then only, we shall be able to curb this. We have cut across by setting up special courts in this Bill. But that is not all. After all, he still has a right to appeal to the High Court and the Supreme Court. This itself will take years before the accused can be punished. The judicial structure today in this country, I am sorry to state—is heavily loaded against the poor. Although, we have provided for payment of travelling allowances and miscellaneous expenses for witnesses and the victims, still it is the duration of the actual crime committed and the punishment given which is detrimental to such happenings occurring again and again. This is why, I feel that it is time when the Government itself thought about the restructuring of the whole judicial process whereby the right to appeal is restricted.

It is a very welcome sign that the provisions have been made to rehabilitate the victims of such atrocities to an extent possible. What is needed is that, as rightly pointed out by Shahabuddinji, we have to fix the quantum of the rehabilitation and the compensation paid. Otherwise, it may differ from state to state and according to the whims and fancies of different persons.

As I pointed out earlier, untouchability is an offence under the present law. But it is being enforced? Have we eradicated untouchability from our country? I am sorry to state that we have not. Still in the villages we have separate wells for Harijans, separate temples of Harijans. Why have we not been able to take action against those persons who are practising untouchability in the rural areas? I am sorry to say, a person of the stature of Sankaracharya of Puri openly advocated untouchability through the Press and he did not contradict that report. We have not taken action against him. We want more Jayendra Saraswathis in this country—the Sankaracharya of Kanchi—who are working for the uplift of the Harijans and working against untouchability.

It is the responsibility of the caste Hindus to see that atrocities are not committed against SC and ST people. We have to change our frame of mind and accept them as brothers. Then only will we be able to make progress on this issue.

I feel that some of the provisions made are a little harsh. Simply throwing of waste in front of the house of a Harijan has been made a cognizable offence. Those people who know the village closely would realise that this would be a daily occurrence. How many cases will you register? This would give way for the police officers at *thana* level to harass people. So we have to reconsider this. Throwing of agriculture waste is not such an offence as could be made cognizable; this could be deleted from the Act.

I strongly support the stringent penal provisions made regarding the usurping and the wrongful occupation of the land allotted to the SC and ST. There is ample scope for this provision because we find that the land allotted in the rural areas has been by and large taken away by the powerful people. It is there even in Madhya Pradesh. I should be ashamed of myself to come from a state where the highest atrocities take place in this country. We have taken a very positive step in the state of Madhya Pradesh whereby through a special programme of *Adhikar Abhiyan*, we have taken up restoration of land to the title holder. You would be happy to know that 62000 people who were not in possession of their land and were only holding Pattas has been given land under this programme.

The problem is more socio-economic than prohibitive or regulatory. We realise that sixty-six per cent of the rural landless in this country are from SC. What is needed is mass oriented agrarian reform, faithfully implemented and monitored by specially constituted land tribunals and manned by people belonging to the SC and ST or by persons who have a definitely known leanings for the SC and ST. Then only will we be able to implement faithfully these land reforms.

Today, although we have fixed the minimum wages, they are not being given. Although we have fixed minimum wages. I know from any experience, they are not being given. Until and unless such things are monitored closely by some special committees or by the land tribunals, we will not be able to justify our intentions.

Land absorbing and land augmenting technical innovations have to be made. You would agree with me that most of the disputes which arise in the rural areas are through non-payment of wages or poor payment of wages. The Government has to step in where we provide adequate work for at least about hundred days in a year. We are very happy, the Hon. Prime Minister Rajiv Gandhi has come out with special programmes under the *Jawahar Rozgar Yojana*. The other point is politically decenation until we politically decentralise power and give power directly to the elected representatives of the people, we will not be able to enforce these laws and all these programmes.

Another thing is the grass-root mobilisation of the Scheduled Castes and the Scheduled Tribes and bringing about an awareness amongst them that they enjoy fundamental rights under the Constitution, and that they enjoy civil rights under the Civil Rights Act. Until and unless they know the provisions of the Act, we will not be able to bring them up to the mainstream.

Administrative restructuring and planning from below is another feature which is important. Rajivji has rightly taken the initiative to decentralise the power to *Panchayati Raj* and also provide work for the landless. Now that we have taken the initiative, the ball is in the court of the state leaders—the politicians in the state capitals to implements these laws and regulations.

I would like to say a word about the tribals. We have a large tribal population and especially in may state of Madhya Pradesh, they are about 22.5 per cent. The Jharkhand movement has been going on for a very long time. We have to give a serious thought to it. I congratulate the Hon. Home Minister for starting a dialogue with the Jharkhand leaders. What are they asking for? They want to be the masters of their own destiny. What are they asking for? They are only asking for self-rule. If we can give it to the Gorkhas of the Darjeeling, why cannot we give it to the tribals of the Central India? It is a serious thing which we have to consider with an open mind. Let us reject it outright. After all, you cannot deliver the goods at the lowest level until and unless you have the people's involvement in the system, people's involvement in the delivery of the schemes, policies and the programmes. Therefore, I faithfully urge upon the Minister to convey my feelings to the Hon. Prime Minister and to the Home Minister to consider this very seriously.

Prof. N.G. Ranga (Guntur): Your Chief Minister also. That is the real trouble.

Mr. Digvijaya Singh: Certainly, Sir, I have said it earlier. The ball is in the court of the Chief Minister because ultimately they are the people who are to implement the laws at the grass-root level.

In the end, I once again congratulate the Hon. Prime Minister. He has shown by his actions—whether by filling the vacancies in the Scheduled Castes and the Scheduled Tribes quota or by giving reservations in the *Panchayati Raj* System and now with the present Bill he has brought forward—that he is cast in the same mould of the Congress giants like Pandit Jawaharlal Nehru, Mahatma Gandhi who have brought in a revolution in this country. Here, of course, what remains will be eradicated by this Bill.

Mr. P.M. Sayeed (Lakshadweep): Mr. Chairman, Sir, I congratulate the Hon. Minister for having brought this Bill before this House. It is a well-thought-out Bill. It deals with almost every aspect regarding the atrocities committed against the Harijans and Adivasis in our country.

As you know, we have passed many laws in this very House on eradication of untouchability, civil rights and many other laws.

But, why is it that the atrocities are on the increase? My humble view is that, of late, on account of the increase in the percentage of literacy and also of the improvement in the economic field, the Harijans and Adivasis are trying to assert their rights. Naturally, they will assert their rights. Some old feudal, affluent, powerful, high-caste sections of our society will naturally resist with more vigour to see that the rights these communities want to assert get defeated. When these atrocities are going on in this country what are we do to do? The point I want to make is that this Bill after having been passed should not meet the same fate as the earlier Acts like eradication of untouchability and civil rights had met with.

There are many salient features in the present Bill which is proposed to be passed. For example, for the first time we are fixing the responsibility on the officers who are going to implement this piece of legislation at the grassroot level. Supposing this piece of legislation also meets the same fate as the earlier ones then what do we propose to do. My suggestion for that would be that at least, in the first instance, you will be in a position to know such atrocity prone areas in the country where atrocities are committed on the Scheduled Castes and Scheduled Tribes. Now such are as will get identified. Secondly the officers who have got sympathy towards these communities must also be identified and some awards should be given to them whenever they implement the provisions of this Bill in letter and spirit.

Mr. Chairman, Sir, I would also like to congratulate the Hon. Prime Minister for this. He has toured the length and breadth of this country and seen the plight of the Harijans and the Adivasis. Even the Hon. Minister herself has arranged so many seminars, conventions, meetings of the Scheduled Castes and Scheduled Tribes MPs and MLAs and other experts. After having studied the problem in depth she has brought this measure. We only hope that this will meet the requirements of the country. It is really very sad even after forty years of independence the Scheduled Castes and Scheduled Tribes population of our country – which is about twenty-five per cent – are not able to assert their rights and we are not in a position to give them their due share. The intention of the Government is very well spelt out in this measure. I would have been happy if the opposition had been here and participated in the debate and given their suggestions. Instead of that they have chosen to remain outside and accuse the Government of bringing in all thése measures with an eye on the coming general elections. The other day when the Panchayati Raj Bill was being discussed many Hon. Members had touched this point. For four long years that aspect had been deliberated upon and fifteen thousand experts had cooperated and discussions were held at length. After that, it was brought before the House. The Harijans and Adivasis are now going to be given reservation in each village panchayat according to their population. Why should we not ask the State Governments to make such laws to see that these measures are implemented through them? There will be an inbuilt mechanism through which they themselves can spot out where exactly the troubles are taking place.

I feel that it is good measure and has to be endorsed by one and all in this house. I think, if it is implemented with the same intention with which this has been brought before the House, the age-old atrocities and other inhuman things which are being inflicted by various high-castes, powerful and affluent sections of the rural society, will definitely be checked. Therefore, I wholeheartedly support this measure and congratulate the Prime Minister once again. Thank you very much.

Mrs. Basavarajeswari (Bellary): Mr. Chairman, Sir, I am happy to thank the Hon. Minister for having brought forward this historic and revolutionary Bill. We have already passed the historic *Panchayat Raj* and *Nagarpalika* Bills.

Most of us refuse to become the Minister of Social Welfare—myself and Dr. Rajendra Kumari Bajpai being exceptions. When ministerships are offered, most of them would like to become Industry Minister, Finance Minister or Minister for some other department. But nobody is willing to become Minister for Social Welfare unless he or she is very much sympathetic and can involve in the welfare of the poorer sections of the society. In that way, I congratulate Madam Bajpai for having taken charge as minister for Welfare and having 'brought this historic Bill. I too was Minister for Social Welfare in Karnataka State. I know something about the atrocities on and welfare of the people belonging to the Scheduled Castes and Scheduled Tribes.

Prof. N.G. Ranga: So, we congratulate you both.

Mrs. Basavarajeswari: We have already taken several

measures to uplift the socially and economically backward people. But still we could not overcome this problem. We have taken up a lot of antipoverty programmes like IRDP, NREP, RLEGP. But what benefits have reached them? I am very sorry to say that the benefits have not reached them fully. There are various reasons which I am going to explain shortly.

As stated by the Hon. Minister, we have given scholarships for their education. We have distributed the surplus land for their socio-economic gains. We ask them to cultivate the wasteland wherever it is available. We have asked them to cultivate forest land wherever it exists. We have worked out so many schemes for the welfare and economic upliftment of these sections. But what is going on? The real fact is that the schemes through which we are doing our best to help them, are not reaching them. The reason behind this. Unless and until we bring total prohibition in this country, I don't think we would be in a position to bring them on par with others. Whatever amount we give and whatever wages they earn and whatever economic benefits we give for them are being misused by this section of the society. The first and foremost thing which we have to think is of total prohibition in this country. We may lose some revenue by this. But we should not mind. We are the followers of Gandhiji and so, we should be proud to say that we are going in for total prohibition in this country. If we want the poor ladies to be protected from all these evils, this is the only measure. By this measure, we can make them economically and morally well-off.

The next point is about education. We are trying our best to give education to everybody. We have been implementing the ICDS project for the welfare of children and also nutrition programme. I would like to know as to many centres have been started in the colonies. So many 'anganwadis' have been started under the ICDS project but I find that very few of them have been started in Harijan colonies. When we start more and more 'anganwadis', we should try to see that children who are brought in one environment are shifted to another environment. Only then, the whole scheme will be successful. We have to change their environment first. How best to change their environment will depend on starting more and more 'anganwadis' in the colonies instead of doing the same in the towns where there are more facilities to enjoy. We should try to see that more 'anganwadis' and health centres are started in the tribal areas and Harijan localities and so also the schools. We have started more schools under the new education policy. We are going to strengthen secondary education under this new education policy. There are a number of single-room schools in the Colonies. There are hundreds of children studying in such schools. We should try to strengthen education in these colonies by providing more and more schools and more and more teachers. We should make it compulsory for children to attend their schools. I would like to know from the Hon. Minister as to how many drop-outs are there. You try to make a survey of the whole subject and try to find the number of drop-outs. Children attend schools at the most upto fourth or fifth standard or SSLC. After that, very few go to college due to poverty. And for the same, parents are not in a position to send their children to college. We have to provide them with some alternatives so that they need not depend upon the wages of their children. They take their children to the fields just to supplement their income. How can we create a feeling among people that they can live without the wages of their children?

These things should be taken care of. Moreover, they have their own differences, such as, they belong to this group or that group. I do not understand as to why there are disparities. Whenever I visit them, I have been telling them not to try to establish such kinds of disparities and we all belong to the same nation and they all belong to the same weaker sections of the society. And if they fight among themselves, what will be the outcome? We must remember Madam Gandhi on the floor of his House. She had brought the political awareness among the minorities, backward classes and Harijans. She had taught us about our rights. But till now, we are not utilising those rights properly. Minister stated, while defining atrocity, that when we ask for our rights, atrocities are committed on us. What has happened in Karnataka? We are painted to see that such things still continue in this country. In Karnataka there was a reformer in the 12th century, Lord Basava. Prof. Ranga knows that. He wanted to eradicate social evils in our society. He made revolutionary reformation in Karnataka. He was a great reformer. He made one Harijan girl marry a Brahmin boy. But he was so much harassed and tortured that he had to leave the kingdom and he committed suicide. He did his best in those days in the 12th century. And today, in the

20th century, we are shameful to see that such things are being practised. As Shahabuddin said, this is not to be viewed politically. It is a national issue. Everybody should take it that we are all one in these matters. We should try to love each other.

As survey was undertaken and it revealed that persons who belonged to the same community, Scheduled Castes or Scheduled Tribes, once they achieved something, they were not very much in favour of developing their own brothers and sisters. Why is it so? Why do they forget their own brothers and sisters? The survey also revealed that they were ashamed to go to their own colonies. Why should it be so? In fact, they should be involved more in these kinds of things. We must put an end to this sort of attitude.

Then, under the Land Reforms Act, surplus land has been given to these poor people. Wherever we have given land, there should be some checks and balances to find out whether the land given to these people is being cultivated by them. Legally, their name may be there in the record, but who is the person actually cultivating it? The fact is that it is being cultivated by somebody else. Who takes the amount of fertilizers given to them? The moment they get the fertilizer, they sell it. What about the implements and seeds being given to them? That is not going into their hands. What is the reason for that? You should find out and set these things right. You should not think only one line, you should think the other way also.

What about the facilities being extended to them under the various schemes like IRDP? We give them buffaloes, cows, bulls and so many other things. If you go and see next day, you will not find them there. That is why we are not achieving the development that was anticipated by us. The real benefits are not reaching the beneficiaries. You should try to find out the reason. You must have a check on the persons who are not utilizing the aid being given to them. Unless we do this, I do not think, the benefits will reach the proper persons. We should be very careful in these things.

Dr. Ambedkar, during the days when the Constitution was being drafted was awake at 2 o'clock in the night one day. I read that in one of the books. When one of his friends asked him why he was awake at that time, he said: "How can I sleep unless my poor people can sleep during the night?" There is still a lot to be done. Poverty is still there; so many social evils are still prevalent in our society. Even today the devdasi system is very much prevalent. Girls are being offered in the name of God freely. Such social evils need to be eradicated. Devdasi system, nude processions etc. in the name of God are very much prevalent in States like Maharashtra and Karnataka. Unless we put an end to these systems, I do not know how we can call ourselves as civilized persons. We are ashamed to see that our sisters are being offered in the name of God freely, which ultimately leads to prostitution. These things should be immediately curbed. Some of the States, I think, enacted laws to rehabilitate these unfortunate devdasis and their children, but that has not proved effective. Those devdasis and children are very much there. Some serious thought has to be given, so that these ladies and children are rehabilitated and kept in proper and good environment, so that the children can be given proper education. Unless these evils are checked, I don't think by bringing this legislation we are going to improve the entire social and economic structure of this community. The word 'atrocities' has been defined very nicely but the only thing is that it has to be implemented also by way of morally as well as legally enforcing the law. At the same time people should be given proper education and teachings. All the 'swamijis', 'gurus', Lords and 'dharmagurus' should come forward to teach the people that we are all one. Unless our leaders come forward and give a call to the nation, we don't think that we can enact it firmly and the condition of these people will improve. With these words, I thank you very much.

[Translation]

Mr. Manikrao Hodlya Gavit (Nandurbar): Mr. Chairman, Sir, I am grateful to you for providing me an opportunity to express my views on Scheduled Castes and Scheduled Tribes (Prevention of Atrocities) Bill. The Hon. Minister has taken a good step by moving this Bill. I would like to thank her for this step. In view of the provisions made in this Bill and the views expressed by the Hon. Members of the Parliament, I can say that if the provisions of this Bill are implemented properly by the Centre and the State Governments, the Scheduled Castes and the Scheduled Tribes will get justice.

Mr. Chairman, Sir, as you also belong to Maharashtra, you are well aware of the atrocities being committed on the people belonging to Scheduled Castes and Scheduled Tribes in almost all States of the country. It is known to all the Hon. Members of the

House including myself being a Scheduled Tribes, besides other people, police personnel also commit atrocities on them. Despite enactment of laws, atrocities are still being committed by the public as well as the police. Whenever a victim of atrocities goes to police station to lodge a complaint he is confirmed in police lock up where he is threatened to the extent that he loses his confidence in lodging a complaint. Such types of atrocities are not reported. In the tribal society in my district, exorcism is practised. The exorcist is called 'Bhagat' in local dialect. These *Bhagats* often have long hairs on their heads and treat the people of their diseases. A complaint was lodged against a *Bhagat* of my area that he had stolen a thing from the field. Despite the fact that *Bhagat* owns 27-28 acres of land, the police dragged him by the hair, and lodged him in the police lock-up. He was only beaten but he was also made baldpated by the police. When he made a complaint, it was not lodged. When I came to know about it and enquired from the Superintendent of Police, he did not deny the fact that the complaint had not been registered. Whenever a poor man or a tribal goes to the police to lodge a complaint, his complaint is registered but later on it is said that no atrocities has been committed. It is said that when the Department of Welfare was a part of the Ministry of Home Affairs, it had more say in the States. But now it has been made an independent department. So I would request the Hon. Minister to do the needful so that the Department could exercise more authority over the States.

The Minimum Wages Act has been made for the poor and the Scheduled Castes and Scheduled Tribes. But it has not been implemented properly in many states. Attention should be paid to this also.

Recently, our Hon. Prime Minister Rajiv Gandhi has made an extensive tours of the areas inhabited by the people belonging to Scheduled Tribes. We visited the huts of these poor people. He saw there the magnitude of poverty and felt their needs. For this reason, this Bill has been brought here.

The Hon. Prime Minister has instructed that the backlog of reserved vacancies for the persons belonging to Scheduled Castes and Scheduled Tribes under the Government of India and the State Governments should be cleared. Their quota of reservation as provided in the constitution should be fulfilled. Recently, I have received a complaint that the postal department in Maharashtra has advertised some posts under special drive in a newspaper named *Lok Satta.* Applications were to be sent within seven days. I would like to submit to the Hon. Minister that how a candidate can send his application within seven days. No candidate belonging to these categories would apply to the post. As a result thereof, backlog will not be cleared and the officer concerned will write to his superior that "candidate not available". When a super class I officers in Maharashtra circle have this type of attitude towards us, what can we expect from the lower level officers? Our Hon. Prime Minister wants that the backlog should be cleared. But how it can be cleared when they are given 7 days' time to send applications. Attention should be paid in this regard. The time schedule as directed by the Hon. Prime Minister for clearance of the backlog should be extended further. The last date by which backlog is to be cleared is 31st October, 1989. It should be extended further.

I have heard that special courts have been set-up for tribal of cases of the atrocities committed on the people belonging to Scheduled Castes and Scheduled Tribes. When their complaints are not registered in the police stations, who will heed to their complaints in the court?

A big irrigation project by the name of Sardar Sarovar Project is being setup on Narmada river at a place where borders of Madhya Pradesh, Maharashtra and Gujarat meet. Land of 33 villages of Maharashtra and some tribal villages of Gujarat is being acquired for this project. Nothing has been done so far for their rehabilitation. Neither any alternative land nor adequate compensation for their land is being given to them. They are given land by the Government, on town planning rate, whereas the land of poor is acquired at throwaway prices at Rs. four to five thousand an acre only. The Government is in favour of doing something in this regard. Unless Government takes some steps justice cannot be done to the people belonging to the Scheduled Castes and Scheduled Tribes.

District Rural Development Agencies have been formed to implement all these programmes. This agency is also responsible for implementing the schemes under the *Jawahar Rozgar Yojana.* The funds provided to the *Gram Panchayats* under *Jawahar Rozgar Yojana* will be spent through this agency. I would like to submit that officers of clean record only should be posted in these agencies, all the money will be pocketed by them and the tribals and the poor will get nothing. That is why I am giving stress time and again on the fact that the government should take steps to provide justice to the poor with much alacrity.

I would also like to submit that a large number of persons belonging to communities other than the SC/ST have availed of facilities by producing bogus caste certificate. On the basis of bogus certificates, they got admission in various educational institutions such as ITIs, medical colleges and engineering colleges, etc. These bogus tribals living in cities are enjoying facilities meant for the tribals living in hill areas. They obtain caste certificates on the basis of affidavit. Thus the genuine tribals are deprived of their facilities. I urge upon the Government to weed out bogus tribals. In 1977, the Government of India removed the area restriction. Because of this decision, a number of non-eligible persons could get caste certificates showing themselves as tribals. Those certificates as still valid.

Recently a Central Minister paid a visit to a Department of Central Government. He said there that the caste certificates should be issued on permanent basis. I told him that I am a tribal myself and I never heard such thing. Such authority helps the bogus people.

In the end, I would like to submit that if the Hon. Minister is really sincere to check the atrocities on Harijans and Tribals, then he should give a serious thought to my suggestions.

Mr. Janak Raj Gupta (Jammu): Mr. Chairman, Sir, the disease got aggrated with every dose of medicine. It is not for the first time that we are confronted with the fact that a lot of atrocities are committed on the Harijans. There is hardly a State where this malady is not present. Of course, somewhere it is in lesser degree and somewhere it is in acute form. A number of laws have been enacted from time to time by the Government to check atrocities on the Scheduled Castes and Scheduled Tribes. There is no doubt that it has been checked to some extent. The Bill moved by Shrimati Bajpai is the need of the hour. It was a long felt demand of the people. Provisions of this Bill needs to be implemented strictly.

Before I could say something about the provisions of the Bill, I would like to draw the attention of the Hon. Minister towards Section 3 of the Bill. In this connection I would like to suggest an amendment. In Section 3 (A), for "whoever, not being a member of a Scheduled Castes or a Scheduled Tribes,...". The word "whoever" is sufficient and words "not being a member of a Scheduled Caste and Scheduled Tribe" should be deleted. Only then the purpose of this Bill will be served. Suppose, an officer belonging to Scheduled Castes and Scheduled Tribes commits atrocities on Scheduled Castes and Scheduled Tribes and tries to deprive them of their rights he will not be punished under the provision of this Bill as many of our learned Members have stated that as soon as economic conditions of a person belonging to the Scheduled Castes and Scheduled Tribes improves, he does not want to live in the colony or locality in which he used to live earlier with his other brethrer.

(English)

Mr. Chairman: It is already 4 pm. The House shall take up discussion under Rule 193. So, you can continue next time. You, please resume your seat.

The Minister of State of the Ministry of Welfare (Dr. Rajendra Kumari Bajpai). Madam, I beg to move:

"That the Bill to prevent the commission of offences of atrocities against the members of the Scheduled Castes and Scheduled Tribes, to provide for Special Courts for the trial of such offences and for the relief and rehabilitation of the victims of such offences and for matters connected therewith or incidental thereto, as passed by the Lok Sabha, be taken into consideration."

This House is aware of the deep concern that our Prime Minister and our Government have for the welfare of Scheduled Castes and the Scheduled Tribes. Many new initiatives have been taken particularly in the last few years to improve the lot of the Scheduled Castes and the Scheduled Tribes. Since we got independence Pt. Jawaharlal Nehru and then Mrs. Indira Gandhi and now our Prime Minister have been trying to improve the economic and social condition of the Scheduled Castes and Scheduled Tribes. In trying to discharge a mandate of the Constitution. Poverty Alleviation Programmes which provide special attention to the Scheduled Castes and Scheduled Tribes have been expanded and intensified. First the IRDP and other programmes were improved considerably and now these have been replaced by a bigger scheme of the *Jawahar Rozgar Yojana*. Drinking water wells and irrigation wells have been provided for this group. The needs of housing have been met by the *Indira Awas Yojana.* The programme for liberation of scavengers has been given a greater impetus. The education of Scheduled Castes and Scheduled Tribes which is of crucial importance to their growth and development has received much greater attention. The number of students studying beyond the Matriculation stage has gone up to 13 Lakhs. Coaching centres have been increased. A special drive is currently on for filling up the backlog which had arisen as a result of non-fulfilment of reserved seats for SC/ST. And that drive is continuing. Efforts are also being made to free them from bonded labour and to find land for cultivation. As you all know among the landless labourers about forty-eight per cent are from the Scheduled Castes and Scheduled Tribes.

We are witnessing today the sign of fruits of development reaching the Scheduled Castes and Scheduled Tribes. With greater spread of education and with the socio-economic condition improving the relations in society sometimes come under tension as a result of this change. Higher caste groups something do not like the change in the socio-economic structure and tensions develop. The demand for justice, for equality for a human living standard, for knowledge, for education and freedom leads, in some cases, to retaliation by groups which are not enlightened enough to recognise the healthy signs of growth.

Madam, previously also the Government of India has tried to remove untouchability. In the Constitution we have abolished untouchability. But to remove it completely from the society, in 1955 the protection of Civil Rights Act was passed and again, to give it more teeth, some more clauses were added in 1976. Now we find that is not enough. This Act was passed specifically for the removal of untouchability and against those who are practising untouchability. The Bill I am bringing here is especially against atrocities. For the first time, we have defined atrocities in this Bill. There are 15 types of atrocities which we have identified. I will not read it. I will mention only two or three points. The Bill defines as follows:

> "If somebody forces a member of the Scheduled Caste or Scheduled Tribe to drink or eat any inedible or obnoxious substance; or
>
> forcibly removes clothes from the person of a member of a Scheduled Caste or a Scheduled Tribe or parades him

naked or with painted face or body or does any similar act which is derogatory to human dignity; or

wrongfully occupies and cultivates any land owned or allotted to or notified by any competent authority to the Scheduled Caste or Scheduled Tribe or gets the land allotted to him transferred; or

wrongfully dispossesses a member of a Scheduled Caste or a Scheduled Tribe from his land or premises or interferes with the enjoyment of his rights over any land or premises or water; or

compels or entices a member of a Scheduled Caste or a Scheduled Tribe to do *begar* or any other similar form of forced or bonded labour other than any compulsory services for public purposes imposed by Government."

So many other things are there. So, for the first time, we have identified and defined atrocities.

Then we have made the punishment more stringent. We have said that all these kinds of atrocities shall be punishable with imprisonment for a term which shall not be less than six months but which may extended to five years with fine. In the previous Act, it was only one month and like that. We know the most of the atrocities are due to land. They insist on their minimum wages which they are denied. When they insist on the minimum wages, then these powerful people who engage them, torture them and inflict atrocities on them. Now we are witnessing today the signs of fruits of development reaching the Scheduled Castes and Scheduled Tribes. With greater spread of education and improvement in the socio-economic conditions, the relations in society sometimes come under tension as a result of this change. Higher caste groups sometimes do not like change in the socio-economic structure and tensions develop. The demand for justice, for equality, for a humane living—what I said in the Bill—for knowledge, for education and freedom leads in some cases to a retaliation by groups who are not enlightened enough to recognise the healthy signs of growth. We can say that these are especially in the rural places where atrocities or a variety of offences are committed on members of the Scheduled Castes and Scheduled Tribes. I have had occasion to tell this House regarding the recent trend, the increase of such offences against members of the Scheduled Castes and Scheduled Tribes because often the question is asked in the House. During 1988, there were a little over 15,000 offences against the Scheduled Castes and 3,300 cases in respect of Scheduled Tribes. Of these, heinous offences such as murder, rape and grievous hurt accounted for about 3,200 cases in respect of Scheduled Castes and 783 in respect of Scheduled Tribes. The nature of these offences in many States indicated that these were not isolated instances but represented a trend in the country. In cities, towns and areas where the society was generally aware about the need to bring about such changes, the upward socio-economic mobility of the Scheduled Castes and Scheduled Tribes was accepted, and tensions did not arise. But in the countryside, in the rural India, tension exists still. But in certain rural areas tradition seems to be difficult to be dislodged and from State to State it differs. In the north, due to some customs, it is more severe. And in some parts of the south also, it is something like that. The Government hence thought that certain special measures would be necessary at this point of time. So, the Bill has come. The cases of such incidents were related generally to land or to continued exploitation by enforcement of traditional demeaning practices. It is regrettable that instances had been reported such as in Kerala where a member of the Scheduled Castes was forced to eat human excreta. There are reports of a bridal party being chased and the houses of this community razed to the ground merely because the bridegroom was riding a horse through a village street when the *baraat* was going on.

The efforts of Government to provide land have been frustrated in many cases by forcible dispossession or illegal occupation of such land. In Madhya Pradesh recently, the Government launched a special programme to see that possession or effective restoration of land is made to the members of the Scheduled Castes and Scheduled Tribes who have been given 'pattas' of the land. But we received this complaint from every State that 'pattas' are given but the possession is not given. And those who are powerful people in the villages are occupying the land and the Scheduled Castes people or the Scheduled Tribes people are not given. And non-tribal people have purchased tribal land, and in fake names they are occupying that land. So, these are some of the atrocities committed on the poor people. In some unfortunate incidents, the womenfolk of the Scheduled Castes and the Scheduled Tribes are sought to be dishonoured and assaulted with the object of teaching a lesson to that community. Even before the family members, before the parents, even young girls are molested or raped. So, this type of human acts and atrocities are committed. I am saying all this in justification of this Bill.

In tribal areas, incidents of sexual exploitation are known to have occurred where willingness of innocent tribal women is secured by exercise of authority or influence. The community is sometimes sought to be pressurised by denying them access to public places, for easing themselves, for cremation or to the source of water, etc. These are the acts of atrocities that are committed against them. Instances have come to notice about fouling of water source by dumping carcass in the vicinity of their houses. All this taken together forms a pattern which calls for more stringent measures. So, we have in this Bill before the House, sought to classify most of such instances atrocities on the Scheduled Castes and the Scheduled Tribes, perpetrated by others.

Although many of these offences could probably be covered under the normal law of the land, we are witnessing today a difference in degree which calls for a differentiation in kind in respect of these offences. The Bill hence proposes to specify higher punishments as also laying down some minimum punishment for such offences. The Bill also provides for forfeiture of property—these are salient features of this Act—whether movable or immovable which may have been used for the commission of an offence under this law. The dominant position of certain vested interests embolden them to continue perpetration of atrocities on the Scheduled Castes and Scheduled Tribes. The provisions are expected to have salutary effect of such tendencies.

Prevention is better than cure and the Bill looks after the preventive measures. If an area is declared prone to atrocities—we will identify these areas—it will become the bounded duty of the law and order machinery to take all possible measures for instilling a sense of safety and security.

We are, for the first time, putting responsibility on the officers. If an officer is found wanting, we will take action....(*Interruptions*).

Mr. N.E. Balaram (Kerala): We agree with the Bill, but she is not giving a real picture. I agree with the Bill without discussion.

Mr. Parvathaneni Upendra (Andhra Pradesh): It is not a controversial thing. We welcome this measure.

Mr. Vishvjit P. Singh (Maharashtra): With such a new-found spirit in the House is it also possible to pass the Constitutional Amendment Bills in the same manner?

Dr. Rajendra Kumari Bajpai: Schemes would be formulated under the general guidance of the Government of India to provide for such measures as also for providing prompt and adequate relief and rehabilitation in the unfortunate event of atrocities taking place.

So, this is also for the fist time that we are doing it.

Then another features is that special court is now being set-up. There is going to be special responsibility on the public servants. That is another feature of the Bill. The Bill places a special responsibility on the public servants who are not members of SC/ST to take action to protect the interests of the Scheduled Castes and the Scheduled Tribes against atrocities being committed, and for taking preventive measures.

With these words, I move that the Bill to prevent the commission of offences of atrocities against the members of Scheduled Castes and Scheduled Tribes, to provide for special courts for the trial of such offences and for relief and rehabilitation of the victims of such offences and for matters connected therewith or incidental thereto, as passed by the Lok Sabha, be taken into consideration.

The question was proposed.

Mr. Parvathaneni Upendra: Madam, while welcoming the Bill, I just want to say this. Mere legislation is not enough. There should be a political will on the part of the Union Government and the State Governments to implement it. We have already the Act relating to untouchability but, still untouchability is being practised. Therefore, all of us should see that the provisions of this Bill are implemented strictly.

The Deputy-Chairman: The question is:

"That the Bill to prevent the commission of the offences of atrocities against the members of the Scheduled Castes and the Scheduled Tribes, to provide for special Courts for the trial of such offences and for relief and rehabilitation of the victims of such offences and for matters connected therewith or incidental thereto, as passed by the Lok Sabha, be taken into consideration."

The motion was adopted.

The Deputy-Chairman: We shall now take up the clause-by-clause consideration of the Bill.

Clauses 2 to 23 were added to the Bill.

Clause 1, the Enacting Formula and the Title were added to the Bill.

Dr. Rajendra Kumari Bajpai: Madam, I move:

"That the Bill be passed."

The question was put and the motion was adopted.

What constitutes atrocity has not been defined but the offences directly or indirectly flowing from the practice of untouchability are described in detail. The inclusion of Scheduled Tribes in this Act deserves special notice. In this connection, what Dr. C. Parvathamma has stated in her book *Scheduled Castes and Tribes: A Socio-economic Survey* (1984), is relevant. She opines that "Untouchability" generally does not apply to the Scheduled Tribes, who live apart in isolation. But when they come out of their habitation and develop contact with the people of plains they are equated with the "Scheduled Castes and untouchables". With the enactment of these two Acts, the prohibition of Untouchability in the Constitution has been given a realistic and effective shape.

This Act specifies the atrocities which are liable to penalties under the Act. According to the Act atrocities includes: forcing the eating of noxious substances, dumping waste matters on land, denudation, wrongful occupation of land, dispossession, bonded labour, intimidation during the voting, mischievous litigation, false information, public humiliation, outrage of modesty, sexual exploitation, fouling of water source, obstruction of entry to a place of public resort, eviction from habitation, mischief with explosives, destruction of buildings and suppression of evidence. These offences under the Prevention of Atrocities Act carry heavier penalties than similar offences under the Indian Penal Code. The offences of custodial rape, highway robbery and house breaking by night which carry a minimum punishment of 10 years under the Indian Penal Code are punishable with imprisonment for life and with the fine under the prevention of Atrocities Act. The Act also provides for forfeiture of property, externment and collective fine.

The Scheduled Castes Prevention of Atrocities Act 1989 (PAA) came into force on January 1, 1990. It is still too early to review its operation or to assess its effectiveness. The purpose of this chapter is only to look at this new Act against the background of the atrocities which have been discussed in the chapter.

Reasons and Objectives

Initially, the Government wanted to restore justice, liberty, equality, status, opportunity for all and fraternity by peaceful means. The statement of objects and reasons accompanying the Bill succinctly gives the rationale behind the Act. Despite various measures to improve the socio-economic condition of the Scheduled Castes and the Scheduled Tribes, they remain vulnerable. They are denied a number of civil rights. They are subjected to various offences, indignities, humiliations and harassment. They have been deprived of their life and property. Serious crimes are committed against them for various historical, social and economic reasons. It is because of the awareness created among the Scheduled Castes and the Scheduled Tribes through spread of education, etc. that they are trying to assert their rights and this is not being taken very kindly by the others. When they assert their rights and resist practices of untouchability against them or demand statutory minimum wages or refuse to do any bonded and forced labour, the vested interests try to cow them down and terrorize them.

When the Scheduled Castes and the Scheduled Tribes try to preserve their self-respect or honour of their women, they become irritants for the dominance of their might. Occupation and cultivation of even the Government allotted land by the Scheduled Castes and the Scheduled Tribes is resented and more often these people become victims of attacks by the vested interests. Of late, there has been an increase in the disturbing trend of commission of certain atrocities like making the Scheduled Caste persons eat substances like, human excreta, mass killings of helpless Scheduled Castes and Scheduled Tribes and rape of women belonging to these groups. Under the circumstances, the existing laws like the Protection of Civil Rights Act, 1955 and the normal provisions of the Indian Penal Code have been found to be inadequate to check these crimes. A special legislation to check and deter crimes against them committed by non-Scheduled Castes and non-Scheduled Tribes has, therefore, become necessary. This Bill is very important. Earlier, the Protection of Civil Rights Act was passed for protecting the Civil Rights of SC and ST and removal of untouchability but they were not properly implemented and now again for the achievement of almost similar objectives, the present Act has been introduced. The main objective is to check atrocities. The

Government of India has initiated many new programmes and schemes for the improvement of SC's and ST's since independence.

Pandit Jawaharlal Nehru and Mrs. Indira Gandhi tried to improve the economic and social condition of the Scheduled Castes and Scheduled Tribes. The Integrated Rural Development Programme and other similar programme helped to improve the socio-economic condition of the SC and ST considerably and now these have been replaced by bigger schemes like the "*Jawahar Rojgar Yojana*". Drinking water well and irrigation wells have been provided for this group. The housing schemes have been started under the *Indira Awas Yojana*. The programme for liberation of scavengers has been given a greater impetus. Education of Scheduled Castes and Scheduled Tribes which is of crucial importance to their growth and development has received much greater attention. Efforts are also being made to free them from bonded labour and to allot them land for cultivation.

Among the landless labourers, about forty-eight per cent are from the Scheduled Castes and Scheduled Tribes. The Minister of State in the Ministry of Welfare stated that the Bill to prevent the commission of offence of atrocities against the members of the Scheduled Castes and Scheduled Tribes, to provide for special court for the trial of such offences and the relief and rehabilitation of the victim of such offences and for matters connected therewith or incidental thereto, be taken into consideration. A separate Welfare Ministry was created in 1985, specially for the welfare of the weaker sections of the society.

Many new initiatives have been particularly in the last few years to improve the status of Scheduled Castes and Scheduled Tribes, in trying to discharge the mandate of the Constitution. Poverty alleviation programmes, which provided special attention to the Scheduled Castes and Scheduled Tribes, have been expanded and intensified. A special drive is currently being made for filling up the backlog which has arisen as a result of non-fulfilment of reserved seats for SC/ST. As we all know about forty-five per cent of the Scheduled Caste population is landless labourers and they are mostly living below poverty line. They will be freed by the Bonded Labour Act and will be rehabilitated by the grant of land and money as well. An important problem that Parliament had to face in relation to the Scheduled Castes and Scheduled Tribes was the practice of untouchability. Untouchability resulted in the creation of an inferiority complex among these classes. Parliament, thus, passed the Untouchability (Offences) Bill in 1955 in accordance with Article 17 of the Indian Constitution. Article 35 points out the law which has to be made in respect of making the various forms or aspects of untouchability an offence and they have to be passed only by Parliament. Many laws were enacted in various States of India between 1937 and 1950.

To have a uniform system of laws, the Government called for the views of the State Governments in February 1950 asking whether untouchability in any form was practised in the States. The Bill declared untouchability as an offence which is punishable.

The backward classes were boycotted by the villagers. Dr. Ambedkar wished that some provisions were made for removing this social boycott. The Maharashtra Government had appointed a committee for the purpose and Thakkar Bappa was its member. This commitee noted that fear of open violence against the backward classes by orthodox society made no progress in achieving the object. The Untouchability (Offences) Bill of 1955 provided for punishment to deter the offender from repeating the offence and also to prevent him to adopt a criminal career.

Dr. Ambedkar suggested that there should be no alternative in the punishment because the offender could pay and be free. He suggested that the Government should take security for good behaviour as there was a provision in Sections 107, 108, 109 and 110 of the Act. The Centre should administer the law and the burden of expenditure also should be borne by the Centre. In exercise of the power conferred by Article 35, Parliament enacted the Untouchability (Offence) Act (UOA), 1955 and the Untouchability (Offences) Amendment and Miscellaneous Provisions Act 1976 (Article 106 of 1976). The title of the Act is changed to the Protection of Civil Rights Act.

The Act prescribed punishment which may extend to imprisonment of six months and a fine which may extend to five hundred rupees or both. The Scheduled Castes Prevention of Atrocities Act 1989 (PAA) came into force on June 30, 1990. It is still too early to review its operation or to assess its effectiveness. The purpose of this chapter is only to look at this new Act against the background of the atrocities.

The Scheduled Castes and the Scheduled Tribes (Prevention

of Atrocities) Act, 1989 (No. 33 to 1989) short title, extent and commencement;

1. This Act may be called the Scheduled Castes and the Scheduled Tribes (Prevention of Atrocities) Act, 1989.
2. It extends to the whole of India except the State of Jammu and Kashmir.
3. It shall come into force from such date as the Central Government may, by notification in the official Gazette appoint.

Definition

1. In this Act, unless the context otherwise requires:

(a) "atrocity" means an offence punishable under Section 3.
(b) "Code" means the code of criminal procedure, 1973 (2 of 1974).
(c) Scheduled Castes and Scheduled Tribes shall have the meanings assigned to them respectively under Clause (24) and Clause (25) of Article 366 of the Constitution.

What Clause (3) of the Constitution (Scheduled Castes) Order, 1950 contemplates is that for a person to be treated as one belonging to a Scheduled Caste within the meaning of that order, he must be one who professes either Hindu or Sikh religion. A declaration of one's belief must necessarily mean a declaration in such a way that it would be known to those whom it may interest.

Therefore, if a public declaration is made by a person that he is ceased to belong to his old religion and has accepted another religion, he will be taken as professing the other religion. In the face of such an open declaration, it would be ideal to enquire further as to whether the conversion to another religion was efficacious. The word "Profess" in the Presidential order appears to have been used in the sense of an open declaration or practice by a person of the Hindu (or the Sikh) religion. Where, therefore, a person says, on the contrary that he has ceased to be a Hindu, he cannot derive any benefit from that orders. There would have been no need to make a mention of the Sikh religion distinction.

From the fact a special mention is made of the Sikh religion it would follow that the word "Hindu" is used in the narrower sense of the orthodox Hindu religion which recognizes castes and contains injunctions based on caste.

Determination whether a caste is included in Scheduled Caste:

To determine whether a particular caste is a Scheduled Caste within the meaning of Article 342, one has to look at the public notification issued by the President on that behalf.

Bhaiya Lal V. *Harikishan Singh* (1965) 2 SCR 877:AIR 1965 SC 1557 Caste (*Chammar*) mentioned in Part X of the order it can be said to include a nonspecified caste (*Mochi*).

Parsasram V. *Shivchand* (1969) ISCC 20. Dohar is a sub-caste of *Chammar*.

In the present case, the notification refers to *Chammar, Jatav* or *Mochi,* and so in dealing with the question in dispute between the parties, the enquiry which the Election Tribunal can hold is whether or not the appellant is a *Chammar, Jatav or Mochi.* The plea that though the appellant is not a *Chammar* as such, he can claim the same status by reason of the fact that he belongs to the Dhor caste which is sub-caste of the *Chammar* caste, cannot be accepted. It appears to us that an enquiry of this kind would not be permissible having regard to the provisions contained in Article 341 (*Bhaiya Lal V. Harikishan Singh* (1965) 2 SCR 877: AIR 1965 SC 1557).

(d) "Special Court" means a court of session specified as a special court in Section 41.

(e) "Special Public Prosecutor" means a Public Prosecutor specified as a special public prosecutor or an advocate referred to in Section 15.

(f) Words and expressions used but not defined in this Act and defined in the Code or the Indian Penal Code (45 of 1860) shall have the meanings assigned to them respectively in the code, or as the case may be in the Indian Penal Code.

2. Any reference in this Act to any enactment or any provision, thereof shall, in relation to an area in which such enactment or such provision is not in force, be constructed as a reference to the corresponding law, if any, in force in that area.

Offences of Atrocities

Punishment for Offences of Atrocities

1. Whoever, not being a member of a Scheduled Caste or a

Scheduled Tribe:

(i) forces a member of a Scheduled Caste or a Scheduled Tribe to drink or eat any inedible or obnoxious substance;

(ii) acts with intent to cause injury, insult or annoyance to any member of a Scheduled Caste or a Scheduled Tribe by dumping excreta, waste matter, carcasses or any other obnoxious substance in his premises or neighbourhood;

(iii) forcibly removes clothes from the person of a member of a Scheduled Caste or a Scheduled Tribe or parades him naked or with painted face or body or commits any similar act which is derogatory to human dignity;

(iv) wrongfully occupies or cultivates any land owned by, or allotted to, or notified by any competent authority to be allotted to a member of a Scheduled Caste or a Scheduled Tribe or gets the land allotted to him transferred;

(v) wrongfully disposes a member of a Scheduled Caste or a Scheduled Tribe from his land or premises or interferes with the enjoyment of his rights over any land, premises or water;

(vi) compels or entices a member of a Scheduled Caste or a Scheduled Tribe to do begging or other similar kinds of forced or bonded labour than any compulsory services for public purpose imposed by Government;

(vii) Forces or intimidates a member of a Scheduled Caste or a Scheduled Tribe not to vote or to vote for a particular candidate or to vote in a manner other than provided by law;

(viii) institutes false, malicious or vexatious suit or criminal or other legal proceedings against a member of a Scheduled Caste or a Scheduled Tribe;

(ix) gives any false or frivolous information to any public servant and thereby causes such public servant to use his lawful power to the injury or annoyance of a member of a Scheduled Caste or Scheduled Tribe;

(x) intentionally insults or intimidates with intent to humiliate a member of a Scheduled Caste or a Scheduled Tribe in any place within public view;

(xi) assaults or uses force on any woman belonging to a Scheduled Caste or a Scheduled Tribe with intent to dishonour or outrage her modesty;

(xii) being in a position to dominate the will of a woman

belonging to a Scheduled Caste or a Scheduled Tribe and uses that position to exploit her sexually to which she would not have otherwise agreed;

(xiii) corrupts or fouls the water of any spring, reservoir or any other source ordinarily used by members of the Scheduled Castes or the Scheduled Tribes so as to render it less fit for the purpose for which it is ordinarily used;

(xiv) denies a member of a the Scheduled Caste or a Scheduled Tribe any customary right of passage to a place of public resort or obstructs such member so as to prevent him from using or having access to a place of public resort to which other members of public or any section thereof have a right to use or access to;

(xv) forces or causes a member of Scheduled Caste or a Scheduled Tribe to leave his house, village or other place or residence, shall be punishable with imprisonment for a term which shall not be less than six months but which may extend to five years and with fine.

2. Whoever not being a member of a Scheduled Caste or a Scheduled Tribe:

(i) gives or fabricates false evidence intending thereby to cause or knowing it to be likely that he or she will thereby cause, any member of a Scheduled Caste or a Scheduled Tribe to be convicted of an offence which is capital by the law for the time being in force shall be punished with imprisonment for life and with fine; and if an innocent member of a Scheduled Caste or a Scheduled Tribe be convicted evidence, the person who gives or fabricates such false evidence, shall be punished with death;

(ii) gives or fabricates false evidence intending thereby to cause, or knowing it to be likely that he or she will thereby cause, any member of Scheduled Caste or a Scheduled Tribe to be convicted of an offence which is capital but punishable with imprisonment for a term of such years or upwards, shall be punished for a term which shall not be less than six months but which may extend to seven years or upwards and with fine;

(iii) commits mischief by fire or any explosive substance intending to cause or knowing it to be likely that he will thereby cause damage to any property belonging to a member of a Scheduled Caste or a Scheduled Tribe, shall be punishable with imprisonment for a term which shall not be less than six months but which may extend to seven years and with fine;

(iv) commits mischief by fire or any explosive substance intending to cause or knowing it to be likely that he will hereby cause destruction of any building which is ordinarily used as a place of worship or as a place for human dwelling or as a place for custody of the property by member of a Scheduled Caste or a Scheduled Tribe, shall be punishable with imprisonment for life and with fine;

(v) commits any offence under the Indian Penal Code (45 of 1960) punishable with imprisonment for a term of ten years or more against a person or property on the ground that such person is a member of Scheduled Caste or Scheduled Tribe or such property belonging to such member, shall be punishable with imprisonment for life and with fine;

(vi) knowingly or having reason to believe that an offence has been committed under this chapter, causes any evidence of the commission of that offence to disappear with the intention of screening the offender from legal punishment, or with that intention gives any information respecting the offence which he knows or believes to be false, shall be punishable with the punishment provided for that offence; or

(vii) being a public servant, commits any offence under this section shall be punishable with imprisonment for a term which shall not be less than one year but which may extend to the punishment provided for that offence.

3. Punishment for neglect duties :

Whoever, being a public servant but not being a member of a Scheduled Caste or as Scheduled Tribe, wilfully neglects his duties required to be performed by him under this Act, shall be punishable with imprisonment for a term which shall not be less than six months but which may extend to one year.

4. Enhanced punishment for subsequent conviction:

Whoever, having already been convicted of an offence under this chapter is convicted for second offence or any offence subsequent to the second offence, shall be punishable with imprisonment for a term which shall not be less than one year but which may extend to the punishment provided for that offence.

5. Forfeiture of property of certain person:

(i) Where a person has been convicted of any offence punishable under this Act, the special court may in addition to awarding any punishment by order in writing, declare that any property, movable or immovable or both belonging to the person which has been used for the commission of that offence shall stand forfeited to Government.

(ii) If any person is blamed for an offence of practising untouchability, the special court may confiscate his property both movable and immovable during the period of investigation. If the trial turns into conviction, this property may be forfeited in order to compensate for the fine.

6. Presumption as to offences :

In a prosecution for an offence under this Act, if it is proved that—

(a) the accused render any financial assistance to a person accused of, or reasonably suspected of committing, an offence under this Act, the special court shall presume, unless the contrary is proved, that such person had abetted the offence.

(b) a group of persons committed an offence under this Act and if it is proved that the offence committed was a sequel to any existing dispute regarding land or any other matter, it shall be presumed that the offence was committed in furtherance of the common intention or in prosecution of the common object.

7. Conferment of power:

(A) That State Government may be at its best to prevent any offence against the untouchables, through the Special Court and Police Officer.

The Special Court offers the Police Officers power to investigate, assert and prosecute the offender in their specified area.

(B) All officers of police and all the other officers of Government shall assist the officer referred to in sub-section (1) in the execution of the provision of this Act or any rule, scheme or order made thereunder.

(C) The provisions of the code shall, so far as may be applied to the exercise of the powers by an officer under sub-section (1).

Externment

8. Removal of a person likely to commit offence:

Where the special court is satisfied, upon a complaint or a police report that a person is likely to be included in 'Scheduled Areas' or 'Tribal Area' as referred to an Article 244 of the Constitution, it may be order in writing, direct such a person to remove himself beyond the limits of such area, and not to return to that area from which he was directed to remove himself for the specified period, not exceeding two years, as may be specified in the order.

9. Procedure on failure of a person to remove himself from area and enter thereon after removal:

(A) If a person to whom a direction has been issued under Section 10 to remove himself from any area;

(a) If the person banished by the special court for temporary period, returns to the specified area before the specified time, the Special Court may give order for his arrest.

(b) The Special Court can, any time, order the person to return to the specified area from which he has been banished, for a temporary period.

10. Taking measurements and photographs, etc. of persons against whom order under Section 10 is made. The Police Officer can take the measurement or photograph of a person against whom an order has been passed under Section 10.

11. Penalty for non-compliance with order under Section 10.

Any person contravening an order of the Special Court made under Section 10 shall be punishable with imprisonment for a term which may extend to one year with fine.

12. Special Court as per the Chapter IV 14X22 for the purpose of providing for speedy trial, the State Government shall, with the concurrence of the Chief Justice of the High Court, by notification in the Official Gazette, specify for each district a court of session to be Special Court to try the offences under this Act.

13. Special Public Prosecutor.

For every Special Court, the State Government shall by notification in the Official Gazette, specify a Public Prosecutor or appoint an advocate who has been in practice as an advocate for not less than seven years, as a Special Public Prosecutor for the purpose of conducting cases in that court.

Miscellaneous

14. Power of State Government to impose collective fine:

The Provision of Section 10A of the Protection of Civil Rights Act, 1955 (22 of 1955) shall, so far as may be, apply for the purposes of imposition and realization of collective fine and for all other matters connected therewith under this Act.

15. Preventive action to be taken by the law and other machinery:

The District Magistrate and the Police Officer may take necessary actions to prevent any atrocities likely to be caused by the people other than Scheduled Castes and Scheduled Tribes of his jurisdiction for maintaining peace and order.

16. Duty of Government to ensure effective implementation of the Act.

The Atrocities Act enables the common man to avail himself of justice. It also provides the expenses to the victims and witnesses during investigation period. After the trial rehabilitation of the victims is done, special officers are appointed for that purpose for effective implementation. The committee is appointed by the State Government. Safety and security measures are to be taken for the victims of the atrocities. The Central Government also takes necessary steps and helps the State Government in this process for the well being of the victims.

1. The Atrocities Act enables the common man to avail himself of justice.
2. This Act offers the expenses of travelling and maintenance to the witnesses and victims during the period of investigation.
3. The victims are provided economic and social rehabilitation by this Act.
4. During the period of prosecution of investigation, this Act appoints the officers.
5. This Act declares it to befit to set different committees at the State Government level.

6. For better implementation of this Act, there is a provision of periodic survey.
7. This identification of the locality where the members of Scheduled Castes and Tribe are, is subject to the Atrocity Act.

17. Protection of action taken in good faith:

If the State or the Central Government takes certain measures in good faith, no legal action is taken against them.

18. Power to make rules.

1. The Central Government may, by notification in the Official Gazette, make rules for carrying out the purposes of this Act.
2. Every rule made under this Act shall be laid, as soon as may be after it is made, before each House of Parliament, while it is in session for a total period of 30 days. If both Houses agree in making any modification in the rules or both Houses agree that the rule should not be made, the rule shall thereafter have effect, only in such modified form or be of no effect, as the case may be; so, however, that any such modification or annulment shall be without prejudice to the validity of anything previously done under that rule.

Measures for Improving Impact of the Prevention of Atrocities Act

The Scheduled Castes and Scheduled Tribes (Prevention of Atrocities) Act, 1989 came into force on January 30, 1989 but it should be remembered that the same class of persons who perpetrated atrocities in the past would have to be tackled under the new law. These persons belong to power groups in society and especially in rural areas they would continue to have the power to influence investigation. The present study has shown that a large number of atrocity cases have been characterized by delay in visits to the scene of crime, and tardy investigation, lukewarm prosecution, protracted pendency and a high percentage of acquittals. If the same fate is not to befall atrocity cases under the PAA, special steps will have to be taken on the following lines:

(i) Publicity. A leading commentator on human rights in India has stated, "It is a sad commentary on our commitment in justice that the historic measure seeking to restore democratic human rights to the Scheduled Castes and Tribes has virtually passed unnoticed".

Widespread publicity will have to be done through all the media highlighting the offences and punishments covered by the Act.

(ii) Translation. An enactment in the English language will not be understood by the common man, especially Scheduled Castes and Tribes in the rural areas. Translation into Hindi and the regional languages should be speeded up.

(iii) Printing and Distribution. A sufficiently large print order should be given and copies of the Act should be distributed so that they are available in every police station in the country.

(iv) Training. Orientation training in the provisions of the Act should be arranged for magistrates, prosecutors and police. Seminars should be arranged in which the objective of the Act and the manner of its implementation are fully discussed.

Working of the Act

According to Section 15 A (4) of the Act, the Central Government is required to place on the table of each House of Parliament every year, a report on the measures taken by itself and the State Governments to ensure that the rights accruing from the abolition of "untouchability" may be availed of by the concerned persons. The latest report pertaining to the years 1989 and 1990 states, *inter alia* that:

1. The problem of untouchability still continues to exist in the rural areas in spite of many efforts being taken to eradicate it.
2. The enactment of laws alone will not bring about the desired results for ameliorating the socio-economic conditions of Scheduled Castes. A new strategy having the three components of:
   (a) special component plan for Scheduled Castes by the States/UTs and the Central Ministries.
   (b) Special Central assistance, and
   (c) State Scheduled Castes Development Corporation was involved in Sixth Plan and has been functioning since then.
3. In 1990, the number of cases registered in many States has gone down considerably, as compared to 1989. In the cases of other States, however, it shows that untouchability is still practised in many parts of the country. There is, therefore, an immediate need for gearing up and

strengthening the existing machinery for effective implementation of the Act.

A statement giving details of cases under Untouchability (offences) in pursuance of Protection of Civil Rights Act, 1955, relating to three years commencing from 1988 is given below. It will be observed that there is no significant variation over the years either in the fresh cases registered by the police or pending at the end of the year awaiting disposal. This calls for special scrutiny and initiation of the appropriate measures to bring down the occurrence of offences. Another aspect needing attention is gearing up of disposal machinery, for it is noticed that unsettled cases are mounting up.

Analysis of the Act

The Protection of Civil Rights Act, 1955 and the Scheduled Castes and the Scheduled Tribes (Prevention of Atrocities) Act, 1989, are the two major legislations that concern with untouchability offences and check commission of crimes on Scheduled Castes and Scheduled Tribes. Fifty-seven Special Courts for trial of offences under the PCR Act have been set up in eight States. Similarly, for implementation of the Scheduled Castes and Scheduled Tribes (Prevention of Atrocities) Act, the State Governments and the Union Territory Administration have directed existing district and session courts as Special Courts for trial of offences under this Act. Exclusive Special Courts have also been set up by some States like Andhra Pradesh and Rajasthan.

Monetary relief and rehabilitation assistance continue to be provided to the victims of atrocities. Various State Governments operate schemes to encourage inter-caste marriages and to provide legal aid. Programmes have been developed through the media against the evil practice of untouchability. The voluntary organisations receive financial assistance to propagate against the practice of untouchability. Periodic research surveys and awards to *Panchayats* are some of the other schemes being operated by some. In spite of all these, a lot more needs to be done. This will be clear from what the Eighth Five Year Plan (1992-97) document of the Planning Commission stated. It is recorded that "untouchability stands abolished by virtue of Article 17 of the Constitution and its practice in any form is punishable. But social discrimination against Scheduled Castes still continue to linger in various parts of the country.

It is a matter of great concern that in spite of legal measures in the form of protection of Civil Rights Act, 1955 and the Scheduled Castes and the Scheduled Tribes (Prevention of Atrocities) Act, 1989, 748 cases of atrocities against persons belonging to Scheduled Castes and one hundred and one cases of atrocities against Scheduled Tribes were reported during the years 1986 and 1990. Of these 3,328 cases were of murder, 5,339 of rape and 4,325 of arson." The document recommends that, "In the nineties there has to be an intensification of attempt to bridge the gap in the levels of development of the Scheduled Castes, and other sections of the population so that by the turn of the century these disadvantaged sections of the population are brought on par with the rest of the society in all spheres of national endeavour."

One member in the Lok Sabha made a statements that in a welfare state there should not be any castes and classes. Thus, the success of the Bill was to depend upon the enforcement of the law and this responsibility rested upon the police. One of the members in the Lok Sabha commented that the Objective of abolition of untouchability would be realized only if the social conscience as a whole is changed.

Cases Under Protection of Civil Rights Act, 1955

Sr. No.	*Categories*	*1988*	*1989*	*1990*
1.	Cases brought forward from the previous year	7401	7505	8433
2.	Fresh cases registered by the police during the year	3722	3700	3730
3.	Cases disposed of by the courts during the year ending in			
	a. Conviction	303	410	128
	b. Acquittal	1402	1463	906
4.	Cases pending at the end of the year 1990	7504	6765	8879

The Deputy Minister in the Lok Sabha assured that the law would be enforced properly. He informed that the penal code, the criminal laws, etc. would be made by the States to administer the provisions of the Bill. In addition, Special Courts were established for deciding whether the cases of atrocities were compoundable or not. The opposition thought the Bill to be a non-controversial one but they warned that a correct approach was needed in implementing the Bill.

It was doubtful whether the police would be serious about executing the provisions of the Atrocities Act. The Minister informed that the police were given power to arrest any person found guilty under the Atrocities Act, because the Scheduled Castes would not go and file the complaint. A resolution moved by a member of Rajya Sabha indicated that a survey be conducted to see how far Atrocities Act had been effective in the States. The member also suggested that a commitee be set up for the purpose. The Minister, however, informed the House that all the States had appointed committees for the purpose and that the States were very co-operative in this connection.

The major flaw in the implementation of the Bill was that the Home Ministry and Ministry of Welfare depended upon the States and the non-official organizations for removing atrocities. This made the progress very slow. The Minister argued on the point that this issue was a deep-rooted one and it would take a long time for social disabilities to disappear. A Scheduled Caste member commented that objective of the Ministry of Welfare was good but the implementation was slack, thus the policy of making Atrocities Act an offence shows no results.

States on the whole were co-operative in implementing schemes for the welfare of the Scheduled Castes and Scheduled Tribes. One of the members from Lok Sabha read the statement of objects and reasons, which says that "despite several measures to improve the socio-economic conditions of the Scheduled Castes and the Scheduled Tribes, they remain vulnerable. They are subjected to different offences, indignities, humiliations and harassment. They have, in many brutal incidents, been deprived of their life and property. Serious crimes are committed against them for different historical, social and economic reasons. It is because of the political awareness amongst the Scheduled Castes and the Scheduled Tribes, through spread of literacy, etc. That they are trying to assert their rights and this is not being taken very kindly by the others when they make efforts to assert their rights and resist practices of untouchability against them or demand statutory minimum wages or refuse to do any bonded and forced labour.

The vested interests try to cow them down and terrorize them. When the Scheduled Castes and the Scheduled Tribes try to perserve their self-respect or the honour of their women, they become irritants for their dominance and might. Occupation and cultivation of the Government allotted land by the Scheduled Castes and the Scheduled Tribes is resented and generally these people become victims of attacks by the vested interests." The civic, the executive and the police authorities are not really very sincere to implement these measures and go against the very aim and vision of the Government.

We have already enacted many Acts but the whole question is unsolved still. The Judiciary is silent in this regard. It takes several years for a case to get settled. These poor people cannot afford to pursue the cases year after year. The result is that the offenders go scot-free, is putting the people to a lot of harassment. No doubt, this Act will give some benefit and relief to the SC and ST members. Whenever a crime, atrocity, torture, etc. is committed against the members of the SC/ST, first of all they have to go to the police station to lodge an FIR. Nothing has been mentioned in the Act about the police officers, crimes. The police officers do not easily record the FIR, and maintain silence on the matter.

At the first instance, we fail to understand why the previous Bills have not proved effective. One of the members from Lok Sabha feared as to whether this Bill would also meet the same fate. The main reason is that the persons who are supposed to implement the provisions of the Bill effectively, oppose it, and are prejudiced. They do not want to protect the rights of the Scheduled Castes and Scheduled Tribes. The people from whom we expect that they will protect their rights, intentionally ignore them. In such, a scenario, it would be impossible to implement the provisions of the Act effectively when a person belonging to the Scheduled Castes is victimized as soon as he goes to the police station to lodge an FIR. He is rebuked and asked to go away. If at all an FIR is lodged, then some lacuna is left so that the culprits may not get any punishment. Unless, the Government checks such corrupt practices of providing shelter to the culprits by way of giving them protection in one way or the other, the Scheduled Castes and Tribes (Prevention of

Atrocities) Bill can never prove to be effective. Hence, provision should be made to penalize the officials who indulge in such practices. The Bill would not be useful if it gives protection to such people in any way. The officials make it a point to exploit the person if he happens to be a Scheduled Caste.

Therefore, the Government should pay attention to it. At some places, the State Governments follow the policy of suppressing the incidents of atrocities committed on the people belonging to Scheduled Castes and Scheduled Tribes. Our ideology is clear and the intention of our Government is also good, but the implementation of these laws is the responsibility of the State Governments and they do not fulfil it. We enact the laws, but they are rarely implemented effectively. The fact was also corroborated by the Hon. Member of Lok Sabha that the laws for the weaker sections are not properly implemented.

Uplifting the status of Dalits is the responsibility of the Central Government. So monitoring cells should be setup at the district level instead of State level to keep a close watch on the atrocities in many areas on different sections for the continuous flow of information. The Commissioner of Scheduled Castes and Scheduled Tribes provides all the necessary information to the Government. Various laws have been enacted and forwarded to the State for implementation but before reaching the district level, these laws become handicapped.

The provisions to prevent atrocities have been made in the Bill and they are good too. But if we look at the already existing provisions made in the Constitution or in the Indian Penal Code, we shall find that in a case of atrocities on Harijans, chargesheet has to be produced in the court within a maximum period of ninety days. But we have seen that police officers take one year or more to produce chargesheet in the courts, as a result of which the cases are dismissed in the absence of proof or final reports. The Bill should also ensure that chargesheets relating to incidents of atrocities committed on the Harijans should be produced in the courts within a maximum period of ninety days. If this is done, the cases pertaining to atrocities will definitely be on the decrease. More courts need to be set up at places where the incidents of atrocities are more and only then justice will be rendered in the real sense and the provisions of the Bill be implemented properly.

This type of Bill is so essential in the beginning of 21st century, is very regrettable. The so called high caste people and the land owners are the main culprits for atrocities on Scheduled Castes and Scheduled Tribes. It is a pity that despite many steps taken by the Government, all these facilities have not reached the rural areas at the grass-root level. We must find out the reasons behind it. Besides enacting this legislation we must also consider the effective implementation of measures taken for uplifting their status because atrocities are closely interrelated to it. There are some good provisions in this Bill. But simply passing of the Bill and making an Act will not be able to stop atrocities on Scheduled Castes and Scheduled Tribes.

We have to find out the main cause for the atrocities, which are being perpetuated on them. If we make a proper examination of it, we will see the social, economic and educational backwardness are the root cause as to why atrocities are being perpetuated on them. The entire Scheduled Castes and Scheduled Tribes population in the country is not educated. Owing to their illiteracy they are not well informed.

Since the economic condition of these people is very weak, they are not able to get respectable status in the society. Of course, our Government has launched many schemes for uplifting the status of the SC/ST.

The Government wants to enhance their status in the society by conferring many economic benefits through different schemes. The Government must see whether the scheme launched for the welfare of SC/ST are effectively implemented or not and funds earmarked under these schemes are properly utilized or not. Today it is a challenge to our politicians, the educated and the youth of our society. If we could not generate a feeling of brotherhood in the society and enforce these laws, we would not be able to provide economic, social and legal protection to the Harijans and Adivasis. The Atrocity Act here has been dealt with thoughtfully and effectively. The focal point in this chapter is on the provisions and plans for the welfare of the Scheduled Castes by the Central Government.

Atrocities Act: Some Contradictions

In order to prevent commission of atrocities on Scheduled Castes and Scheduled Tribes, the Scheduled Castes and the Scheduled Tribes (Prevention of Atrocities) Act was passed in 1989 by the Indian Parliament. The Act provides for setting up the special courts for the trial of the offences under it and also the relief and rehabilitation of the victims of such offences. The Act has been in operation since then, and quite a few anomalies and ambiguities have come to light during the period of its implementation. The apparent contradictions in the provisions of the Act and their implementation has been tried by the author as a layman purely on academic planes. The contention do have sound base of a number of reported cases in the media to substantiate the points. It is in this regard that the following issues are brought up.

The term 'Atrocity' has been defined variously as 'Savage enormity' 'Horrible' and 'heinous wickedness' by the Oxford dictionary'. Taking the literal meaning of the term as given in the dictionary, an act of savageness of extreme proportion or an act which strikes horror of heinous nature are covered under the term 'atrocity' . Act 33 of 1989 which was assented by the President of India exactly after six years one month and four days i.e. on Sept. 11, 1989 has defined 'Atrocity' as an offence punishable undr Chapter II section 3 of the Act. Clause (1) of section 3 of the Act enumerates the nature of offence committed by the members of other castes of Scheduled Castes and Scheduled Tribes. Under this clause not all the offences can be said to connote the dictionary meaning of 'Atrocity' as some of them are more in the nature of desisting people from dispossessing members of Scheduled Castes and Scheduled Tribes of their lands and properties, or forcing these members to vote or not to vote for a particular candidate in elections or denial of customary right of passage through public places. These offences fall in the category of Social Justice based on equity rather than in the category of Atrocity. Clause (2) of Section 3 provides the punishments for the above offences and enumerates some more offences including offence under Indian Penal Code, 1860 along with their punishment. Here again very rare enumerated offences fall under the dictionary meaning of 'atrocity' and, therefore, the capital punishment or life imprisonment to such offenders becomes a subject matter of discussion and debate. Section 4 details the punishment to be given to the members of classes other than SC/ ST belonging to public services in case of willful neglect of their duties and Section 5 deals with the second and subsequent offences and their punishment.

Sections 6, 7, 8 and 9 give application of some provisions of

Indian Penal Code, forfeiture of property of accused persons, presumption as offences, and conferment of powers under this Act on any officer, respectively. At this juncture, it can be argued that beside some of the offences not coming into the category of 'Atrocity' as defined by the Oxford Dictionary, some of them have been covered in other Acts as well. e.g. section 3 (1) (vii) Which reads "forcing or intimidating a member of Scheduled Caste or Scheduled Tribe not to vote or vote to a particular candidate or to vote in a manner other than provided by law." This is an "electoral offence" punishable under the Indian Penal Code/Criminal Procedure Code. But by listing it here, it has to be published under this Act denoting the duplicacy of the law and leaving it to the enforcement authority to arbitrariness of the law. Another noteworthy discriminatory provision is that the Act prescribes the offences committed by the members of other castes on the SC and ST by giving detailed account of offences and their punishments. It is silent on the offences of atrocities as enumerated in the Act committed by the members of SC and ST by giving detailed account of offences and their punishments. But does not say anything on the offences of atrocities as enumerated in the Act committed by the members of SC and ST on the brethren, i.e., by one subcaste on the other subcaste. It is common knowledge that members of one subcaste, being a little higher in the caste hierarchy due to their economic, political or muscle power, unleash a reign of terror on the members of other subcaste.

Examples of stripping of their women folk, 'beggar', chopping of hands, social boycott and the like are quite common. These offences are administered under general laws applicable to all communities and not under this Act. In other situations where a combined group of members of both SC/ST as welll as other castes have been charged for committing an offence under this Act, the people belonging to other castes are punished according to the provision of this Act while members belonging to SC/ST are punished under other relevant laws. Here, the punishment awarded to these two set of offenders under different laws differ considerably; the punishment under this act being more severe and intense.

The administration of legal as well as judicial system becomes discriminatory in such cases much against the time honoured dictum of 'Rule of Law' explicity demanding equal punishment for same offence to all classes of people. The predicament of such people belonging to lower social hierarchy in the SC/ST is nerve ending in the absence of and provision under this Act for taking care of offences committed by their own subcastes. This needs rethinking by the political power that be, if it desires to implement the provision of this Act sincerely and equitably. Last, but not the least, the unscrupulous members of SC/ST take recourse to the provision of the Act to humiliate the member of other castes or to settle their score by fabricating charges punishable under this Act. It has been noticed and reported in quite a few cases. Therefore, it is very expedient and prudent that the provisions of the Act may be attracted against a member of other caste only when a prima facie case is established through preliminary enquiry and investigation.

Analytical Appraisal of Dalit Atrocities

Dalits in India present a picture that is of considerable complexity and magnitude. There are about 779 Scheduled Castes in India which are further sub-categorised as untouchable and touchable castes. However, it is very difficult to state how many of Scheduled Castes are touchable and how many of them are untouchable. It is not known largely due to the fact that one caste may be untouchable in one state and touchable in another state. Further, the phenomenon whether a caste is touchable or not, depends on occasion and situation. But, whatever the criteria to call a caste as untouchable, it is certain that there are considerable perceptual and actual differences among these groups of Scheduled Caste communities. Moreover, the dynamics of touchability and untouchability is not only confined between forward castes and Scheduled Castes but also operates between various groups of Scheduled Castes.

The problems of untouchability, sub-human social existence, abject poverty, economic exploitation, a sub-culture of submission, political powerlessness, etc., have been haunting these castes since ancient times they have been suffering from the psycho-economic pressure of social conformity and, thus, constitute the weakest segment in the Indian social structure. Of course, the spread of western education and the impact of western humanitarianism, liberation and rational ideas have helped the Indians to understand the value of freedom and independence. As a result of this influence, some of the Indians were able to dispel the cringing and slavish mentality and the old superstitions and caste rituals. Therefore, the social reformists such as Raja Ram Mohun Roy, Swami Dayanand Saraswati, Swami Vivekanand, M.G. Vende, Jyotiba Phule, R.G. Bhandarker revolted against social evils and particularly against the system of untouchability. But, the movement of the reforms and the political awakening undertaken for the welfare of Scheduled Castes during 19th century were urban and mostly remained as upper caste affairs. With the growth of nationalism and anti-British feelings towards the end of 19th century, of census reports, which highlighted the numerical strength of Scheduled Castes, helped to realise the significance of Scheduled Caste masses by the Muslim and Hindu political leaders. Hence, Gandhiji considered the removal of social, psychological and political inequalities necessary for launching a struggle against the British. In 1919 he said, "Swaraj is unattainable without the removal of the sin of untouchability as it without Hindu-Muslim unity". It is interesting to observe that the consciousness of Scheduled Castes rose up as a result of Gandhian movement and the work done by the voluntary organisations like Ram Krishna Mission, the Servant of Indian Society, the *Harijan Sevak Sangh,* the All India Scheduled Castes Federation, the Bharatiya Depressed Class League, etc.

Finally, Dr. B.R. Ambedkar as the Law Minister and Chairman of the Draft committee for the Constitution of India managed intelligently to introduce the provisions of removal of untouchability and other safeguards to protect Scheduled Castes in the constitution of India. The Preamble which secures justice; social, economic and political; liberty of thought, expression, belief; faith and worship; equality of status and opportunity for all the citizens of country clearly negates the concept of disability arising out of the practice of untouchability. Not only this, Article 17 states, "untouchability is abolished and its practice in any form is forbidden. The enforcement of any disability arising out of untouchability shall be an offence punishable in accordance with law.: Thus, it confers upon and guarantees social justice and dignity to all untouchables and prescribes punishment for actions of the state and individuals in their private and official capacity with respect to the practice of untouchability.

Besides, Preamble and Article 17, there are several other

constitutional provisions which either directly or indirectly provide for the welfare/development/protection from exploitation of these under-privileged people. Following Art. 17 the Parliament passed the Untouchability Offence Act (UOA) in 1955 to make the practice of Untouchability as a cognizable offence in 1955 which came into operation in December 1956. The Untouchability Offence Act 1955 was criticised as it was not upto the expectation to serve the purpose for which it was enacted.

There are several loopholes in the Act and therefore, a Commission was appointed under the chairmanship of L.Elaya Perumal in 1965 to study the different aspects of Untouchability Offence Act, 1955. The commission submitted its report in 1969 and consequently a Bill to amend the Untouchability Offence Act was introduced in April 1972. This Bill with comprehensive amendment as proposed by the Joint Select Committee of Parliament was passed by the Parliament in September 1976 with certain modifications in order to plug the loopholes in the working of the Act. This new Act was called the Protection of Civil Rights Act 1955. But "it is not surprising that untouchables who seek extra legal support may not find the Act a promising means of redress and may, instead, resort directly to executive officers or political figures rather than to police and the courts." The provision made under 15 A (2) of the Protection of Civil Rights Act, 1955, led to a number of special Courts (special mobile courts) having been set up in the States of Andhra Pradesh, Rajasthan, Madhya Pradesh, Tamil Nadu, Orissa, Karnataka and Bihar. Officers have also been appointed in seventeen states to man the special Cells/squads for initiating or exercising supervision over prosecution of PCR Act cases. Committees with Officials and non-official members in 18 states have been set up to review/supervise the working and implementation of the PCR Act 1955.

In spite of efforts made by the Government, the evil custom of untouchability persists in varying degrees in the country. The Government has introduced certain measures to remove untouchability as well as to protect Scheduled Caste and Scheduled Tribe masses from atrocities being incurred on them. These measures include: special legislation for deterring atrocities; strengthening of existing police cells including mobile squads: rising the number of special/mobile courts including the courts for trying atrocity cases; survey of untouchability and atrocity prone areas; legal aid and relief; encouraging inter-caste marriages; strengthening, monitoring and evaluation; publicity and propaganda; and setting up committees at different levels to look into the untouchability and atrocity cases. The Scheduled Castes and Scheduled Tribes (Prevention of Atrocities) Act, 1989 was enacted by Parliament to prevent atrocities against the members of Scheduled Castes and Scheduled Tribes and to provide for special courts for the trial of such offences and for the relief and rehabilitation of the victims of such offences.

Thus, at present both the Protection of Civil Rights Act, 1955 and Scheduled Castes and Scheduled Tribes (Prevention of Atrocities) Act, 1989 are being executed to protect them from the sufferings of untouchability and stop atrocities arising out of their lowest position (both socially, and economically) in social hierarchy. The social discrimination against Scheduled Castes still goes on in various parts of the country. The eighth plan states that, "It is a matter of concern that in spite of legal measures in the form of Protection of Civil Rights and Scheduled Castes and Scheduled Tribes (Prevention of Atrocities) Act, 1989, 76748 cases of atrocities against persons belonging to the Scheduled Caste and 17101 cases of atrocities against the Scheduled Tribes were reported between 1986 and 1990. Of them 3328 cases were of murder, 5339 of rape and 4325 of arson." The effectiveness of administration for prevention of atrocities against Scheduled Castes may be ascertained if the answers to the certain questions are affirmed.

These questions are: Is there any appropriate legislation to stop atrocities; what type of administrative set up has been evolved or entrusted with to implement the Act to prevent the atrocities?; what kind of impact does it have on the officials who are entrusted to implement the Act?; whether the Act has been able to encourage new patterns of behaviour among the aggrieved sections of the society and made the people of Scheduled Castes and Scheduled Tribes to come forward to report to the competent authority about the atrocities being committed to them?; does it deter the offences?; does it provide an effective remedy for the aggrieved poor people?; Do the poor people find the procedure of redressal of grievances from atrocities simple, unexpensive and accessible under the provisions of the Act?; Is the judicial process prescribed under the Act quick and encouraging to the Scheduled Castes and Scheduled Tribes for getting judicial relief? And lastly does the Act work to create humane conditions in the society obstructing the people not to commit atrocities on the poor and under-privileged people of Scheduled Castes and Scheduled Tribes. The Act, under section 9 (i) confers powers "on any officer of the State Government....exercisable by a police officer under the code in such district or part thereof, or as the case may be, for such cases or class or group of cases, and in particular, the powers of arrest, investigation and prosecution of persons before any special Court."

Further, Sections 14 and 15 of the Act provide for the Special Courts and appointment of a Public Prosecutor for each district. Thus, the police and the institution of magistracy at the district level (or part thereof for police) form the administrative machinery for the implementation of this Act. Therefore, the effectiveness of the Act depends on their working. They are supposed to be honest, vigilant and free to any social, political and economic pressures. It has been reported that the members of Scheduled Castes and Scheduled Tribes who are prone to atrocities and are living in rural areas are very poor and often economically dependent on the higher castes.

The assertion of their rights or to voice against atrocities may result into social boycott, eviction from village, denial or grazing rights, etc. Moreover, if they report, they may not be able to produce witness due to their economic disabilities. In such a circumstance, the administration finds itself ineffective and crippled. Section 17 (1) provides that "a district Magistrate or Sub-Divisional Magistrate or any other Executive Magistrate or any police officer not below the rank of a Deputy Superintendent of Police may, on receiving information and after such enquiry as he may think necessary, has reason to believe that a person or group of persons...likely to commit an offence or has threatened to commit any offence under this Act can take appropriate preventive measures of its own." It clearly reveals that an officer can take initiative but only to take preventive measures. The officer/officials are not empowered to take initiative on their own due to the lack of witness or mass support. Therefore, it becomes necessary to create awareness in the society, including the upper castes, so that all the cases of atrocities may be reported to the police and the members of the society become ready to be witnesses. This Act, no doubt, has the provision to pay travelling allowance to the witnesses but that is not enough. Further, the Village Bardhan/*Sarpanch* should be entrusted with the duty to report such incidences of atrocities to the police within stipulated time and this accountability has to be approximately inserted in the *Panchayati Raj* Act. If this type of provision is made in the legislation and appropriate steps to ensure mass participation for the removal of atrocities are undertaken, only then the administrative machinery would become able to implement this Act effectively. Section 4 of the Act states, "whoever being a public servant but not being a member of Scheduled Caste or Scheduled Tribe wilfully neglects his duties required to be performed by him under this Act, shall be punishable with imprisonment for a term which shall not be less than 6 months but may extend to one year".

However, the experiences in the implementation of PCR Act, 1955 reveals that in various cases, the untouchables seek extra legal support for redressal of their grievances instead of resorting to executive officers. This is equally true for the cases of atrocities and the provision under Section 4 of the Act stated above may not help the Government to make the officials more effective in implementing the provisions of this Act or to take effective steps by the officials to prevent the atrocities on Scheduled Castes and Scheduled Tribes. Moreover, this provision has made the non-Scheduled Caste or non-Scheduled Tribe officials susceptible for misuse by the unscruplous political leaders and deters the honest officials entrusted with these duties to take interest in this/their job. Further, it is very difficult to prove that the certain official is neglecting his duty wilfully, therefore, it may not serve the purpose of streamlining the administration engaged in the prevention of atrocities. This penalty may be substituted by certain disciplinary action such as stoppage of increment, denial of promotional opportunity, etc.

Besides, this negative measure suggested in this section against the official also discriminates him on the caste-line, which certainly creates tension among the non-Scheduled Caste and Scheduled Caste officials and as per sub-section 2 of the Section 9," all other officers of the police and all the other officers of Government" shall not "assist the officer referred to in Sub-section (1) in the execution of the provision of this Act or any rule, scheme for order made thereunder.

Therefore, it has been recommended that positive steps for officials have to be inserted in the Act so that the officials have to be inserted in the Act so that the officials become more committed and willing to protect the Dalit people from atrocities. It is also not necessary that the officials who belong to Scheduled Caste or Scheduled Tribe will certainly perform their duties, regarding the implementation of the Act, with commitment and integrity. It has been evident that the problem of untouchability is also prevalent among the various castes of the Scheduled Castes. The members of some of the Scheduled Castes, and incidentally who happened to belong to the privileged castes of the Scheduled Castes get educated and, hence, in employment on higher positions in administration or police, consider the other lower castes as untouchables. They do not have a brotherly sentiment towards them. Further, many officials belonging to Scheduled Castes or Scheduled Tribes are prone to the pressure of unscruplous political leadership often dominated by the upper castes. Thus, the bureaucracy, mainly composed of upper caste people, political leadership dominated again by higher caste people, and absence of complete cohesiveness among the different Scheduled Castes or Scheduled Tribes will hinder the effectiveness, commitment, integrity and willingness of the Scheduled Caste or Scheduled Tribe officials who have been entrusted with duties underlined in this Act. Therefore, there should not be any discrimination between officials on caste line, as provided in the Act. A perusal of the Act also shows that effective implementation of the Act mostly depends upon the police officials entrusted with such duties under the Act.

Nevertheless, the image of the police officials is such that the poor people are reluctant to file complaints about cases. Even if, it is reported to the officials, he has the right to investigate into the matter before submitting it to the special court designated for the purpose under the Act. The investigation Part of the procedure for redressal of grievances is most difficult to cross by the poor Scheduled Caste people which in several cases results in extra legal compromise. In case there is no extra legal compromise honesty and integrity of the police official or seriousness of the atrocity or interference of political leadership/political party or voluntary organisation or a group of persons, then the case is tried by the special court established as per the provisions of Chapter IV and Section 14 of the Act and the sessions court at the district level is designated by the Government as the special court with the purpose of providing speedy trial. First of all, the special courts have not been established in all the districts of the country. Secondly, the working of these courts is not substantially different from other courts particularly with reference to the speed of disposal of cases.

Thirdly the lack of witnesses in the atrocity cases, and ignorance of judicial process, etc. have been obstructing in the effectiveness of the judicial process and the Special courts. Thus, it is noted that the Act has not been able to influence the behaviour of Scheduled Caste or Scheduled Tribe masses upto certain level to take legal redressal from the court in case of atrocities committed on them.

Therefore, more simple and speedy mechanism, to avoid extra-legal compromise and for speedy trial of cases, must be evolved so that the behavioural pattern of these people can be changed upto a desired level.

Section 3(1) and 3(2) shows that only the person/persons who is/are punishable under the Act. But, what about the person who is the member of Scheduled Caste or Scheduled Tribe and commits atrocities as per the provisions contained in the above stated section. It cannot be accepted at the present juncture of time that the member of Scheduled Caste or Scheduled Tribe who belong to the affluent section of society are not exploiting their brothers and incurring atrocities on them.

This opinion is expressed on the basis of experiences gathered during a study on trial development in Rajasthan by the author and through newspaper reports. The tribal villages having no population of non-Scheduled Tribe people were being exploited by the rich Scheduled Tribe who mostly happened to be educated and holding the office of *sarpanch* in the village. Therefore, the Act should also prescribe the provision for punishing the Scheduled Castes and Scheduled Tribes along with the non-Scheduled Caste and non-Scheduled Tribe people if they offend the provisions of the present Act. Section 7(1) and 7(2) of the Act provide for the forfeiture of property of a person who has been convicted for an offence or the person is accused of any offence under Chapter 11, (offences of Atrocities) of the Act. No doubt, these provisions may help in deterring the offences, but simultaneously, there will be more and more chances of Misuse for political and economic gains. The present trend of politician-bureaucracy-criminal nexus provides the reasons for it. Therefore, Section 7(2) should be made more soft towards the accused person under this Act. Despite this, the Scheduled Castes and Scheduled Tribes (Prevention of Atrocities) Act, 1989 Act will certainly help in preventing the atrocities on them. Although the Act does not provide total redressal from atrocities, but it attempts to punish those found guilty under the Act.

It would be much better if the Act might have the provision relating to the rehabilitation of persons who have suffered from the atrocities. Lastly, attempts have been undertaken to make the judicial process inexpensive and speedy for the trial of atrocity cases but still much more is required to be done in this direction.

9

Constitutional Identification of Dalits

Our Constitution does not contemplate reservations and special treatment as a general principle of operation. Such treatment is authorized only for the limited purpose of advancing the backward. Who, then, are the legitimate recipients of such preferential treatment? The Constitution permits preferences for three categories of groups: (a) Scheduled Castes – i.e., "untouchables", (b) Scheduled Tribes; and (c) other (Socially and educationally) backward classes. The term "backward classes" is generally used in two senses: (1) as a generic term including the Scheduled Castes and Scheduled Tribes as well as the so-called Other Backward Classes; or (2) as a designation of those backward groups not included in either of the first two categories (i.e., as equivalent to "Other Backward Classes."). The Constitution itself does not define these groups, nor does it provide detailed standards by which they may be determined.

In the case of Scheduled Castes and Tribes, it does prescribe an agency and a method for designating them. Not only are Backward Classes left undefined in the Constitution, but no such method or agency for their determination is provided. Before taking up the more complex issues that have arisen in the designation of the Backward Classes, one shall have to trace the problems of identifying the Scheduled Castes and Scheduled Tribes. The Scheduled Castes and Scheduled Tribes form the bulk of those receiving preferential treatment, and they receive a larger quantum of preferences than Other Backward Classes. The Scheduled Caste and Tribe categories are intended to comprise those who were at the bottom or the margins of the Indian social order – those groups who due to their low ritual status in the traditional Hindu hierarchy or their spatial and cultural isolation were subjected to imposition of disabilities and lack of opportunity.

The Constitution prescribes that the Scheduled Castes and Tribes shall be designated by Presidential Order in the first instance, with later modification only by the Act of Parliament. It further provides that the President shall appoint a special officer to investigate all matters concerning the safeguards for the Scheduled Castes and Tribes and report to the Parliament on their working. Accordingly, the office of the Commissioner of Scheduled Castes and Scheduled Tribes was established in 1950 as a continuing body with coordinating and reporting functions but did not included administrative functions.

The Term 'Schedule Castes'

"Scheduled Castes" is the most recent of a long line of official euphemisms for "untouchables.". The Scheduled Caste category is intended to include those groups isolated and disadvanced by their "untouchability"—i.e., their low status in the traditional Hindu caste hierarchy which exposed them to invidious treatment, severe disabilities, and deprivation of economic, social, cultural, and political opportunities. In the early years of the century the "depressed classes" (as they were then called) became an important category to focus on among reformers. After 1901, fears of diminished Hindu majorities and proposals for special legislative representation for these classes propelled "untouchability" from the realm of philanthropy into the political arena. As concern about untouchables and political demands were made in their behalf, there was sharp disagreement about the number of persons who belonged in this category. From 1908 on, it was claimed by numerous writers that untouchables numbered 50 millions or more—about 24 per cent of the Hindu population or just under 16 per cent of the total population of India according to the 1911 census.

Although Madras compiled a list of depressed classes during the 1920s, the Government of India refrained from any official classification (until 1936) on the ground that it would be unfair to stigmatize these groups by official acknowledgment of their low status. But different governmental bodies tried to assess their numbers. The first official estimates in 1917 and 1918 arrived at the figure of about 30 millions for British India. The Franchise (South-borough) Committee, which was setup to advise on the franchise under the 1919 reforms, found 42.2 millions in British India. Since there were presumably one-quarter to one-third as many more in the princely states, this seem to touch the 50 million figure. The 1921 census and the Reforms Enquiry (Muddiman) Committee of 1924 arrived at comparable figures. However, in 1928, official estimates reverted to the lower range: two officials identified the number of untouchables as 28.5 millions and 29 millions, and the Hartog Committee set the number at 29.76 millions. A new round of counting had started with the impending of further constitutional changes. In 1929, the Indian Central (Nair) Committee, set up to advise the Simon Commission, arrived at a figure of 44.5 millions, and the Simon Commission itself estimated the number at 43.6 millions. (See Table 9.1) The Indian Franchise (Lothian) Committee, set up to advise on the franchise under the new reforms, received conflicting estimates from a number of quarters.

The 1931 Census Commissioner estimated untouchables at 31.2 millions excluding Bengal; the Provincial Governments supplied somewhat lower figures, totalling 37.45 millions. The Provincial Committees, setup to advise the Franchise Committee, produces figures that were less than half of the then-current estimates (18.62 millions). The dissenting members of the Franchise Committee reduced the number even further to 14.42 millions. The Franchise Committee itself was unable to arrive at a firm figure. The various estimates are presented in Table 9.1.

TABLE 9.1
Percentage of Untouchables in British India

Province	*Number of Untouchables (Millions)*	*Percentage of Hindu Population*	*Percentage of Total Population*
MADRAS	6.5	18	15.5
BOMBAY	1.5	11	8.0
BENGAL	11.5[a]	57	24.5
UTTAR PRADESH	12.0[a]	31	26.5
PUNJAB	2.8	42	13.5
BIHAR AND ORISSA	5.0[a]	20	14.5
CENTRAL PROVINCES	3.3	33	24.5
ASSAM	1.0	24	13.0
TOTAL	43.6	28.5	19

Source: Indian Statutory Commission 1930a: 40.

There was little dispute (Table 9.2) about who were the untouchables in southern and western India – Madras and Bombay Presidencies and the Central Provinces. The dispute was about northern and eastern India. Which groups there ought to be treated on a par with the untouchables of the south and west? This, in turn, depended on how the depressed classes were going to be defined – whether strictly in terms of specific indicia of ritual and social exclusion or more broadly in terms of low status. Earlier investigations had tended to proceed on the assumption that untouchables throughout India were set off by some uniform and distinctive pattern of practices and that a test could be applied that would identify them on an all-India basis.

Thus, the Government of India's 1919 Despatch, criticizing the inadequacy of the Southborough Committee recommendations for representation for the Depressed Classes, pointed out that "though they are defined in varying terms, [they] are broadly speaking all the same kind of people. Except for the differences in the rigidity of their exclusion they are all more or less in the position of Madras *Panchamas,* definitely outside that part of the Hindu community which is allowed access to their temples." However, this assumption proved difficult to apply in northern and eastern India. Touch and distance pollution extended across the caste system in the south, while in the north touch and distance pollution were not expressed uniformly enough. The Simon Commission, a decade later, conceded that in Bengal, the United Provinces, and Bihar and Orissa, there was a big margin for possible error. In these provinces, "the connection between theoretical untouchability and practical disabilities is less close, and a special investigation might show that the number of those who are denied equal rights in the matter of school, water and the like is less than the total given for the depressed classes in these areas. This vastly different nature of the matter in the north was brought out nicely in the testimony before the Indian Franchise Commission of Mr. G.S. Pal, representing the United Provinces Hindu Backward Classes League, which had submitted a list of 115 castes (estimated to make up over sixty per cent of the population) for inclusion as Depressed Classes in the United Provinces.

Dr. Ambedkar. My point is this. Is this a list of what might be called backward communities, economically backward and

TABLE 9.2
Estimates of Untouchable Population in British India by Various Official Bodies, 1917–1941

	Sir Henry Sharp	Provincial Governments	Franchise Committee (Southborough)	1921 Census	Reforms Enquiry Committee (Muddiman)	Hartog Committee	Indian Central Committee	Indian Statutory Commission (Simon)	Census Commissioner 1931	1931 Census	Provincial Governments	Provincial Committees	Indian Franchise Committee (Lothian)	Indian Franchise Committee (Dissent)	SC Order	1936 List according to 1941 Census
YEAR	1917	1917-18	1919	1921	1924	1928	1929	1930	1931	1931	1932	1932	1932	1936	1941	
SOURCE	A	B	C	D	E	F	D	G	C	H	I	I	I	J	K	L
MADRAS	5.7	6.48	6.4	6.4	6.4	6.53	6.50	6.5	7.0[a]	7.2	7.1	7.1	7.1	7.1	...	8.06
BOMBAY	1.6	1.63	0.6	2.8	2.8	1.46	1.47	1.5	1.8	1.8	1.7	1.7	1.7	1.7	...	1.85
BENGAL	6.7	6.74	9.9	9.0	9.0	6.64	11.50	11.5	N.A.	6.9	11.20[a]	0.07[a]	...	0.07	9.125	7.37
UTTAR PRADESH	8.4	8.37	10.1	9.0	9.0	7.89	13.00	12.0	12.6	11.3	6.8[C]	0.6	...	0.6	10.526	11.71
PUNJAB	2.1	...	1.7	2.8	2.8	1.70	2.80	2.8	1.3	1.3	1.3	1.3[b]	...	1.0	1.420	1.24[d]
BIHAR AND ORISSA	1.2	1.10	9.4	8.0	8.0	2.53	5.00	5.0	3.7[d]	5.7	5.8	4.3	4.3	0.4	4.526	5.57

Contd.

Contd.

CENTRAL PROVINCES	3.0	3.06	3.8	3.3	3.3	3.01	2.67	3.3	2.9	2.8	2.9	2.9	2.9	2.9	...	3.05
ASSAM	2.7	...	0.3	2.0	2.0	oe	1.55	1.0	0.65	0.65	...	...	0.65	...	...	0.67
TOTALS	31.5	...	42.2	43.3	43.3	29.76	44.50	43.6	31.21[c] (Plus Bengal)	39.1	37.45	18.62	...	14.42	...	39.92

Sources: A: Indian Statutory Commission 1930: 1350–53: B: Indian Statutory Commission 1930: 1341ff: C: Indian Constitutional Reforms 1919:I, 119; D : Indian Central Committee 1929 : 367; E: Reforms Enquiry Committee 1925: 56; F: Indian Statutory Commission (Hartog Committee) 1929 : 218; G: Indian Statutory Commission 1930a : 40; H: Census of 1931. Table reproduced in Hutton 1961: 199; I: Indian Franchise Committee 1932 I, 111ff.: J: Indian Franchise Committee 1932:1 219: K: Singh 1947. Appendix I: L: Census of India 1941, I. Pt. I. Tables. P 98.

Notes: Figures are in millions

[a] Noted in source as approximate, tentative under investigation, or under revision.

[b] Figures from minority; Majority gave no figures.

[c] Described as not polluting, but deserving of special representation.

[d] Excluding Ad Dharmis (.34 million).

[e] "Practically none."

educationally backward? Or is this a list of castes which are called untouchables, whose touch causes pollution? Is this a list of castes which are touchable but which are educationally and economically backward or which are untouchable and also educationally and economically backward?

Mr. Pal. I respectfully submit that this is a list of all the castes which in the opinion of the league are depressed classes; untouchability in the sense in which it is understood in Madras or Bombay does not exist here. Bhangi is the only caste that is universally untouchable, pollution by whose touch is regarded as something very undesirable. Here untouchability exists, of course, but in a very mild form or exists in some form or another in all the castes I have enumerated.

Sir Sunder Singh Majithia. How would you define depressed class people?

Mr. Pal. Not in the sense of the definition in Bombay and Madras but apparently here the Hindu class is divided into high and low castes. The problem is very acute, as acute as untouchability is in Bombay and Madras. I apply three tests, the first is we are socially despised; then there is economic backwardness; and educational bankruptcy.

In the most elaborate effort to specify criteria by which to identify untouchable groups, J.H. Hutton, the 1931 Census Commissioner, proposed a series of tests which centre around the incidence of disabilities:

1. Whether the caste or class in question can be served by Brahmans or not.
2. Whether the caste or class in question can be served by the barbers, water-carriers, tailors, etc., who serve the caste Hindus.
3. Whether the caste in question pollutes a high-caste Hindu by contact or proximity.
4. Whether the caste or class in question is one from whose hands a caste Hindu can take water.
5. Whether the caste or class in question is debarred from using public conveniences, such as roads, ferries, wells or schools.
6. Whether the caste or class in question is debarred from the use of Hindu temples.
7. Whether in ordinary social intercourse a well-educated

member of the caste or class in question will be treated as an equal by the high-caste men of the same educational qualifications.

8. Whether the caste or class in question is merely depressed on account of its own ignorance, illiteracy or poverty and but for what, would be subject to no social disability.
9. Whether it is depressed on account of the occupation followed, and whether but for that occupation it would be subject to no social disability.

However these tests are not entirely, free from difficulty. They include terms like "clean Brahmin" and "high-caste Hindu" which have only a local and comparative reference. And whether a caste is "polluting" or "debarred" from public facilities or temples may admit of no unequivocal answer, since pollution and debarment may exist in grades or degrees. Some may be forbidden to approach a temple, while others are only excluded from the inner sanctuary. Debarment from wells might imply use of adequate but separate water supply or onerous exclusion from any decent water supply. Tests 7 and 8, as Lelah Dushkin points out, "seem a bit academic, since the [Census] Superintendents were often in no position to find out whether they applied or not...." Whether a caste "can be served" is not essentially the same as whether it is habitually served unless one assumes correspondence between local learning on the matter and local practice that does not invariably obtain. However, the tests clearly indicate the incidence of disabilities as the crucial test. "It is at least clear that occupation, 'ignorance, illiteracy or poverty' or any other such forms of 'backwardness' were not intended to enter into the definition process." Hutton suggested.

From the point of view of the State the important test is the right to use public conveniences—roads, wells, and schools—and if this be taken as the primary test, religious disabilities and the social disabilities involved by them may be regarded as contributory only. Some importance must be attached to them, since obviously if the general public regards the persons of certain groups as so distasteful that concerted action is resorted to in order to keep them away, persons of those groups do suffer a serious disability.

But the "right to use public conveniences" might be one of

the most difficult and fruitless tests to apply, since roads were normally open to all, practices concerning schools and wells were subject to much local variation and came in a number of gradations, and finally, because practice might diverge sharply from "rights".

The existence of multiple (and ambiguous) criteria permitted regional variation by giving the Census superintendents scope for discretion. Each provincial superintendent was told to draw up his own list, taking these tests into account, "and to reckon as depressed only those castes who definitely suffer from serious social and political handicap on account of their degraded position in the Hindu social scheme."

The final reckoning, then, did not apply Hutton's test pure and simple. Some castes were excluded which were theoretically untouchable, but who, by virtue of prosperity and vigorous organization, "have built up for themselves a strong position which obviates the need of any special measures for their social, political or religious protection." Conversely, some groups were included even though theoretically they were not untouchables. The total of Depressed Classes reported by the census was 39.1 millions in British India and 11.1 millions in the States and Agencies—making a total of 50.2 millions. The insufficiency of any single test to identify the untouchables provoked various responses on the Franchise (Lothian) Committee.

Dr. Ambedkar, the leading untouchable spokesman, points out that the objective is demarcate those who suffer from the contempt and aversion of higher caste Hindus: "It is a fatal mistake to suppose that differences in tests of untouchability suggest differences in the conditions of the untouchables." The crucial common element is the odium and avoidance of the higher castes. Once this element is present "the whole of the class of untouchables so ascertained must be taken into account for the purpose of representation without any further distinction between rich and poor, advanced and backward, educated and uneducated..."

Both of these points were negated by the dissenters, S.B. Tambe, C.Y. Chintamani, and R.R. Bakhale. They find that outside of Madras, Bombay, and the Central provinces, untouchables do not have any distinct and separate identity in the population. In the other provinces "untouchability ... is the adjunct not of a person but of the occupation he occupies." The majority of the Committee, adhering to denial of access to temples and causing pollution by touch or approach as commonly accepted tests of untouchability, reiterated its conviction that the depressed classes should include only untouchables and not "those Hindus who are only economically poor and in other sense backward but are not considered as untouchables." But in the face of conflicting estimates it confessed its inability to reach any conclusions about the untouchable population in the north and east. The groups in this category were finally listed (i.e., scheduled) in 1936 for the purpose of giving effect to the provisions for special electoral representation in the Government of India Act, 1935.

The list finally promulgated did not correspond exactly to any of the earlier estimates: it hewed closely to the low figures for Assam, the high figures for the United Provinces and Bihar and Orissa, and adopted a middle course in Bengal. In the event, the list reflected definitions of untouchability with an admixture of economic and educational tests and considerations of local politics. Lelah Dushkin observes that "the authorities who made up the final list made quite a departure from the original strict criterion of untouchability... many castes listed in the North would not have been included in the South. However, whatever the criteria were, all of the castes included in the final list were socially the lowest Hindu castes in their particular provinces and they were listed partly, at least, on that basis." The list contained over forty million persons. The 1941 Census enumerated 48.8 million members of the listed groups (very close to the 50 million figure current at the inception of the debate a quarter-century earlier). They constituted over nineteen per cent of the Hindu population and 12.6 per cent of the total population of undivided India. (See Table 9.3)

TABLE 9.3
Population of Scheduled Castes in 1941

	SC Pop.(mils.)	*Percentage of Hindu Population*	*Percentage of Total Population*
British India	39.92	20.90	13.49
Madras	8.068	18.85	16.35
Bombay	1.855	11.20	8.89
Bengal	7.378	29.44	12.23
Uttar Pradesh	11.717	25.57	21.39
Punjab	1.248	16.53	4.38

Contd.

Bihar	4.340	16.37	11.49
	5.578	16.74	12.37
Orissa	1.238	18.12	14.18
Central Provinces	3.051	23.57	41.34
Assam	0.676	16.04	6.62
N.W.F.P.	–	–	–
Sind	1.191	15.58	4.22
	SC Pop.(mils.)	*Percentage of Hindu Population*	*Percentage of Total Population*
Ajmer-Merwara	–	–	–
TOTAL	39.80	20.87	13.45
States and Agencies	8.892	13.86	9.78
Cochin	0.141	15.73	9.92
Hyderabad	2.928	21.99	17.92
Mysore	1.405	21.03	19.16
Rajputana	...	...	...
Travancore	0.395	11.15	6.50
Totals (throughout India)	48.81	19.15	12.62

Source: Census of India, 1941, I. Part I: 98

Notes: [a]Greater than sub-totals, owing to omission of minor units.

[b]Some units omitted.

The Constitution Scheduled Castes

The Constitution makers refrained any attempt at a connotative definition of untouchability and adopted the same kind of solution as had the British. Lists were to be compiled for each area of those castes which were considered as needful and deserving of such treatment. Rather than provide any standard of selection for these groups beyond the general understanding that they were the "untouchables," the Constitution provided only a procedure for designating them. The President is empowered to specify, after consulting with the Governor of a state, those "castes, races or tribes or parts of or groups within castes, races and tribes which shall for the purpose of this Constitution be deemed to be Scheduled Castes in relation to that state..." Once promulgated, this list can be changed only by an Act of Parliament. A Scheduled Castes Order was promulgated by the President in 1950 which basically re-enacted the 1936 list. The major additions were four Sikh castes and the provision for the first time of lists for areas which had none previously, (notably Rajasthan, Gwalior, and Madhya Bharat).

A few changes were made in 1951, but these were of the nature of adjustments and elimination of anomalies rather than any basic change in policy. The 1951 census revealed that the Scheduled Castes contained over 52 million members. More discrepancies, errors, and oversights came to light, and in 1956 the lists were revised once again. Major changes were the addition of about a million persons each in Rajasthan and in UP and the inclusion now of all Sikh untouchables. The revised list came to the figure of 55.3 millions (using 1951 census figures). In the 1971 census, the Scheduled Castes contained eighty millions (14.6 per cent of the population). (See Table 6.4) The changes in the list have been more in the nature of removing anomalies and correcting oversights: moving groups from the Scheduled Caste to Tribe lists, sorting out discrepancies and errors, rationalizing administration.

There have been no significant policy departures (other than inclusion of the Sikhs). Indeed, there has been no further effort to formulate any criterion for inclusion. In the first report the Commissioner for Scheduled Castes and Tribes observed that Hutton's 1931 census criteria seems to hold good for purposes of specifying the Scheduled Castes. Although there was no specific indication that they were applied any more literally than in 1931 or 1936, no one seemed troubled. In the late 1950s the Commissioner remarked that the criteria for classifying a caste as scheduled were "fairly definite." Formally, the power to make and change the lists lay with the President (and later with Parliament), but it seems that the dominant role was played by the executive, centre and state. The lists remained in charge of the Ministry of Home Affairs except for an interval from 1964 to 1973 when this task was housed in the erstwhile Department of Social Security (later Social Welfare).

Although the role of the state is formally consultive, designation appears in fact to be a two-stage process in which centre or state proposes and attempts to get consent of the other. Where the state is unwilling, listings favoured by the centre can be held up for years. On the other hand, where states have proposed changes in the list, especially inclusions, these have been rejected due to lack of any supporting data. The selection of Scheduled Castes, then, had done without benefit of a single connotative definition. The selection has proceeded primarily on the basis of

TABLE 9.4

Scheduled Caste Population (in Million) and Percentages 1950–1951, 1956, 1961, 1971

	According to 1950 and 1951 Orders			*According to 1956 Orders*		*1961 Census*			*1971 Census*		
	Total Popula-tion (1951)	*SC Popula-tion*	*SC % of total Popula-tion*	*SC Total Populati-on*	*SC % of Total Population*	*Total Populati-on (1961)*	*SC Populati-on*	*SC % of Total Populati-on*	*Total Populati-on 1971*	*SC Populati-on*	*SC % of Total Populati-on*
Source	A	A	A	A	A	B	B	B	C	C	C
Andhra Pradesh	31.3	4.406	14.09	4.415	14.3	36.0	4.973	13.50	43.50	5.774	13.26
Assam	9.0	0.424	4.68	0.424	4.68	11.9	0.732	6.16	14.96	0.912	6.01
Bihar	38.8	4.913	12.66	4.913	12.67	46.5	6.563	14.04	56.35	7.950	14.10
Bombay	48.3	5.130	10.62	5.202	10.78						
Gujrat						20.6	1.367	6.63	26.70	1.825	6.81
Maharashtra						39.6	2.226	5.61	50.41	3.025	5.99
Jammu & Kashmir	4.4	N.A.	...	0.156	3.54	3.6	0.263	7.55	4.62	0.381	8.24
Kerala	13.5	1.254	9.25	1.207	8.81	16.9	1.422	8.40	21.35	1.772	8.29
Madhya Pradesh	26.1	3.502	13.43	3.912	15.01	32.4	4.245	13.12	41.65	5.453	13.08
Madras (Tamil Nadu)	30.0	5.391	17.98	5.381	17.95	33.7	6.072	18.00	41.20	7.315	17.74

(Contd.)

	According to 1950 and 1951 Orders			According to 1956 Orders		1961 Census			1971 Census		
	Total Population (1951)	SC Population	SC % of total Population	SC Total Population	SC % of Total Population	Total Population (1961)	SC Population	SC % of Total Population	Total Population 1971	SC Population	SC % of Total Population
Mysore (Karnataka)	19.4	2.589	13.33	2.583	13.34	23.6	3.117	13.20	29.30	3.850	13.14
Orissa	14.6	2.639	17.95	2.629	17.95	17.5	2.763	15.71	21.94	3.310	15.08
Punjab	16.1	3.062	18.97	3.490	21.64	20.3	4.139	20.32			
Punjab									13.55	3.348	24.72
Haryana									10.04	1.895	18.82
Rajasthan	11.0	1.584	9.91	2.502	15.67	20.2	3.359	16.62	25.77	4.075	15.79
Uttar Pradesh	63.2	1.855	18.75	13.100	20.72	73.7	15.417	20.90	88.34	18.548	20.99
West Bengal	26.3	4.855	18.56	4.743	18.04	35.0	6.950	19.84	44.31	8.816	19.90
Union Territories	4.1	0.57	13.83	0.664	16.23	7.8	0.916	11.74	6.34	0.750	11.82
Totals	61.2	2.2	14.5	55.3	15.32	39.1	54.504	14.64	47.95	79.995	14.59

Source: A: RCSCST 1956–57: II, 15; B: RCSCST 1961–62: II, 74; C: Census of India, 1971, Series I, Part II–A (ii): xxvii–xxix.
Note: Totals include minor units not given here.

"untouchability"—measured by the incidence of social disabilities—but this criterion has been combined in varying degrees with economic, occupational, educational, and residential and religious tests.

The ensuing list, then, designates all of those groups who in the view of Parliament need the special protections provided by the Constitution: it defines who may stand for reserved seats and enjoy benefits and reservations for the Scheduled Castes. But it does not necessarily include every person or group that might be regarded "untouchables" by any conceivable definition. It omits some groups which historically suffered disabilities (e.g. Ezhuvas) or which would be untouchables in terms of the 1931 census tests. And it excludes non-Hindus (other than Sikhs) who would clearly appear to be untouchables within the juridicial test of "origin in a group considered beyond the pale of the caste system." There is, thus, no single inclusive list of all groups considered untouchable, much in the same way as there is no single criterion for identifying them. In spite of the absence of definitive criterion (or perhaps due to it), the lists have remained stable. Some groups continue to petition for inclusion. The commissioner points out that "there has been a tendency of some castes and communities to use every opportunity for pressing their claims for inclusion in the list of Scheduled Castes/Scheduled Tribes." But the process of getting on is so cumbersome that few have succeeded. If the pre-independence figures of 12.3 per cent are adjusted to allow for the failure of some areas to have lists at all and for the removal of predominantly non-Hindu areas by partition, the 1971 figure of 14.6 per cent (the same in 1961) represents very little change in overall proportion. There have been no notable inclusions (other than the Sikhs).

The changes that have occurred have been rationalizations and extensions of existing criteria to overlooked groups and areas previously omitted, rather than any change in criteria. Nor have there been any major exclusions with the exceptions of the "voluntary" departure of the converts to Buddhism. There has been no litigation about inclusion or exclusion of any group challenging the "untouchability" criterion or its application—but litigation has been made on the religious and residence tests. With whatever admixture of other factors, the Scheduled Castes have been chosen primarily by the criterion of low social and ritual standing. In the selection of Other Backward Classes, the use of social and ritual status as a criterion of the backwardness of the group has been severely limited by the courts. But such criteria have been predominant in the selection of Scheduled Castes, who have been chosen precisely on the ground of their low social and ritual status in the traditional social hierarchy.

The justification for employing low status and attendant disabilities as a criterion for preferences is that these groups are mostly the lowest in income, education, health, cultural resources, and economic opportunities. Generally, more than a simple correlation is implied. These castes are, in the prevailing view, backward because they were subject to disabilities which impeded advancement by individual effort and denied them opportunities for group social mobility. This stress has endured over the years. In the debate preceding passage of the 1976 amendments to the Scheduled Castes order the view surfaced that "it is basically the economic and social backwardness of a caste which should entitle it to be categorized as a Scheduled Caste. But the Home Minister was emphatic in reiterating that the concept of Scheduled Castes is one of backwardness stemming from untouchability. It is not neglect, it is not just poverty, it is not mere backwardness that entitles man to come under the Scheduled Castes. However, to the extent that the legislative prohibition of disabilities and changing social practice result in a lessening of disabilities, and to the extent that preferential treatment raises educational attainments and economic opportunities, the correlation between low ritual standing and economic and social backwardness will be weakened. If "untouchability" is a useful criterion for identifying those groups which are at the bottom in terms of economic, educational, and cultural resources and opportunities, the very success of redistributive measures might cause a discrepancy between ritual standing and the other indicia of backwardness.

It would appear that Parliament's power to designate Scheduled Castes is reasonable broad to permit the use of standards which would decrease the role of ritual standing and disabilities and increase the stress on educational, economic, and cultural criteria. There is room for eventually changing the mix of ritual and other factors in the selection of Scheduled Castes. There has been some discussion about changing the mix—at least to the extent of applying economic and educational tests to de-schedule those groups which have allegedly been so benefitted that the correlation no, longer holds. In June 1965 a committee was appointed by the Government to advise on revision of the existing lists of Scheduled Castes and Scheduled Tribes, under the chairmanship of B.N. Lokur, the Law Secretary. The Lokur Committee presented its report promptly on August 25, 1965. It found that in view of the constitutional abolition of untouchability, it would indeed be inappropriate ... to apply the sole test of untouchability in preparing the list of Scheduled Castes...Nevertheless, having regard to the historical background, we have, in revising the list, adopted the test of extreme social, educational and economic backwardness of castes, arising out of the traditional custom of untouchability. The committee observed with satisfaction that untouchability was "fast disappearing, more so in cities and towns, and even where it is practised, it is considerably diluted in form. They observed that the line of demarcation between high castes and low castes, which was fairly clear in the past, has tended to become blurred."

Asserting that "a lion's share" of the most benefits and preferences were "appropriated by the numerically larger and politically well organized communities" on the list, and noting the deleterious effects of creation of "vested interests" in the listing, they remarked that "the time has come when the question of descheduling of relatively advanced communities should receive serious and urgent consideration." The Committee devoted most of its attention to several technical changes in the lists, including a number of minor exclusions and inclusions. On major de-scheduling, though, they curiously left to utilize any of the fresh and abundant 1961 census data. Instead, they cautiously put forward a list of communities adjudged to be "relatively forward" by "many persons who appeared before us, including eminent social workers."

In addition to 14 tribes, this list included 28 Scheduled Castes listings, ranging from the insignificant to such numerous groups as the *Chamars* (Bihar, UP, and Punjab) and the related Jatav (Madhya Pradesh); the *Dhobis* (West Bengal; Orissa, Bihar and UP); the Mahars (Maharashtra and Madhya Pradesh); the Malas (Andhra Pradesh); and the Namasudras and Rajbanshis of West Bengal. In a kind of dim reflection of the disputes of the early 1930s, the proposals would have left the southern Scheduled Castes virtually intact, but practically halved population of the Scheduled

Castes population in the north. In addition, it would have eliminated about a fifth of the Scheduled Tribes.

Dushkin exposes the thinness of the committee's handful had literacy rates higher than the average for Scheduled Castes in their states; over half and literacy rates lower than all-India rate for Scheduled Castes.

The report was received with angry resistance by Scheduled Castes spokesman. At a tumultuous meeting with the Law Minister (then in charge of the Social Security portfolio), Scheduled Caste Members of Parliament agreed with some inclusions but would not agree to any exclusions from the list. The Minister was reported to have retreated. Scheduled Caste leaders and Government officials concurred that the report was dead. After the 1967 elections, the question again came up—now with the added dimension of the impending debate on whether to extend the reserved seats because of expire in 1970.

TABLE 9.5
Estimated percentage of Scheduled Castes and Scheduled Tribes in Each state who would have been de-scheduled if the provisions of the Lokur Commission had been implemented

	Scheduled Castes	*Scheduled Tribes*
Andhra Pradesh	34.8	–
Assam	32.01	40.48
Bihar	34.07	–
Gujarat	11.35	–
Kerala	4.51	–
Madhya Pradesh	66.69	57.98
Madras	0.04	–
Maharashtra	35.12	20.32
Mysore	8.60	–
Nagaland	–	98.91
Orissa	9.6	4.95
Punjab	38.56	–
Uttar Pradesh	62.22	–
West Bengal	31.81	–
All India	33.88	20.29

Percentge of SC recommended to be de-scheduled in four southern states: 13.34.
Percentage of SC recommended to be de-scheduled in the rest of India: 40.44.
Source: Computed from Census 1966.

In the meantime, Congress (the principal political beneficiary of reserved seats) had become considerably more dependent on the adherence of the occupants of the reserved seats, who now supplied its much narrower plurality in the Lok Sabha. The Congress plurality was 38 seats (279/520); Congress held 72 of 114 reserved seats. On August 12, 1967, a bill to amend the lists was presented by the Government; the bill's proposed list included every one of the groups whose possible deletion had been recommended by the Lokur Committee.

A Joint Parliamentary Committee established to review the lists submitted its report in November 1969. Among the amendments proposed by the Joint Committee were the inclusion in Scheduled Castes women who married Scheduled Caste men, the exclusion from Scheduled Tribes of converts to Christianity and Islam, and the elimination of all area restrictions on Scheduled Caste status. The conversion proposal caused a great controversy, and neither it nor the removal of area restrictions were accepted by the Government, which proposed a host of amendments to the Joint Committee's version when the bill was taken up in November 1970. Mired in controversy, the bill lapsed with the dissolution of the Fourth Lok Sabha in December 1970. A new version, brought forward during Emergency Rule and finally passed in August 1976, eliminated most intra-state area restrictions, adding about 2.5 million to the Scheduled Castes population and over three million to the Scheduled Tribes.

Scheduled Castes and Scheduled Tribes (Amendment) Act, 1976 (Act 108 of 1976). Only 64 of 1,126 intra-state area specifications were retained. The additions to the Scheduled Castes and Tribes population can be seen in the following table:

TABLE 9.6

Increases (and Decreases) in Scheduled Castes and Tribes Population due to 1976 Act (in lakhs)

State	*Scheduled Castes*	*Scheduled Tribes*
Andhra Pradesh	+ 0.41	+ 5.68
Bihar	+ 4.35	
Gujarat	+ 0.64	+ 0.23
Himachal Pradesh	+ 0.38	
Karnataka	+ 4.27	+ 0.31
Kerala	+ 2.30	- 0.76
Madhya Pradesh	+ 2.98	+ 14.28
Maharashtra	+ 1.51	+ 8.87
Orissa	- 0.04	+ 0.03
Rajasthan	+ 1.40	+ 0.09

Tamil Nadu	+ 0.22	+ 1.38
Uttar Pradesh	+ 5.46	
West Bengal	+ 0.84	+ 0.70
Total	+ 24.76	+ 31.57
	+ 0.04	+ 0.76

Source: RCSCST 1975-77:I, 16.

Besides this, the Act maintained the status quo: there were no major inclusions or exclusions. It did not address any of the touchy issues of personal status (of wives, converts, or migrants) which had come to surround the application of the lists.Castes continued to be the primary basis for designating the Scheduled Castes. Caste plays a dual role in the selection of Scheduled Castes: castes in the sense of a social units are typically the groups which are listed, and it is caste in the sense of rank or status in the socio-religious hierarchy which forms the criterion for choosing these groups. But caste is not the only factor in the selection: two other factors are explicitly employed—territory and religion. Scheduled Castes are designated by state and sometimes by districts or regions within states. The same caste may be scheduled in one state but not so in an adjoining state, or one district but not in an adjoining district. The power of the President to specify Scheduled Castes by districts has been upheld on the ground that the social and educational backwardness of a group may change in degree in different areas. Specification by states has been held to be constitutionally needed.

A postal clerk residing and working in Orissa was a member of the Konda Kapus, a group listed as a Scheduled Tribe in neighbouring Andhra Pradesh but not in Orissa. After being appointed to a higher post against a reservation for Scheduled Tribes, he was reverted on the ground that Konda Kapu was not a Scheduled Tribe in Orissa of which he was a permanent resident. He argued that he should be accounted a Scheduled Tribe anywhere for purposes of central government employment, since central legislation clearly outlawed state residence requirements for central government jobs. The High Court, turning to the constitutional provisions for designating Scheduled Tribes [Art. 3421], found that the phrase "shall be deemed to be Scheduled Tribes in relation to that State" means that in order to get the benefit of being a member of a Scheduled Caste or a Scheduled Tribe in matter of public employment, the person claiming it should be a member of such caste or tribe relating to the particular area or state where he is residing and where he seeks employment. Thus the court took a restrictive reading of residence rules to be a constitutional requirement. On various occasions, officials and political leaders have taken the view that only a constitutional amendment could abate these restrictions. However, the area limits have been troublesome. There is some doubt as to whether they correspond with any exactness to the different levels of deprivation and need. (Indeed, the decision not to collect caste-wise census data for any groups other than those already listed as Scheduled Castes or Tribes makes this exceedingly difficult to determine.) Troubling still are the difficulties presented by cases of spatially mobile members of these groups. The Scheduled Castes Order reads rather obscurely that castes shall "be deemed to be Scheduled Castes concerning members thereof resident in the localities specified in relation to them respectively."... In his first report in 1951 the Commissioner of Scheduled Castes and Scheduled Tribes noted that the provision was ambiguous. Taking the example of the *Khatik* caste, which is a Scheduled Caste in Punjab but not in neighbouring Uttar Pradesh, he put forth the following questions: When, if at all, does a U.P. Khatik who moves to Punjab become a member of a Scheduled Caste in relation to Punjab? Is a Punjab Khatik who moves to U.P. no longer a member of a Scheduled Caste in relation to Punjab or in relation to concessions granted by the Central Government? In a markedly unhelpful interpretation the Ministry of Law opined that "each case will have to be decided on its facts." But since "residence at the time in question" was the "determining factor," they inclined to the view that the Punjab Khatik would not be a Scheduled Caste while residing in U.P. The Commissioner's example includes a series of puzzles which we might usefully sort out and label. First, there is the problem of out-migration. Suppose an X leaves a state where Xs are a Scheduled Caste and goes to a state where they are not so listed. Such persons are excluded from any benefits by the prevailing reading of the Order. Thus a *Dusadh* who moved his residence from Bihar (where *Dusadh* was a Scheduled Caste) to Madhya Pradesh (where it was not) was not a member of the Scheduled Castes for purposes of making a lower deposit when filing a nomination paper.

The same rule is applicable to inter-state territorial limitations.

A railway worker resident outside the taluks listed for his tribe was held properly denied eligibility for reservation in promotion. There is the converse problem of immigration. Suppose a member of group X migrates from an area in which the Xs are not scheduled to an area in which they are.

Here the residence test emphasised by courts and officials would appear to argue for inclusion. But the one court that has addressed it decided the other way. *Suryabashi* was listed as a Scheduled Caste in Jabalpur District. But a *Suryabashi* migrant to Jabalpur who hailed from an area where *Suryabashis* were not Scheduled was held ineligible for benefits on the ground that "only Suryabashis residing in Jabalpur district...were declared to be Scheduled Castes under the Presidential Order." Apparently the court is looking beyond residence to some notion of origin in the designated groups, a test that proved inadequate in the out-migration cases. These issues are decided entirely by textual interpretation without any consideration of policies which might provide some guidance here. For example, in-migration involves the enlargement of the number of beneficiaries, whereas out-migration does not.

Again, extension of benefits to in-migrants might induce mobility that was not otherwise economically justifiable; but extension of benefits to out-migrants might be required in order to stop the inhibiting of economically justified moves. The logic of these cases points to an even more grostesque result in the case of lateral movement. Suppose a member of group X migrates from state A where the group is scheduled to state B where it is also scheduled. According to the residence argument of the out-migration cases, he is no more entitled to any benefits as an X of state A. Nor, according to the origins argument of the in-migration case, is he entitled to any benefits as an X of state B. One feels that administrative failure to give full effect to the logic of the cases, perhaps augmented by some dissimulation on the part of the migrants, has tempered the effect of these rules and accounts for the low frequency with which these issues have come to court. That migrant members would lose their Scheduled Caste benefits remained troublesome.

In 1959, the Commissioner had raised the matter again, this time regarding the case of a *Dhobi* whose family origins were in U.P. (where *Dhobi* is a Scheduled Caste) but who was born, brought up, and employed in Bombay (where *Dhobi* is not a Scheduled Caste). He claimed that his ancestral property, house, etc., were in U.P. and that he had no property or house in Bombay, but lived there only for the sake of his employment.

This case was referred to the Law Minister, who again read the order so that he was excluded—a result that the Commissioner anomalous, in the light of the fact that such persons may actually continue to suffer from all the disabilities resultant from the practice of untouchability as they may have to maintain all ties with their relations in the home State. He recommended that migrant Scheduled Castes and Tribes should be eligible for benefits from the Central Government and their home state at least for a generation. No relief of inter-state migrants has been forthcoming. In 1965 the Lokur Committee recommended that removal of inter-state area limitations on the ground that they inhibit mobility. The Scheduled Castes and Scheduled Tribes Orders (Amendment) Bill, 1967, proposed that when a caste is Scheduled for one area of a state, members from that area shall continue to be included so long as they reside anywhere in that state.

The 1976 amendments of the lists did not contain this provision, but the requirement for it was largely dispelled by the abandonment of almost all intra-state area restrictions. The conferring of scheduled status on a group is a monopoly of the Centre. The 1950 Scheduled Tribes Order list for Maharashtra included an item for Halba from six specified taluks in three districts. In 1967 the Government of Maharashtra ordered that the *Halba Koshtis* of the whole of Vidarbha region be treated as belonging to the Scheduled Tribes. A *Halba* railway worker from outside the listed *taluks* was deleted from a promotion panel on the ground that he was not a member of the Scheduled Tribe. His challenge was repulsed by the Bombay High Court, which held that the state's pronouncement could have no effect on his status as a Scheduled Tribe regarding any of the affairs of the Central Government. The court left open the question whether the state might treat him as a Scheduled Tribe regarding state services. This issue has never been fully addressed. While it might be desirable to allow state the employ its better-informed judgement about local conditions, there is of course the danger that state use of this power could dilute benefits to those deemed deserving beneficiaries by national policy.

The most prominent example of this—Maharashtra's treatment of the Buddhists on a par with Scheduled Castes—has not been challenged in court. Religion was introduced as a qualification into the first Scheduled Castes Order in 1936, which provided that no Indian Christian (nor, in Bengal, those professing Buddhism or a tribal religion) should be deemed a member of a Scheduled Caste. Earlier, it was often recognized that there were comparable depressed groups among Christians and Muslims. But in the disputes leading up to the listing of Scheduled Castes, it was agreed that Muslims and Christians should be excluded. This execution was readily understandable, for the major objective of the list was to provide for electoral representation, and Christians and Muslims were the beneficiaries of special electoral treatment as minorities.

In spite of the constitutional ban on religious discrimination, the elimination of separate representation for religious minorities and the change in purpose of the list from electoral to administration of welfare, the religious qualification (or, more appropriately, disqualification) was retained after Independence. The President's 1950 Order provides that "no person professing a religion different from Hinduism shall be deemed a member of a Scheduled Castes. An exception was made in the case of Sikh members of four castes. In 1956 it was broadened to include all Sikh untouchables. The religious test for Scheduled Castes is used, not as a positive test for selecting appropriate groups for inclusion, but as a disqualification of individuals and groups who otherwise meet the criteria, thereby inevitably discouraging conversion. There is reason to think that this was at least part of its purpose. It does not operate as an encouragement of Hindu orthodoxy, for the legal definition of Hinduism is so broad that few individuals are likely to have difficulty with this test other than those who explicitly convert to a non-Hindu religion. In *Punjabrao versus Meshram,* the Supreme Court rejected the argument that Buddhists were included in the meaning of Hindu.

The courts have upheld the exclusion of non-Hindus without digging the broader question of religious discrimination. Nor have the courts addressed the factual question of the effect of conversion in dissipating the conditions that lead groups to be listed as Scheduled Castes. Persistent legislative efforts to include the Buddhists, either by dropping the religious qualification or by specifying that "Hindu" be read to include them, have unsuccessful—as has a recent effort to extend the religious qualification to the Scheduled Tribes.

Since we shall be analysis the impact of the courts on the working of the policy of "compensatory discriminations", it is worth noting that the role of the courts in the process of designating the Scheduled Castes has been very negligible. The search for a uniform criterion that could be followed throughout India to distinguish untouchables from other Hindus proceeded without any assistance from the courts. Although Scheduled Castes were identified on the basis of the disabilities they suffered, the jurisprudence of disabilities was too spotty and too enmeshed with local variations. Although untouchables could be readily identified with the lower end of the *varna* scale, the traditional jurisprudence of *varna* standing was of little help in identifying the groups which were supposedly untouchable. Modern "untouchability" bore little correspondence to the *chandala* category of classical law. In reference to determinations of customary rights, courts had sometimes employed *varna* categories. Untouchables had sometimes, particularly in South India, been referred to as a fifth *varna*, below the Sudras. But in other places they were considered as *Sudras*, albeit "unclean" ones.

For purposes of applying Hindu personal law, the courts had never to distinguish untouchables from Sudras; all Hindus other than the twice-born were lumped together as Sudras. Even where untouchables were popularly considered Sudras, they could not be equated with them, since there were non-untouchable groups belonging to this category. Thus the tests used for distinguishing Sudras from the twice-born could not be used as a satisfactory measure of untouchability. Once the lists were promulgated, the courts contributed little to their refinement. Although on at least one occasion, judicial demands for precision helped to give an opportunity for re-examination, courts have contributed nothing to the critical understanding of the lists for criteria that underlie them.

Although it might appear that identification of "untouchable" groups would proceed from the definition of "untouchability" in order to select those who suffer from it, in fact the opposite process has taken place. The contemporary legal treatment of untouchability has derived from the listing of these groups (which in turn are chosen, as we saw, with at least one eye to an ill-defined notion of untouchability). The term "untouchability" had no technical legal meaning before the Constitution abolished it. The few judicial encounters with the concept have not been able to define it in a way that would be useful in identifying untouchable groups. The courts have suggested that untouchability does not include all instances in which a person is treated as ritually unclean and a source of pollution. It does not include such temporary and expiable states of pollution as those suffered by, for instance, women at childbirth, menstruating women, mourners, persons with contagious diseases, persons who eat forbidden food or violate prescribed states of cleanliness. Nor does it include that "untouchability" which arises from incidents of personal history. Nor does it refer to situational or relative impurity, such as that between ordinary worshipper and priest or temple attendant. It does not include every instance in which a person is stigmatized as unclean, polluting, or inferior due to his origin or membership in a particular group–i.e., where he is subjected to invidious treatment due to difference in religion or membership of a lower or different caste.

The "untouchability" with which Article 17 is concerned is that which "refers to those considered as untouchables in the course of historical development" and which is related to the relegation of persons "beyond the pale of the caste system...on the ground of birth in certain classes." Thus, untouchability is limited to disabilities imposed upon groups commonly considered "untouchable," and its meaning is to be determined by reference to those who have traditionally been regarded as untouchables.

But it is, as we have seen, no easier to define untouchables than to define untouchability. "Beyond the pale of the caste system" is a misleading and unworkable formulation. Even the lowest castes are within the traditional system of reciprocal rights and duties, though they had more of the latter and fewer of the former. Their disabilities and prerogatives are articulated to those of other castes. Presumably, the court that devised this standard meant outside the four *varna* of the classical lawbooks. But, as we have seen, the *varna* test is not workable either–although it often crops up in discussions of untouchability.

Thus, the courts have not developed any learning on "untouchability" that could be employed in refining the criteria of selection of the Scheduled Castes.

However, there is the chance that as the correlation between low ritual status and economic and educational condition breaks down, some of the learning developed by the courts in addressing the problems of identifying the Other Backward Classes will be utilized in the Scheduled Castes and Tribes area.

The Scheduled Tribes vis-a-vis the Scheduled Castes

There has been much less dispute about the identification of the Scheduled Tribes (ST) than about the Scheduled Castes (SC) or the Other Backward Classes (OBCs). The general notion is that this category should include those groups distinguished by "tribal characteristics" and by their spatial and cultural isolation from the bulk of the population. The British tried to protect these "aboriginal" people by placing areas in which they were concentrated outside of ordinary administration to permit a policy of insulating them from exploitative or demoralizing contact with more sophisticated outsiders. These enclaves, known as Excluded Areas and Partially Excluded Areas in the Government of India Act, 1935, were placed outside the operation of general law and were the object of broad executive powers to provide special protective regulation. Some provinces had undertaken a policy of protective treatment of tribals outside these areas. In the 1935 Act, for the first time, provision was made from some representation for "Backward Tribes" in the reformed Provincial Legislatures, and a list of Backward Tribes was promulgated in 1936 for all of the provinces with the exception of Punjab and Bengal. The 1941 census counted 25.4 million tribal people (6.58 per cent of the total population). The Constitution carried forward this dual treatment of tribal areas and tribal people in a set of provisions for their protection and advancement far more elaborate and detailed than the provision for the other categories of backward classes.

Along with reservations in legislatures and services comparable to those for the Scheduled Castes, there are provisions for direct Central control over administration, for direct Central financial responsibility, for annual reports to be presented by the Governors to the President, for extensive executive power over Scheduled Areas to insulate them from the application of inappropriate law and to fashion protective regulation (especially regarding allotment and transfer of land

and money-lending), and for the formation of Tribal Advisory Councils to take part in the formulation of policy. The formal mechanism of designating the Scheduled Tribes is identical with that for Scheduled Castes.

The President may specify, after consulting with Governors, the "tribes and tribal communities or parts of or groups within tribes or tribal communities to be the Scheduled Tribes for each state. Once promulgated, the list can be changed only by the Act of Parliament. The Scheduled Areas are to be ordered by the President, who is empowered to alter or de-schedule them. In 1950, the President promulgated the list of Scheduled Areas and a list of Scheduled Tribes, apparently by adding some more to the 1935 list of Backward Tribes. (Some list of the ST must have been in use earlier, for the Central Government's scheme of post-matriculation scholarship included ST starting with the academic year 1948-49).

Some groups that had been listed as Scheduled Castes in Bengal were now moved to the ST list. The 1951 census counted to 19.1 millions in these groups (5.30 per cent of the total population). Some tribes had been omitted; about a million members of these "left out" tribes were temporarily included in the Other Backward Classes category until 1956, when the Scheduled Tribes Order was amended, adding 2.5 million tribals, mostly in Rajasthan and Madhya Pradesh, bringing the total to 22.5 millions (6.93 per cent of the total population). In 1971 these groups numbered over 38 millions (6.93 per cent of the total population). In 1976 over three million persons were added, bringing the total to almost 40 millions. Although the lists contain groups throughout the country, the tribal population is mostly concentrated in central, eastern, and north-eastern India.

Unlike the relatively dispersed Scheduled Castes population, about ninety per cent of the tribals are found in nine states. Three states had less than one per cent Scheduled Tribes 1961, while Orissa and Madhya Pradesh had more than twenty per cent. More than one-third (10.6 millions) of the Scheduled Tribes population lived in the Scheduled Areas (where they formed less than two-thirds of the population). (See Table 9.7). More than half of the Scheduled Tribes lived in parliamentary constituencies where they formed a majority of the population.

TABLE 9.7
Scheduled Tribes Population

	1950 & 1951 Orders		1956 Order		1961 Census		1971 Census	
Source	A	A	A	A	B	B	C	C
State	(mils.)	%	(mils.)	%	(mils.)	%	(mils.)	%
Andhra	0.766	2.45	1.149	3.68	1.324	3.68	1.657	3.79
Assam	1.735	19.18	1.761	19.48	2.068	17.42	1.920	12.84
Nagaland					.343	93.03	.457	88.46
Bihar	3.827	9.86	3.880	10.00	4.204	9.02	4.932	8.74
Bombay	3.671	7.60	3.743	7.76				
Gujarat					2.754	13.34	3.734	13.97
Maharashtra					2.397	6.03	2.954	5.85
Jammu and Kashmir	No Scheduled Tribes							
Kerala	.074	0.54	0.134	0.99	0.207	1.23	0.270	1.26
Madhya Pradesh	3.859	14.79	4.844	18.58	6.678	20.62	8.387	20.11
Madras	0.060	0.20	0.136	0.45	0.252	0.74	0.311	0.75
Mysore	0.045	0.23	0.080	0.41	0.192	0.81	0.231	0.78
Orissa	2.967	20.25	3.009	20.55	4.223	24.02	5.071	23.11
Punjab	0.002	0.01	.002	0.02	0.014	0.06	...	...
Haryana						...	...	...
Rajasthan	0.348	2.18	1.744	11.11	2.309	11.02	3.125	12.11
Uttar Pradesh	No Scheduled Tribes						.198	.21
West Bengal	1.386	5.27	1.566	5.96	2.063	5.91	2.532	5.70
Totals	19.147	5.30	22.511	6.23	29.846	6.80	38.015	6.93

Sources: A: RCSCST 1956–57: II, 15; B: RCSCST 1961–62: II, 74; C: Census of India, 1971, Series I, Part II-A (ii): xxx-xxxi.

Note: The totals may be slightly higher than the columns indicate, because of inclusion of Scheduled Tribes in the Union Territories.

The Scheduled Tribes were defined partly by habitat and geographic isolation, but even more so on the basis of social, religious, linguistic, and cultural distinctiveness—their "tribal characteristics." Just where the line between "tribals" and "non-tribals" should be drawn has always been under cloud. We shall see that there are still problems of overlap classified with the caste order and controversy about whether a specific group is more appropriately classified as a Scheduled Tribes or a Scheduled Caste. In any event, not all tribal peoples were listed, but only those whose primitiveness, backwardness, or isolation made them deserving of special treatment. No religious test was specified. A recent attempt to exclude converts failed to gain acceptance.

TABLE 9.8
Scheduled Areas Population

State	1961 Total in SA Pop.	1961 ST Pop. in SA	1961 ST in SA as % Total SA	1961 ST in SA as % Total ST
	(mils.)	(mils.)	%	%
Andhra Pradesh	...	0.438	...	33.08
Bihar	5.257	2.929	55.71	69.67
Gujarat	1.987	1.306	65.60	47.42
Maharashtra	1.165	0.856	63.26	35.71
Jammu & Kashmir	No Scheduled Areas			
Kerala	No Scheduled Areas			
Madhya Pradesh	3.395	2.147	63.52	32.15
Madras	No Scheduled Areas			
Mysore	No Scheduled Areas			
Orissa	3.950	2.392	60.50	56.64
Punjab	0.020	0.014	68.90	100.00
Rajasthan	0.877	0.564	64.31	24.42
Uttar Pradesh				
West Bengal	No Scheduled Areas			
Totals	16.659	10.647	61.28[a]	35.70

Source: RCSCST 1965-66: 186.
Note: [a]Andhra Pradesh not included in total.

The Commissioner in 1951 noted that no uniform test for distinguishing the Scheduled Tribes had been formulated. He circularized the State Governments for their opinions. After surveying the divergent responses, which included racial, religious, linguistic, and cultural tests as well as tests of political, economic, and social organization, and degree of contact, isolation, or assimilation/distinctiveness, the Commissioner proposed as the common elements: tribal origin, primitive way of life, remote habitation, and general backwardness in all respects. Whatever theoretically imperfections may underlie the lists, nothing takes on fixity so readily as a rough approximation made to solve an immediate and intractable problem.

A few years later the criteria for Scheduled Tribes seemed wholly unproblematic. The Home Minister in 1956 referred to the "well-defined and easily ascertained" criteria for distinguishing them. By the time the Dhebar Commission reported in 1961, it felt no need to deote any attention to the problem of identifying the tribes. The Lokur Committee in 1965 reported that, in revising the lists, "we have looked for indications of primitive traits, distinctive culture, geographic isolation, shyness of contact with the community at large and backwardness; we have considered that tribes whose members have by and large mixed up with the general population are not eligible to be in the list of Scheduled Tribes." The provisions for Scheduled Tribes are distinct not only in their scope but also in intent, for preservation of their separate integrity, rather than complete assimilation, is one element in solicy toward them.

In the case of Scheduled Castes, the Other Backward Classes, and the Denotified Tribes; it is hoped that the disabilities and disadvantages that separate them from their compatriots will eventually be overcome by the preferential treatment. That is, the objective of the policy is to eliminate their distinctiveness by dispelling all of the differences that set them apart from other Indians. The objective of Scheduled Tribes' Policy is more complex—to balance improvement of their condition and a degree of assimilation with preservation of their distinctiveness and a measure of autonomy. Special treatment of the Tribes will, it is hoped, foster development "along their own lines."

Due to this difference in purpose (and due to their geographical separation), the objections that have been made against the use of communal criteria in other categories of backward classes have not been made with the same force in concerning Scheduled Tribes. Although Scheduled Tribes share with Scheduled Castes a number of reservations—in legislatures, government service, and educational institutions—the principal schemes for the Tribes have been protective and developmental (economic, educational, health, and communications). Tribal aspirants have not pressed hard on the reservations; many have remained fulfilled. With the exception of a few election cases creating problems of tribal membership, tribes have hardly been involved in litigation about compensatory discrimination. They have had little effect on the law, which is being developed in cases involving the Scheduled Castes and the Other Backward Classes.

The Early-History of the Other Backward Classes Category

The Other Backward Classes for whom preferential treatment are authorized are not defined in the Constitution, nor is any exclusive method or agency for their designation provided. For all the uncertainty surrounding the term "Scheduled Castes" (and its predecessor "Depressed Classes"), its central objective is clear: to identify the victims of "untouchability." At the time of Independence, the term "Backward Classes" had a fixed and definite reference. The term had been around for some time, but it had a number of referents, it had shifted rapidly in meaning, and it had come to mean different things in different places. With the objective of tracing these varied meanings in the following discussion, we may portray some of the variety of meanings in schematic form. In 1917 the Majaraja of Kolhapur recounted to Mr. Montagu that he had "been taking very keen interest...in uplifting the Backward Classes and especially the untouchables". Soon after, the term appears in the terms of reference of the Southborough Committee, which was to advise on steps to secure representation of "minorities, of special interests, or of backward classes." But the Committee did not describe any such groups in its report, other than Depressed Classes [Denotation 1?].

The Joint Select Committee of the British Parliament which reviewed the Southborough Report mentioned in passing the significance they attached to "the educational advancement of the depressed and backward classes." There is no intention that the term was meant to include anyone apart from the depressed classes.

"Backward Classes first got a technical meaning in the Princely State of Mysore. In 1918 the Mysore Government appointed a committee to enquire into the question of encouraging members of the "backward communities" in public service. In 1921 preferential recruitment of "backward communities" was instituted, and they were defined as "all communities other than Brahmins, who are not now sufficiently represented in the public service." The Reforms Enquiry Commission (1924) did not find an occasion to use the term, but the Ministry Report refers to its use as a synonym for the Depressed Classes (untouchables) and in contradistinction to "non-Brahmins."

Although "Non-Brahmin" and "Maratha" were much more frequently used in the setting of the Bombay "non-Brahmin" movement of the 1920s, the Backward Classes rubric was employed both popularly and officially in a broad meaning, somewhat similar to that in Mysore. In 1925 a Government Resolution defined Backward Classes as all except Brahmins, Prabhus, Marwaris, Parsis, Banias, and Christians [Denotation 9?]. Reservations in government service were provided for this group. The Hartog Committee (1928) defined Backward Classes in their glossery as "Castes or classes which are educationally backward. They include the depressed classes, aboriginals, hill tribes, and criminal tribes."

The Indian Central Committee in 1929 distinguished the problem of the 'backward classes,' among whom may be counted aboriginals, criminal tribes and others among the less advanced of the inhabitants of British India" [Denotation 5]. Apparently the Committee not only excludes the Depressed Classes but includes, in additions to tribals, some strata of the caste population, for they refer to an estimate of sixteen million backward classes in UP (excluding the untouchables). But the category is not used as expansively as the Mysore or earlier Bombay usage, as it did not include the Madras non-Brahmins or Mahrattas in Bombay, who were discussed separately. The term could not have been a familiar one, for the Report finds it necessary to distinguish Backward Classes from untouchables many times. In a separate note, Mr. M.C. Rajah, an untouchable spokesman, refers to Backward Classes only as a confusing synonym for Depressed Classes [Denotation 1]. In 1930 the Starte Committee in Bombay devoted careful consideration to the question of nomenclature. They observed that in 1924 the term Depressed Classes had been accorded a wider meaning to include "aboriginal tribes and the Criminal Tribes and some other wandering and backward Castes... [which had] resulted in much confusion of thought in this Presidency, as in ordinary usage the phrase Depressed Classes is taken as meaning the untouchables...whereas they do not form half of this new and enlarged grouping of Depressed Classes."

The Committee made recommendation that "Depressed Classes" should be used in the sense of untouchables, a usage which "will coincide with existing common practice." They proposed that the wider group should be called "Backward Classes", which should be subdivided into Depressed Classes (i.e., untouchables); Aboriginals and Hill Tribes; Other Backward Classes (including wandering tribes). They note that the group then currently called Backward Classes should be renamed "intermediate classes."

In addition to 36 Depressed Classes (approximate 1921 population 1.475 millions) and 24 Aboriginal and Hill Tribes (approximate 1921 population 1.323 millions), they list 95 Other Backward Classes (estimated 1921 population 1.041 millions). The Simon Commission, though it refers to "intermediate castes" and takes note of the non-Brahmin movement, does not mention Backward Classes. But shortly after, in the early 1930s, we find a flowering of the term. In the hearings held by the Indian Franchise Committee in the United Provinces, the term recurs in the testimony in a number of significations. Thus a note by Dr. S. S. Nehru, I.C.S., presents a list of Depressed Classes of which portions are designated "Vagrant Tribes" and "Backward Classes". Presumably these are the groups who least fit the "untouchability criterion.

However, the memorandum of Pandit Sheokaran Nath Misra (Deputy Collector of Fyzabad) recommends that "depressed classes should include untouchables as well as backward classes." He equated Depressed Classes roughly with all *Sudras* excepting *Kayasthas* [Denotation 4]. The United Provinces Hindu Backward Classes League (founded in 1929) submitted a memorandum which indicated that the term "Depressed" carried a connotation "of untouchability in the sense of causing pollution by touch as in the case of Madras and Bombay" and that various communities were reluctant to identify themselves as depressed. The League suggested the term "'Hindu' 'Backward'" as a more suitable nomenclature. The list of 115 castes submitted included all candidates for the untouchable category as well as a stratum above [Denotation 4]. "All of the [listed] communities belong to non *Dwijas* or degenerate or *Sudra* classes of the Hindus." They were described as low socially, educationally, and economically and were said to be over sixty per cent of the population. This inclusive usage was adopted elsewhere. Travancore in 1937 abandoned the Depressed Classes nomenclature and substituted the term

"Backward Communities" to include all educationally and economically backward communities [Denotation 3].

However, in Madras and elsewhere the term "Backward Classes" was used to refer to the strata above the untouchables. The Madras Provincial Backward Classes League, consisting of the less forward non-Brahmin communities, was founded in 1934 for the purpose of receiving separate treatment from "the forward non-Brahmin communities." According to the list they presented to the Madras Government in 1944, the Backward Classes included more than a hundred communities with about 25 million people (more than two-thirds of the non-Brahmin category and fifty per cent of the total population of the Presidency). In November 1947, separate reservations in the Madras services was made available for these "Backward Hindus." In the meantime, the Objectives Resolution of the Constituent Assembly, moved by Jawaharlal Nehru on December 13, 1946, had resolved to provide adequate safeguards for "minorities, backward and tribal areas, and depressed and other backward classes." [Denotation 5?6?]. Thus, the term had never acquired a definite meaning at the all-India level.

There had been no effort to define it or employ it on the national level, and there were no nationwide backward classes organizations or spokesmen. The term had definite meanings in local contexts, although these differed somewhat. After the listing of Scheduled Castes, the usage as a synonym for untouchables drops away. Two main species of usage emerge: (1) as the more inclusive group of all those who require special treatment (2) as a stratum higher than the untouchables but nonetheless depressed. This double usage continues even today: the former in the usage of backward classes in the wide sense (including Scheduled Castes and Scheduled Tribes); the latter in the usage as equivalent to "Other Backward Classes." We are now concerned with the other here.

The Constitutional Design

By the time of the Constituent Assembly the usage of the term "Backward Classes" to refer to some larger or smaller portion of the population deserving of special treatment was familiar in various parts of the country. In the Assembly, delegates from the north expressed confusion at the provisions for "Backward Classes," (in what came to be Article 16 (4). It struck them as vague, and some thought it was meant simply as a synonym for the Scheduled Castes, while others were concerned that it might mean more.

But representatives from Madras, Mysore and Bombay assured their colleagues that Backward Classes was a distinct term having a technical meaning. Instances were quoted of Mysore where Backward Classes included all but Brahmins, of Madras where it referred to a stratum of non-untouchable Hindu castes, and of Bombay where it included not just Scheduled Castes and Tribes but also others who are economically, educationally and socially backward. A representative from Bihar (which had the most active Backward Classes movement in the north) elaborated that Backward Classes were a section of society between the highest castes and the Scheduled Castes: "the third [section] occupying the middle position...and consisting of a large portion of our people is what may be termed the Backward Class....No doubt they are not treated as untouchables. Mr. K.M. Munshi assured the House that the term would include the Scheduled Castes, when doubts were expressed, and explained that it was "necessary to find a generic term." "It signifies people—touchable or untouchable, belonging to this community or that, who are so backward that special protection is needed in the services." Although one speaker pointed out that the classes were not necessarily castes and that literacy might be the test of backwardness, it was often envisioned that the backward classes would be communities. When asked what is a backward community, Dr. Ambedkar, defending the draft, explained; "we have left it to be determined by each local Government. A backward community is a community which is backward in the opinion of the Government." However, the matter was not so clear as this might indicate. The most prophetic statement was Mr. T.T. Krishnamachari's prediction that the clause would be "a paradise for lawyers." It was anticipated, then, that the backward classes other than the Scheduled Castes and Tribes were to be designated at the local level. The delegation to local authorities undoubtly reflected an acceptance (at least temporarily) of the divergence of existing practices, a willingness to preserve flexibility, and an awareness of the difficulties of prescribing universally applicable tests of backwardness in the light of the varying local conditions. It may also have been presumed that "Backward Classes" were reasonably potent politically to look out for their own interests on a local level, and unlike Scheduled Castes and Tribes, central control of their designation was not needed to insure the inclusion of the deserving.

However, the central government was not entirely excluded from the process. The President is instructed to appoint a Backward Classes Commission "to investigate the conditions of socially and educationally backward classes...and the difficulties under which they labour and to make recommendations as to the steps that should be taken by the Union or any State to remove such difficulties and to improve their condition..." No special central machinery for supervision of programs for backward classes is provided in the Constitution, but Article 338 (3) provides that the Commissioner of Scheduled Castes and Tribes shall include in his duties such other groups as the President may specify on receiving the report of the Backward Classes Commission.

It is, however, not clear from the text that this Presidential specification was meant to be exclusive. Even before the Constitution became effective there was a great expansion in the employment of the Backward Classes category. Several states created such a category for the first time, and of those who already had it, expanded the benefits conferred upon the Backward Classes. The Central Government was pressed to extend its scheme of post-matriculation scholarships to the Other Backward Classes, and when it did so, it compiled lists of Backward Class in each state for this purpose.

Backward Classes organizations emerged; a national federation was formed. Apart from the central scholarships, provisions for Other Backward Classes roughly followed a regional pattern as indicated by Table 9.9. In South India and in Bombay, provisions for Other Backward Classes flourished. In the north, there were mostly a scatter of educational concessions, and many states did not have any lists at all (other than those compiled for purposes of the central post-matriculation scholarship scheme). It remained unclear just how many people were included in the Backward Classes category. The never-completed 1951 census enumeration, based in part on the existing state lists, counted 67 millions (18.9 per cent of the total population). The Planning Commission in July 1951 estimated that the Other Backward Classes were approximately twenty per cent of the population, but in late 1952 noted that "these other backward classes...are believed to number about [54.6 millions]."

TABLE 9.9

Concessions for Other Backward Classes, 1951–1952

STATE	*Education: fee concession, stipends, training facilities, etc.*	*Reservations in Educational Insts.*	*Other Welfare*	*Recruitment to Government Posts.*	*Expenditures 1951-52 (lakhs)*	*Expenditures, 1953-54*
Andhra	—	—	—	—	—	4.36
Assam	X	O	O	O	18.04	2.49
Bihar	X	O	O	O	6.22	10.26
Bombay	X	X	X	X	24.95	50.15
Madhya Pradesh	O	O	O	O	0	0.77
Madras	X	X	X	X	13.04	41.25
Orissa	O	O	O	O	0	0
Punjab	O	O	O	O	0	0
Uttar Pradesh	X	O	O	O	4.75	6.29
West Bengal	X	O	O	O	...	5.86
Hyderabad	O	O	X	O	36.27	1.70
Madhya Bharat						0
Mysore	X	?	X	X	?	9.14
P.E.P.S.U	O	O	O	O	0	0
Rajasthan	X	O	O	O	0.29	...
Saurashtra	O	O	O	X[a]	0	6.44
Travancore Cochin	X	?	?	X	?	8.71
Ajmer	X	O	O	O	0	0
Bhopal	O	O	O	O	0.05	0.05
Bilaspur	O	O	O	O	?	...
Coorg	O	X	O	O	...	0.06
Delhi	X	O	O	O	...	...
Himachal Pradesh	O	O	O	O	3.47	...
Kutch	O	O	O	O	...	3.7
Manipur	O	O	O	O	..	...
Tripura					0	...
Vindhya Pradesh	O	O	O	O	...	...
Central Government	X	O	X?	O		

Source: This table is a composite of information found in RCSCST 1952: 202–5 with introductory chapters X, XI. The 1953–54 expenditures are taken from I BBC 146.

Note: [a]OBC lumped together with SC and ST.

Other observers predicted a smaller list, address to the inaugural meeting of the Backward Classes Commission is reported to have mentioned the figure of 70 millions. A pair of Supreme Court decisions in April 1951 shattered the legal foundation of the system of communal quotas which prevailed in South India. *State of Madras v. Champakam Dorairajan* struck down the Madras reservations in educational institutions and by implication barred all preferential treatment outside the area of Government employment. *Venkataramana v. State of Madras* struck down the Madras quotas in government posts for all groups other than the Scheduled Castes and "Backward Hindus," confining potential recipients to those who could qualify as the "backward classes" mentioned in Article 16 (4). These decisions caused a political furore in South India and occasioned the prompt addition of Article 15 (4) to the Constitution. The debate over the amendment centered on the desirability of providing educational preferences to the backward classes, and it revolved in part around the question of who were the Backward Classes.

Although the Scheduled Castes and Tribes were equally discomfited by *Champakam Dorairajan* and presumably equally concerned with educational preferences, there was little mention of them in Parliament. The question worrying the house was the identity of Backward Classes and the possible abuse of the new provision by advanced groups. In an attempt to confine the possible meaning of Backward Classes, the wording of Article 15 (4) was keyed to that of Article 340, which provided that the not yet established Backward Classes Commission should list the "socially and educationally backward classes of citizens." Some speakers drew assurance from the notion that the listing by the Commission and subsequent presidential specification would be determinative.

Others assumed that the identity of the Backward Classes would remain a question for the State Governments and counselled trust in their good faith. Examination of the debate makes it quite clear that the Backward Classes, by whomever designated and according to whatever tests they were chosen, were expected to be a castes or communities. Dr. Ambedkar, then Law Minister, fortrightly observed that the amendment was required precisely because "what are called backward classes are...nothing else but a collection of certain castes." There was considerable concern that the provision should not permit communal quotas to be enjoyed by more advanced groups.

While there was discussion of the economic backwardness of the groups who deserved preferences, it was not just the poor that the drafters and speakers had in mind. (Indeed, if they had, an amendment would hardly have been needed.) Some speakers opined that preferences should be directed to the economically poor, but the predominant concern was to provide some special treatment to offset and remedy specifically those social inequalities of caste and community which were seen as underlying and compounding economic differences. The *Venkataramana* case had suggested that the "Backward Classes" included only those caste groups of whose backwardness there was some assurance. In spite of some unflattering observations about that judgment, there was nothing in the proceedings to suggest that Parliament sought to overturn it.

Indeed, it was considered as the foundation for judicial protection against unwarranted use of the power to confer preferences. Upon passage of the amendment, Madras revised its former system of communal quotas to accord with the new needs; the situation in other states remained unchanged.

Lack of Data and Other Difficulties set up

The Backward Classes Commission was setup in 1953 and directed to, "determine the criteria to be adopted in considering whether any sections of the people...(in addition to the Scheduled Castes and Tribes...) should be treated as socially and educationally backward classes; and, in accordance with such criteria to prepare a list of such classes..." The directions express an expectation of centrally-established uniform standards and a central master list of Backward Classes. Accordingly, the Commission, after two years of work, presented a list of 2,399 backward groups and recommended several measures for their economic, educational, social, cultural, and political advancement. It was estimated that these groups totalled more than 116 million members (about thirty-two per cent of the total population of India). This does not include women as a separate group, although the Commission recommended that all women in India made a Backward Class. Nor does it include Scheduled Castes and Scheduled Tribes, who in 1951 made up over fourteen and six per cent respectively of the total population. It had been generally anticipated, if not universally approved, that the "classes" designated by the Commission would

TABLE 9.10
Estimates of Population of Other Backward Classes, Early 1950s

	1951 Census				*Backward Classes Commission*		
State	*Total Population (lakhs)*	*Enumerated Pop. of OBC*	*Percentage of Enum. to Total Pop.*	*Estimated Pop. of OBC*	*Percentage of Est to Total Pop.*	*Estimated Pop. of OBC*	*Percentage of Est. to*
Assam	90.44	18.84	20.8	26.15[a]	28.9	28.66	31.7
Bihar	402.26	62.76	15.6	66.90	16.6	153.21	38.1
Bombay	359.56	44.90	12.5	16.13	4.5	110.10	30.6
Madhya Pradesh	212.48	66.48	31.3	56.04[a]	26.4	79.3	37.2
Madras (& Andhra)	570.16	197.16	34.6	263.95	46.3	126.81	22.2
Orissa	146.46	41.73	28.5	15.85	10.8	13.56	9.3
Punjab	126.41	N.A.	N.A.	7.89[a]	6.2	25.56	20.2
Uttar Pradesh	632.16	41.51	6.6	41.51	6.6	269.10	42.6
West Bengal	248.10	13.59	5.5	1.81	0.7	22.66	9.1
Hyderabad	186.55	94.13	50.5	122.85	65.9	137.66	73.8
Madhya Bharat	79.54	13.68	17.2	13.25	16.7	19.37	24.4
Mysore	90.75	17.53	19.3	20.62	22.7	59.64	65.7
P.E.P.S.U	34.94	...	...	3.79[a]	10.8	4.42	12.7
Rajasthan	152.91	32.16	21.0	34.30[a]	22.4	34.31	22.4
Saurashtra	41.37	15.78	38.1	11.06	26.7	12.16	29.4
Travancore-Cochin	92.80	4.16	4.5	2.85	3.1	9.12	9.8
Ajmer	6.93	0.35	5.1	0.35	5.1	2.98	42.9
Bhopal	8.36	1.25	14.4	1.35	13.5	2.98	35.2
Himachal Pradesh & Bilaspur	11.09	...	...	2.38[a]	21.4	3.15	28.4
Coorg	2.29	0.69	30.3	0.68	29.7	0.64	27.8
Delhi	17.44	N.A.	N.A.	2.41[a]	13.8	3.18	18.2
Kutch	5.68	0.01	0.2	1.08	19.0	2.01	35.4
Manipur	5.78	...	...	...	...	0.35	6.1
Tripura	6.39	0.30	4.7	4.12	64.5	0.69	10.1
Vindhya Pradesh	35.75	7.40	20.7	...	...	13.56	38.5
Andamans & Nicobars	.30	...	...	...	...	...	...
India	3568.29	674.39	18.9	730.01	20.5	1135.10	31.8

Source: III BCC 14–15. (All figures in lakhs).

Note: [a]Represents estimated 1951 population of educationally backward classes. (The source is not entirely clear regarding Assam.)

be castes or communities. While indicating its willingness to avoid perpetuating the evils of caste and its eagerness to avoid caste, the Commission "found it difficult to avoid caste in the present prevailing conditions."

The Commission felt it was "not only correct but inevitable" to interpret its terms of reference "as mainly concerning to social hierarchy based on caste." As general criteria of backwardness the Commission listed trade and occupation, security of employment, educational attainments, representation in government service, and most emphatically, position in the social hierarchy. It used these standards, not directly to identity categories of backward persons, but to identify backward communities. The units to which these tests were applied were for the most part caste and sub-caste groups. In identifying the backward, the Commission used caste in two ways: first, it used caste groups as the units or "classes" to be classified; and second, it used the position or standing of these groups in social hierarchy as the main criterion for determining their backwardness. In classifying communities, the Commission aimed to take into consideration, "the social position which a community occupies in the caste hierarchy, the percentage of literacy and its general educational advancement; and its representation in Government service or in the industrial sphere. The economic backwardness also had to be kept in view...as also the recent trends in its advancement as a result of various [Government] measures...during the past one or two decades. The Commission was deluged by communities claiming to be backward. But it found that the paucity of data fully matched the immensity of its task. The State Governments were found not to have relevant data, "administrators and census officers expressed their inability to supply the relevant material," and figures supplied by the communities themselves were chiefly guesswork.

The decision to de-emphasize caste in the 1951 census operations had left the Commission without any data on the literacy, income, or occupation of the various communities. The Commission had no facilities for generating data themselves. In the face of these obstacles, the Commission plowed bravely on: "In the absence of reliable facts and figures, the only course open to us was to rely on the statistics available from the various Governments and the previous census reports, and to go by the general impressions of Government officers, leaders of public opinion and social workers. In some cases no data was available at all and "the decision to be taken on the strength of the name of the community only, on the principle of giving the benefit of doubt."

The commission did not undertake to document the application of its tests to the communities on its list, for which it provided only names, traditional occupations, and approximate population. In addition to listing the Backward Classes, the Commission was instructed to investigate the conditions of all such socially and educationally backward classes and difficulties under which they labour and make recommendations

(i) as to the steps that should be taken by the union or any state to remove such difficulties or to improve their conditions;

(ii) as to the grants that should be made. True to its charge, the Commission recommended a vast array of schemes for the protection and advancement of the backward, including a number of major changes in rural life: redistribution of land, protection of tenants, help to the small agriculturalists (credit, price supports, irrigation etc). They suggested the creation of a separate ministry for Backward Classes' Welfare. They proposed reservations for Backward Classes in government service of at least twenty-five per cent in Class I, 33 $\frac{1}{3}$ per cent in Class II, and forty per cent in Classes III and IV.

In addition there were various aids to the education of these groups and a reservation of seventy per cent in medical, scientific, and technical colleges. In a last minute *volte face*, the chairman virtually repudiated the Commission's work, concluding that "it would have been better if we could determine the criteria of backwardness on principles other than caste. He finds the caste test repugnant to democracy and inimical to the creation of "a casteless and classless society" (in the then fashionable phrase) by perpetuating and encouraging caste division. It is not quite clear what he would put in its place. He recommends that backwardness be ascertained by residential, economic, educational, and cultural criteria. Apparently he repudiates not only caste standing as the test of backwardness but also the use of caste units.

At several places in his covering letter he recommends that only individuals and families should be the units whose backwardness is ascertained. Elsewhere, however, he recommends policies which seem incompatible with this position (e.g., that where an income test in employed, members of backward communities should be given priority). The chairman's last-minute desertion foreshadowed (and perhaps augmented) the negative reception that awaited the report.

The spectacle of numerous groups vying to display their backwardness, the feeling that caste classifications were divisive and unfitting, the casualness of the Commission's application of its criteria, the vastness of the number they found backward, and the expansiveness of the preferences they proposed laid open their work to widespread criticism. The Commission's report was laid on the table of both Houses of Parliament on September 3, 1956, accompanied by a withering critique from the Minister of Home Affairs, showing disappointment with its criteria and its conclusions.

The emphasis on caste, the Minister asserted, displayed the "dangers of separatism." Not only was the caste basis unfair to the backward outside these communities, but the caste system was undeniably "the greatest hindrance in the way of our progress toward an egalitarian society, and the recognition of specified castes as backward may serve to maintain and perpetuate the existing distinctions on the basis of caste." The Commission's standards other than caste were, no doubt vague. They very expansiveness of the Commission's list undermined its usefulness, for if everyone "barring a few exceptions, has thus to be considered as backward, the really needy would be swamped by the multitude and hardly receive any special attention...Thus the Commission failed to find "positive and workable criteria." "Further investigations will have to be undertaken so that the deficiencies that have been noticed in the findings of the Commission are made good and the problem is solved with due consideration to the requirements of Art. 340..."

The State Governments were requested to undertake *ad hoc* surveys to determine the numbers of Backward Classes and in the meantime to "give all reasonable facilities" to the Backward Classes according to their existing lists and also so such others who in their opinion deserve to be considered as socially and educationally backward in the existing circumstances. Thus the matter went back to the states; the Commission's report remained on the Table, and in spite of occasional agitations, was not taken up by the Parliament until 1965. When the replies from the State Governments "were not found helpful," the Central Government requested the Office of the Registrar General to conduct *ad hoc* surveys to ascertain suitable criteria. It was hoped that the Registrar General could determine occupational tests of backwardness. On the basis of a three-state sample survey, an occupational test with an income ceiling was tentatively proposed. The Home Ministry's recommendation that the states adopt such an occupational criterion enjoyed a mixed reception. However, this attempt failed when the Deputy Registrar General reported that it would be impossible to draw up a precise and complete list of occupations whose practitioners were socially and economically backward. Those who entertained hopes of generous preferential treatment for the Other Backward Classes (OBCs) found some encouragement in the late 1950s. State expenditures on schemes for the OBC increased (particularly in education, where they were substantial), although the expansion of the Central Government's scheme for postmatriculation scholarships slowed down after 1955-56. Apparently at some point in 1957 the Government of India instructed all State Governments to extend the benefits of different welfare schemes to the OBC, using the Ministry of Education lists, pending finalization of a list of OBC.

Furthermore, it requested the State Governments to fill-up the unused vacancies in seats reserved in educational institutions for Scheduled Castes and Tribes with students from the OBC, a measure found very gratifying by the All-India Backward Classes Federation (AIBCF), which noted that "at long last the voice of the Federation is being effectively heard." By the beginning of the 1960s the tide was running strongly against definition of the Backward Classes by community. Opposition within the government came in the shape of criticism from academics and much of the national press, who voiced a common suspicion of the caste criterion.

For the first time since 1951, a court intervened to strike down a scheme for Backward Classes in a decision widely regarded as a blow at casteism. Revulsion from communal criteria was reinforced by reports of their abuse. In a situation where several thoughtful persons were increasingly concerned about the dangerous potentialities of social cleavages, the alleged divisive tendencies of the communal criterion appeared to pose a serious threat to national unity and integration. While a "casteless and classless society" remained the avowed aim of the Congress and a wide section of the intelligentsia, there had been a subtle change in notions of how this aim was to be achieved.

A decade before, it was widely thought that special redistributive measures were required specifically to offset inequalities associated with caste, even while general development programmes addressed other aspects of inequality. The notion of caste differentials are themselves a major kind of inequality needing special Government attention to eliminate their effects gave way to a notion that the salient differences were economic; specific redistributive measures directed at caste differences were not required, since overall development would raise the general level. Recognition of caste differences in order to offset their effects was replaced by an enhanced reluctance to recognize them at all; indeed, any recognition of such differences was noticed as itself a violation of egalitarian principles and productive inequality. In May 1961 the cabinet took decision a that no national list of Other Backward Classes should be drawn up, and the states were informed that in the view of the Government of India "it was better to apply economic tests to go by caste.

At the end of May a conference of Chief Ministers to consider matters concerning National Integration "agreed that economic backwardness rather than community or caste would provide an appropriate criterion for giving aid to individuals in matters of education including professional and technical training." In August 1961 the Home Ministry informed the State Governments of the Centre's decision not to list Backward Classes. In the Ministry's opinion the very expansiveness of such proposed enumerations as that of the Backward Classes Commission militated against them: "If the bulk of the country's millions were to be considered as coming within the category of Backward Classes, no useful purpose could be served by separate enumerations of such classes." Furthermore, the caste criterion was objectionable: "the remedies suggested based on caste would be worse than the evil of backwardness itself." But subsequent efforts to discover usable criteria on economic lines "did not yield any useful results." Whereas in 1956 the Home Ministry had acknowledged an obligation to compile a list in accordance with the needs of Article 340, it now pointed out that the Constitution did not need the Centre to draw up a list. Since, even if it were to do so, "it will still be open to every State Government to draw up its own lists, any all-India list would have no practical utility."

More important, the "crying need" of the day was social cohesion and emotional integration. There was the grave danger that different treatment of the "backward" would foster divisive tendencies and would undermine attempts for general economic uplift and the reduction of disparities between various classes. The states were urged to emphasize the expansion of welfare and educational benefits to all of the poor, using economic rather than communal categories. The withdrawal of the Central Government from involvement in preferences for the Other Backward Classes was confirmed by the omission of any provision for them in the central sector of the Third Five Year Plan. The amount contributed by the Central Government for post-matriculation scholarships for OBC, which had risen steadily since 1949, was frozen at the 1958–59 level. And starting in 1963, the state lists of OBC used in administering this scheme were abandoned in favour of a test of family income. The Central Government's campaign for economic criteria in the states was given by the first (since 1951) intervention of the Supreme Court into the matter of who are the Backward Classes. In September 1962 the Supreme Court struck down the Mysore Backward Classes list, whose defects involved exclusive reliance on caste standing as a measure of backwardness, adding the onus of constitutional disrepute to the caste criterion.

The Court's judgment, which warmly commended economic tests, was widely acclaimed and widely interpreted as outlawing entirely the use of caste tests. This case marked the rise of the judiciary as the institution within which the problem of who are the Backward Classes was most carefully and coherently addressed. In 1965, when the Report of the Backward Classes Commission was finally discussed in Parliament, the Central Government's spokesman firmly reiterated its opposition to communal criteria. Caste criteria were not only administratively unworkable, but were opposed to the "first principle of social justice" in their unfairness to the other poor. They were contrary to the Constitution, would perpetuate caste, and would create in the recipients both vested interests and a sense of helplessness. The Centre endorsed economic criteria, but stopped short of enforcing it on the states, preferring "the path of persuasion." Eight states were said to have adopted the economic criterion. Backward Classes Organizations continued to fight for greater benefits and for a revival of central responsibility and interest in the Backward Classes. In particular, they petitioned for a restoration of the caste basis, for implementation of the report of the Backward Classes

Commission, and for creation of a ministry to attend to the problems of the Backward Classes.

Organizations of particular communities and some composite Backward Class organizations at the local level (especially in the south and in Bihar) continue to flourish, but several of the local composite organizations have become moribund. After a period of desuetude, the national AIBCF had a brief revival in the late 1960s.

The Varied State Patterns

As the Central Government's role in designation of Backward Classes changed from an attempt to prepare a single nationwide list to recommend standards to the states, courts involved in litigation over Backward Classes lists made it clear that the Constitution did not confer on these central proposals any conclusiveness in the identification of the Backward Classes. While the state might make special provision for "any" Backward Class, it is under no constitutional obligation to make such provision for every class designated as backward by the Backward Classes Commission or by any other agency. Indeed, the State may not depend on the findings of the Backward Classes Commission to ascertain conclusively that a given class is backward. On the other hand, preferences may be given to a group which does not appear on the Commission's list. State power to provide preferential treatment to the backward is not restricted to those listed by the Commission or any other agency.

The original expectation that the Commission's list or some part of it would be confirmed by presidential specification has gone unfulfilled. Of course, this failure does not invalidate other listings of Backward Classes, for the courts have held that presidential specification would not exhaustively define the Backward Classes for purposes of preferences under Articles 15 (4) and 16 (4). Central proposals may, of course, carry some persuasive weight with the states (or, as guides to "reasonableness," with the courts). But it is the "State" in the broad sense of all Governmental organs that retains the power of designation. Preferences and who is to receive them may be provided by executive (as well as by legislative) action—and they almost always are. With the abandonment of Central attempts to define the Backward Classes, and the relinquishment of whatever control might accompany central funds for Other Backward Classes, the matter came upon the states. The composition of the OBC, the scope of preferential programmes, and the level of benefits continued to vary widely from state to state. Some of the varying state practices for selecting Backward Classes are summarized. For all its incompleteness and oversimplification, this list gives us a rough profile of who were the Backward Classes in the late 1970s. But at this point it is worth noting a few of the salient characteristics of this profile. Caste and communal units remain the predominant "classes" deemed backward.

Caste lists range in magnitude from those which include a substantial portion of the state's population to those constituting a narrow stratum just above the untouchables. Income tests are also employed in several cases, sometimes independently and sometimes in conjunction with communal units. The level of benefits ranges from none through scholarships and fee concessions to an array of reservations in various Government posts and medical college admissions. There is a significant regional variation noticed. For convenience we may think of three contiguous groupings. First, there is what we might call the peninsular bloc comprising the four Dravidian states (Andhra Pradesh, Karnataka, Kerala, and Tamil Nadu) and Maharashtra.

In these states the Backward Classes categories have a long history descending from pre-Independence arrangements; there are a wide range of benefits; and (except in Maharashtra) a major segment of the population – from thirty-eight to fifty-five per cent is included, and a major segment of scarce opportunities are reserved for them. In stark contrast is what we might call the eastern-middle band, stretching across India from Assam in the north-east through West Bengal and Orissa, across Madhya Pradesh to Rajasthan (Gujarat recently moved from this category to a pattern like that of Maharashtra). In these states there is no major or vital Backward Classes category. The northern tier of states reveals an intermediate pattern. Jammu and Kashmir, with its history of communal quotas, resembles the southern pattern. The admixture of geographical criteria there is similar to one found in Punjab and Uttar Pradesh along with use of communal categories. Bihar, like Jammu and Kashmir, approximates the peninsular pattern. The Backward Classes are selected on a communal basis and form a sizable portion of the population, but the benefits accrued have not been as extensive as in the south. Extension of benefits to reservations of government posts in 1978 set off a political crisis.

What the Central Government tried in 1965 to portray as a trend toward substitution of economic for communal criteria was even then largely a rhetorical artifact albeit one built around two substantial items – the abandonment of communal units in Andhra and in Mysore. From the vantage point of the late 1970s this "trend" seemed as a transient deflection from the main line of development of Backward Classes lists. That line of development has been one of continuing use of communal units, but with increasing relinement and restraint.

Under pressure from the courts, almost all the State Governments that made extensive use of Backward Classes category, setup commissions to identify the Backward Classes. From 1965 to 1976, such commissions submitted their reports in Kerala, Jammu and Kashmir, Andhra Pradesh, Tamil Nadu, Kerala again, Karnataka, and Gujarat. All of these commissions, and the Government orders based on their recommendations, use communal units to designate the Backward Classes. But Jammu and Kashmir relies heavily on occupational and territorial groups, and Kerala uses an income cut-off.

The selection of communities is more sophisticated: "the commissions efforts to collect (and some generate) evidence about occupation income, and education as well as status and disabilities. Most of them make to eliminate the well-off. In some cases, the number of groups designated is more modest than earlier. Benefits are recommended for a limited span of time, and there is always concern about termination and re-assessment. The best of the recent commissions display an industry and a sophistication in gathering and analyzing data that is a far cry from the uncritical and suppositions compilations of some of the early reports on backward classes. As we shall see State Governments are not always receptive to the critical assessment of their commissions. Perhaps some of this state activity came as a response to the animadversions of the Centre on communal criteria, but more directly palpably it was a response to the courts. In some areas it was a response to courts actually striking down schemes; in others, to courts threatening to do so if they were not refined; in still others it was to the implicit threat of litigation. The states aligned their schemes with the prescriptions of the courts rather and not with the pronouncements of the central authority.

TABLE 6.10
A Profile of Other Backward Classes in the Late 1970s

State	Year	Name of Group	Criteria	Est. of Pop.	Posts	Medical College Admission	Other	Comments	Source
Andhra Pradesh	1975	BC	92 listed communities	38%	25%	25%	Scholarships: fee-concessions	"Other" benefits only for those with income under Rs. 3,600	A.C.
		Economically BC	All with income under Rs. 1,500	...	None	None	Scholarships. hostels		A
Bihar	1979	BC	Members of list of 128 communities whose		20%	N.I.	N.I.		
		Economically BC	annual income is less than Rs. 12,000. All with income under Rs. 12,000 annually, other than		3%	N.I.	N.I.		B. R
	1977	BC	SC/ST/ OBC N.I		N.I.	10%	N.I.		C
Gujarat	1978	BC	82 listed communities		5% 10%	N.I.	N.I.	Classes I & II Classes III & IV	R.S.
	1972	Economically	Income less than Rs. 4,800/year		None	None	Scholarships. etc.		D
Haryana	1978	BC	N.I.	N.I.	2% 2%	N.I.	N.I.	Direct recruitment promotion in Class III & IV	

Contd.

Contd.

State	*Year*	*Name of Group*	*Criteria*	*Est. of Pop.*	*Posts*	*Medical College Admission*	*Other*	*Comments*	*Source*
Himachal Pradesh	1978	BC	N.I.	N.I.	10% 2%	N.I.	N.I.	Direct recruit-ment promotion in Classes III and IV I seat of 60	R
	1973	BC	N.I.	N.I.	N.I.	2%	N.I.		E
Jammu and Kashmir	1973	Socially and educationally BC	1. Occupations 2. 19 communities 3. Border & poor areas	N.I. N.I. 8%	42%	N.I.	N.I.		F
Karnataka	1979	BC	List of 16 communities. 129 castes & 62 tribes.	[45%]	40%[a]	N.I.	N.I.	Direct recruitment	G.T. [N]
		Economically BC	All with annual income under Rs. 4,800	N.I.	15%	N.I.	N.I.		U
	1977	BC		N.I.	N.I.	28%	N.I.		C
Kerala	1977	Socially and emotionally BC	Members of listed communities with income less than Rs. 10,0000		N.I.	25%	N.I.		C. [H]
				N.I.	N.I.	N.I.	Scholarships. loans		I
	1972	Socially and Educationally BC	Members of listed communities with income less than Rs. 6,000	N.I.	40%	N.I.	N.I.		O
	1970	BC	Members of 560 listed communities with income iess than Rs. 8,000						

Contd.

Mahara-shtra	1977	OBC	N.I.	N.I.	N.I.	10%	N.I.		C
	1966	OBC	List of communities	12%	14%	N.I.	Scholarships. loans, etc.	Exclusive of reservations for Nav-Buddhas and some tribals	J
				...					
Meghalaya	1978	BC	N.I.	N.I.	5%	N.I.	N.I.		R
Punjab	1978	BC	N.I.	N.I.	5%	N.I.	N.I.		R
	1977	BC	[List of communities]	N.I.	N.I.	5%	N.I.		C
		Backward Areas		N.I.	N.I.	2%	N.I.		[P]
Tamill Nadu	1972	BC	List of 105 communities (plus add'l. list for Kanya Kumari District]	[51%]	31%	31%	Hostels: special training		K.Q.
Uttar Pradesh	1978	BC	List of 58 communities	N.I.	16%	N.I.	N.I.	Initial	L
					15%			recruitment	M
	1977	Hill Areas	...	N.I.	N.I.	3%	N.I.	Promotion	C

Notes: [a]It is probable that this figure is an overstatement in that it fails to distinguish between the groups and the Economically Backward Classes noted just below. Of the 40% total. 5% may be a reservation for the Economically Backard Classes and thus a partial Duplication of the 15% reservation for that group.

[b]Struck down as unconstitutional in *Chottey Lal v. State of U.P.*, A.I.R. 1979 All.

In part this may be so because the Centre offered so little, besides commending the income test. In retrospect it is surprising that the Centre never attempted to formulate a workable quantitative standard for selecting backward communities—e.g., those groups whose average income and average literacy were less than one-half of the state average. It may have been experienced that practically such a course was foreclosed by the decision to omit castewise data on the censuses of 1951 and 1961, but the absence of such efforts indicates that the animus against communal tests eclipsed any consideration of making them more workable. What comes out of the intersection of State Governments, commissions, and courts are the lists of communal groups, with some admixture of geographic and income factors, chosen on the basis of low status, low educational attainments, and poverty.

We might generalize very tentatively about the magnitude of the Backward Classes category: the lists tend to converge on something like the second and third lowest quintiles of the population—in terms of "traditional" status—supposing the Scheduled Castes and Tribes make up roughly the lowest quintile. Northern and southern states arrive at this position from very different starting points. In the peninsula (and in Jammu and Kashmir) the commission process represents a pruning away of the more prosperous and powerful groups from a comprehensive list that approximated a regime of communal quotas. In the northern tier, however, provision for this stratum is added slowly, first in education, then in government jobs, converging on a somewhat similar position. Through the course of this development the term "backward classes" has acquired a multiplicity of meanings. It is used to describe the totality of groups entitled to preferential treatment on the basis of their "backwardness"—i.e., the Scheduled Castes and Tribes as well as "Other Backward Classes"—but *not* those given special treatment due to temporary or situational disadvantage (e.g., disaster victims, refugees, defense personnel). The term also refers specifically to those backward groups *other than*, the Scheduled Castes and Tribes. There remain fundamental, even if rarely articulated, disagreements about who these groups are. Some would confine this category to the lowly—those "far below" the mean in welfare and resources, or those whose deprivations are comparable to those of the Scheduled Castes and Tribes; others use the term Backward Classes to describe a wide middle stratum of Indian society, who need and deserve special help because they are lagging behind the most advanced groups.

There is, as we have seen, further disagreement over whether the term refers to the less well-off in all communities or whether it encompasses only those communities that suffer "backwardness" as a group. The question of who were the Scheduled Castes was debated and roughly settled before Independence within the executive and without the courts participating. But who are Backward Classes is a post-Independence question which the constitutional recognition of the category made one of all-India scope.

The Constitution left the matter with the executive at the state level with an option for the Centre to unify it. When the executive at the centre first failed and then refused to provide a resolution, the question reverted to the states. In the wake of the Janata victory in the 1977 elections, the Backward Classes returned to the national political agenda. Pursuant to its electoral promise, the Janata Government appointed a new Backward Classes Commission in Februrary 1978. Northern state governments under Janata control substantially enlarged the scope for Other Backward Classes, leading to massive violence in Bihar. In its declining days, the Janata caretaker Government came very near to instituting job reservations for Backward Classes in Central Government service. During the hiatus of central involvement, what the states did was increasingly subjected to the examination of the courts. It has been the Supreme Court rather than the Central Government which had more of the unifying and limiting influence.

Index

P

R

T

U

V

W